Philip II

European History in Perspective
General Editor: Jeremy Black

Benjamin Arnold   *Medieval Germany*
Ronald Asch   *The Thirty Years' War*
Christopher Bartlett   *Peace, War and the European Powers, 1814–1914*
Robert Bireley   *The Refashioning of Catholicism, 1450–1700*
Patricia Clavin   *The Great Depression, 1929–1939*
Mark Galeotti   *Gorbachev and his Revolution*
Martin P. Johnson   *The Dreyfus Affair*
Peter Musgrave   *The Early Modern European Economy*
J. L. Price   *The Dutch Republic in the Seventeenth Century*
A. W. Purdue   *The Second World War*
Francisco J. Romero-Salvado   *Twentieth-Century Spain*
Matthew S. Seligmann and Roderick R. McLean
Germany from Reich to Republic, 1871–1918
Brendan Simms   *The Struggle for Mastery in Germany, 1779–1850*
David Sturdy   *Louis XIV*
Peter Waldron   *The End of Imperial Russia, 1855–1917*
James D. White   *Lenin*
Patrick Williams   *Philip II*

European History in Perspective
Series Standing Order
ISBN 0–333–71694–9 hardcover
ISBN 0–333–69336–1 paperback
(*outside North America only*)

You can receive future titles in this series as they are published by placing a
standing order. Please contact your bookseller or, in the case of difficulty, write
to us at the address below with your name and address, the title of the series and the
ISBN quoted above.

Customer Services Department, Macmillan Distribution Ltd
Houndmills, Basingstoke, Hampshire RG21 6XS, England

PHILIP II

Patrick Williams

palgrave

First published 2001 by
PALGRAVE
Houndmills, Basingstoke, Hampshire RG21 6XS and
175 Fifth Avenue, New York, N.Y. 10010
Companies and representatives throughout the world

PALGRAVE is the new global academic imprint of St. Martin's
Press LLC Scholarly and Reference Division and Palgrave Publishers Ltd
(formerly Macmillan Press Ltd).

ISBN 0–333–63042–4 hardback
ISBN 0–333–63043–2 paperback

This book is printed on paper suitable for recycling and
made from fully managed and sustained forest sources.

A catalogue record for this book is available from the British Library.

Library of Congress Cataloging-in-Publication Data

Williams, Patrick, 1943–
    Philip II / Patrick Williams.
        p.   cm. – (European history in perspective)
    Includes bibliographical references and index.
    ISBN 0–333–63042–4 (hardcover) – ISBN 0–333–63043–2 (pbk.)
        1. Philip II, King of Spain, 1527–1598.   2. Spain – History – Philip II,
    1556–1598. 3. Spain – Kings and rulers – Biography.   I. Title:
    Philip the Second. II. Title. III. Series.

DP178 .W55   2000
946′.043 – dc21   00-048347

10 9 8 7 6 5 4 3 2 1
10 09 08 07 06 05 04 03 02 01

Printed in China

In loving memory of my parents,
George and Freda

Acknowledgements

Special thanks to John W. Tobias, who first introduced me to Philip II, and to Helmut Koenigsberger and John Lynch, who encouraged me to study him, and to David Davies, Dámaso de Lario, Hugo O'Donnell, Robert Oresko, Helen Rawlings, Rob Stradling, I. A. A. Thompson, Lorraine White and Phillip Williams who advised me on the text and who saved me from many errors. Over many years it was my privilege to discuss Philip II (and so much more) with Albert Lovett, and it is a great sadness that his premature death has, among its lesser consequences, deprived me of the pleasure of demonstrating to him how much I learned from him. My thanks, too, to Gabriella Stiles, Terka Bagley and Jane Robertson for their expert help in the production of the book.

LIST OF CONTENTS

vii

Part III   The Imprudent King

LIST OF MAPS AND TABLES

Maps

Tables

Explanatory Notes

CURRENCY

The gold ducat of Castile, the coinage of governmental calculations, is used throughout. It was worth 375 *maravedís* (the normal coinage of account). The *real* was worth 34 *maravedís* and the *escudo* was worth 400 *maravedís* from 1566. American silver was calculated in *pesos*, worth 1.375 ducats. The Aragonese *libra* and the Catalan *lliura* were each worth about one ducat.

DATING

Spain adopted the Gregorian Calendar in 1582, adding ten days to the date (See chapter 7) and this 'New Style' is used here. January 1 is taken as the beginning of the year rather than 25 March as in the Julian Calendar.

NAMES

I have used English versions of names of well-known people such as Philip II himself and Don John of Austria but otherwise have used Spanish names.

PART I
The Emperor's Son

1

PREPARATION FOR POWER

Philip II of Spain was born on 21 May 1527 in Valladolid, the first child of the emperor Charles V and his wife Isabella. Charles was present at the birth and when he was given his son to hold for the first time he joyously roared 'God make a good Christian of you!'.[1] It was a proud and challenging dedication, for Charles was the greatest ruler in Christendom and he had already assumed (at least in his own eyes) the status of a crusader, leading the defence of Catholic Christendom against its enemies – against the heretics who were beginning to suborn it within Europe; against the infidels who were launching a terrifying onslaught on land and at sea; against the pagans who in the New World of the Americas were resisting Christianisation; and, most invidious of all, against the king of France, who while boasting the title of 'The Most Christian King' cynically allied himself with Protestants and even with infidels in order to oppose the power of the Emperor. It was to the continuance of this multiple task that Charles dedicated his newborn son; Philip's would be a crusading kingship.

It would also be supranational, for by 1527 Charles ruled more of Europe than any man had done since the emperor Charlemagne (reigned 800–14) and he was ruler, too, of an empire in the Americas that was expanding literally by the day. It was the proud boast of the house of Habsburg (of which Charles became the head in 1519) that it won more lands by diplomatic alliances than others did by war, but not even the Habsburgs' most optimistic advisers could have foreseen, much less

3

planned for, the accretion of territories that came to Charles in the years 1506–19. Four separate inheritances were involved, and in time Charles passed three of these on to his son.

Charles received the first two inheritances in 1506 when his father Philip died and his mother Juana was struck mad in her grief; Charles succeeded his father to the family claim on the ancient dukedom of Burgundy and by virtue of his mother's incapacity he became king of Castile (although technically he was merely Juana's co-ruler until her death in 1555). Duke of Burgundy and king of Castile – the territories were far apart, but their joint tenure defined much of Charles's kingship and came in time to be a dreadful curse on that of his son. Burgundy had been one of the leading states of Europe in the High Middle Ages and had boasted the continent's most resplendent court but the greater part of its territory had been absorbed into the kingdom of France in 1477. In 1506, therefore, Charles inherited only a rump of the great duchy, the three separate territories of the Franche-Comté, Luxembourg and the 'Low Countries'; to the end of his life he was committed to recovering the lands that his family had lost in 1477. He had been born and raised in the Low Countries and he passed on to his son his own profound obsession with the Burgundian inheritance. Indeed, he named him for it, and in honour of the father whom he had barely known: 'Philip' was a Burgundian and not a Spanish name.

Castile was the largest and most populous kingdom in Spain. It occupied two-thirds of the Iberian peninsula and had a population of 4.5 million people at the time of Philip's birth (see Table 1.1). Already it

Table 1.1   The Population of Spain, 1530–91

	1530	%	1591	%
Castile	4 485 389	78.39	6 617 251	81.48
Crown of Aragon[1]	902 003	15.76	1 132 002	13.94
Northern States[2]	334 478	5.85	371 084	4.56
	5 721 870		8 120 337	

Notes: 1 Kingdoms of Aragon and Valencia and Principality of Catalonia.
    2 Provinces of Vizcaya, Guipúzcoa, Álava and kingdom of Navarre.
Source: Felipe Ruiz Martín, 'La Población Española en los Tiempos Modernos', Cuadernos de Historia, I (Madrid: 1967), p. 199.

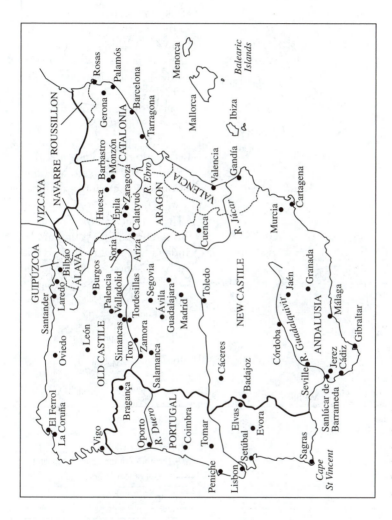

1 Spain in the sixteenth century

2   Western Europe in the 'Age of Philip II'

owned some significant possessions overseas: a few strategic outposts along the North African coast, the Canary Islands in the Atlantic, and the lands discovered by Christopher Columbus in 'the Indies' in the years from 1492. Adjacent to Castile and technically separate from it were the kingdom of Navarre and the provinces of Guipúzcoa, Vizcaya and Álava. These had a total population of about one-third of a million but they had strategic importance on land and sea out of proportion to their size. Their peoples had, too, a wealth of maritime experience – of ship-building and of seamanship – that was to prove invaluable to the kingdom of Castile.

In 1516, Charles succeeded to the third of his inheritances when on the death of his maternal grandfather Ferdinand II he became king of the 'Crown of Aragon'. This was a composite monarchy, consisting on the mainland of the kingdoms of Aragon and Valencia and the princi-pality of Catalonia; the three states had a population of just under one million people. The Crown of Aragon also had some strategically impor-tant possessions in the Mediterranean – the Balearic Islands, Naples, Sicily and Sardinia. Although Ferdinand and his wife Isabella had jointly ruled Aragon and Castile the two crowns had retained their separate identities. On succeeding to the 'Crown of Aragon' in 1516, therefore, Charles became the first individual to rule over the whole of Spain. He arrived to claim his new crowns in 1517. He was seventeen years of age and could not speak any Spanish.

Almost before he had taken possession of his Spanish realms, Charles received the fourth of his inheritances and with it the titular headship of secular Europe – the Holy Roman Empire itself, vacated in 1519 by the death of Charles's paternal grandfather, Maximilian I. Strictly speaking, the imperial title was elective, but in practice the Habsburg family main-tained its hold on it by dispensing massive bribes to the seven electors. Charles's advisers were true to this tradition; effectively, they bought the imperial title for him. As emperor, Charles assumed responsibility for a vast swathe of lands in central and eastern Europe and although his power over these territories was often more theoretical than real his imperial title gave him undoubted pre-eminence among the secular rulers of Europe and he proudly styled himself 'Caesar'. In doing so, he consciously revivified the medieval imperial ideal, identifying himself as the secular leader of Christendom.[2]

Charles was able to do this the more convincingly because the imper-ial title also devolved upon him the responsibility for leading the defence of Christendom against the Ottoman Turks. The Ottoman Empire had been expanding dramatically before Charles's accession to the imperial crown; making use of its apparently inexhaustible reserves of manpower it was assaulting Christendom on land and at sea. In 1453 Mohammed II ('The Conqueror') had taken Constantinople itself, one of the four historic capitals of the Christian world; the great city was renamed 'Istanbul' in recognition of new political and religious realities. Suleiman the Magnificent (reigned 1520–66) then unleashed the most systematic and ferocious onslaught that Christendom had faced since the early eighth century. In 1522 he captured the island of Rhodes and in 1526 he virtually dismembered the kingdom of Hungary. In 1529, Suleiman's troops besieged Vienna itself; the imperial capital only just survived. It fell to Charles of Habsburg to lead the West's defence against Suleiman. Spain had special reason to fear Suleiman's advance because the Mediterranean possessions of the Crown of Aragon stood directly in his path. Moreover, Ottoman expansionism reminded Spain of what had been lost when in a few bewildering years after 711 the Muslims of northern Africa had conquered virtually the whole of Spain. The task of driving the 'Moors' out of Spain – the *reconquista* – had only been completed in 1492 and had been the formative experience of the Spanish people. Was the *reconquista* now to be undone ?

In 1519, just as Charles became emperor, Hernán Cortes began the conquest of Aztec Mexico in the name of Castile and, unwittingly, Charles began to acquire an even greater empire overseas than the one that he ruled in Europe. The Castilian Crown was entitled to one-fifth of all mineral wealth produced in its lands, and by 1527 the precious metals of 'New Spain' (as Mexico was now called) were setting Charles on the path to become the richest monarch of his time. But he would have obligations, too, for the divine providence that showered these lands on Spain demanded that their peoples should be Christianised; commitment to this task was implicit in Charles's proud dedication of his son as 'a good Christian'.

The extraordinary array of territories ruled over by Charles V found their unity only in his person and already by 1527 his rule was proving to be ceaselessly peripatetic as he moved urgently from one territory to another, dealing with crisis after crisis. Indeed, his departure from Castile in 1520 to claim the imperial title itself precipitated a major revolt against him – the 'revolt of the *Comuneros*' of 1520–1 – and when he returned in 1522 he felt obliged to bring with him a small army of German mercenaries. Spain – and more particularly, Castile – was thereby secured for the house of Habsburg; that Charles married in Spain (and that his son and heir was born in the country) emphasised the primacy of Spain among his states.

The Emperor chose as his bride Isabella, princess of Portugal; he married her in Seville in March 1526. In forming a marital alliance with Portugal, Charles was pursuing the traditional policy of the kings of Castile in the hope that one day Castile and Portugal would be united under his successors. But in marrying a woman who was his cousin Charles was also taking a genetic risk that was itself almost a tradition in the house of Habsburg; both he and Isabella were grandchildren of Ferdinand and Isabella and their marriage was therefore a reminder of the dangerous predilection of the Habsburgs for marrying their own kin. Happily, Philip was free of any mental or physical debility, although he suffered from weaknesses in his digestive system which may have been hereditary.

It was especially unfortunate that as the celebrations of Philip's birth began the news should have arrived that Charles's own army had sacked Rome and driven a terrified pope (Clement VII) to flee for his life. The festivities were cancelled as Charles pondered how to respond to the dreadful news. The devotion of the Habsburgs to the Roman Catholic Church was unquestioned but it often seemed secondary to their commitment to the maintenance of their secular power. Philip was heir to this dilemma; he was born into a multinational dynasty which had an obsession with power and an unparalleled ability to absorb and extend it. It was not altogether accidental that in time his first war was with a pope.

Charles exercised his power with unwonted energy; it has been calculated that over the forty years of his reign he spent one day in four travelling and slept in some 3200 beds. There was true heroism in his determination to deal personally with crisis after crisis across the face of his territories in Europe, but ultimately Charles wrecked his own health by these ceaseless travels (and also, it must be admitted, by an appetite for food and drink that was truly imperial). He stayed with his newborn son for two years before leaving for the Empire in July 1529. Charles never spent as long in Spain as he had done in the years 1522–9; indeed, he spent a total of only sixteen years in all in Spain, and after 1529 he returned only four times as king, never remaining for more than two years at a time: April 1533 to April 1535; December 1536 to February 1538; July 1538 to November 1539, and November 1541 to May 1543.[3] The fears of the Castilian rebels of 1520 were validated; Castile *was* subordinate to the demands of the Empire. Soon after his departure in 1529

Charles reached a momentous decision; overwhelmed by the problems confronting him in the Empire he handed on to his brother Ferdinand the responsibility for preventing further Turkish advances in the East. Two years later, he had Ferdinand elected as 'King of the Romans' or emperor-elect so that he could organise the defence of Christendom in the east with due authority. In doing so he effectively secured for his brother the succession to the imperial title. Philip of Spain would not now become Holy Roman Emperor.[4]

THE EDUCATION OF A CHRISTIAN PRINCE

Isabella presented Charles with four children after Philip. Two girls, María (born 1528) and Juana (1538), both lived into adulthood; they grew up with Philip and became deeply attached to him, and he to them. They were his constant companions until they married – María in 1548 and Juana in 1552. However, two boys did not survive infancy; Juan lived for only five months in 1538 and if Fernando survived his birth in 1539 it was only for a few hours. Isabella was so weakened by Fernando's delivery that she herself died (1 May 1539). Charles was devastated for he had come to love his wife dearly.[5] He never remarried, and so after 1539 Philip was his only legitimate male heir. However, the Spanish thrones could pass in the female line and it may have been the fact that his daughters could succeed him that explained Charles's curious – and on the face of it, irresponsible – decision not to remarry when he was left with only one legitimate son.

Philip had precious little personal contact with his father during his formative years; between the ages of five and sixteen he spent a total of only six years or so in his father's presence. In consequence, the Emperor became almost as distant a figure to him as he was to his other subjects, not so much a real presence in his life as a legendary, almost mythical one. During childhood and adolescence Philip had to content himself with hearing what his father was up to in far-distant lands rather than with knowing him as a real person. He learned of great triumphs and of great defeats, of terrible enemies who were themselves figures of mythic stature: Suleiman the Magnificent and Barbarossa, his admiral, who sailed deep into the western Mediterranean to devastate Christian shipping; and Martin Luther, the German heretic who broke the unity of Christendom. Philip heard, too, of the cynicism of Francis I of France (1516–47), who allied himself with Lutherans and infidels to combat

Charles's power. Perhaps, indeed, Philip came to realise that his father's triumphs seemed inevitably to be followed by defeats as his enemies united against him whenever he won great victories. But above all else, Philip grew up in the certitude that he would inherit enormous power and that in his use of it he would be measured against the giant shadow of his brilliant, energetic and charismatic father. Philip was never to escape from the burden of that legacy. He was the Emperor's son.

But – and it is sometimes forgotten – Philip was also the Empress's son. In his formative years he spent much more time in his mother's company than he did in his father's. Isabella was a formidable and imperious woman, known for her iron self-control, and from her Philip inherited his extraordinary self-discipline and his regal composure; never were the inner feelings of a public man more impenetrable than his. Philip also inherited from Isabella a love of Portugal and its people that he retained throughout his life. Indeed, his greatest joy in his own kingship came when in 1580 he united Portugal with Spain. It was doubtless under Isabella's tutelage – and perhaps to consciously honour her memory – that Philip developed that deep affection for Portuguese men and women that was to be so enduringly characteristic of him. The first of the beneficiaries of this was a personable young Portuguese who had come to Spain with Isabella in 1526 as a page-boy, Ruy Gómez de Silva. Philip began a deep and lasting friendship with Ruy Gómez.[6] Isabella's sudden death in 1539 affected Philip deeply and his loyalty to Ruy Gómez may well have been inspired in part by his need to hold on to his mother's legacy.

Charles entrusted the supervision of his son's formal education to the joint care of Juan Martínez Siliceo, a low-born churchman who was responsible for Philip's moral and spiritual development, and Juan de Zúñiga, an untitled younger son of the count of Miranda, who instructed Philip in the courtly and equestrian arts. Siliceo and Zúñiga in turn brought in distinguished scholars to guide Philip's academic development. Chief among them were three men who jointly conversed with Philip in Latin and who took special responsibility for parts of his curriculum – Honorato Juan for Greek and Latin, Juan Ginés de Sepúlveda for History, and Cristóbal Calvete de Estrella for History and Geography. They had variable success. Philip grew up to be fascinated by geography and history; from an early age he showed an insatiable interest in the factual details of a problem for he had an enquiring mind that was avid for knowledge. He loved books deeply and in time became one of the greatest collectors of them in Europe; the foundations for his library were laid by Calvete de Estrella in 1540–7. Philip showed an early interest in painting, as a practitioner as well as a collector; again he would build up a collection of extraordinary range and depth. He developed, too, a love of music, guided by Antonio de Cabezón, Spain's leading organ composer, and by the clavichord-player, Francisco de Soto. But he had less interest in languages; unlike his father, who was famously adept at them, Philip had no aptitude for modern languages and made little effort to master any of them. He spoke Latin tolerably well and had some facility in Italian and Portuguese. But if his linguistic skills were underdeveloped Philip did by his mid-teens have the accomplishments of a gentlemen; he was a skilful horseman and huntsman, and he took real pleasure in his abilities, finding in the equestrian arts a release from the cares of public life.[7]

Philip's tutors left their mark upon him in two other important respects. Siliceo passed on to Philip his fierce concern for doctrinal purity while Zúñiga provided him with a cherished friend in his own son; Don Luis de Requesens y Zúñiga was appointed as a page to Philip in 1535. Luis de Requesens – he took his mother's name rather than his father's – was born in 1528, and he and Ruy Gómez de Silva (who was twelve years older) were Philip's childhood playmates. They grew up with him, playing and learning together.[8] As the boys grew to manhood, their friendship deepened into trust and when Philip acquired the authority to do so he raised both Ruy Gómez and Luis to senior offices. Both rewarded him with distinguished service, but both died young – Ruy Gómez at fifty-seven years of age in 1573 and Luis at forty-eight in 1576.

Charles V returned to Spain in November 1541 and stayed until May 1543. Those months were precious for both Charles and Philip, for it was then that they really came to know each other well as Charles guided his son into his first political and military actions. In 1542 Philip attended the Cortes (or parliament) of Castile in Valladolid (January) and then went on to those of the Crown of Aragon, which by tradition met in the small and remote town of Monzón in the province of Huesca (May). Philip had been sworn in as heir to the throne of Castile as an infant in 1528 and he now took the oaths to the eastern kingdoms. It was significant of the difference between the two kingdoms that Philip was allowed to take the oath in Aragon only on condition that he did not wield any power until he had returned as an adult to take the oath in the cathedral of Zaragoza. But if he learned something of the singlemindedness with which the Aragonese clung to their historic privileges, Philip at least became in a legal sense the heir to all the thrones of Spain. From Monzón he proceeded to the eastern foothills of the Pyrenees to observe the progress of the siege of Perpignan by the French army. This was a symbolic rite of passage for him, his introduction to that science of war that was so fundamental to the art of kingship. He was guided and instructed by his father's senior general, Fernando Álvarez de Toledo, third duke of Alba. The venture was a success; the French withdrew. In future years, Philip's relations with the duke would be less felicitous; indeed, much of the first half of his reign would be complicated by his inability to cope with Alba's overpowering personality.

It was during this stay in Spain that Charles promised his son that he would hand over to him as his first territory the duchy of Milan, which was an imperial fief. The duchy commanded the whole of northern Italy and stood as a bulwark against French attacks by land on Naples. It was populous enough to provide a constant supply of men for Charles's armies – the city of Milan with over 120000 inhabitants was one of the five largest cities in Europe – and it also served as the *plaza de armas* for Charles's European military strategy; from Milan troops could be despatched eastwards to the Empire and northwards to the Low Countries. Securing control of Milan was one of the key achievements of Charles V's reign, and in promising to endow the duchy upon his son the Emperor gave Philip the key to maintaining Spanish power in Italy and to moving his troops throughout Europe. Philip understood full well how important Milan would be to his future and when his father toyed with the idea of selling the duchy he skilfully used his councillors of State to argue his case for him. He carried the day; Milan was not sold.[9]

As he prepared for his departure in the northern Catalan town of Palamós Charles signed two sets of instructions for Philip on 4 and 6 May 1543. Philip would reach adulthood on his sixteenth birthday on 21 May and Charles intended that he should act as regent for him in Spain. He therefore gave him detailed instructions on how he was to conduct himself. In the letter of 4 May Charles emphasised the confidence that he had in Philip, thanking God for having given him 'such a son'. He insisted that Philip's first obligation was that he 'should never allow heretics to enter into your kingdoms' and enjoined him to support the Inquisition to ensure that they did not do so. He urged Philip to administer justice impartially and to keep a vigilant eye on the honesty of his officials. As to Philip's personal conduct, Charles insisted that he should be moderate in all things and never take any decision in anger. Philip paid devoted attention to his father's guidance; he lived his life by these rules. Charles went on to urge that Philip make full use of his own senior

servants, stressing, for instance, that he was not to sign papers before
Francisco de los Cobos, his chief secretary of State, had advised him on
their contents. Similarly, Philip was to follow the judgement of Alba in
matters of war and to make the very fullest use of Juan de Zúñiga in all
areas of government. To ensure his son's compliance, Charles ordered
that these Instructions were to be read to him in the presence of Zúñiga
himself.

The letter of 6 May was by contrast strictly confidential, an intimate
letter from a father to a son. Its very existence was to be known to no
one except Philip himself. Revealingly – at the age now of forty-three! –
Charles confessed that he was anxious about his advancing years. He was
fearful that the journey that he was about to undertake to the Empire
was 'the most dangerous that there could be for my honour and reputation, for my life and my financial resources' but stressed that he could
not fulfil his responsibilities if he did not go. He wrote of the burden he
felt at having to leave Spain 'in such extreme need'. To help Philip
govern, Charles gave him highly personalised – and brilliantly shrewd –
characterisations of his chief ministers. Although Philip was nominally
regent of Spain it was these men, notably los Cobos, Alba, Zúñiga and
Juan de Tavera, cardinal-archbishop of Toledo and Inquisitor-General,
who were to assume the responsibility for taking decisions.[10]

As part of the settlement of his affairs, Charles had arranged for Philip
to marry his Portuguese cousin María Manuela but he could not spare
the time to stay in Spain for the marriage. Philip, nevertheless, was very
enthusiastic about the agreement and wrote joyously to Charles describing his preparations for the ceremony and for his first sight of his bride.[11]
He was not disappointed in María Manuela; her shyness and her beauty
captivated him. The young couple took their vows in Salamanca on 15
November 1543. On 8 July 1545, after an horrific delivery that lasted two
full days, María gave birth to a son who had an abnormally large head.
She died four days later, only eighteen years of age. The boy was named
after his grandfather, Don Carlos. As for Philip, he had grown up quickly;
at eighteen he was a widower and the father of a son whose physical and
mental condition was to cause grave anxieties. Philip was deeply shaken
and retired to a monastery for three weeks to reflect upon the tragedy.[12]

Philip could not, however, abandon his responsibilities as regent. He
kept in touch with his father through a detailed and lengthy correspondence and soon displayed a mature ability to immerse himself in the
details of government.[13] Responsibility pressed the more heavily on Philip
because the men whom Charles had appointed to supervise his political

education died in rapid succession – Cardinal Tavera in 1545; Juan de Zúñiga in 1546; and los Cobos in 1547. Charles replaced Tavera with two men – Siliceo became archbishop of Toledo and García de Loaysa was appointed as Inquisitor-General. García de Loaysa died within a few weeks and Charles then named Fernando de Valdés as his successor.[14] The combination of Siliceo in the primatial see and Valdés in the Inquisitorship-General had profound implications; stern, unyielding men, they represented the triumph of the forces of reaction in the Spanish Church. Siliceo immediately imposed a statute of purity of blood ('*limpieza de sangre*') on the cathedral chapter of Toledo, by which men who had Jewish blood in their veins (or who were accused of having such blood) were debarred from holding office.[15] The use of this statute at the very heart of the Spanish Church encouraged many other institutions to follow suit. Valdés was even more extreme; he took advantage of the Emperor's absence to extend the power of the Inquisition over all aspects of national life. Within a few years, Valdés's ambitions for the Inquisition were threatening to distort the very balances within the Spanish state.

Charles confounded his own fears by emerging triumphant in his war in Germany; on 23 April 1547 he inflicted a crushing defeat upon the Franco-Protestant army at the battle of Mühlberg in Saxony.[16] It was the greatest of his military triumphs and he celebrated it by commissioning two works of art from Italian masters – a statue from León Leoni and a painting from Titian. Both pieces proved to be among the greatest works of their time and so Charles's triumph at Mühlberg became part of the iconography of European artistic achievement: Leoni's *Il Furore* depicted Charles triumphant over Tumult, while Titian's equestrian portrait became the supreme image of Charles and has dominated posterity's view of the Emperor as the resolute crusader solemnly confronting his destiny.[17] However, Titian's painting also showed that Charles was old beyond his years; the truth was that Charles was not at the height of his power but that psychologically he was at its end, worn out and prematurely aged. Charles was subsequently to claim that he had wanted to abdicate after Mühlberg; his reputation would have stood higher had he done so, for in the years after 1547 he was in physical decline, and as his health crumbled so too did his will to govern.

Unnoticed in the crisis of the months before the great battle a German woman named Barbara Blomberg gave birth to a son by the emperor; the child became known as Don John of Austria. It would be years before Philip knew officially that he had a half-brother. He certainly knew already that he had a half-sister; in 1522 Charles had a daughter,

Margaret, by a Dutch woman, Johanna van der Gheyst. In 1536 Charles arranged the marriage of Margaret to Alessandro de Medici, duke of Florence. Alessandro was assassinated in the following year and so in 1538 Charles had Margaret marry Ottavio Farnese, grandson of no less a figure than Pope Paul III. In Rome on 27 August 1545 Margaret presented the Emperor with twin grandsons, who were christened Carlo and Alessandro. To celebrate the continuation of his family line Paul III created the duchy of Parma and Piacenza for Ottavio's father, Pierluigi. Carlo died in infancy, but Alessandro was taken to Brussels to be educated in Philip's household, and a Spanish garrison was stationed in Piacenza; both measures ensured that the Farneses stayed loyal to the Habsburgs.[18] Young Alessandro became in time the greatest soldier of his age; he is known to us as Alexander Farnese.

THE FIRST JOURNEY ABROAD: THE LOW COUNTRIES, 1548–51

Triumphant after the battle of Mühlberg and conscious of the need to put his affairs in order before he abdicated, Charles ordered Philip to join him in the Low Countries so that he could familiarise himself with his Burgundian territories and be presented to his future subjects. As part of the preparation for his son's journey, Charles ordered that Philip's household be remodelled in the Burgundian fashion. This was a major innovation which had far-reaching consequences for it imposed a much more formal life on the court.[19] Philip's household was to be controlled by a *mayordomo mayor*, or chief steward, and no less a figure than the duke of Alba was appointed to the post. On 15 August 1548 Philip appeared in public for the first time surrounded by his *mayordomos*. The studied formality of the Burgundian court could have been designed for Philip, who was calm and controlled and hated being in a crowd. But the introduction of the new *etiquetas* also stressed the foreignness of Habsburg monarchy in Spain. This was especially unfortunate at a time when Philip himself was poised to leave Spain for a long journey to northern Europe, emulating his father's journey north in 1520 – a journey which had of course provoked the *comuneros* to revolt. For Philip, the new *etiqueta* was to be a daily reminder of his father's obsession with recovering control of the duchy of Burgundy. Charles also arranged the betrothal of Philip's cousin Maximilian to his sister María; they married in Valladolid on 14 September and remained in Spain to serve as regents while Philip was away in northern Europe. Philip sailed for Italy from Rosas in northern Catalonia on 19 October.[20]

Philip's journey took the form of a grand tour *par excellence*. Accompanied by well over a thousand courtiers, churchmen, nobles and servants, he travelled through many of the key strategic, commercial and cultural centres of Europe. He began in Genoa, which from about the time of his birth had provided the major banking and credit services for the Spanish Monarchy; here, he was introduced to the glittering wealth and architectural splendour of Italy. He went on to the duchy of Milan and paid homage to his father by visiting the site of the battlefield of Pavia, where in 1525 Charles's troops had taken Francis I prisoner. He proceeded to Trent, where the great council of the Roman Catholic Church was defining its counter-attack on the forces of the Protestant Reformation. He then passed through the cities of Innsbruck, Munich, Augsburg and Heidelberg before arriving in Burgundian territory in Luxembourg. In each of these cities Philip was welcomed not only in his own right but as the emperor's son in the confident expectation that he would inherit his father's personal qualities along with his states. Philip's journey from Genoa to Luxembourg was a celebration of the power and prestige of his dynasty and a reaffirmation that the greatness of the house of Habsburg was in his keeping.[21]

On 1 April 1549 Philip entered Brussels and was reunited with his father. It was almost six years since Charles had seen his son and he wept with joy. Philip also met Charles's redoubtable sisters, the dowager queens of France (Eleanor) and of Hungary (María). The aristocracy of the Low Countries were assembled in Philip's honour and he encountered for the first time men who were to play major roles in his own career – men such as William of Nassau, Prince of the house of Orange; Lamoral, count of Egmont, and Philippe de Montmorency, count of Hornes. Charles and Philip spent two months together in Brussels before Philip began another journey. Between July and October 1549 he travelled the length and breadth of the seventeen provinces of the 'Low Countries' and was sworn in as heir in each of them.[22]

The journey around the seventeen provinces was one of the formative experiences of Philip's life. Like Spain, the Low Countries achieved their unity in the person of their ruler. Each province had its own constitution and there was not even a common language to bind them to each other; French was spoken in the south while German dialects predominated in the north. The provinces had, too, different economic interests; the northern provinces chiefly earned their living from the sea, while those in the south had an agrarian and industrial economy. The Low Countries were heavily urbanised; there were about 200 towns and cities and one-third or so of the population of three million people lived in them. By far the largest city was Antwerp, with a population of 80000 people. Ninety kilometres inland on the River Scheldt, Antwerp was a great port, open to the North Sea and serving a rich hinterland in the Low Countries, the Empire and France. It had developed a variety of commercial and financial functions to complement its trading activities and led Europe in many of them. Calvete de Estrella, who accompanied Philip and wrote a detailed account of the journey, was almost overwhelmed by the splendour of Antwerp, describing it as 'the very richest' of cities.[23] Heavily populated and urbanised, rich, cosmopolitan and diverse, intellectually vibrant: the Low Countries were utterly different from Spain and Philip was fascinated by them. But he never came to love them as his father did – and from the outset he was deeply suspicious as to their orthodoxy in religion.

In the Low Countries Philip was introduced to the elegant courtly ceremonials of northern Europe; in each of the major towns and cities he was formally received in 'joyous entries' which celebrated the legitimacy of his rule and his princely virtues. As the cities competed with each other to welcome Philip, some of the celebrations became the stuff of proverb, notably those organised by María of Hungary at Binche ('more splendid than the festivals of Binche'). But the celebrations were not simply about princely power and majesty; they pointedly reminded Philip that he was obliged to be a just and benevolent ruler, that there was a social compact between ruler and ruled. The unstated corollary of this was that political obedience was contingent upon princely benevolence.[24] Charles V himself had found it difficult even to understand the demands of his countrymen for political expression much less to accommodate them; Philip, who was a Castilian, was to find it still harder. But for all that, Philip paid the most particular attention to the bewildering wealth and variety of the civilisation of the Low Countries; in his understated way he noted the elegance of their buildings, the logical and precise arrangement of their gardens, the lively realism of their paintings and the rhythmic subtlety of their music, and he waited for the opportunity to introduce all of these into Spain. As to political liberty, of this he was less admiring. It was in his view the business of subjects to be ruled, not to make compacts with their lawful sovereign and much as he was enchanted by the Low Countries he never changed that view.

Charles had decided only in 1548 that he would incorporate the Low Countries into Philip's inheritance. Accordingly, he now constitutionally separated the seventeen provinces from the Empire. Charles had several reasons for uniting the Low Countries and Spain under his son's rule, far apart as they were. There were strong economic connections between them; about two-thirds of Castilian wool was exported to the Low Countries and there were trading and fishing contacts. Politically, the union made a great deal of sense; from the Low Countries Philip could exert pressure on France, the Empire and England and keep a close eye on the Baltic trade, which was vital to Spain as a source of naval supplies and grain. Most especially, he could put an army into France and be at once only a couple of days' march from Paris. But of course there were also disadvantages to the union, chiefly those created or accentuated by the distance between Spain and the Low Countries. There was, too, the rapid spread of Calvinism to be dealt with in the Low Countries. Sectarian heresy was nothing new in these cosmopolitan lands – Anabaptism had developed alarmingly in the previous generation – but Calvinism was organised and disciplined in a way that other heresies were not and it appealed to a much broader section of society. Directed from Geneva by John Calvin himself, it spread along the rivers and it flowered in the towns and cities of the Low Countries. Charles's later years witnessed the rapid growth of Calvinism there, and with it came all the portents of civil unrest. Charles responded ruthlessly, clamping down on dissent and executing heretics in large numbers.

As he began the process of divesting himself of power, Charles determined that Philip and not Ferdinand should succeed him as emperor. In 1551 he therefore summoned his senior relatives to Augsburg in the hope that he could persuade them to agree to undo the decision that he had taken twenty years before to have Ferdinand succeed him. However, Ferdinand refused to yield and the divisions between the two brothers became so bitter that for a time they were not even on speaking terms. Charles had to compromise, and it was agreed by what became known as 'The Habsburg Family Compact' of 9 March 1551 that Ferdinand would succeed Charles as emperor but that he would then do what he could to ensure that Philip succeeded him. Philip would then in turn facilitate the succession of Ferdinand's son Maximilian to the imperial throne and would himself marry one of Ferdinand's daughters.[25] Philip's future was now clear; he would be king of Spain and her possessions and ruler of the Low Countries. He would also be the master of Italy, ruling

Naples and Sicily in the south and Milan in the north as well as the fortresses (*presidios*) that were scattered along the coast. Genoa, while not
a Habsburg possession, was bound by identity of interest to the Spanish
Habsburgs and the duchy of Parma was tied to Spain by the marriage
of Philip's half-sister Margaret. The imperial title would revert to Philip
when Ferdinand died. He would then be the leading prince in Europe.
It must have been with quiet satisfaction that he left his father to return
to Spain.

However, the destiny of a great part of Europe could no longer rest
in the hands solely of the Habsburg family and by the time that Philip
arrived in Barcelona (12 July 1551) the plans made at Augsburg were
unravelling fast. Within months they were effectively annulled; in January
1552 Henry II of France formed a league with leading German Protestants to prevent Charles from imposing his settlement on Europe. War
began in the spring of 1552; Henry II invaded Lorraine with an army of
35 000 men and occupied the three French-speaking bishoprics of Metz,
Toul and Verdun while Maurice of Saxony marched into southern
Germany in pursuit of the Emperor himself. In the face of Maurice's
rapid advance, Charles had to flee for his life; he was carried out of his
Empire in a litter by candlelight over the Brenner Pass to Villach (19–28
May 1552).[26]

Charles attempted to regain some of his prestige by besieging Metz in
October 1552 but he failed abysmally and had to lift the siege in January
1553. Taken together, the flight to Villach and the failure at Metz cost
Charles much of his reputation and in all probability convinced him that
it was time to abdicate. Certainly, the two events marked the end of his
grandiose plans for settling the future of the continent.

Nevertheless, the Emperor's wars had still to be fought and on resum-
ing the regency in Spain Philip was obliged to find the resources to help
his father fight on in Germany. 'There is no money here, nor do we have
the means with which to acquire it,' wrote Ruy Gómez de Silva in the
spring of 1551, but with brutal effectiveness Philip found the money that
his father insisted upon; in the years 1551–4 he conjured up some eleven
million ducats in the form of loans and subsidies. Virtually all of this
money came from Castile, and it was raised by making use of a variety of
expedients which tested Philip's scruples as much as his ingenuity and
singlemindedness: forced loans from bankers, the alienation of substantial revenues from the royal domain and the seizure of treasure arriving
at Seville from the Indies.[27] The territories of the eastern states of Spain
contributed only token amounts to the war chest. Philip presided in 1552

over the joint Cortes of the Crown of Aragon; he found it no more con-
genial a task than he had done in 1543 and he failed to produce any
significant funds for the war.[28]

KING OF ENGLAND, 1554–8

The opportunity to salvage some imperial prestige arose when Edward
VI of England died suddenly (6 July 1553) and was succeeded by his half-
sister Mary, Henry VIII's daughter by Katharine of Aragon. Henry had
divorced Katharine when he fell under the spell of Anne Boleyn and
managed to convince himself that his marriage to Katharine had been
canonically invalid. To make his divorce possible Henry had broken with
the papacy. Disowned by her own father, illegitimised by Parliament,
Mary had grown up as the very personification of Catholicism in England.
She had clung tenaciously to the only certainties available to her – her
love for her Spanish mother and her deep religious faith. When she
found that her right to succeed to the throne was challenged by the duke
of Northumberland and his daughter-in-law, Jane Grey, Mary demonstrated a cool nerve in outfacing the duke and rallying her own supporters. Northumberland and Grey went to the block and so Mary
became the first queen regnant in English history. She had no doubts
about her destiny – to restore England to the Catholic faith – and she
had no doubts either about the means by which she would achieve it; in
October 1553 an agreement was made with Charles V's agents for her to
marry Philip of Spain.[29]

The negotiations were conducted with uncommon haste for both
parties had much to gain. Mary was already thirty-six and if she died childless the throne would pass to her half-sister Elizabeth and England would
then in all probability revert to Protestantism. The religious destiny of
England therefore hung in Mary's view upon her ability to produce a
legitimate heir; not even her father had been more desperate to produce
a male heir than she was now. As for Charles V, he had jettisoned the
idea of marrying Philip to one of Ferdinand's daughters when the
Habsburg Family Compact had fallen apart and he now saw the marriage
of Philip to Mary as the means through which he could rekindle the old
Anglo-Burgundian alliance. He acted, therefore, with such unwonted
alacrity in agreeing the terms of the marriage that he quite failed even
to inform his son of the details. Not until January 1554 did the count of
Egmont write from London to inform Philip of the agreement.[30]

Philip was bitterly angry when he read of the terms that his father had agreed, for he had himself all but concluded an agreement to marry another Portuguese princess (who was, coincidentally, also named María). His father's agreement stipulated that any child of his marriage with Mary Tudor would succeed to the English throne and to the Low Countries and would also inherit Spain and her territories in Europe and the Americas if (as was quite probable) Don Carlos failed to produce an heir. When the marriage took place, Philip was to have the title of king-consort of England, but he was not to exercise any regnal powers. The agreement also precluded any English involvement in the wars of the house of Habsburg. Philip resented being married off to a woman of comparatively advanced years, of whom it was widely known that she was unlikely to be able to bear children and he certainly dreaded the prospect of being a king-consort in a foreign land without power or influence, of starting his kingly career as a cipher. The prospect of a further marriage with a young Portuguese princess which would in all probability have led in time to the unification of Spain and Portugal was an infinitely more attractive proposition for him. But his father's dynastic ambitions prevailed: Philip's second bride would be Mary of England not María of Portugal.

Within weeks of signing the treaty Mary was confronted by a rebellion; Sir Thomas Wyatt raised an army of 4000 men and marched on London to force Mary to abandon the Spanish match. However, London held firm for the queen, Wyatt went to the block and perhaps a couple of hundred of his followers were summarily executed. Princess Elizabeth (who had played no part in the rebellion) was despatched to the Tower and was for some time in fear of her life. Wyatt's defeat cleared the way for the marriage, which took place on 6 March 1554. Egmont stood proxy for Philip.

It was with deep foreboding that Philip prepared to travel to England. He was at once anxious about the terms of the agreement and concerned for his physical safety in England. On the day before he formally accepted the terms of the marriage he signed a secret paper asserting that his signature was null and void because some of the provisions in the treaty had been agreed against his will. Philip's sister Juana, who had been widowed in 1554, was summoned to Valladolid to serve as regent of Spain. She brought with her a large contingent of Portuguese servants, men and women who came to play a most significant political role during her regency (and indeed after it). Juana left her infant son, Sebastián, in Lisbon to be brought up as the heir to the Portuguese throne. Philip met his sister and entrusted Don Carlos to her care. He then hurriedly set the government of Spain in order and sailed from La Coruña on 12 July in a fleet of 125 ships commanded by Don Álvaro de Bazán.[31] Philip took with him many of his leading nobles such as the dukes of Alba and Medinaceli and the counts of Feria, Chinchón, Aguilar and Olivares. He was also accompanied by the counts of Egmont (who had travelled to Spain for the purpose) and Hornes. Philip sailed with the intention of being away from Spain only briefly but in the event he remained in northern Europe for five years and found himself king of Spain when he returned.[32]

Philip disembarked at Southampton after a week at sea. He proceeded to Winchester where, on the feast-day of Spain's patron saint, St James, (25 July) the marriage was formally ratified. Before the ceremony took place an Imperial Act was read out in which Charles invested Philip with the titles of king of Naples and duke of Milan.[33] Philip now had the kingly rank that was appropriate for his marriage. He did his best to show his pleasure at becoming king of England but graciousness did not come easily to him, the more so because Mary herself proved to have aged rather more than the Spaniards had been led to believe; Ruy Gómez, usually the most delicate and tactful of men, went so far as to describe her in a letter as 'old and flabby'.[34] Worse followed; the bride's sexual inadequacy was soon the talk of Philip's household, and there could only have been one source for the story of Philip's unhappiness.[35]

Mary was blithely unaware of her husband's disappointment. She took Philip to Windsor, where she installed him as head of the chivalric Order of the Garter, and on to London, where they made a splendid 'joyous entry' on 18 August. Philip was gratified by the reception given him in London; he wrote to Juana that 'I was received with every sign of love and contentment from everybody'.[36] He attended Mass at Westminster Abbey and after a week in London left for Hampton Court, where he stayed for a month (and during which time he probably met Princess Elizabeth, newly released from imprisonment).[37]

Mary now turned to her major political work, the recatholicisation of England, and she did so in the conviction that she was pregnant; indeed, she even felt her child move in her womb. It was calculated that she would give birth early in May 1555; if the child was a boy, the success of the queen's life's work would be assured, for England would be ruled once again by a Catholic dynasty.[38]

The Reformation in England had been brought about by Acts of Parliament and so it could only be formally undone by Parliament; in

November, both houses of Parliament humbly petitioned to be allowed to enter once again into communion with the Roman Church. Philip was present on 30 November when Cardinal Reginald Pole, as papal legate, formally pronounced the absolution of the kingdom of England from schism. Philip was proud to have played a role in this historic process and when emissaries went to submit to the pope in the spring of 1555 Philip noted that they went 'in the name of the Queen and myself for the whole of this kingdom'.[39]

Mary now began the great persecution which has earned her the sobriquet 'Bloody Mary' and she did so with the full support of her husband. Parliament had revived the heresy laws and on 4 February 1555 John Rogers became the first person to be burned alive under Mary. On 12 March, Philip wrote approvingly to Juana that 'things have been going from good to better and some heretics have been punished'.[40] About 280 people followed Rogers to the stake in the next three and a half years. Most of them were of low birth and they tended to be from the southeast of England. About sixty of them were women. The most notable of all of them was Thomas Cranmer, archbishop of Canterbury; he went to the stake on 21 March. On the following day Reginald Pole was consecrated as his successor.[41]

Brutal though Mary's policy was, it might not have been of permanent consequence had she produced an heir, and by the summer of 1555 she was proudly displaying all the signs of pregnancy. Much more than the fate of the English throne now hung on her condition, for the death of Juana *la Loca* on 11 April had finally made it possible for Charles to proceed with his abdication. However, Philip could not leave England until his wife had given birth and so Charles's abdication, and with it the settlement of much of western Europe, had to wait on the birth of Mary's child.

But there was no child. In her determination to become pregnant Mary had convinced herself that she had successfully conceived when she had not done so. It may well be that the symptoms that Mary took for pregnancy were in fact those of the beginning of cancer of the uterus from which she was to die in 1558. By the autumn of 1555 it was no longer possible for her to hope or to pretend. Humiliated beyond endurance – for he too had genuinely believed in the pregnancy – Philip left England at the beginning of September 1555. At least he found that fortune favoured him on the sea; he crossed the Channel in less than three hours. He remembered in years to come that the crossing of the Straits of Dover could be accomplished so quickly and so easily.[42]

2

KING OF SPAIN

THE ABDICATIONS OF CHARLES V, 1555–6

Charles V greeted Philip in Brussels on 8 September; once again, the emperor was reduced to tears by a reunion with his son. On 25 October 1555 in the Great Hall of the Palace of Brussels, in one of the most romantic ceremonies in European political history, Charles renounced the Low Countries in favour of Philip. He spoke movingly of the forty journeys that he had made on land and sea and of the wars that he had fought against infidel and Christian. He exhorted Philip to have regard above all his other responsibilities for the maintenance of the Catholic religion and for the execution of justice. As a separate but ancillary act, Charles had three days earlier handed over to Philip the command of the Order of the Golden Fleece, the chivalric order founded in 1430 that was the embodiment of Burgundian culture. He now formally confirmed that endowment, emphasising in the most public manner the commitment that he was imposing upon his son to maintain the Burgundian heritage. Replying in Spanish, Philip insisted that he would have preferred Charles to have remained in office until his death, but he swore to execute the responsibilities that now fell to him 'to the utmost' of his power. He and Charles embraced emotionally. The audience, or much of it, was moved to tears. Philip then had to address the assembly but because he could not speak more than a few words of French or Flemish he had Antoine Perrenot de Granvelle, bishop of Arras, perform the task for him. It was a moment as poignant as it was embarrassing: the Low Countries had passed into foreign hands.

The scene in the Great Hall of Brussels has enchanted history, bathing Charles in the glow of achievement and in the nobility that accrued from an unprecedented and voluntary renunciation of great power. The reality was that the abdication was a brilliant theatrical production which sought to disguise the fact that Charles was exhausted by his labours and that he had been psychologically broken by the disasters of 1551–3. He was a sadly diminished figure.[1] Among those who were not fooled by the spectacle was Philip himself. No word of reproach for his father ever escaped his lips but he learned one lesson from the abdication and forty years later applied it with absolute determination – he himself would *never* give up power.

Charles continued on occasion to act as if he had not abdicated at all, summoning his son to discuss affairs with him and holding meetings of his council; he seemed at pains to make it evident that Philip was ruler of the Low Countries by default. It was nearly a year before he finally dragged himself away.[2] It was a wretched beginning for the new ruler, to be undermined by his own father.

On 16 January 1556, Charles abdicated as king of Spain. This time there was no public ceremony and Charles merely handed over the titles to the Spanish kingdoms to Philip as if they were property deeds. He spoke for an hour but said much more than was wise, professing that he had wanted to renounce his kingdoms since 1547. Cruelly, Charles reminded his son that he had not wished to marry and have children and had done so only because Ferdinand had failed to produce sons.[3] Despite such insensitive behaviour, Charles broke down in tears once more as he placed the renunciations of the Spanish kingdoms on his desk and signed them; three times, after each signature (for Castile, Aragon and Sicily), Philip kissed his father's hand. In the summer, Charles handed over to his son control of the remnants of the dukedom of Burgundy. However, he retained the imperial title. Charles formally bade farewell to Philip on 28 August 1556 but contrived even then to put off his departure from the Low Countries until 16 September. On arrival in Spain the emperor was carried slowly in his litter to the Jeronimite monastery of Yuste, where he arrived in February 1557. He died there on 21 September 1558.

Philip was energised by his father's departure and threw himself with relish into his duties. He conducted business with that diligence and unfailing courtesy that were to become his hallmarks; he knew better than to make promises that he might not be able to keep and he assiduously cultivated the practice of listening with grave courtesy to petitioners but giving no immediate response to them. He relaxed by hunting, and on one occasion was injured in a boar-hunt. He was even prepared to joust in a tournament to decide whether the women of Brussels were more beautiful than those of Mechelen and keenly watched some of his courtiers playing games on ice. While maintaining his kingly reserve, therefore, Philip made a considerable effort to create a favourable impression on his new subjects. But he was also very conscious of the need to be seen to be providing a lead in religious matters. He left no one in doubt as to his devotion to the doctrines and rituals of the Catholic Church, attending Mass assiduously and playing his full part in religious ceremonies.[4]

WAR WITH THE PAPACY AND FRANCE

This made it all the more unfortunate that Philip had to postpone his return to Spain because he found himself forced into a war with the papacy and France. In May 1555, the College of Cardinals elected Gian Pietro Carafa as pope, clearly with the intention that he should serve a short and uneventful term of office, for he was seventy-nine years of age. However, Carafa (who took the name of Paul IV) had the energy and ambition of a man half his age and he was animated by a lifelong and unyielding hatred for Charles V and for the house of Habsburg. Since Charles now lay beyond his reach, Paul IV vented his spleen on Philip. He found this task the more agreeable because he knew that Philip had used his influence in the College of Cardinals to oppose his election.[5] Paul therefore offered to secure the transfer of the duchy of Milan and the kingdom of Naples to two of the sons of Henry II of France in return for an alliance against Spain. In doing so, he placed Philip in a dreadful dilemma, for while Philip could not contemplate allowing the French to re-establish themselves in Italy it seemed unthinkable that he could begin his reign with a war against the pope himself. He was, after all, the Catholic king. Philip's nerve was equal to the challenge, however; 'I am determined to maintain all my realms', he wrote in April 1557.[6] Shortly afterwards he insisted that he would go to war with Paul IV and Henry II 'for the sake of undeceiving the world, and especially his enemies with regard to their opinion of his being cowardly and spiritless'.[7] Philip understood only too well that for a monarch, reputation was everything. He appointed the duke of Alba to command his armies in Italy.[8]

So determined was Philip to pursue the war effectively that he returned
to England to secure Mary's support, crossing from Calais to Dover on
18 March 1557.[9] There was deep hostility in the English Privy Council to
the idea of fighting a war on behalf of Spain even if it did have the attrac-
tion of being against France. Mary secured the backing that she needed
from her councillors by calling them in one by one to declare their
position to her; intimidated, they agreed to go to war. An extraordinary
stroke of good fortune followed; in April a madcap Englishman in
the pay of France, Thomas Stafford, seized Scarborough Castle in
Yorkshire and proclaimed himself 'Protector of England'. It was easy
now for Mary to declare war on France, and she did so on 7 June. Philip
returned across the Channel on 6 July, taking with him 5000 English
soldiers.[10]

The war was fought in Italy and on the borders of the Low Countries
and France. Francis, duke of Guise, led an army of 13 000 men into Italy
but then wasted a month enjoying the pleasures of Rome before moving
on to Naples in April 1557. His self-indulgence allowed Alba, not for the
last time, to win a campaign by refusing to engage his enemy in battle.
Alba simply let plague and expense – the traditional enemies of French
invasions of Italy – devastate Guise's army. When in the autumn Guise
was called urgently to the front in Flanders, Alba invaded the papal states,
put the town of Anagni to the sword and marched on Rome itself.
Memories of the Sack of Rome in 1527 were still painful but Alba had no
intention of taking his army into Rome and with Philip's explicit approval
made peace with Paul IV in the only way that formidable pontiff could
understand – by submitting unconditionally to him. On 27 September
1557 Alba entered Rome and made his way to the Vatican between two
files of papal soldiers. There, he fell on his knees and formally asked
Paul IV for forgiveness for having waged war against him. Despite the
humiliation of his general (which he bore with stoic resolution) Philip
stood now as the undoubted master of Italy. He had triumphantly passed
the first test of his kingship.[11]

He was equally successful on the northern front. On the feast of
St Lawrence, 10 August 1557, at St Quentin, forty kilometres north of
Paris, Philip's army crushed the French under Anne of Montmorency,
Constable of France. The army consisted of 35 000 infantry – including
7000 who were brought by sea from Castile – and 12 000 cavalry, and
it was truly cosmopolitan; it was commanded by the redoubtable
Emmanuel Philibert, duke of Savoy, and the cavalry (which played the
decisive part in the battle) was led by Egmont. The English soldiers

played a conspicuous part in the victory. Indeed, it was a triumph; the French lost 14 000 men – 3000 of them killed – while the Constable and four of his sons were among those taken prisoner. The Constable was joined in his captivity by Gaspar de Châtillon, seigneur of Coligny, Admiral of France. Philip was not present during the battle and arrived on the following day to survey the carnage. He was horrified by the blood-letting but he had the deep satisfaction of knowing that he had established his martial qualities at the outset of his reign; he never went to war again in person, both because he found the spectacle repugnant but also because he did not wish to risk losing the prestige that he won at St Quentin.[12] To celebrate his triumph Philip had the Dutch master Antonis Mor paint him as a warrior in armour, tempered and triumphant. Mor's painting did full justice to Philip's new standing as a great warrior prince, now a major European figure in his own right.

Philip did not hazard his new laurels by marching on Paris, fearing that his forces might become over-extended. His caution, however, allowed the French to regroup, and on 6 January 1558 they regained national honour by taking Calais (which had been in English hands since 1347). Philip felt the loss keenly and was forced yet again to postpone his return to Spain: 'what has happened at Calais has obliged me to abandon the plan for the present'.[13] A further Spanish success when Egmont defeated the French at Gravelines in July 1558 then enabled the combatants to wind the war down with honour mutually satisfied. Peace could now be made.

The process of ending the wars was facilitated by the deaths of Philip's father and wife. On 1 November 1558 Philip learned in Brussels of the death of Charles, and on 17 November Mary Tudor died. Their deaths brought Charles's grand design for a Burgundian–English alliance to a convenient close and were a major landmark in Philip's own life, setting him free to plan his future without regard for Charles's priorities. Philip honoured his father's memory with obsequies in Brussels which set a new standard for courtly grandeur (29 December 1558) but he did not mourn Mary Tudor, contenting himself with letting it be known that he had 'felt a reasonable regret for her death'.[14]

In England, Mary was succeeded by her half-sister Elizabeth, now twenty-five years of age. The new queen had lived a life marked by uncertainty and often by terror. She would one day proclaim in all sincerity that she did not want to look into men's souls but her terrifying experiences had taught her the art of looking into men's minds, of analysing their motives. Elizabeth had learned, too, how to hide her own purposes, to dissimulate and to prevaricate without shame or embarrassment. Two things were widely believed of her at the outset of her reign – that she would take England in a Protestant direction despite her submission to Rome under her sister's rule, and that she would marry to have children and secure the succession.

Philip shared these perceptions and was so determined to maintain Spain's friendship with England that he duly let it be known to Elizabeth that he was prepared to marry her. Elizabeth professed herself gratified by his suit but for political and religious reasons she could not seriously entertain a Spanish match. However, she fully shared Philip's commitment to maintaining Anglo-Spanish friendship, convinced as she was that she had more to fear from France than from Spain. Both monarchs therefore determined not to antagonise each other and so they now fenced elegantly, proclaiming their affection and regard for each other. In January 1559 Elizabeth inevitably but gently rejected Philip's suit.[15] He was, in truth, relieved, but he remained committed to securing English support against France and to strengthening the economic links between England and the Low Countries. He therefore set himself to protect Elizabeth. As the new queen moved with baffling unclearness of purpose to impose a Protestant settlement upon England, it was Philip who did most to prevent the papacy from pronouncing the sentence of excommunication against her that would have forced her Catholic subjects to choose between their faith and their country. Philip knew how to distinguish his political from his religious objectives. In this sense he and Elizabeth were kindred spirits.

THE PEACE OF CÂTEAU-CAMBRÉSIS

The wars of Charles V were brought to an end by the two treaties which were signed on 2 and 3 April 1559 between France and England and between Spain and France; together they became known (after the somewhat dilapidated chateau in Picardy in which they were negotiated) as the Peace of Câteau-Cambrésis. The agreements recognised that a generation of dynastic warfare had placed colossal strains upon the social and political structures of the monarchies of western Europe, and most especially upon those of Spain and France. The Peace acknowledged, too, the anxieties that each of the three rulers had about the religious stability of their kingdoms. Henry II already had good reason to fear the links that the Huguenots were establishing with noble factions in France and

with their co-religionists abroad. Calvinism had made dramatic progress
in France in the 1540s and 1550s and the Huguenots had even presumed
to hold an inaugural National Synod in Paris in 1557 and to formulate a
'Confession of Faith and Ecclesiastical Discipline'. Philip, already anxious
about the situation in the Low Countries, was profoundly shaken to learn
that the Spanish Inquisition had in 1558–9 identified two groups of
Protestants in the cities of Seville and Valladolid. He could delay his
return to Spain no longer. For her part, Elizabeth was calculating to what
extent she dared reveal her Protestantism – or indeed, whether she could
survive on her throne if she chose not to do so. The three monarchs
were, therefore, united in their conviction that they needed a period of
peace in order to establish (or to re-establish) control over their kingdoms. Accordingly, after some routine haggling, agreement was reached
quite easily.

The most important of the provisions of the Peace confirmed Spain's
pre-eminence in Italy. France accepted Philip's rule over Milan, Naples
and Sicily and dropped her claims to Savoy and Piedmont. She retained
only the fortresses of Turin, Saluzzo and Pignerol in the peninsula.
Emmanuel Philibert of Savoy joined in Spain's triumph; his services as
Governor of the Low Countries and as commander at St Quentin were
rewarded by the restoration of the dukedom of Savoy (which had been
overrun by the French in 1536). The re-establishment of the dukedom had
the substantial advantage for Spain of creating a barrier against further
French attacks on Italy. However, at the very moment that alliance with
Spain brought his dukedom back to him, Emmanuel Philibert now agreed
to a French alliance, to be reinforced by his marriage to Henry II's sister
Margaret. Known as 'Ironhead' because of his strength of purpose,
Emmanuel Philibert was a remarkably clear-sighted statesman. He understood that it was only by balancing Spain with France that he could remain
secure in his dukedom. He would be Philip's ally, never his slave.

France's failure in Italy was compensated for to some degree in northern Europe. She retained Calais (although in theory for only for eight
years) together with the imperial cities of Metz, Toul and Verdun, while
the recovery of St Quentin and the other fortresses lost in 1557 meant
that she would be able to threaten the Low Countries in the future as in
the past. The amity with Spain was sealed in the customary manner with
a marriage agreement; it was agreed that Philip would marry Henry II's
young daughter Elizabeth. Until the very last day of the negotiations it
had been uncertain whether Elizabeth would be betrothed to Philip
himself or to Don Carlos, and in taking her for his own bride Philip may

well have tacitly acknowledged the unsuitability of his son for marriage (see below, chapter 3). The marriage was celebrated in Paris on 22 June; Alba stood proxy for Philip II.[16]

The celebrations came to a dramatic end when Henry II was mortally injured in a jousting accident at a tournament to celebrate the marriages; he died on 10 July. Henry's death transformed the political situation in France. He left a widow, Catherine de' Medici, and seven children – four boys (Francis, Charles, Henry and another child named Francis) and three girls (Claude, Elizabeth and Margaret). Although France's Salic Law forbade the succession of females, the Valois dynasty seemed to be secure enough. However, the boys were all young and none of them enjoyed robust health. The eldest now succeeded to the throne at the age of sixteen, as Francis II. Far from finding stability under the strong and experienced Henry II, therefore, France was in 1559 thrown into political and religious chaos that lasted for a generation. The death of Henry II and the political, religious and social turmoil that it gave rise to made possible what has become known as 'the Age of Philip II', the period of nearly half a century during which the power of Spain was pre-eminent in European politics. All the advantages that the French monarchy had enjoyed over Spain – a population twice as large, a position that was much more central to the European heartland, natural resources that were immeasurably richer – now counted for little in the scales of European power-politics.

Central to the weakening of French monarchical power was the destructive factionalism of the three great landed families, who competed with each other for power at court and who even sought to dominate the crown itself: the Guise, the most powerful of all, whose lands lay chiefly in the north-east; the Montmorency, whose lands were in the south-west; and the Condé or Bourbon-Vendôme, landholders in the centre and the south. Rivalry was complicated – and further embittered – by religious conflict, for the Guise family prided itself on being the secular leader of Roman Catholicism in France while the Bourbon family had already, in the person of Jeanne d'Albret, begun its conversion to Calvinism in 1560. Jeanne's husband, Antoine de Bourbon, was a prince of the blood and had a claim on the throne should the Valois family die out. Antoine wobbled in his religious faith but although he just about remained inside the Catholic Church his son and heir, Henry of Navarre, was brought up as a Calvinist and he stood next in line to the throne after the royal princes.[17]

The accession of Francis II led to the replacement of the Montmorency by the Guise as the dominant clan at court, for Francis was married to

Mary Stuart, Queen of Scotland, and she was the niece of Francis, duke of Guise. The Guise family found it convenient to denigrate the Peace of Câteau-Cambrésis as a humiliation from which they (and the new king) freely dissociated themselves. More than this, they cast covetous eyes on the throne of England, for Mary Stuart was descended from Henry VIII's sister Margaret and had the strongest claim on the English throne if Elizabeth died childless. The new pre-eminence of the Guise family in France had, therefore, profound implications for the balance of power in western Europe; France, far from accepting the verdict of Câteau-Cambrésis, might now seek to undo it by destabilising or even conquering England and thereby constructing a power bloc of France, Scotland and England that would more than rival Philip's monarchy. In consequence, Philip was obliged to seek a tacit diplomatic understanding with Elizabeth and to protect her even as she edged England towards a Protestant settlement and undid the great triumph of his time as king-consort – the re-catholicisation of England. Within weeks of signing the treaties at Câteau-Cambrésis, the Catholic Peace had given way to a situation in which the two great Catholic powers might well go to war over the future of Protestant England.

THE KING'S MEN

It was among the most solemn duties of the king of Spain to take advice from well-qualified men. Philip found no shortage of men competing to win his favour as he took up the reins of government, for he could choose from the leading figures of no fewer than three courts – his own in England and then in the Low Countries; Charles V's in Brussels; and Juana's in Spain. When it became known that Charles intended to abdicate the men in all three courts gravitated towards Philip. But by then it was already too late for many of them; the men who had gone to England with Philip in 1554 had the inside track and they dominated the government of Spain during Philip's first fifteen years or so in power. In a very real sense, what took place in the later 1550s was a transfer of power not just from the Emperor to his son, but from Charles's generation to Philip's, and that in turn was a transformation which was not simply determined by age but by attitude – the men who came to power under Philip were men of his own age and his own stamp. With the singular exception of the Portuguese Ruy Gómez de Silva, they were Spaniards – or, more properly, they were Castilians.

Charles's court in Brussels naturally included the most senior men, but few of them were Spanish. The leading figure was Perrenot de Granvelle, Bishop of Arras. Granvelle had been born for power; his father had been Charles V's chief minister and he himself had managed important affairs of state for the Emperor before he was out of his twenties. In 1550 he had become Chancellor in succession to his father, and when in the abdication ceremony of 1555 he took the oath in Philip's name he confidently expected to have similar pre-eminence under the new king. However, Granvelle's self assurance – indeed, it was arrogance – intimidated Philip. That Granvelle was Charles V's leading servant, that he expected to wield power under Philip, and that he sought indeed to instruct the new king in the exercise of power: these were the characteristics that debarred him from office as far as Philip was concerned. When Philip travelled to Spain in 1559 he left Granvelle behind and it did not satisfy the bishop's overweening pride that he held the rank of first minister to the regent, Margaret of Parma.

The leading nobles of the Low Countries – men such as the Prince of Orange and the counts of Egmont and Hornes – had of course no interest in travelling to Spain with Philip, but they expected to be accorded proper acknowledgement of their status in the Low Countries. Philip realised, however reluctantly, that he could not govern the Low Countries without the active support of the senior aristocracy. Accordingly, he allowed Orange, Egmont and Hornes to retain their seats on the Council of State in the Low Countries after his departure.[18] It suited his purpose that Granvelle and the native aristocracy were deeply antipathetic towards each other. When Philip sailed for Spain, therefore, he left behind him his father's four leading servants, men who had embodied the cosmopolitan nature of Charles V's rule. That each of the four – Granvelle, Orange, Egmont and Hornes – were deeply resentful of the way in which Philip had treated them did not augur well for the future.

The only leading figure from the Emperor's court who travelled to Spain to take up a position of power was Francisco de Eraso, a career-administrator of humble birth. Significantly, Eraso was Spanish, born in Navarre. He had made himself indispensable to Charles, and three times in the months between September 1554 and March 1555 was sent by the Emperor on missions to Philip's court in England. He took advantage of the opportunity to consolidate his relationship with Ruy Gómez, and from Brussels he kept Ruy Gómez informed of what was happening in Charles's court. He thereby secured his future; when Philip became king of Spain, one of his first major appointments was to name Eraso as secretary of the Council of Finance (April 1556). Eraso directed the management of crown finances in the early years of Philip's reign.[19]

Eraso recognised that Ruy Gómez had used the years in England to become Philip's chief adviser; indeed, he had become known as 'rey Gómez', in punning acknowledgement of his primacy at court.[20] Technically, his power-base derived from his office of *sumiller de corps*, in which capacity he controlled the working of Philip's household, but in reality he owed his political power to his personal relationship with the monarch. Philip had come to trust Ruy Gómez's judgement and recognised that he needed his moral and practical support as he entered into his kingship. It may indeed have been to prevent Ruy Gómez from exercising too great an influence over Philip that Charles had placed Alba and Gómez in equally strong positions at the head of Philip's household – Alba as his *mayordomo mayor* and Ruy Gómez as his *sumiller de corps*. In England the two men began a struggle for influence that continued until Ruy Gómez's death.

Ruy Gómez and Alba could hardly have been more different in background, temperament or political purpose. Ruy Gómez was a confidant whom Philip trusted as he did no other minister (with the possible exception of Luis de Requesens) while Alba was a servant whom Philip deeply resented and indeed feared but whose services he could not dispense with. Philip's dislike of Alba was well-known – as early as 1551 an informed observer had suggested that Philip would not retain Alba's services in the long term[21] – but he had no other senior aristocrat who was accomplished enough in the arts of war to lead his armies. Ruy Gómez was a courtier, practised in the arts of civility, a man who was able to argue persuasively and to use his considerable personal charm as a political tool; Alba was a domineering, overpowering personality who was accustomed to having his way and who had neither the time nor the temperament for discussion, a man to whom the political arts were largely alien.

Both men regularly left Philip's court on his business while he was in northern Europe, and the nature of their absences made clear the difference in Philip's attitude towards them. Philip was consciously preparing Ruy Gómez for government by broadening his experience while he was simply ridding himself of Alba; indeed, on one occasion, Ruy Gómez triumphantly wrote that 'the King remarks that he has not wished to conclude certain business before having got the Duke out of the country'.[22] In England and the Low Countries, therefore, Philip systematically extended his favour to Ruy Gómez at the expense of Alba. This was of more than purely personal significance, for the two men held starkly opposing views about the structure of Philip's monarchy. Ruy Gómez, himself a foreigner, urged Philip to institute a federal structure, with each state having its own rights and responsibilities within the monarchy, while Alba, the aristocratic and authoritarian Castilian, insisted that Philip impose a Castilian model on his lands, if need be by force. The debate between the two men was to be of profound significance for the future and, leavened as it was by intense personal rancour, it dominated the early years of Philip's reign.

Two friars joined Alba and Ruy Gómez at the centre of power in Philip's court during the years in the north – the Dominican, Bartolomé de Carranza, who was the court's official preacher, and the Franciscan Bernardo de Fresneda, who was Philip's confessor. Their offices gave the two men privileged access to Philip and despite the traditional rivalry between the Dominicans and the Franciscans they worked fruitfully together during the early years in the north. However, they fell out over Fresneda's suspicion that Carranza was seeking the royal confessorship for himself, and their relationship was finally destroyed when in February 1558 Carranza was consecrated as archbishop of Toledo in succession to Siliceo. Carranza was only fifty-five years of age and it was clearly Philip's intention that he should guide the Spanish Church for many years to come. Fresneda found that insupportable and took up opposition to Carranza.[23]

Back in Spain, a third senior churchman was furious at the appointment of Carranza to the primatial see. Fernando de Valdés, Inquisitor-General and archbishop of Seville, had hoped and indeed expected to succeed to the archbishopric of Toledo himself. Valdés wreaked a terrible vengeance on Carranza – and on the king who had had the temerity to appoint him to the office that he regarded as his own by right. Valdés had particular need of the primatial see because he was fighting for his own survival at court. Juana found him to be overpowering and intimidating. Indeed, Valdés seriously undermined the regent's authority by leading a number of senior bishops in refusing to contribute to a voluntary 'gift' to help the crown. This and other provocations led Juana to try to force Valdés to leave the court in Valladolid by insisting that he reside in his archbishopric of Seville. From England, Philip vigorously supported Juana. However, Valdés hung on, knowing that if he left court he would necessarily have to retire as Inquisitor-General. Philip sent his new archbishop of Toledo back to Spain to force Valdés out. Undismayed, Valdés went on the attack; astoundingly, he produced sufficient evidence to force the king and the pope to agree to the arrest of the

Archbishop of Toledo on suspicion of heretical writings. On 22 August 1559, three days before Philip embarked for Spain, Valdés had Carranza arrested.[24]

The imprisonment of Carranza was only the first part of Valdés's counter-attack, and indeed it was the lesser part, for in 1558 he had been triumphantly able to inform Juana that he had uncovered two circles of active heretics in Seville and in Valladolid and that a number of the leading figures among the heretics – notably Agustín Cazalla and Carlo de Sesso in Valladolid and Dr Constantino Ponce de la Fuente in Seville – had travelled with Charles and Philip to the Low Countries and to Germany. It was this evidence, more even than the attack upon Carranza, that saved Valdés, for it clearly made it impossible for the Crown to dispense with his services. That the contagion of heresy had spread from within the circle of men who had travelled abroad with Charles and Philip was further demonstrated by the Carranza affair, for the new archbishop had spent years in the north and had had the tact-lessness to publish his 'Commentaries' not in Spain (where they could have been vetted by the Inquisition) but in Antwerp. In Carranza's mean-dering tome there were scores of errors that zealous inquisitors seized upon; the volume that was meant to celebrate his triumph sealed his doom. But more than this, in conjunction with the evidence gleaned in Valladolid and Seville it established an irrefutable link between travel in northern Europe and the acquisition of heretical opinions. Philip himself had spent years abroad; unspoken in Valdés's savage and brilliant attack was the challenge to the king to demonstrate that he himself was uncontaminated. Truly, Valdés was able to reflect when he uncovered the two 'protestant cells' that 'it appears that God was pleased that I should have been here'.[25] He knew that Philip would now be forced to support the Inquisition even when it questioned the orthodoxy of the archbishop of Toledo himself, a man who was the king's own confidant. So it proved.

There was a further dimension to Valdés's attack upon foreign influence in Spain, for during the 1540s and 1550s the new Society of Jesus had begun to exert a quite astonishing influence in the country. Valdés felt especially threatened by the Society's growth, instinctively fearing the dynamism with which it operated. He was certainly aware that Juana herself was closely bound to the Jesuits (although he probably could not have known that she had been accepted secretly into its membership, thereby becoming the only female Jesuit in history). Founded by the Basque Ignatius Loyola in 1540 to help the development of souls and the propagation of the Catholic faith, the Society was in origin a strongly Spanish order – four of the nine founder members were Spanish – but it committed itself to a vow of total submission to the will of the pope. To many in Spain this made it an object of suspicion. The first Jesuit arrived in Spain in 1541 and the Spanish Province of the Order was formally created in 1547. By the time of Philip's accession in 1556 over 300 Jesuits were active in Spain and the Society had houses in eighteen towns and cities, finding ready support among many churchmen and noblemen.[26] The established religious orders were often deeply suspicious of the Jesuits, fearing their creative dynamism and anxious that their political contacts would give them leverage out of proportion to their numbers. Valdés shared these fears and set himself in the name of Spanish orthodoxy to attack the Society. Taking as his chief ally Melchor Cano, a Dominican theologian who shared many of his own principles (and prejudices), Valdés chose as his chief victim Francisco de Borja, who had renounced his dukedom of Gandia to become a Jesuit. Borja was a confidant of the royal family – he had officiated at the interment of the Empress Isabella, had administered the last rites to both Juana *la Loca* and to Charles V himself and had served as a tutor to Philip. He was among the first to testify for Carranza at his trial and in 1559 he interceded on behalf of one of the families involved in the Valladolid Protestant scare.[27] His actions commended neither himself nor the Society of Jesus to the Inquisitor-General; Valdés, as was his custom, hounded both.

THE FIRES OF THE FAITH: VALLADOLID, 8 OCTOBER 1559

Philip set sail for Spain from Flushing on 25 August 1559. Emmanuel Philibert of Savoy had refused to stay on in the Low Countries and Philip therefore appointed his half-sister Margaret of Parma as Governor-General with Granvelle as her first minister. He attempted to placate the senior nobles by rewarding them with grants of money a few days before he left – the count of Egmont received 50 000 *écus*, the Prince of Orange 40 000, and the counts of Berghes and Hornes 15 000 each. Philip left these men, too, with offices in the provinces that were appropriate to their social station: Orange, for instance, became Stadholder of Holland, Zeeland and Utrecht while Egmont was appointed Stadholder of Flanders and Artois.[28]

At thirty-two years of age Philip was now an experienced and knowledgeable ruler. He had met most of the major statesmen of his time and in his quiet way had made his judgements of them. He had seen for himself the key strategic routes of his monarchy; he had travelled the overland route from Genoa to the Low Countries (what would become known as 'The Spanish Road') and now he sailed across the Bay of Biscay for the second time. He had seen the waters of the Channel that the English claimed as their own and had crossed them three times at their narrowest point. When the time came for him to send his armies and navies along those great arteries he would be able to do so from personal knowledge of them. He had, if only nominally, commanded his army at a great victory over the French and as king-consort of England was able to claim part of the credit for the recatholicisation of England. He had defeated a formidable pope in war. Twice a widower, he was about to marry again.

A studious, reflective man, Philip had used his time in northern Europe to observe and to learn. He committed very few of his plans to paper, preferring to mull over his ideas privately and indeed to discuss them with his advisers (sometimes without telling them what he was thinking of). It is clear from the major structural changes that he made in Spain in the first two years or so after his return – the choice of Madrid as capital, the commitment to build the great monastery-palace of the Escorial and so on – that he had a clear strategy in his mind when he returned to Spain. However, since he kept his plans very much to himself (and also because most of his papers were destroyed in a shipwreck on the return to Spain) we have to follow his actions in these early years after his return in order to reconstruct this strategy. The identities of the men who travelled with him revealed a little of the way that Philip's mind was working; he brought with him, for instance, the painter Antonis Mor and the architect Juan Bautista de Toledo. Philip knew very clearly how he would use these men to present the public face of a kingship that he intended to be both very private and withdrawn and yet overpowering to any who might think of challenging it. Indeed, he had already prepared some of the ground; while in northern Europe Philip had authorised major rebuilding in the palace in Madrid (the Alcázar) and in other royal houses and hunting lodges in the centre of Spain. Quietly, without people realising what he was doing, Philip had prepared the way for his return – and for a style of kingship that would be the very antithesis of his father's.

During his years in the north, Philip had shown a mature and con-trolled command of political affairs. He had accepted the restraints imposed upon him in England by his ill-defined position as king-consort.[29] He had managed, certainly, to exercise most of his rights as king of Spain during his absence. He had shown great diligence in applying himself to his paperwork and had demonstrated unfailing courtesy in dealing with the individuals who flocked to ask favours of him. As to his servants: he valued his close friends, Ruy Gómez de Silva and Luis de Requesens, and his secretary, Gonzalo Pérez, but he had not found it easy to work with Alba and Granvelle, William of Orange, Egmont and Hornes. He had had to abandon Carranza but he would *never* trust Valdés – and he had learned how to play men off one against another. He had clearly decided, too, that he would not allow his senior aristocrats to exercise real political power at the centre of government.

Philip had also, with measured calculation, created a personality for himself that contrasted dramatically with that of his father. Where Charles was outgoing and energetic, Philip was reserved and quiescent; where Charles had always sought to be at the heart of action, Philip had already shown that he could distance himself from it; where Charles was a man for the broad sweep of policy, Philip concentrated obsessively on detail; where Charles often ignored the routine cares of government for his pleasures, Philip was already known for his disciplined concern with the very minutiae of government; where Charles had abused his body in indulging his passions for food and drink, Philip was abstemious in his diet. Philip had in a very real sense constructed his personality to be as different from his father's as possible. As he repeated the journey that Charles had made in 1517, he could be satisfied that he would be a very different king from his father. He disembarked at Laredo on 8 September 1559. He heard Mass and on the following day headed inland for the city of his birth.

On 8 October a giant scaffold stood in the Plaza Mayor of Valladolid so that the enormous crowd could see the men and women who had been convicted by the Inquisition as they heard their sentences proclaimed and awaited their fate. One account had it that 200 000 people were crammed into the Plaza Mayor; it is unlikely that there were quite so many, but the crowd that had gathered was probably of a size that had never been seen before in Old Castile.[30] People had waited months for this moment and they had come from far and wide to witness it. Indeed, so great was the anger against the accused that the Inquisition actually had to protect them lest they be lynched. An earlier *auto-de-fé* in May had been a grand and edifying spectacle: thirty-one people had been dealt with and Melchor Cano had preached to them for an hour before they met their fate. But some of the most important victims had been saved so that they could be dealt with in the presence of the king himself, in celebration of his return to Castile. Now the day had arrived and after a sermon had been preached the man who had organised the event (and who stood to gain the most from it) stepped forward and faced the king. Fernando de Valdés begged for divine help in the fight against heresy and apostasy in Spain. Philip stood up and, holding his sword in his hand, took the oath to give all the support that he could to the Inquisition. It was the first formal act of his reign in Spain and in it Philip was true to the injunction of his father at the moment of his birth that God 'make a good Christian of you'. Charles had repeated that injunction in a codicil to his will written on 9 September 1558, in which he had urged Philip to see that heretics were punished and destroyed 'with all rigour' and without any exception. It was his dying wish that Philip should support the Inquisition.[31] Now, less than a kilometre from the palace in which he had been born, he did so.

An *auto-de-fé* involved only the formal reading out of crimes and of sentences; the punishments themselves were carried out by the secular authorities in a subsequent but separate ceremony. Eighteen people now heard their fate. Chief among them was Carlo de Sesso, an Italian who was known to Philip himself. The story grew up that as he was led past the king, Sesso rebuked him for his cruelty and that Philip replied that if his own son had been as guilty as Sesso was, he himself would pile the faggots at the stake at which he was to die. It is probable that the exchange did not actually take place for condemned men would not be allowed too close to the king of Spain, but if the story must be denied a historical truthfulness it can be accorded a dramatic one, for Philip in his contempt for heresy was fully capable of saying such a thing. He had seen at first hand in the Low Countries how heresy could advance at the expense of royal authority and he had no intention of letting such a thing occur in Spain. Sesso went bravely to his death in the Campo Grande a few minutes' walk away; with two others who had refused to recant he was burned alive. A further nine people, who had recanted their errors, were garrotted before the flames were lit beneath them; five of them were women. The rest were imprisoned. In addition, the bones of Leonor de Vivero were exhumed and ritually consigned to the flames; Leonor was the mother of the Cazalla family, which provided several of the victims in Valladolid and she had cheated the flames by dying in prison. Philip himself was not present in the Campo Grande; he did not need to be, for with his presence in the Plaza Mayor he had done all that was required of him.

News of the *auto-de-fé* of 8 October 1559 reverberated around Europe and has echoed down the ages. It was meant to do so. Philip had on that day made a profoundly important public commitment in the city of his birth; he had demonstrated that he would give the fullest support to the Inquisition and that his reign would be distinguished by his active commitment to the war against heresy. History has often accepted this at face value and seen Philip as a crusader for Catholicism both at home and abroad. This is to misunderstand him; he would lead a crusade to protect Catholicism within Spain and her possessions in the Mediterranean but he would be consistently loath to do the same elsewhere. Philip was in 1559 no crusader; he had a deep devotion to the Roman Catholic Church (in its Spanish form) and he had an enduring revulsion of heresy, but he retained, too, a cool calculation of what his interests were as king of Spain. He would not tolerate heresy in his hereditary dominions. This was the statement that he made in Valladolid on 8 October 1559. Heresy elsewhere was of no particular concern to him; he deplored it but he did not intend to lead a crusade against it. He had other priorities.

PART II
The Prudent King

3

THE RE-ORDERING OF SPAIN

The beginning of a new reign was traditionally a time of joyous optimism, a celebration of the new king, of his good intentions and happy prospects. But there was little to celebrate in Spain in 1559. There was, certainly, widespread relief that the king had returned home but there was also a profound sense of war-weariness and a consciousness of the seriousness of the problems facing the country. Even the climate was hostile, accentuating hunger and famine across Spain. Philip himself seems to have needed time to recover from the emotional impact of the great *auto-de-fé*; he left Valladolid the day after the *auto* and spent a month hunting. He performed one pressing task, when at La Espina near Valladolid he formally acknowledged the existence of his half-brother, Don John of Austria.[1] But it is difficult to escape the conclusion that Philip was overwhelmed by the range of problems facing him. For years he had ached to return to his homeland but as he began now to fully absorb the realities of the situation confronting him in Spain he baulked at the prospect of dealing with them. At the end of 1559 he wrote to Granvelle that 'I confess to you that when I was in Flanders, I never believed the situation could be so bad here.'[2] He took refuge in inaction; in April 1560, an ambassador reported that Philip 'avoids business as much as possible'.[3] It was not the last time that Philip adopted this attitude when confronted by crisis; the carefully contrived appearance of 'prudence' that so impressed contemporaries was, very often, an immobility borne of indecisiveness. But it was also part of the image of majesty that Philip very deliberately created for himself – the image of a king who was coolly aloof and who could not be hurried or pressured into making decisions.

Philip did, however, make one decision while he was in Valladolid that proved to have profound importance and indeed changed the very shape of his monarchy; on 24 September he authorised Fray Andrés de Urdaneta to go on an expedition with two ships that he had ordered the Viceroy of Peru to send to wrest control from Portugal of the 'Philippine Islands' in the Pacific Ocean. Charles V had effectively sold those islands to Portugal in 1529 at the Treaty of Zaragoza, and in a deeply symbolic act Philip determined that he would regain control of them.[4] They had been named for him when he was prince and in a calculated rejection of his father's polity he resolved that he would reclaim them for himself – and that in doing so he would rule an empire that was truly global even though he himself was not an emperor.

THE PREPONDERANCE OF CASTILE

Philip was fully aware of his obligations to each and every one of his realms and did not distinguish between them in any theoretical or legal sense. There is little doubt that Philip intended to return to the Low Countries, but after 1559 he never left the Iberian peninsula again. At the heart of his failure to do so lay his difficulties over the succession, and these were compounded by his personal preferences; Spain was the heart of his monarchy, and Castile – the land of his own birth – stood for him at the very centre of Spain. Here he made his home, and with it the centre of his monarchy. He undertook to find out about his native land in a singularly revealing manner; one of his first actions was to commission the Dutch painter and engraver Anton van Wyngaerde (whom he had appointed as his court painter) to traverse the length and breadth of Spain, painting pictures of the chief cities of the land. Wyngaerde produced a series of exquisite watercolours which are an enduring record of Spain's cities in the early years of Philip's reign. If the king could not visit each of his major cities, he would at least know what they looked like.[5]

At the core of Philip's problems in Spain in 1559 lay the wreckage of his financial resources. In order to free the funds to wage the war against Henry II and Paul IV, Philip had had to suspend payments to his bankers in 1557, to bring about what is normally described as a 'state bankruptcy'. In 1559 he had to begin to make good those payments. Moreover, he had other financial shortfalls to consider. The dispute with the papacy had deprived him of income from the two 'Graces' that he collected with papal permission – the *cruzada*, paid by the laity, and the *subsidio*, a range of taxes on the clergy's wealth. Philip's personal expenses had also increased; he now had to maintain his own court in Spain and pay for the households of his new queen and of Don Carlos. And in 1559 no treasure fleet arrived from the New World.

The crown of Castile's disposable income came to just under three million ducats in 1559. The largest single source of revenue was the *encabezamiento general*, the farm on the sales tax (the *alcabala*), which was agreed with the cities and which brought in about 890 000 ducats annually. This was supplemented by a variety of other taxes: taxes on trade produced *c.* 690 000 ducats; the treasure of the Indies fleet brought about 380 000 ducats for the Crown; the 'ordinary' and 'extraordinary' *servicios* yielded a further 400 000 ducats and the alienations from the royal domain raised a further 280 000 ducats.[6]

The *encabezamiento general*, the ordinary and extraordinary *servicios* and the trade taxes were raised with the approval of the parliament or Cortes of Castile. This body consisted of two procurators from each of eighteen towns and cities and since the Crown required only to have majority support in order to raise or increase taxation it needed in effect to win the support of nineteen procurators to carry out its programme. Even in the earlier years of the reign this was less easy to achieve than might have been anticipated. The Cortes of Castile met twelve times during Philip's reign, and as the Crown's financial needs grew the Cortes were convened more regularly and for sessions that lasted much longer (see Table 3.1). In the years 1559–62 Philip raised his income from Castile by about 1 300 000 ducats annually, some 43 per cent. In the first instance, he took

Table 3.1 Meetings of the Cortes of Castile

1	April–September 1588	7	Jan. 1576–Dec. 1577
2	Dec. 1559–Nov. 1560	8	May 1579–Feb. 1582
3	Feb.–Aug. 1563	9	June 1583–Aug. 1585
4	Dec. 1566–Jan. 1567	10	Oct. 1586–Feb. 1588
5	Feb. 1570–April 1571	11	April 1588–July 1590
6	Apr. 1573–Sept. 1575	12	May 1592–Nov. 1598

Sources: *Actas de las Cortes de Castilla*. I am obliged to Professor I. A. A. Thompson for his assistance in compiling this table.
The towns and cities represented in the Cortes of Castile were: Ávila, Burgos, Córdoba, Cuenca, Granada, Guadalajara, Jaen, León, Madrid, Murcia, Palencia, Salamanca, Soria, Segovia, Seville, Toledo, Valladolid, Zamora

advantage of the goodwill that the Cortes naturally displayed towards him at the beginning of his reign to increase the *encabezamiento general* to 1 216 000 ducats. However, without consulting the procurators Philip then unilaterally introduced new or increased excise and monopoly taxes and resorted to expedients such as selling jurisdictions and titles. His actions provoked fury among the procurators and in 1566 they were moved to condemn what they called 'new taxes' and to attempt to secure their repeal by refusing to grant the ordinary and extraordinary *servicios* until Philip did so. The dispute was smoothed over, but it was a shot across Philip's bows, warning him that he could not take the Cortes of Castile for granted.[7]

The second major source of taxation in Castile was the Church. The death of Paul IV in 1559 cleared the way for Philip to negotiate with his successor, Pius IV (1559–65), for the renewal of the *cruzada* and *subsidio*. Since Pius needed Spanish support in the war against Islam an accommodation was soon reached; Philip promised to support a fleet of one hundred galleys in the Mediterranean and Pius IV renewed the *cruzada* for three years at 300 000 ducats annually. Philip secured another 150 000 ducats on indulgences without affecting the *cruzada*. The *subsidio* was raised again in 1562, to 420 000 ducats annually. With the income granted him from tithes and from a variety of other ecclesiastical sources such as pensions and the tax on the lands of the Military Orders, Philip was by the middle of the 1560s collecting well over 1 500 000 ducats annually from taxes that were raised with the permission of the papacy.

Even with all these extra revenues the Crown still had a shortfall. Philip made up some of the difference by selling government bonds (*juros*) but had to pay more than a million ducats annually in interest charges. And still it was not enough. On 14 November 1560 Philip was forced to default for a second time on his payments to his bankers, converting his debts to them into *juros*.[8] This further weakened the prospects of the Castilian economy and accelerated its decline into a *rentier* economy. In the first years of his reign, Philip had confirmed a pattern that would last for a hundred years; Castile was making a disproportionate contribution to the needs of empire. Castilian resources were being mortgaged years into the future to pay for the needs of the present.[9]

Aragon traditionally paid much less than Castile towards the needs of the Crown. Indeed, since the monarch had to travel to Aragon with his household to hold the Cortes that voted taxes it was generally not worth his trouble to do so; the amounts raised did not justify the expense of the journey. This, together with the lessening of the importance of the border of Aragon after the peace with France in 1559, explained why Philip did not go to Aragon until 1563–4 to be sworn in as king – a prerequisite to securing any grants of money. He then did not travel to the east again until he made a brief visit in 1585–6, and he paid a third and final visit of a few months in 1592. Philip held general Cortes of the three eastern realms in 1563 and 1585 and convened separate sessions of the Corts of Catalonia in 1563 and of the Cortes of the Kingdom of Aragon in 1592. In summoning the representative bodies of his eastern Cortes so infrequently and with a disdain that he barely bothered to disguise, Philip made it clear to his subjects in the Crown of Aragon just how little he valued them by comparison with his subjects in Castile. Therefore, as Castile became more important to Philip, so the states of Aragon received less of his time and attention. The results were predictable – resentment in Castile at the royal demands, fury in Aragon at the royal neglect.

Philip prefaced his journey to Aragon in 1563 by formally laying the foundation stone for his monastery of the Escorial (23 April). He then spent some weeks in Valladolid before heading for Monzón to hold the joint assembly of the three Cortes of Aragon, Valencia and Catalonia. The Cortes opened on 13 September. It was suggestive of the heavy atmosphere under which they took place that Philip felt obliged to apologise for the delay of eleven years since the Cortes had last been summoned. It took the best part of a month merely to examine the powers of the procurators and to have them take their oaths of office. They then duly refused even to consider the Crown's requests for money until they were satisfied on three counts: that the king would promise only to use native-born Aragonese in senior positions in the kingdom; that he would undertake to use natives of the kingdom in his household; and that he would restrict the powers of the Inquisition (which was considered by many in the kingdom to infringe upon their *fueros* or liberties). Philip was so dismayed by the delaying tactics of the procurators that at one stage he had his bed brought into the building in which the meeting was taking place. It was only with the greatest reluctance that he agreed to stay while the procurators concluded their business. The subsidy of 200 000 *libras* that was wrung from the Cortes hardly covered the expenses of the Crown. The meeting was brought to a close in the early hours of 24 January and Philip left immediately for Catalonia.

He arrived in Barcelona on 6 February and was royally entertained – by civic fiestas and then (6 March) by an *auto-de-fé* in which forty men and women were sentenced. Seven of them were burned at the stake.

Philip then welcomed two of his sister María's sons, the archdukes Rudolf and Ernest, who had arrived to be educated at court. It was evident to the Catalans that the king regarded this as the most important part of his business in Barcelona. Certainly, Philip once again found a meeting of a parliament to be an aggravating business and indeed made his feelings clear to the delegates by arriving in riding breeches and with his horse at the ready. He was promised a *servicio* of 300 000 *libras* and then departed so suddenly that no Catalan nobles were able to escort him out of Barcelona. The royal visit to Valencia was even more cursory; Philip made his solemn entry into the city on 14 April and left eleven days later. He did not even convene a Cortes in the Kingdom of Valencia, for to do so would have required him to live there while the Cortes met, and this he was not prepared to do. He arrived back in Madrid on 3 June.[10]

The visit to the eastern states was a political necessity but in financial terms it probably cost more than it raised. Philip had therefore begun his reign by having to depend on the resources of Castile – and by making it clear to the peoples of the eastern states just how little they counted in the balance. And he had not had his son sworn in as heir to the eastern states; Philip had intended that Don Carlos would join him in Monzón but the Prince was not well enough to make the journey. The whole trip was a dismal and condign failure, a portent of Philip's inability to deal constructively with his eastern states – or indeed, even to spare them the time in which he could apply himself to their problems.

THE ROYAL FAMILY: JOY AND TRAGEDY

Elizabeth of Valois arrived in Spain at the end of 1559 and her marriage to Philip was ratified at a splendid ceremony in Guadalajara in January 1560. The new queen was not old enough to consummate the marriage for a couple of years but she enchanted Philip and the court with her delicate beauty and vivacity. Princess Juana was particularly friendly towards Elizabeth and helped to smooth her entry into court society. But more than anybody, Philip himself doted on her and looked after her tenderly. He had barely known his first wife, had been at best indifferent to his second, but from the very beginning he was captivated by Elizabeth and although he was twice her age he seems to have fallen genuinely and deeply in love with her. Elizabeth was a wife whom he could mould, and she brought out the very best in him.[11] Philip even allowed her some political involvement; when in 1565 she travelled to the French frontier for a brief reunion with her mother, Philip encouraged Elizabeth to engage in some diplomatic activity (the 'Colloquy of Bayonne') while insisting that their meeting was 'simply a family meeting of affection'.[12] The results of this extraordinary privilege were somewhat unfortunate; the meeting of Catherine and Elizabeth seemed to many Protestants – and not just in France – to be a harbinger of an understanding between the two great Catholic powers that they would prosecute with vigour the war against Protestantism. No such agreement was made, but the apparent rapprochement between the two great Catholic powers was deeply worrying to many Protestants throughout Europe.

Philip and Elizabeth began their marital life together as soon as Elizabeth reached puberty. She became pregnant but suffered a miscarriage in 1564. In 1566 she was delivered of a girl and the French ambassador reported that Philip behaved during the birth as 'the best and most affectionate husband that could be imagined'. The infanta was christened Isabella Clara Eugenia. In the following year Elizabeth gave birth to another daughter, Catalina Micaela. Elizabeth suffered complications after both births and when she conceived again shortly after Catalina Micaela's birth she was desperately weak. She gave birth to a still-born daughter after carrying her for only four months (3 October 1568) and it was immediately evident that she herself had only hours left to live. Before Elizabeth died she apologised to Philip for her failure to bear him a son. She was twenty-two years of age. Philip was utterly devastated by her death.[13] As he interred his beloved queen he must have reflected on the harshness of the fate that ruled his private life, for his only son had died in terrible circumstances less than three months earlier. At forty-one years of age and after having been married three times, Philip still had no male heir.

The condition of Don Carlos had frightened and depressed Philip from the moment of their reunion, for it was immediately evident to him that his son was deeply disturbed. In October 1559 Don Carlos was disgracefully rude at a court reception and although he was quickly brought to heel by Philip, the damage had been done: Don Carlos's condition became a matter of public comment.[14] Philip had him sworn in as heir to the throne of Castile on 22 February 1560 – he had no alternative – but there was no disguising the backwardness of the prince. By the autumn of 1561, Don Carlos was locking himself in his rooms and beginning to experiment with strange medicines. Tragedy followed; in Alcalá on 19 April 1562, the prince fell down some stairs and landed heavily on his head. The swelling of his crown made it evident that he had suffered some brain damage and he sank into delirium. A variety of remedies were applied and by 20 May Don Carlos was out of immediate danger. However, he never fully recovered even the limited facilities that he had possessed. It took him months to regain his balance and to walk again and his behaviour became increasingly marked over subsequent years by capriciousness and indeed by sadism. During the crisis, Philip threw himself and his son into God's hands, averring that 'God always shows his clemency in such extreme cases'.[15] He was extremely solicitous for his son's welfare; he visited him several times during the crisis in Alcalá and looked after him lovingly.[16] But he could have no confidence that Don Carlos would ever be fit to succeed him. In 1564 an ambassador described Don Carlos as having the intellectual capacity of a seven-year-old. The prince was then nineteen years of age.[17]

In the forlorn hope of inducing some measure of responsibility into his son, Philip had him join the Council of State in June 1565. He also appointed Ruy Gómez de Silva as his *mayordomo mayor* to reassure the world (and the prince himself) that all was well. There was even talk of arranging a marriage for him.[18] But nothing improved Don Carlos's condition. In 1565 he tried to escape from court to go to Flanders to resolve the crisis there. He also threatened the procurators of the Cortes of Castile that he 'would strip them all of all their power' if they meddled in his affairs, and in 1566 he attacked Alba with a knife, furious that the duke rather than he was being sent to Flanders to deal with what was by now a rebellion. When Don Carlos spoke to Don John and others of his intention 'to kill a man', Philip had no choice but to act, for it was well understood that it was he himself who was the intended victim. On 19 January 1568 he led the Council of State into Don Carlos's bedroom and placed him under arrest.

The prince deteriorated rapidly in confinement. He took to damaging himself by sitting near to a hot fire and then showering in cold water, by gorging himself on his meals and then going on hunger-strike. His body, enfeebled since birth, could not support such abuse, and he declined rapidly. He died on 24 July 1568. Philip (contrary to stories that were subsequently circulated by his enemies) went to see him in his final hours.[19] Ashamed and deeply embarrassed by Don Carlos during his life, Philip sank into despair after his son's death.

This failure to secure the succession in the male line was doubtless the more agonising to Philip because the two illegitimate branches of the royal family had produced brilliant young men; Don John of Austria and Alexander Farnese both effortlessly displayed that mastery of the courtly arts in which Don Carlos was so irredeemably lacking.[20] In 1565, when Malta was under siege by the Ottoman Turk (see chapter 5), Don John fled from court to join the relief expedition; he reached Barcelona after the expedition had sailed but he had demonstrated his mettle – he, too, was the Emperor's son – and in 1568 Philip named him General of the Sea, opening the way to the military career that Don John yearned for.[21] It may be that Philip gave Don John this position because he was having to consider the possibility of allowing him to succeed to the throne.

Elizabeth of Valois and Don Carlos were both laid to rest in Madrid, but Philip did not have the time to grieve properly for them. The revolt of the *moriscos* of Granada broke out at the end of 1568 (see chapter 5 below) and Philip travelled south to supervise the military campaign against the rebels. While he was preoccupied with the revolt in Granada Philip made arrangements for his own fourth marriage. Desperate to secure the succession, he ignored the genetic risks of which he must have been acutely conscious after the death of Don Carlos; once again he married within his own close family, choosing for his wife Anna, daughter of his sister María and Maximilian. Anna had been born in Cigales, just outside Valladolid, during her parents' regency in 1549. She arrived at Santander on 2 October 1570 and on 14 November was married to Philip in Segovia.

The new queen was a strikingly elegant young woman and Philip was charmed by her. On 4 December 1571 she was delivered of a boy – the first son to be born to Philip in a quarter of a century – and he was named Fernando. Mindful of the death of Elizabeth after a rapid succession of pregnancies, Philip seems to have practised a discreet form of birth-control, allowing Anna time to recover after each confinement. She was delivered of a succession of children: Carlos Lorenzo in 1573; Diego Felix, 1575; Felipe, 1578 and María, 1580. However, the risk that Philip had taken in marrying his own niece soon brought predictable and tragic consequences, for his children were weak and did not live long: Carlos Lorenzo died in 1575; Fernando in 1578; Diego Felix in 1582 and María in 1583. By that latter date, therefore, Philip was once again left with only one son – Felipe, who was from birth very weak and was not expected to live long. Worst of all, Anna herself died of disease in 1580 (see chapter 7). The succession was once again precarious.[22]

THE CREATION OF A KINGLY ENVIRONMENT:
COURT, CAPITAL CITY AND ROYAL MONASTERY

Philip had no authentic capital city to welcome him home in 1559. In recent decades Valladolid and Toledo had enjoyed capital status, but both were now effectively ruled out of consideration – Valladolid by virtue of the discovery of the 'Protestant cells' and Toledo because Philip could clearly not reside in the city at a time when its archbishop was under arrest on charges of heresy (and when, indeed, he was availing himself of the income of the archdiocese). During the course of 1561, Philip chose Madrid as the site of his capital. The city had many natural advantages. It was situated on the crossroads at the centre of the peninsula – Philip himself had passed through it many times and had come to know it well – and it had a reputation as a healthy and well-provisioned city. It possessed the facilities for a court and capital: a commanding royal palace (the 'Alcázar'); sufficient housing capacity and space to accommodate Philip's nobility, servants and administrators; and a plaza mayor which, if it was rather derelict, could be made suitable for courtly celebrations. Moreover, it was comparatively small – it had only 16 000 inhabitants in 1561 – and could be developed by the king in a way which would have been impossible with larger and more venerable cities.[23]

Philip moved his court into Madrid in the early summer of 1561 but he did so discreetly, without making a formal entry or even announcing that he had chosen the city for his new capital. A few months later he chose the village of El Escorial as the site for his monastery. There has been much debate as to whether the choice of Madrid or the Escorial came first in Philip's mind but the two choices were so closely related as to be inseparable; Philip had decided that he would have not merely a capital city so much as a whole complex of places which would *between them* fulfil the various functions of a capital. Probably he had decided this while he was in northern Europe; the example of London (where the royal palaces such as Hampton Court were separated by some distance from the centre of government at Westminster) might well have been uppermost in his mind. Although he had never seen Paris, Philip would have known that the Valois kings spent most of the year living in the châteaux of the Loire valley and only visited their capital city on rare occasions, sometimes, indeed, for as little as a day or two in a year. He had no intention of adopting such an extreme pattern himself but he certainly did not envisage living in his capital city as a matter of course; what mattered to him was that he should have a whole complex of residences close to each other so that he could move from one to the other as he saw fit. The facilities offered by Madrid and the Escorial were therefore complemented by those of the Casa del Campo on the outskirts of the city and by the royal palaces and hunting lodges of the Pardo and Aranjuez just outside it. Segovia, with its woods and royal houses, was but a few hours' ride away. Court and government could reside in Madrid, while Philip could move between his other residences as he chose. From Madrid, too, he would have ready access to both Old and New Castile.[24]

Two aspects of Philip's choice of Madrid are worthy of note – that he did not discuss it seriously with his senior advisers and that he never formally announced the decision itself. His conduct here presaged what was to become his basic approach to decision-making on major matters, for he took advice from a few chosen advisers while not even letting them know what exactly it was that he was contemplating. Only he saw the whole picture. As late as the middle of April 1561, Gonzalo Pérez – one of his two or three most senior advisers – was admitting that he did not know 'for certain' what was happening and speculated that Philip might be on the point of choosing Segovia as his new capital.[25] Within two months Philip had moved his court and government into Madrid. Philip's conduct is simply explained: he did not want to commit his prestige to the removal of the court to Madrid so that if the new capital proved to be unsatisfactory he could then transfer his court again without loss of face.[26] This behaviour in turn contradicted another of Philip's motives, for he intended to show very deliberately that he was making a new beginning across the whole face of government. There was also a psychological imperative for him behind the choice of Madrid, an affirmation that his monarchy would be very different from his father's, that he personally was reconstructing Spain after the decades of neglect.

The creation of a new capital city was not done at government expense. Philip toyed with grandiose plans to develop the new city but paid for little himself beyond enlarging the Alcázar and its grounds and patronising a few religious foundations. He never cared much for Madrid – for him it was a functional city – and he left it to the corporation of Madrid and to private enterprise to develop the new city. His servants even had to pay to make their own accommodation habitable.[27] The corporation of Madrid, anxious to ensure that the court remained in the city, undertook an expensive programme of public works in the decade after 1561. The city's enthusiasm was shared chiefly by the religious orders; few had as keen an eye for the drift of events as they, and in the years 1561–96 they founded eighteen religious houses in Madrid as testament to their commitment to the future of the city.[28] The aristocracy were more cautious, waiting to see whether the court would remain there before building palaces. Madrid therefore grew relatively slowly until it became evident that it was indeed likely to remain as the capital city; its population of about 16000 (100 per cent) in 1561 had doubled to 34000 (212 per cent) by the end of the 1560s and had trebled to 55000 (344 per cent) by 1584.[29]

While Philip allowed few resources for the growth of Madrid, he positively showered them on the building of his monastery-palace of 'the Escorial'. He admitted to a total expenditure of 5260560 ducats – equivalent to about one half of the Crown's annual free income by the 1580s – for constructing and decorating the monastery, and the actual cost was probably much greater.[30] Philip himself chose the site for the building, at the foot of the Guadarrama mountains a thousand metres above sea level. The monastery was thus built above the mosquito line – Philip had suffered from malaria and did not intend to do so again – and had access to a ready supply of pure, running water. The Escorial was in a healthy environment to which Philip could repair, particularly when the heat of summer built up in Madrid. It was, however, close enough to Madrid to allow him to return to the capital as the need arose; indeed, on clear days Philip could see Madrid from his apartments. The inhabitants of El Escorial scraped a living from iron waste ('el escora'), and so the full name of the foundation became 'San Lorenzo del Escorial'.

The construction of the Escorial was the greatest project of Philip's reign; the king was obsessed by it and, often to the dismay of his ministers, he pored over every detail of the plans and supervised many of the building operations himself. Where he could find it painfully difficult to make decisions on affairs of state, Philip was readily and promptly able to deal with the most complex issues for his beloved monastery. Making decisions at the Escorial was for Philip a joy, a release from the cares of government. He ensured that the best materials were brought from all over his monarchy: every year, for instance, 20000 ducats were reserved for its building costs from the sale of rights over the Indians of New Spain; Philip sent to the New World for precious materials and rare woods with which to decorate it; he assigned rents in his European possessions to pay for it; he negotiated with the papacy for the grant of benefices to pay for work on the monastery; he himself decided which of his workers and artists would be paid and when; he took the closest interest in the conduct of ceremonies and insisted that the very highest standards be maintained.[31]

The ostensible reason for the construction of the building was to com-
memorate Philip's victory in arms at the battle of St Quentin on St
Lawrence's Day in 1557. As it happened, Philip had from childhood a
special devotion to the saint (who had the advantage of being Spanish)
and so it was natural for him to dedicate the monastery to St Lawrence
and to design it in the shape of the gridiron on which he had reputedly
been martyred. Philip also intended the building to serve as a mausoleum
for the earthly remains of his father and the other members of his family.
He chose the Jeronimite Order to rule his monastery because its auster-
ity and discipline most closely corresponded to his own purposes; the
Jeronimites (who had originally been hermits) were at once deeply con-
templative but also active in the world. No doubt Philip also had it in
mind to emulate his father's choice of the Jeronimites for the monastery
at Yuste.[32] However, the Escorial was much more than a monastery, even
if it became the most splendid in Spain. It served as a palace (albeit an
unusual one in that courtiers had no right of entry to it), it housed a
church of cathedral-like proportions and of course it guarded the
remains of the members of the royal family. Among its ancillary functions, it contained picture galleries and a library that ranked among the
most important of their time. All these units were separate from each
other and were yet integrated into the whole building, which was built
in granite and planned on precisely related rectangles. The building
covered an area some 33 000 square metres, and its statistics became the
stuff of fable, known throughout Europe – fifteen cloisters and eighty-six
staircases, nearly one hundred and fifty kilometres of corridors, and
so on. The Escorial was a marvel of organisation and compression. Even
its gardens were innovative, bringing the plants and styles that Philip
had so admired in the Low Countries to southern Europe. To design it,
Philip worked with two architects: Juan Bautista de Toledo (who had
worked on St Peter's Rome under the guidance of Michelangelo himself)
began the work and Juan de Herrera succeeded him on his death in 1567.
Philip consulted with his architects every day as far as his schedule
permitted, and he allowed no changes in any plans without his express
authorisation. The strong probability that Philip had settled on the
idea of a courtly complex while he was in northern Europe was
bolstered by the use he made of Flemish artisans and workers in his
building projects; the influence of the Low Countries permeated his
great monastery-palace.[33]

Construction started on 23 April 1563 and Philip was so enthused by
the project that during the course of 1564 he radically enlarged the scale
of the building, expanding the area of the royal apartments and doubling

the number of monks who were to live in the monastery to one hundred. Thereafter, he made no substantive alterations to the scale of the project. A labour force of over 1000 men carried on its work twenty-four hours a day, using candlelight when daylight gave out. Stone was cut to shape and size in the quarries and was then put into place on arrival at the site. Designers worked in tandem with builders so that much of the interior decoration was ready to be slotted into place as soon as a section of building was completed. It was calculated that this prefabrication saved fourteen years' work. The unremitting and disciplined energy with which the building was constructed was one of the wonders of the age. It also explained the integrity and simplicity of the architectural style itself. The building itself (although not the pantheon, which was begun by Philip's son and finished by his grandson) was finally completed in September 1584.

The basilica church at the heart of the building was built on a scale that rivalled St Peter's in Rome. Its nave was ninety-two metres high. The whole complex housed no fewer than forty-three altars; among its other functions, the Escorial was a working church. A door into Philip's private apartments enabled him to look down in privacy on the divine services at the high altar, giving the building its extraordinary blend of grandeur and intimacy.

Philip marked the dedication of the Catholic faith to the cult of the saints by collecting relics on an unprecedented scale. He had agents at work for him throughout Europe; Guzmán de Silva, for instance, better known as Ambassador in England, formally deposited in 1574 a collection of relics that he had put together at the king's command. The relics whose authentication satisfied Philip were catalogued and put on display. Among the bones in the reliquarium were a forearm of St Lawrence himself and bones from both of his parents. Philip's relics from the early Church also included a shinbone of St Bartholomew and a relic of St Sebastian. Pride of place in the collection went to some hairs from the head of the Virgin Mary herself; Philip displayed them, naturally enough, in a cross made of gold.[34]

Within a decade the building was ready to receive the first royal bodies. The coffins of Elizabeth of Valois and Don Carlos were brought from Madrid in June 1573 and in the following year Charles V and the immediate members of his family (notably the Empress Isabella) were reunited in death. Eventually the corpses of all the members of Philip's immediate family were brought to the Escorial with the exception of that of his beloved sister Juana, whom he allowed to be interred in the convent of the Descalzas Reales that she had endowed in Madrid and to which she had been deeply devoted.

Philip reunited his family, too, in the magnificent lifesize statutes cast in bronze in Milan by Pompeo Leoni, son of León; Charles V, his wife Isabella and his sisters María and Leonor, knelt together on the Gospel side, while Philip and three of his wives – Mary Tudor being conspicuously absent on the pretext that she was not buried in the Escorial – and Don Carlos knelt opposite them, both groups praying intently. The two royal groups, situated at the very heart of the Escorial, were a reminder that in his incomparable building Philip was not only worshipping God but remembering his devotion to his family. Less prominently displayed, so as not to detract attention from the two royal groups, were other series of statues by Pompeo Leoni, of the Evangelists and of leading Apostles and doctors of the Church. Together, they form one of the great collections of European statuary.

It was partly in homage to his family that Philip built up what became the first great modern collection of paintings.[35] He inherited about 200 pictures from Charles V himself, Margaret of Hungary (who was Philip's great-aunt) and María of Hungary, his aunt, and he expanded the royal collection to a total of 1500, two-thirds of which (1150) were housed in the Escorial. This great collection served a number of purposes. In its portraits of Philip's family (past and present) it celebrated the greatness and legitimacy of the house of Habsburg, and in its pictures of religious devotion it stressed the primacy of the dynasty (and indeed of Spain) in the defence and propagation of the Roman Catholic faith. It was also designed in an unashamedly competitive spirit to surpass the other royal collections of Europe – most especially of course that of the Valois kings of France – and bore comparison with the holdings of the Vatican itself.

As in so much else, Philip's journey north in 1548–51 was fundamental to the development of his appreciation of painting; Italy and the Low Countries rounded out his aesthetic education as they did his political education. He met the great Titian and was painted by him in Milan at the turn of 1548–9. Titian (born 1480/85) was already an elderly man but he was undoubtedly the most accomplished and versatile painter of his day and he had worked for Charles V and his family for a quarter of a century. In the Low Countries, notably at Binche, Philip saw the unique collection of Titian's work that María of Hungary had built up; she owned no fewer than nineteen portraits by the master and his followers as well as many religious paintings. Philip met Titian again in 1550 at Augsburg and negotiated a set of commissions with him which substantively employed the artist until a year or so before his death in 1576; in effect Titian was working primarily for Philip throughout the years 1550–75. The two men never met after 1551 but they maintained a correspondence in which Philip's letters were addressed to his 'faithful and beloved friend'.

Titian's work for Philip served a variety of purposes. The formal portraits demonstrated Philip's princely qualities; Titian painted the king as a soldier in his suit of armour but also seated, as if carrying out his functions as a judge. He commemorated the great triumphs of the reign, most notably the *Allegory of Lepanto* (1575) which claimed for Philip and his dynasty the glory for the triumph of the Holy League over the Turk in 1571.

The second service performed by Titian was religious; Philip brought the great *Last Judgement in Glory* from Yuste (where Charles had gazed upon it in his last moments) and placed it in the Escorial. The great painting was complemented by Titian's *Martyrdom of St Lawrence* (1567), which served as the chief altarpiece in the monastery. Philip also commissioned a number of major religious paintings from Titian – the *Ecce Homo* and *The Entombment of Christ* among them. Fray José de Sigüenza, the historian of the Escorial, recorded that Philip often spent hours at a time contemplating the religious mysteries depicted in Titian's religious paintings and that he was on occasions moved to tears by them.

Philip also commissioned paintings of a more private nature from Titian; over the years 1554–62 the painter produced a series of mythological subjects which were known as the *Poesie* in emulation of Ovid's *Metamorphoses* and which were frankly erotic in content. Among them were the *Danaë* – one of the greatest (and most erotic) nudes in European painting – *Bacchus and Ariadne, Bacchanal of the Andrians* and *The Rape of Lucretia*. In the *Venus and Adonis* and *The Organ Player* Titian may even – presumably with the king's approval – have incorporated portraits of Philip himself. At all events, these paintings were exhibited in the royal apartments in Madrid, for they would have been quite unsuitable for the walls of the Escorial. The *Poesie* remind us that if Philip lived as a monk in the Escorial, he maintained in Madrid the style of a thoroughly modern Renaissance prince.

Philip's collection of paintings also reminds us of the enduring impression made upon him by his years in the Low Countries. He had been greatly influenced by the work of Roger van der Weyden (1400–64) and had his *Calvary* brought to the monastery in 1574. He employed Michel de Coxcie (1499–1592) to copy some of the great masterpieces of Netherlands religious painting, among them van der Weyden's *Descent from the Cross* and Jan van Eyck's Ghent altarpiece. Coxcie, who rejoiced in the nickname of 'the Raphael of the North', was employed by Philip as a court painter but most of his work in the Escorial was as a copyist of the paintings of his homeland rather than as an original artist. On the other hand, Philip was so inspired by the paintings of Hieronymous Bosch (*c.* 1450–1516) that he set himself to collect as much as he could of Bosch's extant work; he finished up owning the majority of it. Bosch's fantastic paintings depicted in the most graphic detail what Philip understood to be the realities of sinful life and most especially of the judgement awaiting all men at the end of their lives, be they kings or peasants. Philip displayed Bosch's painting of *The Seven Deadly Sins* in his apartments in the Escorial; the painting was on a tabletop which was hung on a wall and Philip was therefore able to reflect upon its teaching while he was eating – and thus, as it were, to digest the teaching along with his food. Among the other masterpieces by Bosch that Philip acquired were *The Cure of Folly, The Hay Wain, Ecce Homo, The Garden of Earthly Delights* and two versions of *The Temptation of St Anthony.* Some people at court were uneasy about Philip's commitment to Bosch's work, permitting themselves to wonder whether the painter had in fact had heretical leanings, but Sigüenza memorably defended the king's interest by insisting that Bosch's genius was to paint the temptations and agonies of the inner man.[36] It was this that appealed so profoundly to Philip, who himself endured great agonies of self-doubt.

At the heart of Philip's great collection, therefore, were the works of Titian, Coxcie and Bosch, representatives of different parts of his monarchy – and representatives, too, it might well be thought, of different parts of Philip's own psyche. In addition, Philip collected as many paintings as he could by leading Italian contemporary masters; Veronese's *The Annunciation* and Tintoretto's *Nativity* were some compensation for the artists' refusal to come to Spain to work for him. Among other major Italian artists, Philip also formed an attachment to the work of Jacopo Bassano, who specialised in the daringly modern subjects of landscape and scenes of low-life. Philip commissioned Federico Zuccaro to paint the altarpiece for the high altar but the work was too free for Philip's taste and he had it reworked by his own court painters. Zuccaro was despatched back to Italy.

While Philip naturally sought out the work of the most celebrated Italian masters he was committed to supporting the best of his compatriots. Chief among them were Juan Fernández de Navarrete (*c.* 1538–79) and Alonso Sánchez Coello (*c.* 1531–80). Fernández de Navarrete, known as 'el Mudo' because he had been deaf from infancy, was commissioned in 1576 to paint thirty-two small altarpieces for the basilica of San Lorenzo; by the time he died he had only completed nine, notably *The Beheading of the Apostle James* and the *Martyrdom of St Philip.* Sánchez Coello worked at court for thirty years (from 1561) and produced the discreet portrait of Don Carlos and the exquisite full-length portraits of Philip's two daughters, Isabella and Catalina. Sánchez Coello was originally employed in the household of Elizabeth of Valois, and there he shared work with the Italian, Sofonisba Anguisciola (*c.* 1540–1625), unique among the painters of Philip's court in being female. Sofonisba's major work was the portrait of Philip at about the mid-point of his reign that was until very recently attributed to Sánchez Coello, in which Philip appeared as the solemn, reserved king, dressed in black and, devoid of any of the trappings of majesty, telling his rosary, a king of deep sobriety and piety. Juan Pantoja de la Cruz (*d.*1608) also served the king in his later years, painting the moving portrait of Philip at seventy years of age, weary, standing on legs that were so thin that they could barely support his weight. In every one of the portraits painted of him Philip wore the Order of the Golden Fleece: he never forgot his ancestry.

Philip found it difficult to attract foreign masters to live in Spain because so many of them were intimidated at the prospect of becoming involved with the Inquisition; Pompeo Leoni was briefly arrested by the Inquisition as a Lutheran and there is a strong suspicion that Antonis Mor left Spain (in 1560) for fear that he might meet the same fate. However, one foreigner of genius did aspire to the position of court painter to Philip. At the end of the 1570s Domenikos Theotokopoulos came to the Escorial, hoping to succeed to Titian's position as chief painter to the king. 'El Greco', as he was known, had trained in Titian's studio in Venice and he painted the *Martyrdom of St Maurice and the Theban Legion* for Philip (1580) as a parable on the struggle in the Low Countries; the king's Governors-General all appeared as Roman generals. Philip, however, found El Greco's style to be too ethereal for him, but as Sigüenza sagely recorded, he was not alone in this.[37] And although the king did not like the work, he paid the full 300 ducats for it that had been agreed. Paradoxically, Philip's rejection – for which he has been much criticised – proved to be the making of El Greco's career, for the painter moved to Toledo; he fell in love with the city on the hill, idealised it as his Jerusalem and spent the rest of his life there, his genius flourishing in an environment that could have been made for him.

Another artist of genius shared El Greco's fate in having his work rejected by the king. In 1576, Philip acquired Benvenuto Cellini's statue of the Crucifixion and was so excited when he learned of its arrival in the capital that he ordered that it be carried from Madrid to the Escorial because it was too precious to be carted by mules. Unfortunately, when it was unpacked Philip took an instant dislike to the frankness with which Cellini had portrayed Christ and had the statue consigned to a chapel in which it would not be readily seen. Cellini's work was too exotic for the king's taste.

In music as in painting, Philip's taste was broadened and deepened by his two long visits to northern Europe. His parents had contrasting preferences in music – Charles V was always accompanied on his travels by his Flemish chapel while Isabella maintained a Spanish chapel – and Philip inherited his father's taste rather than his mother's. When Philip came back to Spain in 1559 he brought his Flemish singers with him and he employed a long line of Flemish masters at the Escorial – Pierre de Manchicourt (to 1564), Jean Beaumarchais (1565–70), Gérard de Turnhout (1571–80), George de la Hèle (1581–6) and Philippe Rogier (1588–96). It may well be, indeed, that Philip found difficulty with the strong preference of the Council of Trent for plainchant at the expense of polyphony, but he allowed the use of polyphony at the Escorial. It was in acknowledgement of this that the great Palestrina dedicated two books of masses to the king. Philip's strong preference for Flemish over Spanish music meant that Antonio de Cabezón was the only Spanish composer of the first rank whom he employed directly. Cristóbal de Morales died in 1553 before Philip came to the throne and Tomás Luis de Victoria spent most of his life abroad before returning home in 1587 to take up the position of *maestro* at the convent of the Descalzas Reales in Madrid. He served Philip's sister María but not the king himself.[38]

Legend has it that Philip immured himself in the Escorial. He did not. By the 1570s he was able to live there for months at a time but every year he also spent time in Madrid and in his major country houses and hunting lodges. He was known for his accessibility to even the humblest of his subjects when he was on the move between his residences.[39] Certainly, he spent part of every day that he was in the Escorial as a sort of honorary monk, joining in the prayers and ceremonies of the monks. Doing so fulfilled a deep spiritual need in him, and the isolation that he enjoyed in the Escorial allowed him to concentrate on his governmental work. Philip was thereby able to develop the practice of working prodigiously long hours, often stopping only when he was too exhausted to carry on. Locked behind the granite walls of the monastery, he was freed of many of the tiresome routines of monarchy, and in particular he was liberated from the attentions of the aristocrats and petitioners who would have flocked to court in the hope of catching his attention and winning his favour. Living as a monk was essential to the extraordinary diligence with which Philip applied himself to his papers. It was also fundamental to the exaggerated opinions that the world held of him: to his enemies he was the monarch who hid himself away so that he could scheme the more fully, while to his admirers he was the king who was so devout that he lived the life of a humble monk. The polarisation of views that thereby set in has lasted to this day.

THE KING'S COUNCILS

Spain was governed through a system of councils, and like so much else in the country in 1559 they were in a state of disarray. The councils had been founded over the years 1480–1525 and their role was advisory and not executive; they made recommendations to the monarch but could not make policy, for only the monarch could do that. At the head of the system was the Council of State, which Charles V had established in 1523 to advise him on major affairs of war and diplomacy. Appointment to the Council of State was from the outset a personal honour bestowed by the monarch in recognition of distinguished service to the Crown. The majority of men appointed to the Council were senior nobles, for they alone had that experience of the great embassies and viceroyalties which qualified a man to give advice on the highest affairs of state. Leading churchmen such as the king's confessor and the archbishop of Toledo or the Inquisitor-General could also expect to be appointed in acknowledgement of the principle that the Church had to guide and validate secular action. The Council of State had a junior body in the Council of War, which was staffed by lesser nobles and dealt with the logistical rather than the policy-making aspects of war; churchmen ordinarily had no role here, although since councillors of State were entitled to sit on the Council of War, they could attend if they wished. The Councils of State and War were unique among the councils in that they had no legal *ordenanzas* regulating their activities, stipulating how often they should meet and who should attend them. Accordingly, the king could summon them when he chose to, or he could ignore them, again as he chose.

Philip was determined to prevent the Council of State from developing into a regularly functioning part of government. He feared that if it did so his own freedom to make policy would be restricted by the weight of the advice given him at the Council, and that senior aristocrats sitting on the Council would gain that entry into government and policy-making that he was resolved to deny them. True, he chose a group of men as 'councillors of state' on his second journey to northern Europe, but he seems to have done this for courtly rather than political reasons, to confer honour and status upon men who had travelled with him rather than to entitle them to advise him regularly on policy.[40] A number of these men were foreigners, and Philip did not take them with him when he returned to Spain – Granvelle, Ferrante Gonzaga, Emmanuel Philibert of Savoy and Andrea Doria, for instance. The field was therefore left for Ruy Gómez himself and for the leading Spaniards – Alba of course, Juan de Figueroa, the counts of Feria and Chinchón, Juan Manrique de Lara and Gutierre López de Padilla.

On his return to Spain, Philip began to convene the Council when he needed advice on serious problems, and on occasions he summoned it when he wanted to involve his senior advisers in decisions precisely so that he should not bear the sole responsibility for them himself. This latter seems to have been the case, for instance, with the most celebrated meetings of the Council of State in the first decade of his reign – those held 'in the Woods of Segovia' in 1566 that decided on a repressive policy towards the rebellion in the Low Countries (see chapter 5). In those early years Philip drew a crucial distinction between his councillors of State and the Council itself. He sometimes asked councillors for their views on important matters without necessarily convening the Council itself. Indeed, the Council itself met so infrequently that men were often not available when Philip decided that he needed their advice; in June 1565, for example, Gonzalo Pérez informed Philip that 'of the councillors of State, only Don Luis Dávila and the Bishop of Cuenca have remained here (in Madrid) . . .'[41]

Such a situation suited the king ideally, but two developments made it less easy for Philip to ignore the Council of State after the first decade or so of his reign. In the first instance, the involvement of Spain in wars in northern Europe, and particularly the attempt to crush the rebellion in the Low Countries, confronted Philip with such agonising choices that he felt increasingly obliged to have the Council give him the benefit of its advice. Accordingly, by the 1570s the Council of State was beginning to sit more frequently and to have a significant voice in the affairs of government. The fulminating crises of the second half of Philip's reign saw it develop even further. In the second instance, the development of Madrid as the acknowledged capital of Spain encouraged leading aristocrats to build houses in the city, and their proximity exerted a subtle pressure upon the king to use them in government; Philip could not simply continue to ignore them, as he had been able to do when they were living away from the capital.

In the early years of the reign, therefore, aristocrats who did not have access to the king through their positions at court had little opportunity to make their voices heard in government. Pre-eminent among those who did have ready access to the king were of course Ruy Gómez de Silva and the Duke of Alba, and they carried on the contest for influence over Philip that they had begun in northern Europe. Since Ruy Gómez was emphatically in the ascendant at the time of the return to Spain this meant in practice that Alba had to mount a challenge to him. The duke did so with characteristic bluntness; in February 1560 he announced that he would not attend court if Ruy Gómez was there, and so he left. Philip could not allow himself to be dictated to and let it be known that he 'loves [Ruy Gómez] as heartily as he ever loved him'.[42] Alba was forced to return to court, but still he could not endure Ruy Gómez's primacy and in September 1560 he lost his temper in a quite extraordinary incident when he found Philip closeted behind locked doors with Francisco de Eraso, who was Ruy Gómez's leading supporter. As *mayordomo mayor* Alba carried the keys to the palace and had the right to enter any room he chose. He knocked repeatedly on the door and when Eraso eventually opened it, Alba 'let fly a volley of abuse' against him and 'in a violent rage' asked Philip for leave to retire from court. Philip tried to mollify him but Alba insisted on leaving. Even then Philip continued to send to him to ask for advice. This was a serious mistake, demeaning to the king's majesty, and in reporting it the Venetian ambassador noted Alba's motivation: 'he wishes everything to depend upon himself alone, nor can he suffer others, unworthy to be compared with him, to have power equal to his, and superior to it in some respects'.[43] What Alba wanted was to be sole adviser to the king on major affairs and particularly on foreign policy. What Philip showed was that he simply could not control the duke; when, late in October 1560, Philip returned to Toledo after a hunting trip, he brought Alba with him and it was noted that the duke 'occupies the chief place of this court'.[44] Alba had humiliated the king. In 1563 Alba stormed off to his estates once more; he was away for a year.[45] Any assessment of the power wielded by Alba at court must take into account how frequently he was absent from court.[46] For Philip himself, it was a moot question whether he was better off with Alba at court or without him. Certainly, he appreciated that if he had allowed the Council of State to develop into a regularised part of government, Alba (and other aristocrats) would have a forum for their views, and this he was determined to deny them. Weak though he was in his dealings with the duke, Philip must have welcomed Alba's regular tantrums and departures.

Philip took a very different attitude to the professional councils than he did to the Councils of State and War. From the beginning he was determined that he would have their advice on a regular basis, and during his reign the councils developed – at differential rates, it is true – as the central apparatus of the state. These councils divided into two categories. The first had responsibility for governing the constituent parts of Spain: Castile (founded in 1480), Aragon (1494), Indies (1523) and Navarre (1525). In 1559 Philip himself added a council of Italy to this group (and in the 1580s he expanded it further with councils for Portugal and Flanders). The second category of council had responsibility for specific areas of policy: the Inquisition (1481), which was the only professional council to exercise authority over the whole of Spain; Military Orders (1494), administering the lands of the Military Orders of Santiago, Calatrava and Alcántara which had been subsumed into the Crown's patrimony; Crusade (c. 1516), controlling the tax after which it was named; and Finance (1523) which managed the revenues of the Crown of Castile. All these councils were governed by *ordenanzas*, which specified how often they were to meet and what their responsibilities were.

The social composition of the councils reflected their political purposes. The councils of Aragon and Italy represented separate states in Madrid; significantly, therefore, their councillors were called *regentes*. Two *regentes* sat on the Council of Aragon to represent each of the states of the Crown of Aragon (Aragon itself, Valencia and Catalonia). Similarly, two *regentes* sat on the Council of Italy for each of its constituent parts (Naples, Sicily and Milan). On both councils, these *regentes* were normally lawyers by training and they sat with members of the local nobility. On Navarre, the councillors displayed a similar mix of legal and noble backgrounds.[47] The Council of Castile was the supreme judicial tribunal of the kingdom and so its councillors were men with degrees in law. Lawyers also dominated the councils of the Indies and Orders, while most members of the Inquisition had degrees in canon law. At the heart of the conciliar system in Castile itself, therefore, dominating four of the major councils of state, were lawyers, civil and canon.

The Council of Finance was very backward in its organisation in 1556 and the men who served on it were co-opted as often as not for their general administrative expertise rather than because they had any training in financial management. For instance, Ruy Gómez himself was appointed in 1556 as one of three *contadores mayores* who were to administer financial affairs.[48] The consequences of this lack of financial expertise in the councillors of Finance were to be profoundly damaging; throughout his reign, Philip failed to address the basic need for having sound financial advice from experts. Indeed, it was not until his last years that he developed a structure within which the Council of Finance at last had available to it the information that the Crown held as to its resources and its commitments.

As the condition of the Council of Finance implied, the councils were at significantly different stages of development in 1559. Broadly speaking, the most well-organised and important among them were the Councils of Castile, Inquisition and the Indies, and they were so because the Crown had serious need of their special functions: the Council of Castile as a judicial tribunal; Inquisition as the comptroller of faith and morals throughout Spain; and the Indies as the agency responsible for the government of Castile's massive territories in the Americas. These were prestigious and powerful councils and because they were each of them the ultimate court of appeal in their respective jurisdictions they were known as 'supreme' councils. However, the Council of Castile was undermined by a succession of presidential changes in the first decade of the reign, caused for the most part by deaths of incumbents; in the years 1553–65 the council had four presidents and two acting presidents. By contrast, Inquisition stood immobile and unchanging under the leadership of Valdés.

The first major development in the evolution of these councils came in 1565 when Philip promoted Lic. Diego de Espinosa to the presidency of Castile.[49] Espinosa was a priest of fifty-three years of age and his appointment to the presidency was startlingly dramatic, for he had only reached his first significant governmental post (a councillorship of Inquisition) as recently as 1564. He had, therefore, none of the background or knowledge qualifying him for the senior administrative and judicial position in Castile. He did, however, have prodigious energy and organising ability and Philip was so impressed with the impact that he made as President of Castile that when he finally forced Valdés to retire in 1566 he appointed Espinosa as Inquisitor-General as well, with retention of the presidency of Castile. Within two years of reaching the central administration, therefore, Espinosa had become its most powerful figure, exercising unique control over patronage in church and state. A mere priest, he was raised in 1568 to the cardinalate and thereby became a figure of international significance.

Espinosa's remarkable elevation served a number of purposes for the king. Chief among them was Philip's determination to reorganise the government of the kingdom of Castile and its church; Espinosa was charged to do both. It seems clear, too, that Espinosa's power was given to him as part of Philip's preparations for his own return to the Low Countries. By the mid-1560s, the situation in the Low Countries was deteriorating rapidly (see chapter 5) and Philip needed to be able to plan for his journey north secure in the conviction that church and state in Spain (and more particularly in Castile) were in hands that were completely trustworthy, that he would not be again undermined in his absence as he had been by Valdés in the 1550s.

Espinosa's rise to pre-eminence was also surely part of the process whereby Philip sought to emancipate himself from the influence of his childhood friend, Ruy Gómez de Silva, and to provide yet a further counterbalance to the duke of Alba. Ruy Gómez retained Philip's affection until his death in 1573, and was indeed raised to the dukedom (of Pastrana) in 1572. However, Philip distanced himself from his old mentor in a political sense; after the mid-1560s Ruy Gómez no longer exercised a substantive influence on the formulation of policy, and it was indicative of his decline that Francisco de Eraso was dismissed from his major offices for corruption.[50]

It was indeed significant of the new dispensation in government that both Ruy Gómez and Alba went out of their way to accommodate themselves to Espinosa. When Alba wrote to Espinosa congratulating him on his appointment to the presidency of the Council of Castile he urged him 'to always employ me' in his service, assuring him that this would be 'for me a very great favour'. Ruy Gómez insistently sought the President's favour; in April 1566, for instance, he wrote to Espinosa urging him to employ Juan de Escobedo in government, promising him 'there are few if any who can match him for ability and faithfulness'.[51] Espinosa's power astonished observers; the count of Chinchón observed of him that he was 'the man in all Spain in whom the king places most confidence, and with whom he discusses most business, both concerning Spain and foreign affairs', and the French ambassador advised Catherine de' Medici that Espinosa 'can do whatever he wishes with this king'.[52]

Espinosa's all-embracing role provided a focal point for governmental activity. It fell to him to mobilise the resources for the wars in Granada and the Low Countries at the end of the 1560s. Administratively, his dynamic leadership stimulated the Council of Castile and this in turn led to an expansion in the importance of the central councils as a whole. He was also in effect the leader of the Castilian Church; with Archbishop Carranza imprisoned, it fell to Espinosa to implement the decrees of the Council of Trent. He also instituted major reforms of the religious orders and the universities. Above all else, however, Espinosa was the master of the Crown's patronage system, and his voluminous correspondence testified to the growing importance of his role in centralising control of appointments in both church and state. Naturally, Espinosa promoted his own men, and the most important of them – Juan de Ovando and Mateo Vázquez de Leca – became major figures in their own right, carrying on the principles of his work after he himself had been removed from office. The circumstances of Espinosa's decline remain largely unexplained but they probably centred on Philip's fears that the cardinal was becoming too sure of his own power – and on the king's realisation that he would not after all be travelling to the Low Countries and so did not need an *alter ego* to be in charge of government. Philip withdrew his favour from Espinosa shortly before his death in 1572.[53]

Each council had a secretary who organised its paperwork and reported from and to the king. Having access to the king gave conciliar secretaries the possibility of wielding greater influence than the councillors to whom they were nominally responsible. This was the more true because the very backwardness of conciliar development had made it easier for a few individuals to wield substantial influence. It was, for instance, a measure of the comparative simplicity of government in the later 1550s that Francisco de Eraso had responsibility for the papers of the councils of Finance, Castile, Inquisition, Orders and Indies. As Philip's government became more firmly established, so the volume of its work grew and the role of leading secretaries became more important. Power came with the king's confidence. The way was being prepared for the first great secretaries of the reign, Antonio Pérez and Mateo Vázquez de Leca, men of humble origin who acquired great political power because they had daily access to Philip (see chapter 6).

'POPE AS WELL AS KING': ROYAL CONTROL OF THE CHURCH

Philip exercised powers over the Church in his territories that were the envy of many other European monarchs, Catholic or Protestant. Over the years 1486–1523 Isabella the Catholic and Charles V had won *patronatos* from the papacy which allowed the Crown to nominate to all bishoprics in Spain and the Indies, and which prohibited the papacy from even publishing its bulls in Spain or in the Indies without royal permission. Moreover, the Crown exercised important financial control over the Church; it could (with papal approval) levy the taxes of the *cruzada* and the *subsidio* (and, later, the *excusado*) and it controlled the lands and revenues of the three Military Orders of Santiago, Calatrava and Alcántara. More important still, the Crown exercised effective control (after Valdés's removal) over the Inquisition. Philip added new tribunals to the Inquisition for Galicia (1561) and for the two American viceroyalties (1571) to further extend the power of the Crown over church and state.

Philip's determination to control the Church led him regularly into conflict with the papacy. He never flinched from the prospect. This was most notably true of the collision over the fate of Archbishop Carranza. In September 1563, Luis de Requesens arrived in Rome with the task of improving relations with the pope, but within months he was writing that Pius was 'very angry and dissatisfied' with Philip. Soon he was using a military metaphor when writing to the king: 'Yesterday I had an audience with His Holiness and we had a tremendous skirmish, in which His Holiness raised his voice many times and I responded by doing likewise. I managed to retain the respect which the position that he holds demands and yet was able to reply to every point as was fitting.'[54] When in 1564 Requesens was duly excommunicated and prepared to leave Rome, he drily noted that 'the Pope will be very satisfied to find himself without an Ambassador who knows how to talk freely to him'.[55] And all this of a pontiff who was well-inclined to Philip and to Spain!

The Castilian Church underwent some significant structural changes during Philip's reign; the diocese of Burgos was raised to an archbishopric in 1574 while Valladolid became a bishopric in 1595. The Church then consisted of five archdioceses (Toledo, Seville, Santiago, Granada and Burgos) and thirty dioceses. The Church in Aragon was naturally much smaller, but it, too, underwent some important developments; its three archbishoprics (Tarragona, Zaragoza and Valencia) remained unchanged but six new bishoprics were created – Orihuela (1564), Barbastro and Jaca (1571), Elna (1573), Teruel (1577) and Solsona (1593) – bringing the number of bishoprics in the Crown of Aragon to seventeen.[56]

Towering above the whole structure in both size and wealth was the primatial see of Toledo, which had an income of about 200000 ducats by the middle of Philip's reign and was well over twice as wealthy as the second richest archdiocese, that of Seville, which had an income of 80 000 ducats. Among the sees of the Crown of Aragon, only two ranked among the first dozen by value of income: Zaragoza (third with 55 000 ducats' annual income) and Valencia (fifth with 50 000). The wealth of the Spanish Church lay predominantly therefore in Castile. However, there were fewer people in religious orders than has often been supposed; by 1591 the clerical estate in Castile consisted of 74 153 people, comprising only 1.12 per cent of the total population – 33 087 secular clergy together with 20 697 men and 20 369 women who belonged to religious orders.[57]

The seminal factor in the development of the Church in Spain in Philip's reign was the implementation by the Crown of the decrees of the Council of Trent (1545–63). One thousand or so Spanish churchmen were involved in the work of the Council and many of them returned to Spain enthused by its work and determined to implement its decrees. The most important of the sessions of the Council was the third and final one (18 January 1562–4 December 1563); 137 Spaniards were accredited to the Council during this session.[58] Spain was cut off from many of the intellectual currents of western Europe during Philip's reign but was certainly not isolated from developments in Catholic Europe and from the work of the Council of Trent.

The Council redefined Catholic doctrine and practice and sent the Church out to fight for souls in lands which had remained loyal to the Church as much as in those that had rejected its authority. It therefore reinvigorated the life of the Church in countries where the Reformation had already been resisted; this was most notably true of Spain, which under the impress of its own diverse and vigorous Catholic tradition was able to absorb much of the Council's work. The Council insisted that the Mass remain at the heart of Catholic practice and rejected attempts to modify the doctrine of transubstantiation, insisting that Christ was really present in the sacrifice of the Mass. Equally fundamentally, it restated the primacy of the papacy within the Church. The Spanish bishops, led by Archbishop Guerrero of Granada, vehemently argued that the episcopacy was divine in origin and therefore had parity with the holder of St Peter's See, but they were in the event unable to sway the Council and the papal victory effectively established something of a papal monarchy at the head of the Church. By way of compensation, the Council insisted that the bishops – who were, after all, undeniably the direct descendants of the Apostles – had the practical responsibility for promulgating doctrine and for establishing sacerdotal discipline. The Council recognised, too, that the bishops had the responsibility for administering its decrees (and for finding the monies with which to fund the programme) and it therefore charged them to supervise closely the conduct of their clergy and to found seminaries to train new clergy to higher standards than had often operated hitherto. It also instructed bishops to hold regional councils so that they could more readily stimulate and control their local churches. Philip published the decrees of the Council on 19 July 1564 with the revealing caveat that they were not to be implemented if they impinged upon the privileges of the Crown. When Pius IV complained that Philip had abrogated to himself the right of interpreting the meaning of the Tridentine decrees and that 'he meant to be pope as well as king' he was not wide of the mark.[59] As early as 4 December 1564 Philip wrote to his churchmen, somewhat wryly noting that a few of them had seen fit to appeal to the pope himself to have some of the Council's decrees modified or revoked. Philip insisted that there was not to be any 'delay or suspension' in implementing the decrees, noting that they had been promulgated with 'our authority'. He genuinely did regard the pope as a junior partner where the affairs of the Spanish Church were concerned.[60]

Philip was the master of the Spanish episcopal bench and he was determined to remain so. He fully recognised the crucial role played by the episcopacy in the affairs of the renewed Church and he took a close and continuing interest in appointments to bishoprics. Certainly, he was acutely conscious that this was a God-given responsibility and that he would have at his death to account for the quality of the appointments that he had made, but he was also determined that as king of Spain he would control the bishops in his lands, at home and overseas.[61] He nominated 127 men to 172 posts in the Castilian Church, at an average of four or so per annum. He was punctilious in his approach (and in choosing the men whom he trusted to advise him on the appointments). He insisted that his bishops 'should be graduates of theology or canon law from approved universities, of sound judgement, exemplary life style, modest disposition, charitable conduct, worthy reputation, pure-blooded and legitimate birth'. He relied upon the six privileged *colegios mayores* of Salamanca, Alcalá and Valladolid to provide him with nearly half of his bishops and thereby accentuated the role played by those universities – and most especially, of course, Salamanca, which had four of the *colegios mayores* – at the centre of affairs in Spain. Philip's bishops were men of ability and integrity but they were regalists, conscious that they owed their elevation to the Crown and that they looked to it for further advance; they dared not offend the Crown without jeopardising their own career prospects.[62] They enthusiastically implemented the decrees of the Council of Trent and promoted others who would do likewise, but they never forgot their loyalty to the Crown. For his part, Philip always remembered that he was master of the Spanish Church, of its bishops as of its inquisitors.

The chosen instrument of the bishops in implementing the work of the Council were the provincial councils. These were held during Philip's reign in Toledo, Granada, Salamanca, Zaragoza, Valencia and Tarragona. The most important was inevitably that of Toledo (September 1565–March 1566). Philip himself gave permission for it to sit in the 'absence' of Archbishop Carranza and authorised Cardinal Cristóbal de Rojas y Sandoval, archbishop of Seville, to convene it. Trustful though he was of the archbishop, Philip took the precaution of having his own confidant, the redoubtable Francisco de Toledo – the future viceroy of Peru – attend the Council as his 'observer'. The Council of Toledo legislated for the whole of church life: it established archives so that local practices could be codified; surveyed the ecclesiastical buildings of the archdiocese; regulated the way in which children were taught the faith; laid down the disciplinary norms governing the behaviour of the clergy, and so on.[63] The bishops who attended the provincial council were then obliged to organise their own diocesan councils to implement the Tridentine decrees. In this way, the work of the great council was filtered down to the local level. Perhaps the most enduring legacy of Trent in Spain came with the foundation of new seminaries; twenty-one were established between 1564 and 1600.[64] A new elite priesthood was created, a priesthood that was professional and disciplined and which looked after the souls in its charge from the cradle to the grave as it spread the ideals and values of the Council of Trent at the local level.

The most pressing of Philip's problems with the Church on his return in 1559 was to regain control over the Inquisition and to direct it for his own purposes. He signalled his support of the Inquisition by following up his attendance at the *auto-de-fé* in Valladolid in 1559 by being present at *autos* in Toledo (1560) and in Barcelona (1563). He also allowed the Inquisition to exercise some new powers; in 1559, for instance, he ordered that all Spanish students at Louvain University in the Low Countries were to return home and submit themselves to vetting by the Inquisition. He forbade Spaniards to study at foreign universities. More drastically still, he allowed Valdés to issue the Index of August 1559 which took censorship to a new level, banning 670 works.[65] However, once Philip had succeeded in removing Valdés in 1565 (on grounds of dotage and ill-health) he deliberately changed the nature of the Inquisition by appointing Diego de Espinosa as the first of a succession of Inquisitors-General of whose loyalty he could be absolutely certain.[66] From that point, the king was in charge of the Inquisition – and of all his churchmen. Under Espinosa, the Spanish Inquisition once again became a department of state.

The work that the Inquisition did can now be analysed in detail, and the realities separated from the myths. The remarkable research of professors Henningsen and Contreras has demonstrated that in the period 1560–1614 the Inquisition dealt with 27 910 cases. The old enemies had been well and truly defeated; only 1722 (6.2 per cent) of these processes were concerned with allegations of Judaic behaviour and 2244 (8 per cent) involved accusations of Lutheran sympathies or behaviour. The two largest categories now were 'Mahommedanism' (8911: 31.9 per cent) and those offences defined together as 'Propositions', a term which conveniently incorporated the whole gamut of questionable theological ideas (8186: 29.3 per cent). The first of these reflected the continued existence of the *morisco* communities of southern and eastern Spain while the second – which covered everything from blasphemy to sacerdotal misbehaviour – increasingly provided the basis for the Inquisition's work among Christians. Under Philip and his son the Holy Office became the policeman of the nation's morals rather than the persecutor of Jews and their sympathisers (which had been its original justification). Executions in this period numbered 637, with a further 545 people being burned in effigy – a total of 4.3 per cent of the cases, or an average of eleven burnings a year. Cases of 'major' heresy were therefore comparatively rare, and the Inquisition concerned itself now with the daily lives of Old Christians – with their ignorance of Church doctrine (which increasingly came to be seen as an offence in itself) and with their blasphemy and sexual misconduct. At its highest level, the Inquisition became therefore the institution which most fully enforced the decrees of the Council of Trent among ordinary Spaniards, insisting that they know their prayers and make their religious observance. At its lowest, it became not merely brutal but often rather ridiculous – for instance, it was greatly concerned with the widespread practice of prostitution, but seemed to regard consorting with a prostitute as much less of an offence than a refusal to pay for the services that she rendered.[67] Despite such banalities, the Inquisition's prestige was now greater than ever, but there was less for it to do, and as it ran out of victims it became more consumed with its own importance and its apparatus grew (see chapter 9). The Inquisition was suffering one of the classic symptoms of institutional decline, that as it had less to do so its bureaucracy became top-heavy, its concerns increasingly with its own prestige and status rather than with its function.

While the Inquisition refocused its activity, Philip had to resolve the difficulties created by the case of Bartolomé de Carranza, and these were compounded because the archbishop showed that he knew how to fight for himself. Carranza succeeded in having Valdés barred from judging his case on the grounds of his proven hostility towards him and he won the unyielding support of the papacy. Pius IV made extraordinary efforts to reach an accommodation with Philip, despatching no fewer than sixteen nuncios and envoys to Spain in six years. But Pius was resolute in his support for Carranza, and the only compromise that he would make was to allow the archbishop's trial to take place in Spain. Insistently, he reserved the verdict and sentence for himself.

Many of Carranza's fellow bishops were outraged by the attack on him, fearful no doubt that if the Primate himself was vulnerable to the Inquisition then they too were at risk; this may well have been what was behind the remarkable indiscretion of Fernando de Loazes, archbishop of Tarragona, who allowed himself to muse to some villagers in 1560 that 'if the archbishop is a heretic or Lutheran, then we are all heretics or Lutherans'.[68] Abroad, there was less need for discretion: in 1562 the Council of Trent declared that Carranza's Catechism was doctrinally pure. Powerful support came, too, from Francisco de Borja, who testified on Carranza's behalf; his evidence clearly indicated that the Society of Jesus supported the archbishop.

The difficulties created for Philip by the Carranza affair increased dramatically when at the turn of 1565–6 Michele Ghislieri was elected to succeed Paul IV as pope; he chose the name of Pius V. With his election, the Roman Catholic Church acquired one of its greatest and most formidable popes. Pius V (1566–72) never acknowledged the need for compromise in church affairs or in politics and his aims were startlingly simple – to implement the decrees of the Council of Trent and to do all that he could to lead the Church to wage holy war, against Islam in the south and protestantism in the north. For all of this he needed Philip's support and so he granted him unprecedented funds with which to fight Islam. But nothing would force Pius to compromise over Carranza. Not even Philip's will was a match for Pius V's and the king had to give way, agreeing to have Carranza transferred to Rome for judgement. The archbishop arrived there in May 1567. He did so with the satisfaction that Valdés had finally been removed from power in Spain and that he himself was at last out of the Inquisition's clutches.[69] The power of the Inquisition had been bridled.

As the Inquisition stultified, two new religious orders developed profoundly important roles during Philip's reign, the Society of Jesus and the reformed or Discalced Carmelites. Both were created by Spaniards of genius, Ignatius Loyola and Teresa Ahumada. Philip himself had strong reservations about the Society's allegiance to the papacy and treated it with reserve, but he could do little to stem its advance. The Society continued to have a strong Spanish leadership after Loyola's death in 1556: Diego de Laínez (1558–64) and Francisco de Borja himself (1567–72) both ruled it as generals – and under their guidance it naturally paid a special interest to its Spanish mission. Although the Society was not by strict definition a teaching order, by the end of Philip's reign it had colleges in thirty-three towns and cities and more than 2000 of its members were working in the Iberian peninsula, many of them in positions of high influence at court or in noble households.[70] Their influence helped to revitalise Spanish Catholicism and their opponents did not know how to deal with the ubiquitous Jesuits, men who were at once highly individual in their actions and yet utterly disciplined in the service of the Society.

Teresa Ahumada was in many respects similar to the great Jesuit; her personality was every bit as powerful as Loyola's, her willpower quite as uncompromising and her psychological insight into human motives just as penetrating. Teresa spent nineteen or so years as an unremarkable Carmelite nun in the convent of the Encarnación in Ávila but became increasingly dismayed by the laxity within the convent. Encouraged by (among others) Jesuit confessors, she determined to found a convent which would adhere strictly to the Rule but yet allow for personal spiritual development through prayer and reflection. She founded the convent in Ávila itself and dedicated it to St Joseph (24 August 1562). By the time of her death in 1582 Teresa had established a further sixteen convents, all but two of them in Old Castile. Because they adhered to the vow of poverty, Teresa's nuns were known as the Discalced or shoeless ('Descalzas') Carmelites. She also established two monasteries for men. Teresa's foundations quickly became celebrated as centres of rigorous devotion and of practical charitable commitment to the communities in which they lived; they were of prime importance in leading a movement for spiritual renewal at a local level.

Teresa's was a simple but eclectic genius; she was influenced by some of the leading figures of her time – Francisco de Borja, Peter of Alcán- tara, John of the Cross, all of whom were later canonised by the Church – and she showed herself able to cajole and inspire people. However, the very intensity (and success) with which she operated aroused great enmity towards her personally, within her Order and beyond it. When her work was brought to a halt by the opposition of a hostile papal nuncio as well as by the hierarchy of her own Order, she turned to Philip himself for support and in December 1577 she trod her way to the Escorial for an interview with the king. Her account of the meeting provides a fasci- nating insight into Philip's personality. Teresa confessed that she was ter- rified by his 'penetrating gaze – the kind of gaze that goes deep down to the very soul' and which seemed to 'pierce me through and through'. Philip (who was probably quite as intimidated as Teresa) listened to her patiently and dismissed her gently with what she described as 'the most charming bow I ever saw': 'Go away in peace, for everything shall be arranged as you wish.'[71] Teresa was exultant, convinced that Philip would intervene to save her work. And so he did, securing a papal bull in 1580 which separated the Reformed from the Carmelite Order. Teresa's life's work was rescued and her reforms endured.

4

THE WEALTH OF THE INDIES

CASTILE'S INDIES: A DEVELOPING NEW WORLD

Philip inherited territories in the New World that were even more extensive than those he ruled in the Old, stretching some 8000 kilometres from
the northern marchlands of New Spain to the southernmost settlements
in Peru. It was a matter of the deepest conviction to him that he held
these lands both as a political trust that he had inherited from his father
and as a divine grant from God and that, moreover, both his political and
religious rights had been validated by papal sanction. Accordingly, he was
remarkably clear-sighted in defining his objectives in the New World – to
protect and exploit his territories and to convert the Indians to a true
understanding of the Catholic faith – and he was ruthless and unyielding in pursuit of them. Indeed, he was so successful that his management
of the affairs of 'the Indies' is often described as the greatest achievement of his kingship, for he demonstrated an ability to design powerful
systems and a sensitive judgement in choosing the men who would
implement them for him. He demonstrated, too, that he could do in the
Americas what he was incapable of doing nearer home, of giving his
subordinates wide powers and entrusting them with their responsibilities
over extended periods of time.

Philip's reign was a period of consolidation for the Crown in the Indies,
his overriding concern being to properly control and exploit the lands
that he had inherited rather than to acquire new lands. By the time of
his accession the Age of Conquest in the Spanish Indies was substantively
at an end, and Philip's reign saw only two significant additions to his overseas empire – a few settlements on the coast of Florida in North America

(see pp. 88) and, much more importantly, the conquest of the Philippines. The expedition that Philip had planned from the beginning of his
reign did not sail from New Spain until November 1564. Friar Urdaneta
was joined in command by Miguel López de Legazpi, who took charge
of the soldiers on board. The fleet covered 6000 miles in ten weeks and
the Philippines were conquered – virtually without combat – for Spain.
Even before the conquest had begun, Urdaneta undertook the hazardous
return voyage to New Spain, thereby demonstrating that a trading link
could be established between the Philippines and the American mainland. Trade began at once – the first convoy from Acapulco sailed in 1566
– and it proved to be lucrative; silver was worth half as much again in
China than it was in the Hispanic world and the Spanish colonists in the
Americas soon realised that they could buy the goods of China at very
favourable prices. Moreover, it soon became evident that Manila could
serve as a collection point from which many of the precious goods of
the East could find their way to the Americas. The Portuguese, with their
far-flung trading posts and their knowledge of the Far East, proved to
be ideal intermediaries here. The silks of China were therefore joined
on their journey to Acapulco by a variety of other precious goods
from Asia – porcelain, ivory, jewels and spices among them. The return
journey was much less readily accomplished than the outward-bound
one; it often took six months or more, and only the strongest ships
and the most resilient of men survived it. By 1571 the trade was
sufficiently well established for the Spanish to found the city of Manila
as the capital of the archipelago. Over the remainder of Philip's reign
the trade developed substantially until it was absorbing dangerously
large volumes of American silver; in 1597 – the last full year of Philip's
reign – the volume of silver leaving Acapulco on 'the Manila Galleon'
for the first time surpassed the volume of silver going from New Spain to
Seville.[1]

Florida and the Philippines apart, Philip's empire remained in extent
much as he had inherited it. Christopher Columbus had claimed the
lands of 'the Indies' for the Crown of Castile by right of discovery, and
in 1493 Isabella the Catholic had secured from Pope Alexander VI,
himself a Spaniard, the celebrated bull *Inter caetera* which allocated to
Castile all lands more than a hundred leagues west of an imaginary line
drawn from the Azores and the Cape Verde Islands and gave to Portugal
all lands to the east of that line. The papal judgement allowed other
nations no rights at all in the new lands. In 1494, the monarchs of Castile
and Portugal agreed by the Treaty of Tordesillas to accept the papal divi-

sion. At the time, this seemed to be a matter of little consequence for Europe as a whole since 'the Indies' consisted merely of a few scattered islands. However, within a few years it had become evident that an extensive and rich New World existed in the west and that Castile was laying claim to sole authority over the whole of the central and southern Americas with the exception of Brazil (which, being to the east of 'the line', belonged to Portugal). More even than this, Castile was also claiming sovereignty over all lands that were as yet undiscovered to the west of the pope's imaginary line. Castile's *Laws of the Indies* stated that 'by gift of the Holy Apostolic See and by other just and lawful titles, we are Lord of the West Indies, of the Islands and Tierra Firme in the Atlantic Ocean, of both what has been discovered and what is yet to be discovered, and these are incorporated into our royal crown of Castile'.[2] Accordingly, all other nations (including non-Castilian Spaniards) were legally excluded from them. By the middle of the century French and English seamen were beginning to reject this monopolistic claim and to demand their own right of entry into the New World. Two circumstances made it reasonable for them to do so: the status of the New World had been expressly excluded from the Treaty of Câteau-Cambrésis and remained therefore ill-defined, and by the middle of the century many Frenchmen and Englishmen no longer acknowledged the validity of the papal authority upon which Castile's monopolistic claims were based. But for Philip of Castile there was no discussion, much less negotiation: the Indies belonged solely and exclusively to Castile.

The papal sanction also validated for Philip the religious mission that he had inherited, obliging him to convert the pagan Indians to Catholicism. 'Are these not men? Do they not possess rational souls?', the Dominican Montesinos had asked in 1511, outraged by the treatment that the Indians had already received from the conquistadores. After much agonising, the Spanish Crown had decided that the Indians *were* men, but that they were naive and ill-formed in their spiritual development and that it was therefore its own most solemn duty to protect them from exploitation and to convert them to a true understanding of Catholicism so that their souls could be saved. The Crown was genuinely committed to this mission; in 1542 it published the *New Laws* designed to protect the Indians from exploitation and in 1550 went so far as to prohibit any further expeditions of conquest ('*entradas*') in the New World while it deliberated on its own rights over and obligations towards the Indians. In the Instructions given to viceroys at the beginning of their term of office it became customary for the first precept to emphasise the obligation that the Crown felt to protect the Indians and to convert them so that they could attain redemption.[3]

There was no protection, however, against the diseases and illnesses that the Europeans brought with them to the New World, and by the middle of the sixteenth century it was evident that the native population of the Indies had suffered a catastrophic decline and that there was no longer the abundance of native labour that had marked the early colonial period. The precise extent of this decline has been the subject of fierce academic debate because of the lack of detailed information about the size of the native populations of Mexico and Peru at the time of the discoveries. It is likely that the viceroyalty of New Spain had a population of about 22 000 000 people in 1519 and it is known from surveys that Philip himself ordered that by 1568 the Indians numbered only 2 650 000 and that by 1580 they had been reduced to about 1 900 000. By the early years of the seventeenth century the native population of New Spain was less than a million; it had plummeted by over 90 per cent during the course of the sixteenth century. In Peru (for which figures are even more scarce) it is likely that the population was about 9 000 000 in the early 1520s but that it had fallen to about 2 500 000 by the time of Philip's accession and declined further until early in the seventeenth century it was a mere 600 000 or so.[4] The Indian populations of New Spain and Peru had thus been devastated, to the point where their extinction was a real possibility.

These losses, almost incomprehensible in numbers and in scale, came about in essence not through the wars that the Spaniards fought against the natives nor through the cruelty with which they treated them (brutal though that often was) but through the irruption into the New World of the illnesses and diseases of the Old World and through the inability of the immune systems of the native population to resist them; when the physiologies of Europe and the Americas came into contact for the first time catastrophe was inevitable. Serious illnesses such as typhoid or smallpox had devastating consequences on the Amerindians but so too did illnesses that were themselves comparatively insignificant in their European context – measles, mumps and influenza among them. The greatest losses occurred of course in the first years of the conquest but the 1570s saw a series of major epidemics afflicting the natives of New Spain; for instance, in 1576–8 a plague (probably typhus) killed up to 300 000 people.[5]

The consequences were more than shattering; Nathan Wachtel has poignantly referred to the 'destructuration' of the natives' world, meaning that the life-patterns, ideologies and expectations of the natives were wrecked by the devastation imposed upon them by the combination of physiological, political and cultural influences that accompanied the Spanish Conquest.[6] Uncomprehending of what was happening to them, the Amerindians were dislocated in their lives, in their morale and in their hopes for the future – and consequently they were less able to resist exploitation. Other causes added to the 'destructuration'; the Amerindians were forced off their land by cattle ranchers in New Spain and by pig and sheep farmers in Peru, and in both viceroyalties large numbers of Indians were resettled in what became known as 'congregations' and were forced to work in silver mines. With each new epidemic the concentration of Indians was further accelerated; in the 1550s and again after the devastation of the 1570s, the Crown pushed faster ahead with its programme of congregations. Much as it sought to protect the Indians it also needed to exploit them for its own purposes. The silver mines had to be worked: it was the fundamental imperative of Spanish government in the New World. A secondary consequence followed from the collapse of the Indian population; both Crown and colonists began to look elsewhere for an alternative labour supply. They began to find it in Africa; the trade in African slaves in which the Portuguese had long been engaged began now to assume a transatlantic dimension.

The Crown of Castile was entitled by law to one-fifth of all minerals mined in its territories and it naturally extended this law to the Indies.[7] Although the first conquistadores found wealth even beyond their imaginings in New Spain it was not until the 1540s that rich silver mines were discovered, at Potosí in Peru (1545) and at Zacatecas in New Spain (1546). A third great mine was opened up at Guanajuato in New Spain in 1558. Technological development supplemented discovery; in 1557, the 'mercury-amalgamation process' was introduced into the mines of New Spain by Bartolomé de Medina. Precisely as Philip's reign opened, therefore, the means became available to expedite the separation of the silver from the other ores and to increase the speed and volume of production substantially. The discovery of large supplies of mercury at Huancavelica in central Peru in 1564 completed the cycle; Huancavelica produced 7871 quintales of mercury in 1571–4 but the volume had risen to 43 240 by 1580–4.[8] In 1574 the mercury amalgamation process was introduced in Potosí, and production was transformed; during the course of the 1570s, silver production in Peru began to surpass that of New Spain in volume. By the end of the century, Potosí, some 4000 metres high, had a population of 120 000 or so, and even rivalled fabulous Seville as the most rapidly developing boom-town of the Hispanic world (although neither could compare with the population of Naples of about 200000 people).

In the second half of the 1570s, over 20 million ducats of silver arrived in Spain, of which about 8 million were for the Crown – twice as much as it had received in the first half of the decade. By the end of the 1570s the silver from the New World was beginning to transform not merely the economics but also the politics of the Old World, and it was beginning, too, to change the relationships within the Hispanic world. Although contemporaries continued to speak of 'Spanish gold' as the chief product of the Indies, a new age of economic activity had begun in the European world – the 'Age of American Silver'. Gold production shrank in importance after the first generation of conquest and soon became relatively insignificant in comparison with the veritable flood of silver.

From the 1570s, therefore, Philip enjoyed a new kind of wealth, for an abundance – and by the 1580s, a superabundance – of silver enabled him to plan political and military enterprises on a completely new scale. The second half of his reign was therefore very different from the first; by the 1580s he was receiving three times as much silver as in the 1560s, and by the 1590s it was four times as much (see Table 4.1). Philip's vaunted prudence was the first casualty of the flood of silver.

For all that the Crown profited so substantially from the mines of the New World, the greater part of the silver registered at Seville from the 1570s came not as taxes for the Crown but as payments to private indi-

Table 4.1   Official Receipts of Treasure at Seville (in ducats)

Years	Crown	Private	Total
1561–70	7705880 (100%)	27148653 (100%)	34854533 (100%)
1571–80	13678966 (177%)	26414040 (97%)	40093006 (115%)
1581–90	21441498 (278%)	51718461 (190%)	73159958 (210%)
1591–1600	28871791 (375%)	66846583 (246%)	95718374 (274%)

Source: Earl J. Hamilton, 'Table 1 Total Imports of Treasure', *American Treasure and the Price Revolution in Spain, 1501–1650* (Harvard Economic Studies, vol. 43, New York : 1965), p. 34. Hamilton's series has been updated from 1580 by Michel Morineau, *Incroyables gazettes et fabuleux métaux. Les retours des trésors américains d'après les gazettes hollandaises (XVIe–XVIIe siècles)*, (Cambridge: 1985); I have followed Morineau in coverting pesos to ducats at 1.375; Morineau's calculation for total imports in 1581–90 is 55061384 ducats and for 1591–1600 is 77540316, at pp. 72–4.

viduals for goods sent out to the New World. The first generation of Spaniards in the New World had to have most of their goods sent to them from the mother country; theirs was a dependent economy. However, by the middle of the sixteenth century the colonists were beginning to demand a range of products that Spain found it increasingly difficult to provide. These goods – foodstuffs, clothing, tools and the like – had to be bought in northern Europe and then reshipped to the colonies. Trade grew, therefore, through the needs of the settlers as well as with silver production; by the 1580s the gross annual tonnage of the fleets sailing from Seville for the New World was twice as large (80 000 tons) as it had been forty years earlier.

The flood of silver had profoundly important economic and social consequences in Spain, for it helped to push prices upwards as part of the phenonemon known as 'the price revolution' of the sixteenth century. By the beginning of Philip's reign this was beginning to attract notice. Indeed, the classic exposition of the nature of the price rise was published by Martín Azpilcueta Navarro in the very year of Philip's accession to the thrones of Spain: 'We see by experience that in France, where money is scarcer than in Spain, bread, wine, cloth, and labour are worth much less. And even in Spain, in times when money was scarcer, saleable goods and labour were given for very much less than after the discovery of the Indies, which flooded the country with gold and silver.'[9]

The 'price revolution' was not, however, caused wholly or indeed chiefly by American silver, for it accompanied – and was substantially accelerated by – a population revolution in Spain. The population of Spain increased by nearly one-half during Philip's lifetime (see Table 1.1) and the increased pressure on resources pushed prices upwards and did so more in the first half of the century than in the second. It is now evident that the population rise was most pronounced in the 1530s and 1540s and that it had levelled off by the 1580s as the population outgrew the capacity of the land to feed it. Of course, not all specie stayed in Spain; increasing amounts of silver were re-exported (sometimes without even being landed in Spain) to pay for the Crown's imperial and financial commitments. Nevertheless, the amount of silver circulating in Spain was still enormous and it helped to push prices upwards in Spain before they rose in northern Europe. Spain was therefore disadvantaged in her trading activities in Europe precisely by the flood of silver from which she seemed to be benefiting so much, while her people found that the rise in their cost of living was accelerated because there was so much silver in the country – silver to which, for the most part, they had no access.

MONOPOLISTIC CONTROL

From the beginning of the period of conquest, the Castilian Crown had determined to control the exploitation of its American colonies by establishing a monopoly, and for geographical and maritime reasons it chose the city of Seville as the centre from which the monopoly was operated. Although it was an inland port, Seville had well-established trading links with Africa and the Canary Islands, the Mediterranean and northern Europe. With ready access to the summer trade winds of the North Atlantic, Seville was ideally placed to organise the exploitation of the Indies, having relatively easy access to the Canary Islands and the Azores, the key stopping-off points on voyages to and from the New World. Seville was also the largest and wealthiest city in Spain and was the capital of the richest agricultural region in the country. It possessed, therefore, all the expertise – seagoing, commercial, financial and agricultural – that was necessary to exploit the New World and to benefit from it. It governed the trade with the New World through two institutions: the House of Trade (*Casa de la Contratación*), established in 1503 'to establish and perpetuate' the trade with the Indies by registering every item of merchandise and every passenger travelling to or from the Indies; and the Consulate (*Consulado*), formed in 1543 as a merchants' guild to register every item carried on outward- and inward-bound voyages.[10] Philip himself showed from an early age that he understood the importance of the Indies; while still regent, in 1550 and again in 1552, he issued ordinances instructing shipowners to carry artillery on their ships and imposed a time-limit within which they were to acquire the necessary guns so that the ships could properly defend themselves.[11]

The monopoly was cumbersome but it worked and Castile maintained her grip upon her territories in the Americas. About 200 000–300 000 Spaniards passed through Seville in the sixteenth century on their way to the Americas; for the most part they were male, but by the middle years of Philip's reign perhaps a quarter or so of them were women. The population of Seville rose from about 50 000 people at the time of Philip's birth to 125 000–130 000 at the time of his death.[12] By 1598 it was among the six largest cities of Europe and was one-third as large again as Madrid, the national capital.

Within the context of the monopoly centred upon Seville, Philip used four instruments to establish his control over the Indies and the Atlantic routes to and from them: he organised an onslaught on the corsairs operating in the Caribbean and developed a convoy system to protect the fleets sailing to and from the Indies; he reinvigorated the viceregal system in the Americas; he used the authority of the secular church to bolster his authority in the New World; and in Spain he developed the Council of the Indies to exercise overall control over Church and State in the Indies. While, however, he was brilliantly successful in re-establishing and then strengthening the authority of the Crown in the Indies, Philip damaged his own achievements by reforming the Council of the Indies and then by refusing to allow it to operate properly. It was as if he could trust men who were beyond his daily control but he could not prevent himself from interfering with those with whom he worked on a daily basis.

Pedro Menéndez de Avilés and the defence of the monopoly

Philip recognised at the outset of his reign that he had to secure the Caribbean against foreign corsairs and traders. In the years 1548–63 Spain lost eighty-six ships in the Caribbean and on the Atlantic routes. Indeed, in 1554 a complaint was sent to Charles V from Panamá that 'the corsairs are as much the lords of this coast as Your Majesty is the river of San Lúcar, because there is not a ship in all the Caribbean which has not been robbed two or three times'.[13] The attacks upon Spanish shipping in the Caribbean often had religious undertones. In July 1555, Jacques de Sores, a French Huguenot seaman, captured Havana and occupied it for twenty-six days; he desecrated and then destroyed the cathedral and with measured insolence gave the priests' vestments to his men to wear as cloaks.[14] Admiral Coligny, the Huguenot leader, organised expeditions to Florida in 1562 and 1564. The first of these, under Jean Ribaut, founded Port Royal and the second under René Laudonnière established the fort of Fort Caroline on the St Johns River. The leaders and many of their men were Huguenots and the threat to the Caribbean security – and to the integrity of its Catholicism – was real. Philip charged Pedro Menéndez de Avilés to deal with them.

The king had chosen his man well. Menéndez was an Asturian seaman and shipowner whom Philip had come to know and trust during his time as king of England. Indeed, Menéndez commanded a squadron in the fleet that carried Philip to England and had brought Philip many of the troops who had fought at St Quentin, and he commanded the fleet that brought Philip back to Spain in 1559. In 1556, 1560 and again in 1561 Philip appointed him as general of the fleets sailing to the Indies. As early as 1558 Menéndez had warned Philip of the need to fight off the French threat to the Caribbean and to create an effective defensive system in the Indies.[15] When, therefore, the French established settlements in Florida it was natural that Philip should have turned to Menéndez to remove them; on 15 March 1565 he named him *adelantado y gobernador* of Florida and charged him with destroying the French settlements. On the same day a separate contract was agreed by which Menéndez undertook to organise a convoy system so that Spanish trade with the Indies could remain inviolate in the future. The eviction of the French from Florida and the establishment of the convoy system were in effect therefore privatised in the Asturian's hands. Menéndez sailed from Cadiz on 28 June 1565.[16]

He achieved his first objective with brutal alacrity; he destroyed the French settlements in Florida and subsequently slaughtered over 200 Frenchmen, the majority of them after they had surrendered to him, and he established a fort at San Agustín (8 September 1565) from which the coast could be protected. Soon, a couple of hundred settlers were introduced to the settlement. The spot at which the massacre of the French seamen took place henceforth bore the salutary name 'Matanzas' – 'the place of the slaughters'. Menéndez justified his brutality by claiming that he was not able to feed so many prisoners and that he had in any event executed them not because they were Frenchmen but because they were heretics. But he also noted that Ribaut, an accomplished and experienced sailor, could have inflicted profound damage on the Spanish monopoly: 'he could do more in one year than another in ten, for he was the most experienced seaman and corsair known'. It was good enough for Philip; he wrote to Menéndez congratulating him and assuring him of his support.[17] Philip also instructed his ambassador in England to give a full account of what had occurred to Queen Elizabeth, effectively warning her that the same fate could be expected by any Englishmen venturing into the Caribbean: in defending the Spanish Sea, Philip would take no prisoners.[18]

The king had reason enough to advise Elizabeth of the strength of his resolve, for significant numbers of English seamen were beginning to sail into the Caribbean in illicit trading ventures. In particular, John Hawkins of Plymouth systematically breached Philip's monopoly; in 1562–3, 1564–5 and 1567–8, he sold cargoes of African slaves to the Spanish settlers. Hawkins had the cool effrontery to claim that he was merely taking advantage of England's traditional friendship with Spain and that he was paying taxes on them. He also on occasion used sufficient force to allow the colonists to claim, innocently or otherwise, that he had forced them to do business with him. Beneath the insolent façade, what Hawkins was after was Spanish silver, and his activities represented a real threat to Philip's revenue as much as to his authority, the more so since each of his enterprises was more ambitious than the last. However, each voyage forced Philip to show what was to be an abiding characteristic of his management of affairs in the Indies – his ability to repair effectively the inadequacies in his defence systems that were highlighted by the successes of foreign seamen. In the Indies, Philip learned from his mistakes, quickly and to purpose.

The third of Hawkins's voyages was to be a turning-point in diplomatic as well as in colonial affairs, for he organised it in 1567 at a time when Anglo-Spanish relations were under increasing strain (see chapter 5). Elizabeth and her ministers insistently denied to the Spanish ambassador Guzmán de Silva that Hawkins was bound for the Caribbean. The ambassador was not fooled and as a result of his warnings the authorities in the Caribbean were put on alert.[19] Hawkins sailed from Plymouth on 2 October 1567 in a fleet of which the flagship (the *Jesus of Lubeck*) was a royal ship, and he took with him munitions which had been supplied by the royal armourers of the Tower of London. There could be no escaping the challenge that was laid down by the English – seadogs and government – to the Spanish monopoly. Six hundred men sailed with Hawkins, among them his young kinsman Francis Drake.

Hawkins arrived in the Caribbean with 400 or so African slaves and soon found that the authorities were much more resolute in refusing to trade with him than on his previous voyages. He had to resort to force in order to unload his slaves. He allowed Drake to storm the town of Rio de la Hacha on the coast of Venezuela – it was in all probability Drake's baptism of fire – and he himself fired on the royal fortresses in the harbour at Cartagena. The rewards did not justify the effort and Hawkins headed north to leave the Caribbean, realising that the easy-going days of collusive trade had gone for good.

The expedition ran into two violent storms off Cuba and Hawkins decided to call in at San Juan de Ulúa to repair his ships before returning across the Atlantic. He sailed into the port on 15 September and found to his astonishment that he was welcomed by the authorities. The reason did not take long to discover; on the following day, the outward-bound fleet arrived from Spain carrying the new viceroy, Don Martín Enríquez de Almansa. The port authorities had welcomed Hawkins in the belief that his ships belonged to the viceroy's fleet.

What happened next became the subject of bitter dispute between the English and the Spanish but in reality the matter was quite simple. Hawkins refused to allow the viceroy to sail into San Juan unless he gave him an assurance that the English ships would not be attacked. Enríquez grudgingly gave it, but neither man was under any illusion as to what would happen once the viceroy had gained access to his own port. On 23 September the Spanish fleet duly attacked the English ships in the harbour. They sent two fireships against the English which created 'a marvellous fear' and dispersed the English fleet. Drake sailed away, leaving Hawkins to fight on alone. Both sides fought to their strengths, the Spanish attempting to board the enemy ships, the English using their superior artillery to keep the *galeones* at bay. Hawkins managed to use his twenty battery guns to fight his way out of the harbour, destroying the *almiranta* and sinking the *capitana* and another ship in the process. These were very serious losses for the new viceroy to endure, and they marked the end of any pretence at tolerance of English activities in the Caribbean as far as the Spanish government was concerned. Hawkins's losses were in their way quite as severe; he had to abandon half his crew to find their fate in New Spain. After an horrific crossing he arrived back in England on 25 January 1569. The voyage had been a catastrophic failure; Hawkins had lost three-quarters of his men and over a thousand tons of shipping. Francis Drake had perhaps lost more; for the remainder of his life he insistently proclaimed that Enríquez had behaved treacherously at San Juan, and in all probability he proclaimed it the louder because he knew that he had lost his nerve in his first sea battle and had abandoned his commander in his hour of need. Hawkins certainly drew that conclusion, declaiming that Drake 'forsooke us in our great myserie'.[20] Drake never lost his nerve again; he could not afford to do so. For Philip and his new viceroy, the incident at San Juan de Ulúa was a triumphant vindication, a restatement of what Menéndez had taught the French at Fort Caroline: Spain would allow no 'peace beyond the line' to seamen who challenged her monopoly.

Dealing with interlopers was, however, comparatively short-term work. Menéndez's major contribution to the security of the Indies was much longer-lasting, for he perfected the convoy system which for the remainder of the Habsburg period protected the silver fleets, and he constructed a series of fortifications which strengthened Spain's hold over the Caribbean. Convoys had been used since 1542 in times of war and in the later 1560s Menéndez established what was to become the classic form. Two fleets left Spain carrying the goods that the colonists required.

The first, known as the *flota*, left in the spring for New Spain and wintered at Vera Cruz; the second, known as the *galeones*, left in the autumn and wintered at Cartagena. Their arrival in the Indies was synchronised with the preparations to ship the silver back to Spain. The Peruvian silver was brought by sea to the Isthmus of Panamá and carried overland on mules to the Caribbean coast. It was then shipped to Havana, where the fleet with the silver from New Spain was awaiting it. The two fleets sailed back to Spain together in the autumn, usually in heavily guarded convoys of about 60 to 70 ships. Now they presented a target worthy of serious attention. Once again, Philip ensured that the fleet was well protected. As early as 1562 he had established a squadron of eight galleys to protect the approach of the silver fleet around Cape St Vincent and the Gulf of Cadiz – what was to become known as the 'Squadron for the Protection of the Straits' – and from the mid-1560s he ordered that the flagships of the *flotas* and *galeones* should carry 100 tons less than their optimum cargo so that they had space for ordinance with which to defend the fleet. In subsequent years, he progressively increased the armaments of the royal galleons. In 1568 he began the construction of twelve galleons in Cantabria to form the fleet that would protect the homebound galleons – what would become known as the *Armada para la Guarda de la Carrera de las Indias*. The system was very expensive but it was effective; not until 1628 was a Spanish treasure fleet successfully attacked in the Caribbean. By an extraordinary coincidence, the disaster took place off Matanzas itself, where Menéndez had slaughtered his French prisoners.[21]

Menéndez also strengthened the fortifications of the key points in the Caribbean, notably those of Havana and Cartagena, so that they could provide defensive foci for the fleets. However, Francis Drake himself demonstrated the weakness of Menéndez's new system at Nombre de Dios in 1572: it did not protect the silver from Peru at the point where it was carried overland by mules to the Caribbean. Drake reconnoitred in two voyages in 1570 and 1571 and then in 1572, using natives to guide and to supplement his own troops, he captured a mule train carrying the silver across the Isthmus from Panama. He made his fortune and salvaged his reputation from the shame of the incident at San Juan. On the way out of the Caribbean, Drake impudently sailed past a royal fleet at Cartagena and saluted it. Illicit trade had turned to brilliant and savage plunder. Once again Philip reacted promptly, instituting the *Armada de Barlovento*, a fleet of two galley squadrons based in Cartagena and the Greater Antilles, to patrol the Caribbean and protect its shipping.[22] Philip was always quick to absorb the lessons that Francis Drake taught him.

Viceregal government

It was curious that while Castile excluded the subjects of the Crown of Aragon from the Indies she chose to govern her American possessions by making use of the Aragonese institution of the viceroyalty. It was, too, a measure of the success that Castile enjoyed in the New World that she needed only two viceroyalties to govern the whole of her enormous territories – that of New Spain, which covered all territories north of the Isthmus of Panamá and that of Peru, which covered the lands to the south, with the exception of Venezuela. By the time of Philip's accession the two viceroyalties were at very different stages of their development. The viceroyalty of New Spain had been firmly established over a period of thirty years by two brilliant administrators – Antonio de Mendoza (1535–50) and Luis de Velasco the Elder (1550–64) – and although there were difficulties after Velasco's sudden death (31 July 1564) these were soon resolved.[23] Peru, by contrast, was in a primitive condition, at least a generation behind New Spain in its development; the first viceroy, Blasco Núñez Vela, had been murdered by Spanish rebels in 1546 and by the mid-1560s no viceroy had managed to see out the three years that was the normal term of office. Peru had not known stable government, and Philip set himself to provide it. He did so with brilliant economy of effort.

In 1568, on the recommendation of Diego de Espinosa, Philip appointed Martin Enríquez de Almansa to the viceroyalty of New Spain and Francisco de Toledo to that of Peru. The appointments ranked among the most successful that he ever made.[24] Philip recognised that both Enríquez and Toledo were men of real ability and he allowed them to stay in office for twelve years so that they provided the stability of government that had been so lacking, most especially in Peru. A measure of the significance of the length of their tenure of office can be gauged from the fact that the years 1568–80 saw four holders in each of the viceroyalties of Naples and Sicily. It was no accident that Philip allowed Enríquez and Toledo to stay in office for so long for it was precisely in these years that the explosion in the volume of silver production was coming about.

In New Spain, Enríquez showed himself to be a methodical administrator. He organised the *repartimiento* system, whereby settlers were allowed to have a specified number of Indians working for them for given periods, and although he strenuously tried to moderate the conditions under which the Indians worked, the priority that he gave to silver production made it possible for them to be exploited more efficiently. He also secured the roads to Zacatecas so that the silver could be moved more securely and quickly. In 1572, to prevent merchants from profiteering by controlling mercury supplies, he took control of all mercury for the Crown.[25] Enríquez also increased tax yields by introducing the *alcabala* in 1574. He was as concerned with the Church as with the State; he introduced the Inquisition in 1571 and allowed the Society of Jesus to enter New Spain in 1572 – he was himself related to Francisco de Borja – and in 1573 he began the construction of the cathedral of Mexico. Enríquez won the reward appropriate to his achievement; in 1580 he was appointed to succeed Toledo in the viceroyalty of Peru.

Philip had known Francisco de Toledo since his own childhood; once again, he remained loyal to a friend he had come to trust in his formative years. Toledo was a remarkable man, possessed of a powerful intellect and a ruthless determination. He was appalled by what he termed 'the little peace and great disturbance' that he discovered on his arrival in Peru.[26] He found that the Spaniards were exploiting the Indians and fighting among themselves without respect for the royal administration; 'the Indians are enemies of work and the Spaniards who live there are lovers of idleness'. He insisted that royal justice should be imposed sternly and impartially and set an example by peremptorily executing miscreants. He then set out on a tour of the viceroyalty; it took him five years to cover the enormous territory (1570–5). But this was no mere factfinding tour; Toledo completed the conquest of the Incas by slaughtering the army of the last native leader, Manco Inca, in 1572 and by conquering the last free Inca city, Vilcabamba. He then ceremonially had Manco Inca beheaded publicly in Cuzco in formal recognition that the Conquest of Peru had at last been completed.

Toledo increased the production of the silver mines by introducing the mercury amalgamation process and by using forced labour under the *mita* system whereby quotas of Indians were forced to work the mines. Toledo was clearly anxious about his methods, for on returning to Spain he wrote a lengthy exposition justifying his conduct. He described how on arrival he had found the Indians living in dispersed and uninhabitable lands, exploited by the colonists and unable to provide properly for themselves. He recounted how he brought them into communities where they could be properly controlled and taught the Christian faith – 'so that they can better learn how to be men', as he put it, and 'the better to be Christians'. In fact, bringing the Indians into settlements was fundamental to the brutal exploitation that lay behind the increased silver production. By the end of Toledo's term of office the mines of Potosí alone produced more silver than the whole of the Mexican industry. The price was paid by the Indians.

The Church and the Indians

The first missionaries in the New World had been members of the mendicant orders; the Franciscans arrived in 1524, the Dominicans in 1526 and the Augustinians in 1533. By 1559 there were 802 friars in New Spain alone.[27] In their way, the mendicants were every bit as singleminded and as ruthless as the conquistadores and they were just as successful. Indeed, their resourcefulness and independence posed a real threat to royal control over the Church in the Indies. Philip therefore determined to replace them with secular clergy. Since the Council of Trent had stipulated that no one could have cure of souls unless he was subject to a bishop, Philip had the means at hand to control the mendicants. In 1574, therefore, he ordered that each bishop was to control the mendicants in his diocese, and in 1583 he decreed that secular priests were to be appointed to livings in preference to friars. By the mid-point of his reign Philip had put an end to the pre-eminence of the mendicant orders, forcing them to accept episcopal control or to confine themselves to working as missionaries on the farthermost frontiers of their provinces.

Philip had the good sense to appoint able men as archbishops and then to allow them to serve for an extended period; Pedro Moya de Contreras served as Archbishop of Mexico for nearly twenty years (1573–91) and was so successful that Philip allowed him to serve as interim viceroy (1583–5), while Toribio de Mogrovejo served as Bishop of Lima for twenty-five years (1581–1606). In the Indies, Philip knew how to be served, and he knew how to place his trust in men of exceptional ability. Mexican church councils in 1565 and 1585 brought the Church in New Spain into line with practice in Spain by enforcing the Tridentine decrees.[28]

Francisco de Toledo found that few priests and friars in Peru were able to communicate with the Indians in their own languages. He therefore founded a chair of Quechua in the University of Lima to organise the teaching of the language. He appointed an examining officer to licence priests before they were admitted to the exercise of their powers and he spread the priests around the viceroyalty so that each one should be responsible only for 400–500 Indians. He founded two colleges for the education of the children of chieftains so that they could lead the process of Christianisation. Concerned that bishops exercised too much power because of the sheer size of their dioceses, Toledo broke the dioceses up into more manageable units. He also allowed the Inquisition and the

Society of Jesus to establish themselves in Peru as part of his drive to create a Church that was modern in its structure.

Juan de Ovando and the Council of the Indies

Although the Council of the Indies was almost forty years old by the beginning of Philip's reign it had at its disposal very few men who had personal knowledge of the New World. Moreover, the councillorship of the Indies was generally seen as a stepping-stone to appointment to the Council of Castile or to a bishopric rather than as an end in itself. The Council was therefore deficient in both structure and prestige and was accordingly ill-equipped to deal with its responsibilities. In 1571 Philip instructed Lic. Don Juan de Ovando to modernise and restructure the Council.

Ovando had no direct experience of the Indies. He had been born in Extremadura and had begun his career as Administrator of the archdiocese of Seville for Fernando de Valdés while he was serving as Inquisitor-General. On Valdés's death, Ovando moved to Madrid and joined the clientele of Espinosa. The cardinal had persuaded Philip of the need to institute a fundamental reform of the secular and ecclesiastical government of the Indies and Ovando was entrusted with the task of investigating the way in which the Council – and its individual councillors – had conducted themselves. Once again, Philip had chosen well; Ovando had a voracious appetite for properly documented information – it is to him that we owe the salvation of many of Las Casas's private papers, including Columbus's priceless log of his voyages to the Indies – and, protected by Espinosa, he fearlessly set about his task. He began by investigating the records of the Council of the Indies in order to establish the history and practices of the government of the colonies. He then undertook a widespread investigation into the conduct of everyone involved in the administration of the Indies, whether at court or in the Indies. He rounded this out by personally interviewing everyone at court who had first-hand knowledge of the way in which the Indies had been governed, including Philip himself. Ovando even sent a scientific expedition to New Spain, despatching Dr Francisco Hernández de Liévana to investigate the medicinal properties of plants growing there. Hernández de Liévana brought back a wealth of detail, specimens and watercolour paintings; Philip took the closest interest in all of them, excited by the detailed information about the New World – human and natural – for which he was responsible.

Ovando's enquiry established that the Council of the Indies could not be relied upon to make reasoned recommendations to the king because its members were often simply not familiar with the *Laws of the Indies* and that, indeed, the laws themselves were not even properly collected. Accordingly, he recommended that Philip should have the laws collected, codified and printed; the great labour began in 1571 with the publication of the statutes governing the Council itself. Ovando was less successful in persuading Philip to upgrade the status of the Council; despite his strictures, Philip continued to leave the presidency vacant and he failed to make the councillorship of the Indies sufficiently prestigious to attract men in its own right rather than as a port of call on their route to a seat on the Council of Castile. However, Philip did agree to Ovando's recommendation to appoint a cartographer-historian of the Indies to the Council; the position was held by a succession of distinguished men, notably by Juan López de Velasco and Antonio Léon Pinelo, and they built up an archive of material which was fundamental to the governance of the Indies for the remainder of the colonial period.[29]

Ovando's reward was the traditional one for a successful reformer; on 28 August 1571 he was appointed to the presidency of the Council that he had so criticised.[30] A month later, Philip approved the *ordenanzas* of the Council, accepting Ovando's reforms and establishing the structure of the Council that would last throughout the Habsburg period. Philip had instituted a major, clear-sighted and long-term governmental change. However, he then substantially invalidated it by not allowing Ovando to concentrate on implementing his reforms, for he piled a mountain of other work onto his shoulders; in 1572 Ovando succeeded to many of the responsibilities that Cardinal Espinosa had held, and in 1573 was appointed as a founder-member of the *Junta de Presidentes*. There was therefore a rather perverse, if entirely characteristic, logic in Philip's decision of 1574 to put Ovando in charge of the Council of Finance while retaining the presidency of the Council of the Indies.[31] The decision showed at once the king's confidence in Ovando and his failure to understand the need to structure his government in a manner which allowed it to function responsibly, for the Crown's finances were at the point of collapse and their management required the fullest attention; the burdens now placed on Ovando were manifestly too much for one man to bear. Within a year he was dead.

5

CRUSADE, CRISIS AND REVOLT
IN THE LOW COUNTRIES

A. THE MEDITERRANEAN

WAR IN THE MEDITERRANEAN, 1560–5

On 15 June 1559, in Brussels, Philip took the decision to send an expedition to reconquer Tripoli, which had been conquered in 1551 by the celebrated Barbary pirate corsair Dragut.[1] Philip's decision was motivated in part by a perfectly natural ambition to announce the beginning of his reign in Spain with a great victory against the infidel. More generally it emphasised his determination to reverse the successes of the Ottoman Turks and their co-religionists, the Barbary pirates, and to prevent them taking joint action in the western Mediterranean against Spain, her territories and her allies. Charles V had never concentrated fully on the defence of the western Mediterranean, although he had organised occasional large-scale expeditions; he had, for instance, succeeded in conquering Tunis in 1535 but had failed humiliatingly against Algiers in 1541. In consequence, Mediterranean Christendom suffered a rhythmic and escalating series of losses: Algiers had fallen in 1529; La Goletta in 1534; Tripoli in 1551 and Bougie in 1555. Algiers and Tripoli in particular became major pirate lairs and no one trading in the western Mediterranean, or living on its coast, was safe. Ottoman Turkey did not ordinarily send large fleets into the western Mediterranean but in 1558 a small expedition descended on Menorca and took thousands of Spaniards off into captivity. In Algiers it was said to be 'raining Christians'.[2] The assault on Tripoli was Philip's declaration that he intended to fight back – and that he intended in doing so to claim for himself the leadership of

Christian Europe as well as to protect his lands, his subjects and their commerce.

Philip entrusted command of his expedition to Don Juan de la Cerda, fourth Duke of Medina Celi. The Duke was a personal friend and confidant – he was yet another of those men who had travelled with Philip to England in 1554 – and he was of the blood royal. Philip appointed the Genoese admiral Gian Andrea Doria as admiral of the fleet. Doria was only twenty years of age and his appointment emphasised Philip's determination to develop the traditional alliance with Genoa – and to use Genoa's galley fleet in his own enterprises. The expedition was originally designed as a small, raiding assault but Philip allowed it to grow into a large-scale and multinational operation on the pattern of his father's campaigns. The fleet came to consist of more than one hundred ships, sixty of them prime fighting galleys drawn from Spain and her Mediterranean allies (notably the papacy, Genoa and Tuscany) and it carried about 12 000 soldiers. Unfortunately, it took six months to assemble and did not sail from Sicily until 1 December 1559. As if to ensure that everyone knew about it, the expedition then stayed at Malta for ten weeks to make final preparations and only sailed for the island of Djerba (just off Tripoli) on 1 March. The repeated delays cost the expedition dear, for up to 2000 men were lost to the illnesses that festered in the camps.

Initially the expedition seemed blessed by success; Dragut was caught with his fleet in the shallow waters off Djerba. However, he managed to escape, apparently by dragging his galleys over the sand and refloating them away from the Christian fleet. Dragut found that assistance was soon on its way; Suleiman (like everyone else) knew of the Christian fleet and was no doubt determined that he would take the measure of the new king of Spain. He despatched a fleet of seventy-four galleys, each with a hundred janissaries on board. The fleet was commanded by Piale Pasha and appeared off Malta on 11 May, having rowed from Istanbul in an almost unbelievable twenty days. The Christian force, properly led, might well have resisted but Medina Celi and Doria were quite unequal to the challenge and the unexpected arrival of the Turkish fleet created panic among their men. Piale Pasha drove home his advantage with unerring brilliance; his decision to risk attacking the Christian fleet before taking down his own masts has been described by Professor Guilmartin as 'among the great snap decisions in naval history'. The Christian fleet was devastated; twenty-eight galleys were destroyed and the army made little resistance, unnerved by the irruption of the dreaded janissaries. Medina Celi and Doria fled to safety, leaving the remnants of Philip's army besieged in a fort under the command of Don Álvaro de Sande. Philip initially declared that it was his sacred duty to save the men in the fort but when he heard that Medina Celi was safe he ruthlessly changed his mind, abandoning the besieged men to their fate on the grounds that they had sufficient supplies to survive the siege. They held out (despite the reappearance of Dragut with reinforcements) but were forced to surrender on 31 July. On 1 October, when Piale Pasha made his triumphal entry into Istanbul, three Spanish generals rode behind him – Sande himself, Don Berenguer de Requesens and Don Sancho de Leyva (who was accompanied by two sons). Behind them trudged thousands of Christian soldiers, marching into their own servitude. It was not merely the numbers involved that represented a serious loss to Spain, as some 600 or so of these men were skilled mariners and technicians, and the Spanish galley-fleet felt their loss for years to come.[3]

In his humiliation Philip was more fortunate than he deserved to be, for in the years 1561–4 Suleiman concentrated on his war with Persia and did not send his fleet into the western Mediterranean. Even so, affairs went badly for Philip and for Christendom; in 1561 Dragut ambushed seven of the king's galleys and in October 1562 a further twenty-five galleys were destroyed and some 5000 men were drowned when a violent storm overwhelmed them at La Herradura near Málaga. Philip's ability even to defend the coasts of Spain and his Mediterranean possessions was now seriously at risk: in 1559 he had had command of ninety-one galleys but by 1562 only fifty-two remained.[4]

Philip had no choice now but to undertake a major galley-building programme and he did so with superb effectiveness, for this was the sort of task for which he was ideally equipped; he had the singlemindedness to establish a policy and to bend all the resources of his monarchy to its pursuit. He secured grants from the papacy to help fund his expanded fleet and acquired many galleys by making use – forced or otherwise – of the fleets of his allies in the Mediterranean. Most importantly, he set the dockyards of Barcelona, Sicily and Naples to work to build his own galleys. It was a slow and expensive business but by 1574 Philip was supporting 146 galleys; his fleet was now on a par with that of the Turk.[5] This enormous building programme, precise and sustained, represented one of the great achievements of his reign; by the end of the 1560s, Spain had the means to properly defend her possessions in the central and western Mediterranean and to confront the full power of the Turk. Philip's galleys were divided into four squadrons: that of 'Spain', which was based in Cartagena; those of 'Naples' and 'Sicily', funded by the separate kingdoms and operating out of Naples and Messina; and that of 'Genoa', funded now by papal grant.[6]

As early as April 1563 Philip had sufficient galleys to relieve Oran when it was besieged by an Algerian fleet. Encouraged by a defensive success he then ordered his commanders to capture the great rock ('el Peñon') which commanded the eastern approach to Gibraltar. Philip could not risk allowing Islamic pirates to establish a strong base at el Peñon, for they might then be able to threaten the treasure galleons from the Indies as they made their approach to Cadiz and the Guadalquivir. However, the effort failed rather humiliatingly (July–August 1563). Once again, Philip showed that when he had committed his prestige to an undertaking he would not draw back. In 1564 he despatched an expedition of nearly a hundred galleys carrying some 16000 men under the command of Don García de Toledo, and in less than a week the famous rock was captured and a garrison installed.[7] Philip had recovered his prestige – but he had also made it all the more likely that Suleiman would respond, for he too could not tolerate failure.

It was (as Philip recognised) virtually inevitable that the Turkish onslaught would be directed against Malta. The island was not itself a Spanish possession; Charles V had granted it to the multinational order of the Knights of St John of Jerusalem in 1530 to compensate them for having been driven out of Rhodes by Suleiman in 1522. The Knights had turned Malta into one of the major centres of Christian corsair activity. In attempting to conquer the island, Suleiman was pointing a dagger not just at the Knights of St John but at Spain herself, for, tiny though it was, Malta was one of the great natural strongpoints of the Mediterranean. It was certainly a thorn in Dragut's flesh; he referred to it as 'a nest of vipers'. With control of its magnificent harbour, Suleiman would be able to send his fleet to range the western Mediterranean and even the Atlantic Approaches, and he would be able to co-ordinate actions against Spain with his co-religionists in Algiers and Tripoli. His challenge to Philip, and to western Christendom, was unequivocal.

Suleiman sent a fleet worthy of his ambition. More than 140 of his own galleys and 30000 men were despatched against Malta and they were supplemented by a further 55 galleys provided by his allies in Alexandria, Algiers and Tripoli (from where Dragut himself brought 43 galleys). In all, Piale Pasha had perhaps 200 galleys and 36000 men under his command. It was a truly awesome fleet, and it arrived off the island on 18 May. The Knights, commanded by their venerable Grand Master Jean Parisot de la Valette (who had reached the age of seventy in 1564), had only some 9000 men with whom to defend the island.

Outnumbered as they were, the Knights understood just how precious every day's resistance was to their chances of saving Malta and they resisted with ferocious discipline. Their first success came in holding the fort of St Elmo for three weeks, withstanding four major assaults. Although the Knights probably did not know it, they achieved a significant success when the great Dragut was among those who died beneath their walls. Not until 23 June did they capitulate. The sixty or so Knights who had survived were promptly executed, and their bodies were mutilated and floated over to the Christians. La Valette responded in kind; he had his own Turkish prisoners beheaded and fired their heads into the Turkish lines. No quarter was asked or given: this was Holy War.

As the Turks turned to the strongpoints of Birgu and Fort St Michael, La Valette and his Knights looked to Don García de Toledo, viceroy of Sicily, for their salvation. Knowing how much hung on his actions, Don García acted with a careful calculation which puzzled and infuriated the Knights. He organised the first of three relief forces when he sent 600 men under Don Juan de Cardona into the northern part of the island (20 June). The arrival of even a small relief force raised Christian spirits and enabled La Valette to organise a number of sorties which astounded the Turks. An attempt to land a larger relief force at the end of August failed abjectly but on 7 September, with the Knights in their last extremity, Don García himself led the *Gran Soccorso*, consisting of 12000 men and 100 galleys. He managed to put his force on shore 'without', as he put it, 'losing one oar'. His arrival broke Turkish spirits; after three and a half months of ferocious war and great suffering they were faced now with a reinvigorated Christian force. Within five days the Turkish army had embarked and sailed for home. Suleiman had lost perhaps 30000 men in the attack upon Malta.[8] There would be no triumphal procession in Istanbul in 1565.

Nor would there be much generosity between the Christians who had been involved in the great siege. García de Toledo was subjected to vicious and sustained criticism for the slowness with which he had moved. However, Philip was more generously praised.[9] Indeed, his reputation in Europe was transformed, for he had confronted the full might of Suleiman in a battle of the sultan's own choosing and had defeated him decisively. A Frenchman, Pierre de Bourdeille, seigneur de Brantôme, best expressed the king's new standing: 'A hundred thousand years from now, the great king Philip of Spain will still be worthy of praise and renown, and worthy that all Christendom should pray as many years for the salvation of his soul, if God had not yet already given him a seat in Paradise for having so nobly delivered so many gentlemen in Malta, that was about to follow Rhodes into enemy hands.' Philip himself gloried in his triumph: from his hunting lodge in the woods at Segovia he wrote to his ambassador in England that 'the Turk fled shamefully with great damage from the Spaniards and Italians led by Don Garcia de Toledo'.[10] As it happened, Suleiman himself had only months to live when Malta fell; that his last great venture had failed made it only the more certain that his successor would launch an even more ferocious attack upon Spain and the Christian Mediterranean, for Turkish policy, like Philip's, could be motivated by pride as much as by military strategy.

REVOLT IN THE ALPUJARRAS, 1568–70

The crisis over Malta highlighted the existence of what seemed to many to be an Islamic fifth-column within Spain. Philip himself had been deeply anxious that the *moriscos* of Granada might rise in rebellion to support the Turkish attack on Malta, and like most of his subjects the king believed that the Catholicism which the *moriscos* practised was essentially insincere, a religion of convenience. He therefore encouraged Cardinal Espinosa as president of the Council of Castile and Inquisitor-General to pursue aggressively a policy of converting the *moriscos* of Granada, if need be by force. In doing so, Philip drove the *moriscos* to revolt and in their desperation to seek support from the Turk and the Barbary pirates. He brought about, in other words, the very objective that he was trying to prevent but at a time of war with the Turk he could do no other; he had to secure his south-eastern coast against the possibility of a Turkish onslaught. Deepest of all of Philip's fears was the anxiety that his reign might be distinguished by the ignominy of the re-implantation of Islam on Spanish soil.

If Philip's motivation was strategic and religious, Espinosa's was personal and governmental, for as part of his own gathering-up of power at the centre he was determined to extend the authority of the Council of Castile. He did this in Granada by using the Council's subordinate agency, the Chancellery of Granada, to challenge the authority of the captaincy-general of Granada. This office was virtually hereditary in the Mondéjar family – a branch of the Mendoza clan – and was currently held by Iñigo López de Mendoza, Count of Tendilla and Marquis of Mondéjar. Few noble families held more power in their own territories than did the Mondéjars in Granada and they traditionally protected the *moriscos* (if only so that they could exploit them themselves). Espinosa's assault on the *moriscos* and their aristocratic protectors began in 1561 when he instituted an enquiry into land tenure with the obvious intention of dispossessing the *moriscos* of their land when – as was virtually inevitable – they were unable to show evidence of legal ownership.[11]

Espinosa had two men in Granada who proved to be the perfect agents for his policy – Pedro Guerrero, Archbishop of Granada since 1546, and Pedro de Deza, whom Espinosa had had appointed as President of the Chancellery of Granada in 1566. Guerrero was deeply committed to converting the *moriscos*; as early as 1554 he had allowed the Society of Jesus to found a house in the moorish quarter of the city of Granada, the Albaicín, expressly to do battle with the *moriscos*. In 1559 he gave the Society permission to establish a fully fledged House of Doctrine in the Albaicín to serve as a centre for the proper conversion of the whole *morisco* community; children were to be educated by the Jesuits to provide future teachers for their own community. Guerrero also ordered that young *morisca* girls should be brought up by Catholic women in the faith or placed in convents so that they could live Catholic lives 'as if they had been born in Old Castile'.

Guerrero's determination to reconvert the *moriscos* was reinforced by his attendance at the last session of the Council of Trent (where he had led the cohort of Spanish bishops) and on returning home he summoned a provincial church council to support his attack on the *moriscos*; the council opened on 15 September 1565 and Guerrero expressly invited his clergy to launch a succession of calls for action against the *moriscos*. They duly did so, insisting that the *moriscos* had never been sincere converts and that they had now to be dealt with. Guerrero forwarded the petition to Espinosa.

Pedro de Deza arrived in the city of Granada on 25 May 1566 to take up the presidency of the Chancellery. He had served under Espinosa on the Council of Inquisition and he came with instructions from him to implement the new policy of severity against the *moriscos*. He drew up a Pragmatic which detailed the behaviour that was now required of the *moriscos* and had it published, with studied symbolism, on 1 January 1567, the anniversary of Granada's surrender in 1492. The work begun in 1492 was now to be brought to a conclusion.

The Pragmatic stipulated that Arabic was henceforth not to be used either in public or in private and that within three years all *moriscos* were to learn Castilian and to abandon the use of their native tongue. Deza abrogated to himself the authority to decide which books written in Arabic were to be allowed to survive; those of which he disapproved were to be burned. No *morisco* clothing was to be worn and women were to uncover their faces. Marital and other celebrations were to be open to unannounced inspection by the Christian authorities and no moorish names were to be given to infants.

In despair, the *moriscos* made two more appeals. Deza himself curtly swept the first one aside and a mission to Madrid led by Don Juan Henríquez and supported by Tendilla was outmanoeuvred by Espinosa, who had the Council of State insist to Philip that he was under an obligation to convert the *moriscos*. Philip agreed; once again, the Council of State had given him the advice that he sought.[12]

The hiatus between the drawing-up of the Pragmatic and the failure of the mission to Madrid gave the *moriscos* time to organise, and at midnight on 26 December 1568 a small body of them launched an attack on the city of Granada in the hope of precipitating a general rebellion. It was a dismal failure; not even the Albaicín itself rose in support and the authorities held the fortress of the Alhambra without real difficulty. Worse followed, for the *moriscos* of the city of Granada showed that they were bitterly divided against each other; from the outset family feuds prevented them from uniting and indeed two *morisco* 'kings' died at the hands of fellow-*moriscos*. But if the revolt failed in the city of Granada it spread out into the mountains of the Alpujarras with dreadful violence; particularly brutal deaths were devised for many priests who had ministered to the *moriscos*, often after they had been tortured. This treatment served only to deepen Christian resolve and to alienate the few friends that the *moriscos* had among the Christians. This, too, was Holy War.

Philip did not have a standing army to deal with the revolt and was handicapped by the absence of so many experienced soldiers and commanders in the Army of Flanders. He had therefore to use the feudal levy to have cities and aristocracy lead their own men to war; for instance, Mondéjar himself marched out of the city of Seville in January 1569 with 2000 troops provided by the city itself, while 500 men were sent south by the city of Segovia. It was a rag-tag army that was thereby assembled;

Philip had determined to raise an army of 40000 men but by the middle of 1569 he had only 16000 men in the field and they were not for the most part soldiers of quality or experience.[13]

It was, moreover, an army that was badly led. Deza insisted that the Marquis of Los Vélez should command the army because Mondéjar was too closely tied to the *moriscos*. Unfortunately, Los Vélez's connections at court were better than his command of strategy and after he had been responsible for a succession of embarrassing failures Espinosa was forced to insist on his removal. He did so by urging Philip to send a member of his own family to organise and lead the army. The Cardinal was in effect insisting that Philip give the command to Don John of Austria. Reluctantly, the king did so, and once again he charged Luis de Requesens (in conjunction now with Don Luis de Quixada) to guide – and restrain – his brother. Don John was delighted that at last he had been given a command worthy of his blood.[14] The troops celebrated Don John's appointment by attacking *moriscos* and on 18 March 1569 150 or so wealthy men from the Albaicín were slaughtered in the Chancellery, where they had been held as hostages for the good behaviour of the *moriscos*.[15] The despair and hatred of the *moriscos* deepened.

Don John left court on 6 April and soon had 20000 men under his command. Philip travelled to Cordoba to supervise the campaign and in October 1569 published a decree ordering that *moriscos* were to be exiled from Granada and that henceforth the war was to be conducted with 'fire and blood'.[16] There could be no doubt now for the *moriscos* that they faced a fight to the death. Isolated in small and remote communities and with precious few weapons, they had little hope of standing up to the royal army let alone of defeating it. They received virtually no help from their co-religionists in the other kingdoms of Spain, and although some 4000 men came over from Africa they were not sufficient to make any serious impact upon the campaign. Taking their justification from the massacre of priests, the Christian forces now used indiscriminate terror and slaughter against the *moriscos*.

Don John's campaign consisted for the most part of skirmishes rather than battles, but his personal gallantry won plaudits from all and when Luis de Quixada died from wounds received in the battle of Serón in February 1570, Don John was able to claim the full credit for the success of the war on land. In fact, he had found it to be a dispiriting campaign and had spent much of it complaining about the poor quality of his troops and the shortage of money made available to him. The end of the rebellion was facilitated by hunger among the rebels; the harvest of 1570 was desperately poor and many *moriscos* were forced to come down from the mountains and surrender themselves into the hands of Christians because of their hunger. Don John himself left Granada at the end of November 1570, garlanded with the laurels of military triumph.[17]

Having overcome the rebellion, Philip decided to remove the whole *morisco* community of the kingdom of Granada so that never again need he fear that they could open Spain up to Islamic invasion. The deportations began on 1 November 1570; the *moriscos* were led in chain gangs out of Granada and were deposited in each of the major cities of Castile; perhaps 90 000 of them were removed in all. In the cities of Castile, however, they became feared and despised minorities; the deportation that was designed to solve the problem of Granada led to an intensification of resentment against the *moriscos* across the face of Castile. It also, of course, caused lasting damage to the kingdom of Granada; it was to be generations before the land was fully resettled by settlers from other parts of Spain and the skills and techniques of the expelled *moriscos* were lost for ever.[18]

FROM LEPANTO TO TUNIS, 1571–4

Suleiman the Magnificent died in 1566 and was succeeded by his son Selim II. In 1570, with a vigour that belied his unprepossessing nickname of 'the Sot', Selim demanded that the Republic of Venice surrender Cyprus to him. The acquisition of Cyprus was a longstanding Turkish objective – Suleiman himself had coveted the island – and it is probable that Selim was taking advantage of Spain's preoccupation with the revolt of Granada to intimidate Venice into agreeing to his demands, confident that the Republic would not be able to persuade Spain to come to her assistance. Certainly, he must have calculated that the Republic's dependence upon his own goodwill for the maintenance of its trading concessions in the eastern Mediterranean would have encouraged it to acquiesce in his conquest of Cyprus. In the event, the Venetian Senate refused by only a narrow majority to accede to Selim's demand, and in July the first of 50 000 Turkish troops landed on the island; Nicosia fell on 9 September and only Famagusta then remained in Venetian hands. The Republic sent a large relief force but it was not even able to land men: Famagusta's days were numbered.

To Pope Pius V, Turkish belligerence came as a gift from heaven, for it enabled him to persuade Venice and Spain to join him in that 'Holy League' against the Turk that lay at the heart of all his ambitions. He understood that Venice was now forced to respond to Turkish aggression despite fears for her trade while Spain was deeply apprehensive of Turkish intentions, being only too conscious of how narrowly she had escaped disaster at Malta in 1565. A saint he may have been but Pius V was hard-headed enough to realise that Venice and Spain would need practical encouragement to overcome their traditional antipathy to each other and to commit their resources to a major campaign against the Turk. He therefore granted both states the right to tax their clergy to provide the resources for war; the Republic was given the right to levy the tithe while Spain received the *excusado* (which had been agreed in 1567 but not yet levied) and had the *cruzada* and *subsidio* renewed. On 25 May 1571 the Holy League was solemnly proclaimed in St Peter's Square; Pius's crusade had come into being. Spain, the papacy and Venice pledged themselves to join together for three years to defend Christendom against Islam, undertaking to assemble a fleet of 200 galleys and 100 galleons to carry 50 000 troops. Don John was appointed to lead the fleet in recognition of the primacy of Spain's contribution and in the confident expectation that men would flock to his standard because he was the king's brother. Once again, however, Philip discreetly charged Luis de Requesens to guide and to restrain his brother. Don John sailed from Barcelona on 20 July for the rendezvous at Messina. On 4 August Famagusta surrendered: Cyprus was lost to Christendom.

At Messina Don John was joined by the fleets of Venice, Genoa and the papacy and by the end of August he had 207 galleys (although some accounts numbered them as many as 250), about a hundred or so support ships and 84 420 men – 28 000 soldiers; 12 920 sailors and 43 500 oarsmen. In addition, Don John had command of six Venetian galleasses, merchant galleys which were so large that they had to be towed into battle but which carried forty or so heavy guns, capable of withering firepower at close range. The galleasses, ponderous but overwhelmingly powerful, played a decisive role in the battle. The papal galleys were commanded by Marc Antonio Colonna, the Venetian by Sebastian Veniero, and the Genoese by Gian Andrea Doria. One-third of the soldiers (8160) were Spanish by birth and eighty-one galleys belonged to Philip. Among the senior men leading Spanish units was Álvaro de Bazán, who had been raised by Philip to the marquisate of Santa Cruz in recognition of his distinguished service; Santa Cruz was entrusted with Philip's precious galley fleet.

Don John was aided by the over-confidence of his enemy; Ali Pasha, the Turkish admiral, wasted energy and provisions on pillaging forays around Crete and in the Adriatic and was taken by surprise when Don John appeared and offered combat at the narrow entrance to the Gulf of Lepanto. The Turkish fleet included substantial contributions from the Barbary states of Algiers and Tripoli; in all, it consisted of about 250 galleys and sixty-six *galeotes* and probably carried as many as 75000 men, 25000 of them soldiers.

Don John drew up his fleet in three squadrons – the Venetians on the left, close to the shore, the Genoese on the right and the Spaniards in the centre. He ordered Santa Cruz to keep the elite Spanish galleys in reserve to go where the fighting was thickest and he positioned two Venetian galleasses in front of each of the three parts of his fleet. He issued strict orders that the infantrymen were not to fire until they could see the whites of the eyes of the enemy and he had the *Galera Real* parade in front of the whole fleet before battle commenced, showing his troops that he himself would be in the thick of the fight. He gave the Venetian galleasses the honour of opening the battle; their long-range bombardment aimed at the centre of the Turkish fleet threw it into confusion. The galleasses then led the Christian fleet in the attack; they battered their way into the Turkish lines and brought their heavy artillery into play at close quarters to devastating effect. When the fleets joined battle, the fighting was ferocious and was often hand-to-hand on galley-decks; Don John took the *Galera Real* right into the heart of the action and distinguished himself in combat, being wounded in the leg. Twice he attempted to board Ali Pasha's galley and twice he was driven off. On the third assault, the deck was carried. Ali Pasha was killed and his head was brought to Don John; he winced in disgust. Among others who won battle honours was Don John's friend, Alexander Farnese. The battle lasted only for four or five hours but the carnage was dreadful; some 30000 or so of the Turkish force were killed and it was suggestive of the stark brutality with which the battle was fought that only 8000 were taken prisoner. Only thirty-five Turkish galleys escaped and nearly 200 galleys were captured by the Christians, some of them – it is not clear how many – in sound enough condition to be re-used. The Christian fleet lost fifteen galleys and 7650 men were killed and 7784 wounded. These were neatly compensated for by the 12000 or so Christian galley slaves who were freed from the Turkish fleet. The victory was virtually complete, and Ottoman Turkey found itself effectively without a galley fleet.[19]

The psychological impact of the victory was striking and it was permanent. Don John himself wrote to Philip that he had given him 'the best victory that any Christian prince has ever had'. Miguel de Cervantes, who lost his left hand in the fighting, described the battle of Lepanto in his masterpiece *Don Quixote* (1605–10) as 'that most glorious battle' because 'on that day, so fortunate for Christendom, . . . the world and all the nations learnt how wrong they were in supposing that the Turks were invincible on the sea'. It was, Cervantes insisted, the day when 'the insolent pride of the Ottomans was broken for ever'.[20] The chief banners of the Turk were taken in triumph to the Escorial and to Toledo cathedral, and lesser trophies found their way to a host of Catalan towns. Titian himself commemorated the triumph (as El Greco had the original treaty).

At the heart of the triumph stood Philip II. In 1565 he had saved Malta from a full-scale onslaught and now he had surpassed even that triumph, defeating the Turk in the largest naval encounter the modern world had seen. He was now without question the greatest monarch in Christendom. No doubt he reflected in private that he had won laurels that were even more illustrious than those of his father.

Unfortunately, the triumph of the Holy League was not followed up by any decisive campaign and the League itself fell apart. Pius V died on 1 May 1572, and without his energetic inspiration the other partners quickly lost their interest in the crusade; Venice was anxious to resume trade with the Turk while Spain was having to commit resources northwards to the Low Countries. The 1572 campaign achieved nothing and on 7 March 1573 Venice abandoned the League and, swallowing her pride in favour of her pocket, resumed peaceful trading with the Ottoman empire.

In 1573 Don John added to his legend by capturing Tunis on 11 September (at the head of a fleet of 155 galleys) in emulation of his father. Unfortunately, consumed perhaps by a growing belief in his own invincibility, Don John then made the elementary mistake of leaving a garrison in Tunis which was insufficient to defend it but large enough to invite a Turkish attack. Selim was able to build a new fleet with remarkable speed, and in 1574 he despatched a fleet of 220 galleys which recaptured Tunis (and its fortress of La Goletta) without serious difficulty. Lepanto had been avenged and stalemate had been reached between Turkey and Spain. In 1578 a year's truce was agreed between the agents of Selim and Philip; it was renewed regularly until the end of the century.[21] The era of large-scale collisions between fleets representing the fullest strength of Christendom and Islam was over, at least in the short term.

B. WESTERN EUROPE

MARY QUEEN OF SCOTS AND THE ENGLISH SUCCESSION

Philip was able to concentrate on the Mediterranean in the early years of his reign because northern Europe was relatively quiescent in its exhaustion after the Treaty of Câteau-Cambrésis. The situation in the British Isles lay at the core of many of Europe's uncertainties as Elizabeth moved obfuscatingly to reverse the religious settlement of her sister and as Scotland imploded under the stress of noble faction, Presbyterian extremism and French dynastic ambition. By the end of 1558 Philip had tacitly accepted that Elizabeth would be a Protestant monarch. The new queen used her first parliament (January–April 1559) to re-establish the Church of England and to abolish all papal jurisdiction in her realm.[22] Elizabeth dealt smoothly, too, with her first test in foreign affairs, using her navy and army to help the Scottish Presbyterians to drive out the pro-French government of Mary of Lorraine. The Treaty of Edinburgh (6 July 1560) led to the evacuation of French troops and to Mary Stuart, daughter of Mary of Lorraine, agreeing to renounce her claims to the English throne. It was a brilliant first triumph for Elizabeth, notable for its cool judgement and economy of effort. Philip thought of intervening but prudently decided against it; in all probability he welcomed the outcome, for it seriously reduced the ability of France to exercise power or even influence in England and Scotland.

Even more gratifying to Philip was the further destabilisation of France with the sudden death of Francis II in December 1560 and the accession of his sixteen-year-old brother Charles IX. The change of monarch brought the Guises' period of power to an end, and with it the possibility that France and Scotland might be united under Mary, Queen of Scots. The Guises were replaced as the controlling political family by the pro-Huguenot Bourbon-Montmorency clan. Although the new king was technically an adult, it fell in practice to the queen mother, Catherine de' Medici, to maintain the peace of France; yet another woman stepped into the front rank of power. Catherine had disadvantages beyond her sex for she was a foreigner and found it difficult to understand the complex hatreds that increasingly divided French society. She was, however, determined to maintain the peace with Spain that had been sealed by the marriage of her daughter Elizabeth to Philip in 1560; avoiding war with Spain was fundamental to her polity.

In Scotland, the alliance between Presbyterians and nobles soon fell apart. Alarmed by the extremism of the Presbyterian faction, a group of nobles invited Mary Stuart to return and in August 1561 she did so. Mary had left Scotland in 1548 and she soon showed that she had no real understanding of the situation in her turbulent, disordered native land; indeed, she could not even converse in its language. But if Mary had little judgement for politics she had less for men and she began now to systematically destroy her own political position by liaisons with a succession of especially violent men. In 1565 she married Henry, Lord Darnley, but soon tired of him and gave her trust to David Rizzio, an Italian adventurer. Enraged by what he took (probably wrongly) as his wife's adultery, on 9 March 1566 Darnley and his supporters dragged Rizzio away from Mary and killed him outside her door in the palace of Holyrood. Mary was pregnant and she waited until she had given birth on 19 June to Darnley's son (the future James VI of Scotland and I of England) before taking her revenge. She looked for support now to James Hepburn, earl of Bothwell and in January 1567 she took Darnley to recuperate from illness to Kirk o'Field just outside Edinburgh. On 9 February, after Mary had conveniently absented herself, a massive explosion wrecked the house in which Darnley was staying. It was singularly curious that Darnley's body and that of a servant who died with him were found to be undamaged by the great explosion. Few doubted that Bothwell had organised the deed and fewer still that Mary Stuart herself was implicated. Bothwell was duly cleared in a trial but the stain on Mary's reputation was less easily conjured away. And there was no escaping the despairing lunacy of her next act; in May, Mary Queen of Scots married Bothwell.

Mary's marriage cost her the throne for a second time. The Lords of the Covenant, outraged by her promiscuity as much as by her violence, went to war on her and Bothwell. They defeated Bothwell in what was called (somewhat grandly, since little blood was shed) the Battle of Carberry Hill (15 June 1567). Characteristically, the earl fled to Denmark, leaving the queen to her fate. Mary was forced to abdicate and to appoint the earl of Moray as regent for her son (24 July 1567). She escaped from custody in Lochleven but suffered a further defeat in May 1568 and fled to England to save her life.[23]

The presence of Mary Stuart in England changed the very nature of English politics and did much to lead to the slow but inexorable breakdown of England's relations with Spain. Elizabeth was now thirty-five years of age and still unmarried; if she died without heirs, as seemed ever more likely, Mary Stuart would have a serious claim on the throne despite her renunciation of her rights in 1560. Moreover, Mary was a Catholic and as such could hardly avoid becoming the natural focal point for Catholic opposition to Elizabeth. Given Mary's capricious and indeed disordered personality it was inevitable that she would become not merely the object of plots against Elizabeth but the instigator of them. Nothing better expressed the secularism of Philip's foreign policy throughout the 1560s than his determination to oppose Mary Stuart's succession to the English throne; better in his view to have the non-Catholic Elizabeth on the throne than the pro-French Catholic Mary Stuart. He was always genuinely sympathetic to the plight of the English Catholic community and anxious to give it such help as he could but he was determined to do so without jeopardising his relationship with Elizabeth; as late as June 1565 he instructed his ambassador in London to 'miss no opportunity which offers of encouraging and strengthening the said Catholics by all such means and measures as will not scandalise the Queen or her friends' but insisting that he was to behave with 'all the prudence and adroitness' that the case required.[24] Philip was not yet prepared to fight a crusade for Catholicism in England and he would not risk a war with Elizabeth to satisfy the ambitions either of the pope or of Mary Queen of Scots. Accordingly, he continued to protect Elizabeth from excommunication by the pope. However, in 1568–9 a series of events took place quite independently of each other which began to force him to change his policy towards Elizabeth.

THE LOW COUNTRIES: GOVERNMENT FROM SPAIN, 1559–67

When Philip sailed away from the Low Countries in August 1559 he left Margaret of Parma and Granvelle with precise instructions on how they were to govern the provinces until he returned, as he undoubtedly meant to do. He had deliberated long and hard and his plans were carefully thought-out, wide-ranging and precise in their detail. Unfortunately, they made it only too clear that in three fundamental respects he had not really understood the nature of the problems with which he was confronted in the Low Countries: it was not realistic to believe that the provinces could be governed without the active involvement of the native aristocracy; nor that religious dissidence could simply be crushed; nor that a puppet government could operate from Brussels while Philip himself took all major decisions from Spain. Since his father's abdication Philip had learned all the wrong lessons. The programme that he now adumbrated might have had some chance of working successfully at the beginning of an extended royal residence in the Low Countries; imposed as it was at the very moment of the king's departure for Spain it had no great likelihood of doing so. Indeed, it might almost have been calculated to make matters worse, inexorably driving the different strands of the opposition – aristocratic, religious and plebeian – to unite against the authority of the government. This is exactly what happened, and it took less than a decade to do so.

Margaret and Granvelle were instructed to develop and extend the powers of the central government over church and state but it was made clear that they were not to take any major decisions without consulting Philip. The three 'collateral Councils' through which Charles V had governed the Low Countries – the Councils of State and Finance and the Privy Council – were to continue but they were now to be marginalised as power was concentrated in the hands of Margaret and Granvelle and in those of a secret junta that was accountable to them. The leading noblemen were to retain the appearance of power by being given seats on the Council of State but were to be excluded from all substantive discussions on policy-making (which took place in the junta).

Central, too, to the purpose of Margaret and Granvelle was that their government would become self-financing. Philip was determined that Spain, so recently bankrupt, would not be providing subsidies to govern the Low Countries. Philip had, after difficult and lengthy negotiations, wrung a grant of three million guilders from the States General in 1558; it was to last for nine years and so was called the 'Novennial Aid'.[25] Until 1567 at least, therefore, Margaret and Granvelle were expected to achieve all the tasks that Philip had laid down for them without having recourse to the States General. They were also charged with reorganising the ecclesiastical structure so that the authority of the Church could be strengthened and the fight against heresy pursued more effectively. Finally, in order to ensure that this ambitious programme was pursued in secure and peaceful circumstances, the 3000 or so Spanish troops who formed the heart of Philip's army in the north were to remain in the Low Countries.

If the primary flaw in Philip's plan was that he himself was absent while this rigorous programme was to be implemented, the second was that Margaret and Granvelle simply could not work profitably together. Margaret resented the fact that while she was the nominal head of government it was Granvelle who had the king's ear, and she was irritated by the patronising manner in which he dealt with her. For his part, Granvelle regarded Margaret as being weak in a crisis, unable to hold an unpopular line in the face of determined opposition. This was exactly what he himself could do with some relish; Granvelle had the arrogance to court unpopularity, so certain was he of his own judgement. It was indeed in crisis that Margaret and Granvelle fell apart; confronted by resolute opposition, Margaret caved in while Granvelle became more obdurate. In consequence, it was comparatively easy for experienced and resolute opponents to divide them against each other.

From the beginning, the great nobles did precisely that. Men like Orange, Egmont and Hornes had served the house of Habsburg with distinction and had earned the right to be treated seriously by Philip; they were not inclined to take lessons in duty from a royal bastard who was a woman or from a somewhat dissolute chief minister who was a bishop. Philip's determination to exclude them from real power offended them at their most sensitive point; they believed that they had the *right* to be consulted by their sovereign in the daily business of government and they expected, as of that right, to benefit from the royal patronage. There was, in their view, an unwritten contract with their monarch – they would serve him loyally: he would reward them generously. Philip's instructions to Margaret and Granvelle broke this contract and set the great nobility reluctantly on the path to opposition to him. The king should have played on the fears that the leading nobles felt about popular and religious dissidence; instead he crassly alienated them. In consequence, the very people who should have been the Crown's strongest supporters were turned slowly but inexorably against it. The stance of these men to the policies of the government was therefore essentially political and personal rather than religious. They were not involved in the growing religious turbulence in the Low Countries; only Orange would change his faith, and then only slowly and over many years. In 1561 he took a first step towards abandoning Catholicism when he married Anne, niece of the Protestant Elector of Saxony. But Orange remained, at least to appearances, a practising Catholic. Like Egmont and Hornes, he kept his distance from the religious dissidents; as leading aristocrats, the three men were quite as fearful of social revolution as was the king himself.

Calvinist preachers were still comparatively few in number as the 1560s opened but they were highly motivated and disciplined and the cellular organisation within which they worked made it very difficult for the government to deal effectively with them. They were greatly helped in their work by economic circumstance. The economy of the Low Countries, already damaged by the long wars of Charles V, was now suffering from the effects of the closing of the Sound by the war between Sweden and Denmark. Even the climate created difficulties, for these were harsh years; the winters of 1563–4 and 1564–5 were particularly bitter and aggravated the hardship in which most Netherlanders were living.[26] In such circumstances, people were the more prepared to listen to the radicalism of the preachers.

Philip had only to look to the example of France to see how the spread of Calvinism could complicate and embitter political troubles. The collapse of France towards civil war added point to his determination to bring about a radical restructuring of the Church in the Low Countries. The exercise was certainly long overdue; there were only five bishops in the seventeen provinces, and it was quite unrealistic to expect five men to supervise the cure of some three million souls – in Spain, there were nearly fifty bishops to look after the spiritual needs of a population of about seven million people. Before leaving for Spain, therefore, Philip secured the agreement of the papacy to the establishment of three new ecclesiastical provinces and to the appointment of a further ten bishops; with its new structure the Church would be able to undertake its pastoral obligations much more efficiently. The papacy duly issued the Bull in 1559. Practical organisation, doctrinal renewal: Philip's reform was eminently sensible and justifiable.

Unfortunately the root and branch reform of the Catholic Church and the dramatic expansion of its apparatus could not but seem to many Netherlanders to be a part of a coherent and sinister programme on the part of the king that was both religious and political in inspiration. Some of the magnates had good reason to fear that Philip's reforms were intended to bite into their traditional rights of patronage. More generally, many Netherlanders were apprehensive that Philip was restructuring the episcopacy as a prelude to imposing a Spanish-style of Church on the Low Countries and that he intended to introduce the Spanish Inquisition itself. Philip in fact had no such intention – not least because the Holy Office in Spain had fewer powers than its counterpart in the Low Countries – but he had only himself to blame for the fear that his policies created. He had been so determinedly insensitive to the aspirations of his subjects in the Low Countries, so insistent on imposing his own structures – administrators, army and now bishops – that it was only natural that there should be deep suspicion as to his ultimate intentions. He also had to face the legacy of the 1550s, for the fires of Smithfield and Valladolid cast their shadow across the Low Countries; they were now part of the folk-memory of Protestants in northern Europe and were becoming a symbol of powerful political importance, convincing people that Philip was truly engaged on a crusade to destroy Protestantism wherever he found it.

Nor was it only Calvinists who feared Philip's intentions, for the restructuring of the Church had worrying implications for many Catholics: the secular clergy found themselves facing the distressing prospect of having resident bishops who would exercise real control over them; many abbots feared that they would lose substantial powers of patronage; the younger sons of the nobility were anxious that they would be deprived of a traditional avenue of preferment by the new insistence on a university education for high church office. It was a singular achievement for Philip to unite so many strands of opinion against him, aristocratic, Protestant and Catholic. Nor had he finished yet; in 1561 he had Granvelle raised to the primatial see of Mechelen so that he could rule both Church and State; the opprobrium that Granvelle so readily attracted to himself rubbed off on both Church and State, to the grave detriment of both. Moreover, many of the new bishops appointed through Granvelle's good offices proved to be personally inappropriate for the task of providing leadership for the Church.[27]

The arrangements made by Philip for the government of the Low Countries were therefore deeply flawed, but once he had made them he stuck to them, and the more they unravelled in the years after his departure for Spain the more obstinate he became about imposing them. It was the fundamental flaw of Philip's kingship that once he had committed his prestige to a position he found it impossible to retreat from it. Consequently, he was prepared to extend and deepen his commitments rather than be seen to retreat from them and in doing so to diminish the majesty of his kingship. He would only change his policies when forced to do so.

This is precisely what happened as Philip suffered a succession of humiliating reversals in the Low Countries. The first of these came when in January 1561 he was forced to allow the withdrawal of the Spanish troops in the face of the refusal of the States General to release monies with which to pay them: no money, no troops. Encouraged by this evidence of royal weakness, the senior nobility pressed home their attack; in July 1561 Egmont and Orange wrote to Philip protesting against the implementation of the episcopal reorganisation. The king refused to yield and in the spring of 1563 Orange, Egmont and Hornes withdrew from the Council of State in a deliberate challenge to the government and to Philip himself. Again Philip refused to budge, and so in July the nobles declared that they would not return to the Council unless Granvelle was dismissed. In the war of nerves, Margaret broke first. She advised Philip to abandon Granvelle and in December he did so; Granvelle left Brussels in March 1564, ostensibly to visit his elderly mother. He never returned.[28]

The shock of Granvelle's dismissal gave both sides pause for thought and early in 1565 the nobles sent Egmont himself to Spain to persuade Philip of the need for compromise. He stayed in Madrid for six weeks, living in the house of Ruy Gómez de Silva – and thereby giving visible expression to the way in which the situation in the Low Countries was merely one of the issues (if the most important) that were becoming enveloped by the faction-fighting at court. Egmont was received graciously by Philip himself and when he left at the beginning of April he was convinced that he had persuaded the king to allow the Council of State in Brussels to exercise a fuller role in government and to modify the workings of the laws against heresy. Egmont travelled home triumphantly convinced that Philip's policy was changing and that he himself had been chiefly responsible for persuading the king to change his mind. He was accompanied by young Alexander Farnese, travelling to Brussels for his marriage to Princess María of Portugal. Philip took vindictive delight in disabusing Egmont of his confidence; two weeks after the count left Madrid, Philip sent letters to Margaret confirming the sentence of death on six Anabaptists. Egmont arrived in Brussels on 30 April 1565 and found himself humiliated in front of his peers, duped by the king he had served so well.[29] The contemptuous way in which Philip had deceived him also inflicted a damaging blow to the prestige of Ruy Gómez at court.

In the autumn of 1565 Philip retreated to his hunting-lodge at Segovia to await the news about the siege of Malta. He heard of the relief of the island on 24 September and spent the following weeks reflecting intensely about the affairs of his monarchy; the triumph at Malta had given him a breathing space in the south and he could now turn his attention (and perhaps even his forces) to the north. Ambassadors were put on alert for the arrival of special couriers.[30] On 17 and 20 October 1565 Philip despatched two letters to Margaret which he signed in 'the Woods of Segovia'; in them he made it clear that there could be no question of compromise on the religious issue in the Netherlands. The edicts against heresy were to be strictly enforced and Margaret was forbidden to summon the States General until the religious situation had been stabilised. Indeed, Philip made it expressly clear that he had never intended to take advice from the native nobility: 'as to whether I would wish to ask the advice of the private and great councils and of the governors and provincial councils, this would be a considerable waste of time since my mind is made up'. He also made it clear that he would not restrict the activities of the Inquisition: 'If one fears disturbances there is no reason to think that they are more imminent and will be greater when one does allow the inquisitors to perform their proper duties and when one does assist them.'[31] Margaret was so shaken by Philip's stridency that she did not publish the letters for a week and even then she did not dare to have the heresy laws proclaimed until the end of the year.[32] The marriage of Alexander Farnese and María took place in a grimly resentful and apprehensive atmosphere. When the celebrations had concluded the count of Hornes left court, wittily letting it be known that he was going to visit his mother and sister in emulation of Granvelle's departure two years previously; the allusion clearly gave people to understand that he did not anticipate returning to court. Egmont followed soon afterwards, claiming that he was going to visit the frontiers and letting it be known that he was 'deeply grieved' at Philip's decision, which 'had deprived him of the good opinion of his friends and the public'. The Prince of Orange remained at court but spoke sombrely of going home.[33] Egmont and Hornes soon returned to court, but they had made their point; Philip had pushed his leading aristocrats in the Low Countries to the point where they were prepared to publicly dissociate themselves from his service and policy.

The king had made his momentous decision with the slow, grinding diligence that was typical of him. However, not for the last time he was now overtaken by events. While he had pondered, the cauldron of discontent in the Low Countries had simmered and when the 'Letters from the Woods of Segovia' arrived it boiled over. The Letters made it abundantly clear that Philip would not baulk at using force and that it was only now a question of time before he did so. His opponents began to organise themselves for the storm that they knew was coming. The junior nobles reacted first; by the end of the year some 400 or so of them had signed a document known as 'The Compromise of the Nobility', declaring that they would if necessary resort to arms to fight for the moderation of the 'Placards' (which were the instruments by which Philip defined and denounced heresy). The 'Compromise' laid the blame for Philip's actions on his evil advisers and bluntly warned him that he was 'in grave danger of losing the whole of his estate' if he persisted with his support of the Inquisition. On 5 April 1566 some 200 to 300 of them rode into Brussels and forced their way into Margaret's presence, where they thrust their 'Request' upon her in which they spoke of their fears of 'an open revolt and a universal rebellion' against the king's rule. It was indeed the point of rebellion.[34] The 'Confederates' were derided as 'les gueux' ('the beggars'), but, taking pride rather than offence, they abrogated the name for themselves as a token of pride – 'Les Gueux', the fearless opponents of the regime. Terrified almost out of her wits, Margaret published what she called the 'Moderation' (9 April), ordering that the Placards be interpreted more leniently, at the very least while she consulted with Philip. Hoping to buy time, she only encouraged rebellion; the 'Confederates' became more openly hostile as respect for the government crumbled.

The effrontery of the Confederates stimulated all the opponents of the government – aristocratic, popular and religious. Orange, Egmont and Hornes – anxious perhaps at being sidelined by their junior colleagues? – now threatened to abandon court permanently for their estates. They had judged their moment well; desperate not to lose the only people who could still give her regime some practical support Margaret again caved in, promising that she would entreat Philip to allow the senior nobility a real and effective role in policy-making. The three men agreed to stay; insofar as Margaret was now in control of government at all, it was with their consent. Hornes's brother, Floris de Montmorency, baron of Montigny, was sent to Spain to impress upon Philip the gravity of the situation.

In the high summer of 1566, the rebellion of the lower aristocracy gave way with dramatic suddenness to popular religious revolution. The crisis had stimulated the return of many exiles, among them preachers trained in Geneva, men who were determined and disciplined. By July many of these men were holding large meetings across the country with impunity; they attracted large audiences and became known as 'hedge-preachers'. Their activities led to a further escalation of disorder; on 10 August some of the chief towns in the southern provinces experienced a paroxysm of image-breaking. The 'Iconoclastic Riots', as they came to be called, lasted only for a fortnight but they devastated hundreds of churches and religious houses. Moreover, they inflicted profound damage on the reputation of Philip and his government, for they made it evident that Philip could not protect his religious establishments and their inhabitants. While the disturbances were undoubtedly spontaneous for the most part, there may well have been some element of control, with perhaps a few hundred men directing affairs, roving around the country organising mobs and picking targets. Margaret certainly did not see it in this way; in the worst of her panic attacks she informed Philip that over 200000 people were in arms against her authority.[35]

Philip agonised over his response, swaying rapidly from one extreme to the other. On 26 July he decided that the 'Moderation' was to be rejected but five days later he once again signed a letter in 'The Woods at Segovia', and this time it was a letter of retreat; Philip announced the abolition of the Inquisition in the Low Countries and offered a general pardon to the rebels. He justified the abolition of the Inquisition by claiming that the new episcopal structure was 'fully and firmly established'. He also vowed to return himself: 'I will not fail to come, please God. I expect to be with you at the latest next spring and if there is a way of going earlier, be sure that I won't fail to use it.'[36] Panic in Brussels, an agony of indecision in Madrid: the weeks of high summer 1566 brought out the very worst characteristics of Philip's government. The reality of Philip's own position was that the breakdown of order in the Low Countries had dispelled any lingering doubts that he had about the need to use force. However, the decision to send an army into the Low Countries had such profoundly important implications that Philip recoiled from making it by himself. Late in October 1566, he summoned his councillors of State to the Escorial.

At the monastery the councillors held formal set-piece debates which were in effect about the very nature of the monarchy and the direction in which it was now to develop. Ruy Gómez insisted that Philip should travel to the Low Countries to re-establish his authority, and he asserted that the king would need only to be accompanied by a relatively small army. It was not a convincing argument; as Juan Manrique de Lara pointed out, Philip's safety could not be guaranteed in the circumstances that obtained in the Low Countries. Alba urged that a substantial army should be sent to re-establish control before the king could contemplate travelling himself. He won the argument.[37]

There remained the question of who would command the army. Some discussion took place over a few weeks but in reality there was only one candidate; on 29 November 1566 the duke of Alba accepted the post of Captain-General of the Army. Ruy Gómez and his allies continued to argue determinedly against large-scale military intervention but Philip was always immovable once he had dragged himself to make a major decision, and when in the spring of 1567 some Dutch nobles openly took to arms it must have confirmed him in his determination to crush the rebellion. As it happened, Margaret was able to defeat the rebels with some ease but there could no longer be any doubt of the need to send an army (although Ruy Gómez continued to argue against doing so). On 17 April 1567 Alba took his leave of Philip.[38]

The decision to send Alba to the Netherlands with an army in order to crush revolt was described by Professor Wernham, with justice, as 'one of the turning-points of western European history', as the establishment of a major Spanish army at the northern crossroads of Europe changed the face of European politics for nearly a century, until the Peace of the Pyrenees in 1659.[39] Philip's motives in sending Alba were two fold: to crush religious dissent and to reimpose his authority over fractious subjects. Rebellion was an affront to the king's majesty; Philip had been forced to retreat on a number of key issues in the years since 1561: the recall of the Spanish troops; the dismissal of Granvelle; the moderation of the Placards. He had now been driven to the point where he would retreat no longer.

Philip had another motive, and it was one of which he apparently never spoke; the Low Countries were part of the Burgundian inheritance to which his father had committed him. He had been named for that inheritance and was immovably determined that he would preserve what remained of it. In his response to the Dutch rebels the fact that he was defending the Burgundian inheritance was for him of fundamental and of determinative importance. Fernand Braudel has rightly described Philip's policy towards the Netherlands as welling from his being a 'prisoner of Spain'; but before he was that, the king was a prisoner of his Burgundian forbears. Philip could not allow the key part of the Burgundian inheritance to be at risk.[40] To do so would be to betray his very heritage. Alba and the 10 050 men who would form the core of the 'Army of Flanders' entered Brussels on 22 August 1567.

ALBA IN THE LOW COUNTRIES: TERROR AND TAXATION

Alba's march set western Europe by its ears. In France, Huguenot fears that the great Catholic crusade against Protestantism was now really underway precipitated the second War of Religion (September 1567–March 1568). A third soon followed (September 1568–August 1570), and so for the first three years of Alba's rule in the Low Countries the only continental power that could have readily offered significant help to his opponents was almost completely preoccupied with her own civil wars. When Alba met Margaret of Parma on his arrival he made it clear that he had the right to erect fortresses, remove magistrates and to impose punishment for past rebellion. On being asked by Margaret whether he had any other powers, Alba pointedly remarked that time would tell. Margaret resigned her office and left Brussels on 20 December. Alba stood supreme and unchallenged.[41] He began to build up his army so that it was large enough for the purposes that he had in mind, to create 'the Army of Flanders'.

The Duke now acted with a dreadful sense of theatre to intimidate both popular and aristocratic opponents of his regime. He established a 'Council of Troubles' to prosecute individuals responsible for the riots of 1566. It began its work on 5 September 1567. Four days later, the counts of Egmont and Hornes were arrested. The ruthlessness with which the Council operated soon earned it the popular sobriquet 'The Council of Blood': with Alba himself presiding over the more important cases, it investigated 8950 people, sentencing 1105 of them to death or banishment and 9000 or so to have their property confiscated. In the popular mind, the Council carried out many more executions than actually took place but the terror that it inspired was real enough: some 50 000 or 60 000 people – perhaps 2 per cent of the total populace – fled the country during Alba's rule. Among them was William of Orange, and to many it seemed of little consequence, but Granvelle himself sagely observed when hearing of the Prince's escape that Alba's hunt had failed in its chief purpose. But if William was beyond Alba's reach he was not beyond his vengeance; the duke proclaimed him to be an outlaw – thereby effectively decreeing that he could lawfully be assassinated – and he confiscated his property. Worse, he seized his son, Philip William, who was a student at Louvain University and had him sent in February 1568 to be educated in Spain as a Catholic; the boy, aged only thirteen, resumed his studies at Alcalá.[42] He never saw his father again. As the most public statement of the unbridled power that he now exercised, Alba had Egmont and Hornes beheaded on charges of treason in the market square of Brussels on 5 June 1568. Knights of the Order of the Golden Fleece, counsellors of Charles V and of Philip himself, the two men went to their deaths with dignity but with a blank incomprehension of how much the world in which they had lived and in which they now died, had changed.[43] Those who saw their heads roll, and those who heard of it, understood well enough; no one was safe from Alba and no one could expect mercy from him. The government was waging ruthless war on its opponents and it held all the advantages, for the few people who dared to oppose it were disparate and unorganised.

The opponents of the government were also leaderless, for William of Orange now trod a difficult path, professing his loyalty to Philip as his lawful monarch and insisting that he was only opposed to Alba, who was a tyrant, crushing the traditional liberties of the seventeen provinces. He and his brother Louis of Nassau prepared invasion forces in Germany and France for a campaign in 1568 which would be waged against the tyrannical minister rather than against the lawful king. Alba defeated Louis with peremptory ease at Jemmingen in July and then contemptuously made a mockery of Orange's army of 30 000 men – half the size of his own force – by disdaining even to engage it in battle. He merely stalked Orange as he marched up and down the banks of the Maas, waiting until his money was exhausted and his army broke up for want of pay. When, in November, Orange admitted defeat without even having fought Alba, and withdrew into Germany, his credibility seemed to be irreparably damaged. Alba's triumph was complete and he celebrated it by commissioning Jacques Jonghelinck to model a statue of himself that was five metres high, in which his foot was crushing Rebellion in emulation of León Leoni's *Il Furore*. Alba had an inscription placed below the statue boasting that he had 'extirpated sedition, reduced rebellion, restored religion, secured justice and established peace' and erected it in the very heart of Antwerp.[44] The statue represented a grievous error of judgement on the duke's part; to his opponents in the Netherlands it seemed to be the historic liberties and constitutional freedoms of the Low Countries that Alba was trampling upon, while his enemies in Spain were able to use it to insinuate to Philip that Alba was guilty of *lèse-majesté* in comparing himself with the king's illustrious father.

For the moment, however, there was little that Alba's opponents could do to baulk him. In 1569 and 1570 Orange was not able even to mount campaigns. The best that he could do was to use the printing press to urge the people of the Low Countries to resist Alba. On 1 September 1568 he published an open letter warning that unless Alba was resisted worse would surely follow:

it is to be feared that if God does not help us . . . we may see on an even larger scale, how greatly and grievously all the afore-mentioned innovations, proposals, oppressions, inquisitions, persecutions, murders, seizures, executions and tyrannies have increased and multiplied, and how totally inhuman they have become since the duke (in the name of the king and shielding himself with the king's authority) arrived here with his Spanish soldiers.[45]

However, even in apparently complete triumph, Alba had to deal with stark financial reality: his army had to be paid and the Novennial Aid had expired. He therefore turned to restructuring governmental finance so as to make the government of the Low Countries independent of Spanish subsidies. He summoned the States General in 1569 and demanded that they vote three separate taxes: a 1 per cent tax on landed property, a 5 per cent tax on land sales and a 10 per cent tax on all sales. The proposed taxes came to be known as the Hundredth, Twentieth and Tenth Pennies respectively and they had much to commend them: they would be much more egalitarian and probably much more productive than existing taxes. However, the States General were prepared only to vote the Hundredth Penny, for to have voted the other two would have been to vote themselves out of existence since the government would not need to summon them again with perpetual taxes on tap. The States General offered a grant equivalent to two million ducats over two years in lieu of the other two taxes. Reluctantly, and enraged by the opposition, Alba had to agree. Even in military triumph, he could not make the Low Countries pay for themselves; Spain – or, more properly, Castile – would have to do so. In 1567, Spain had sent two million ducats to the Low Countries; in 1568 and again in 1569 she sent twice as much.[46]

'THIS WOMAN': ELIZABETH OF ENGLAND AND THE BREAKDOWN OF ANGLO-BURGUNDIAN AMITY

The determination of Philip and Elizabeth of England to remain on friendly terms initially survived the tensions created by Alba's brutality in the Low Countries. Despite intense pressure Elizabeth refused to budge from her position that the rebellion against Philip was unlawful and therefore lay beyond her support. Elizabeth was more terrified of rebellion than she was fearful of Alba's army; indeed, time would show that she was also more apprehensive of French involvement in the Low Countries than of the reassertion of Spain's power there. Accordingly, she continued to give Philip signs of her friendship; she let him know that she was looking forward to seeing him again when he went to the Low Countries – proof that they had indeed met in England a decade or more before – and when he arrested Don Carlos she went so far as to send him a message of comfort and support.[47]

Philip knew well enough what store to set on Elizabeth's concern for him, but like her he found that during the course of 1568–9 the tradition of Anglo-Burgundian amity was progressively undermined by the tensions caused by three separate and unrelated events: the arrival of Mary Stuart in England in May 1568; the conflict over some Spanish silver sequestrated by Elizabeth in December; and the return home of Hawkins and Drake in January 1569 with their colourful accounts of Spanish treachery at San Juan de Ulúa. Underlining these areas of conflict were tensions created by ambassadors; it did not further Anglo-Spanish relations for John Man, Elizabeth's ambassador in Madrid, to describe the pope as 'nothing but a canting little monk'. Nor did it smooth Elizabeth's temper for Philip to instruct Don Guerau de Espés on taking up his embassy in London that Man was 'a heretic so pernicious and evil-minded'.[48] Embassies were becoming centres of turbulence.

Philip agonised over the dilemmas created for him by Mary Stuart's arrival in England and he tried to resolve them by handing them on to Alba. In September 1568, Mary appealed to Philip for help and he wrote to Alba that he was 'willing to help her in her sufferings' but that he had 'refrained from taking any decision or answering her [letter] . . . until you tell me what you think of her business, and in what way, and to what extent, I should assist her'. Philip urged Alba to write to him 'by the first opportunity' to advise him on the action that he should take.[49]

Relations with England deteriorated with dramatic suddenness at the turn of 1568–9. In December some ships carrying treasure for the payment of the Army of Flanders were forced by storms and pirates to take refuge in English harbours and Elizabeth sequestrated the treasure, claiming somewhat ingenuously that since it had not yet reached Alba it was the property of the bankers and that she had merely borrowed it from them before the duke himself could do so. Furious, Alba imposed an embargo on English trade with the Low Countries. Elizabeth naturally reciprocated and the trade war continued until 1574, to Spain's disadvantage much more than England's. As it began, Hawkins and Drake returned home to denounce the treachery of the Spanish authorities at San Juan de Ulúa. Cool heads – and there were not many in 1568–9 – noted that England had restated its power in the Channel and that Spain had done exactly the same in the Caribbean: England's Channel, Spain's Caribbean.

By February 1569 Philip was sufficiently frustrated to write to Alba of 'the good opportunity which now presents itself to remedy religious affairs in that country by deposing the present queen and giving the crown to the queen of Scotland'. He ordered the duke to investigate 'what foundation there is for this, and what success would probably attend such a design as, if there is anything in it, I should be glad to carry it out'. Astoundingly, he even authorised Alba to take such action as he himself saw fit: 'If you think the chance will be lost by again waiting to consult me, you may at once take the steps you may consider advisable . . . I have so much confidence in your good sense and prudence that I am sure I can safely leave the matter in your hands.' Philip required only that Alba 'keep me well informed'. Alba had problems enough in the Low Countries without getting involved in England and so he duly passed the responsibility back to the king: 'all things considered, I think it would be best to adopt a gentle course', wrote the Iron Duke.[50] Exasperated beyond measure by Elizabeth's contumacy (and perhaps by Alba's refusal to act against her), at the end of 1569 Philip wrote once again to the duke, insisting that 'we are beginning to lose reputation by deferring so long to provide a remedy for the great grievance done by this woman to my subjects, friends, and allies'. Once again, Alba refused to act.[51]

As Philip and Alba tossed the responsibility for succouring the English Catholics back and forth, the Catholics of the north rose in rebellion against Elizabeth and in support of Mary Stuart. The rising, incompetently led by the dukes of Westmoreland and Northumberland, was quickly and brutally put down. Spain's opportunity of encouraging a popular rebellion had gone and Philip confessed himself to be 'deeply grieved' by the failure and ordered his ambassador in England to take instructions from Alba and 'to proceed entirely by his advice and instruction'.[52] Once again, Alba did nothing.

Pope Pius V was not a man to stand on the sidelines; on 20 February 1570 he issued the Bull *Regnans in Excelsis* which excommunicated Elizabeth and thereby proclaimed it legitimate for Catholics to overthrow her or even to plot her death. Philip was withering in his contempt for the pope's action and deeply angered that Pius had not even had the courtesy to inform him of what he was doing; he had first heard of the Bull from Guerau de Espés, his ambassador in England! In his fury, Philip went so far as to write to Elizabeth herself, absolving himself of responsibility for what Pius had done. He also wrote to de Espés to ensure that his version of events would be circulated in England: 'His Holiness has taken this step without communicating with me in any way, which certainly has greatly surprised me, because my knowledge of English affairs is such that I believe I could give a better opinion upon them and the course that ought to have been adopted under the circumstances than any one else.' He noted that the pope had 'allowed himself to be carried away by his zeal' and confessed himself to be fearful that 'this sudden and unexpected step will exacerbate feeling there, and drive the Queen and her friends the more to oppress and persecute the few good Catholics still remaining in England'.[53]

Philip was correct: Pius V's Bull forced 'the few good Catholics still remaining in England' to weigh their loyalty to their queen against that to their faith and it enabled their enemies to smear them all with the charge of treason, real or potential. Philip had struggled for a decade to prevent that situation arising, as in her different way had Elizabeth herself. At a stroke, the pope himself now undid all that work, and he did so in the wake of a rebellion that had already failed. Pius's action also gave legitimacy to all the intrigues of the imprisoned Catholic queen of Scots. It was little wonder that Philip was furious.

There was, however, no escaping the realities created jointly by the failure of the Northern Rebellion and the papal Bull; much as he deplored it, Philip was now forced to recognise that the last vestiges of Anglo-Burgundian amity had been all but broken. He decided that he would approve the marriage of Mary Stuart with an Englishman, preferably the duke of Norfolk. In doing so, Mary would position herself either to overthrow Elizabeth or to succeed her or to allow the child of her next marriage to follow Elizabeth onto the throne. Accordingly, Philip instructed Alba to arrange Mary's marriage to Norfolk or to another Englishman.[54] Elizabeth countered by opening negotiations to marry the French Dauphin, Henry, duke of Alençon. It was probably nothing more than a diplomatic ploy, threatening Philip with an Anglo-French marriage if he persisted with his intrigue with Mary Stuart, but it opened a courtship that lasted for nearly a decade and which became in itself a factor in international relations. Philip himself airily dismissed the prospect of a marriage between Elizabeth and Alençon as 'a mere invention', but he could never be certain.[55]

The opportunity for Philip to overthrow Elizabeth soon appeared to present itself. Roberto Ridolfi, a Florentine banker, had been involved in the plotting before the Northern Rebellion and he now developed a scheme for a new Catholic rising in the summer of 1572 to place Mary Stuart on the English throne. Much if not all of what he was up to seems to have been known to the English government, for the English spymaster Francis Walsingham certainly knew of Ridolfi's plots and probably allowed him to proceed in order to trap the Spanish government into supporting him; Philip himself certainly suspected that this was the case.[56] Norfolk, however, foolishly agreed to meet Ridolfi and to lead a rebellion if Alba arrived with 10 000 troops. Alba had no intention of so doing and fobbed Ridolfi off. Philip was equally determined to wait on events before committing himself. Walsingham knew most of what was afoot and in August 1571 Norfolk was sent to the Tower. After much prevarication by Elizabeth he was executed on 2 June 1572. The English government allowed the evidence of Mary Stuart's complicity in the plot to become public knowledge and thereby fuelled the demands made by many in Parliament and in the Privy Council for her to follow Norfolk to the block. Elizabeth, however, would not execute a fellow-monarch.[57] For his part, Philip was tarred with complicity in the plot even though he had not given any significant help to Mary and Norfolk. As for Mary Stuart herself, failure drove her into ever more desperate measures.

There was a second, and rather curious, aspect to the Ridolfi affair. Philip was approached in the spring of 1572 by an agent of John Hawkins with an offer that Hawkins would desert to Philip with a squadron of ships in return for the release of the shipmates who had been captured at San Juan de Ulúa and for a supplementary bribe. Once again, Walsingham was probably behind the plot, but Philip apparently believed that Hawkins was sincere, perhaps because he was so tempted by the possibility of having Hawkins's ships to escort Alba's troopships across the Channel. In all likelihood it was Hawkins's intention to sink Alba's ships in mid-Channel. The first plan for an invasion of England was hatched. It came to nothing of course. But it was a portent – and it is a historical curiosity that it was hatched by John Hawkins himself.[58]

THE 'SEA BEGGARS' AND THE REVOLT OF HOLLAND AND ZEELAND

In March 1572 Elizabeth ordered that the small and rather rag-tag fleet of Dutch pirates operating in the Channel should be barred from English ports. Why she did this is not altogether clear; the 'Sea Beggars', as they became known, chiefly preyed on Spanish shipping and it may have been as a conciliatory gesture to Philip that Elizabeth expelled them. Certainly, Philip himself took it as such, writing to thank her for her act of friendship.[59] Alternatively, Elizabeth's action may have arisen from her annoyance at the disruption to trade in the Channel that the Beggars had caused. At all events, the Beggars were now suddenly forced to find a new home, and on 1 April 1572 twenty-five or so of their ships under Count William de la Marck landed on The Brill in Zeeland and, finding it undefended, garrisoned it with a force of 600 men. A week later they seized Flushing. Taken almost in a fit of absentmindedness, The Brill and Flushing provided Alba's rebels with two bases, both of which were open to the sea. Flushing was by far the more important of the two; sitting at the mouth of the Scheldt, it offered access to friendly ships from other countries. The action of the Sea Beggars proved to be the spark that ignited revolt across much of the Low Countries; within a few weeks most of the coastal area from Flushing to Groningen, and much of its immediate hinterland, was in revolt. In town after town Calvinists instigated rebellion against the authority of Spain and they reaped rewards beyond their imagining. Alone among the major towns of the north, Amsterdam remained loyal to Philip. The revolt of Holland and Zeeland had begun.

Within a few weeks in the spring of 1572, therefore, the problems facing Alba had changed beyond recognition; he was confronted now not merely with organising a situation in which the king could safely visit his troubled provinces but with a revolt which threatened the very continuance of Philip's rule over them. Alba faced, too, a series of substantial logistical problems, for virtually the whole area now in revolt could be replenished from the sea while his own army could not function effectively in the marshy lands of the north. There would be no easy victories in that terrain. There was also the very real possibility that Spain would be unable to send reinforcements to Alba by sea, fearful of the damage that rebel ships could do to even a large fleet. Moreover, Alba had to contend with the difficulties of overcoming powerful communes that were organised by men who were every bit as ruthless and as single-minded as he was himself.

For all this, it was still evident that the rebels would need to find support from abroad to supplement their efforts. Their chief hope came from France, where Admiral Coligny was urging Charles IX to declare war on Spain in alliance with England and some Protestant German princes. Coligny was disappointed in his hopes of England; Elizabeth agreed to a strictly defensive league with France (Treaty of Blois, 19 April 1572) but she would not go to war with Philip. This made it all the more important, of course, that Charles IX should commit himself to an anti-Spanish war. William of Orange, preparing to launch his first invasion since 1568, waited for the French to declare war and for Coligny to lead an army into the Low Countries. However, his brother Louis precipitated affairs by seizing the town of Mons in order to provide the French with a secure point of entry (24 May). In doing so, Louis forced Alba to abandon any intention he might have had of dealing with the Sea Beggars. For the first time, Alba was having to respond to events rather than control them. He prepared to march from Brussels to recapture Mons. Once again, Europe waited on a march by the duke of Alba.

Orange himself now moved decisively to seize the leadership of his people, publishing in June 1572 his 'Remonstrance' to the States and people of the Low Countries. He described himself as the 'patron of the fatherland and champion of freedom' and assured Netherlanders that 'I will never desert you'. He offered his protection to the opponents of Alba and, sneering at 'this child of unbelieving Jews', challenged his countrymen to rise against the tyrant:

> Chase him away, then, take your revenge, attack that monster, hated by Spaniards, Italians and Germans alike, see that this rogue of rogues, swollen with pride at his triumphs in Lower and Upper Germany, does not escape you, this prototype of utter cruelty, who littered the gates, harbours, and streets of your fine towns with the corpses of your citizens, who spared neither sex, age nor rank, who slaughtered free-born men like cattle, who made children into orphans and accused innocent men, who plunged all your homes into mourning, who either laid out the slaughtered bodies on the wheel or would not allow them to be fetched for burial or at least made it impossible for you to give them a decent funeral.

More substantially, the prince guaranteed freedom of religious practice to the people of those areas which welcomed his army. Although Orange clung to the fiction that he still gave his allegiance to Philip, he had in practice begun to break both with Philip as his sovereign and with Roman Catholicism as his religion.[60] The States of Holland all but followed suit; in July they insisted that Philip was still their lawful sovereign but nevertheless recognised Orange as 'Governor-General of Holland, Zeeland and Friesland' and sought to extend his authority over the other provinces.[61]

Coligny's timetable for the invasion depended upon the marriage that was to take place in August 1572 between Henry, Prince of Navarre, and Margaret, sister of Charles IX. The marriage of the leading Protestant nobleman to the king's sister was testament to the growing power of the Huguenots and Catherine de' Medici naturally feared that she was herself about to be sidelined by Coligny. It is not clear whether Catherine took the lead in making the decision to have Coligny assassinated, but since she was determined to maintain her influence over her son and to prevent war with Spain breaking out it is reasonable to assume that hers was the decisive role. An assassination attempt took place on 22 August, but Coligny was only wounded. Once again, it was probably Catherine who played the leading role in what followed; the decision was taken at court – and authorised by the king – to launch a pre-emptive strike on the Huguenots in Paris before they turned on the Crown itself. They apparently had no intention of doing so, trusting in the good faith of their king. On the night of St Bartholomew (23–24 August 1572) the tocsin was sounded and the royal and Catholic forces of Paris turned on the Huguenots, slaughtering 2000 or more of them. Coligny himself was finished off, and after he was killed his body was castrated and dragged symbolically through the sewers of Paris. Imitative massacres followed in cities as far apart as Bordeaux, Toulouse and Lyons; perhaps twice as many died in these cities as in Paris itself.[62]

On hearing of the massacre in Paris, Philip danced with joy and (like the pope) ordered that a *Te Deum* be sung in celebration.[63] Well might he have done so, for the massacre meant that there would be no French attack on Alba at Mons and in consequence no Franco-Spanish war. The Prince of Orange's hopes lay crushed. Inevitably, France collapsed once again into civil war. But the massacre also dealt a crushing blow to the prestige of the monarchy in France, which had behaved with such murderous treachery. The Huguenots would never again trust Charles IX. In fact, the king himself lived only until 1574 when he died in agony, tormented (it was said) by the screams of the victims of St Bartholomew's night. But if the House of Valois lost prestige, the House of Guise benefited; the coronation of Henry III in 1575 was conducted by the Cardinal of Guise and senior members of the Guise family filled every major post in the ceremony. Everywhere in Europe, Protestants believed after St Bartholomew's night that the great Catholic crusade against Protestantism was now underway, and that it was led jointly by Philip and by the papacy. In this sense, the Massacre of St Bartholomew's Day was a dividing point in European affairs in psychological as well as in political and religious terms. A small consequence, as it appeared: Henry of Navarre was taken prisoner in the French court and, for the fourth time in his young life, abjured his religion. While all around him were consumed by the rightness of their cause, the Prince of Navarre was, it seemed, intent only on his own survival.[64]

William of Orange was compelled to proceed with his plans or to lose such credibility as still remained to him, and on 27 August he invaded Brabant. Once again Alba refused to fight him, but this time because he had so much more urgent campaigns on his hands. He recaptured Mons and allowed Louis and his Huguenot allies to leave, observing the terms of war; it was the last time that he was generous to a defeated opponent. Alba now turned his attention to the rebel towns and unleashed upon them a policy of calculated and systematic terror. By the end of August there were perhaps sixty of them and Alba could obviously not contemplate moving against each of them in turn. He opted therefore to besiege selected towns and to make dreadful examples of them when they capitulated in order to terrorise the rest into submitting without obliging him to mount a siege – in October, Malines; in November Zutphen and in December Naarden. After the last, Alba wrote triumphantly to Philip that 'not a mother's son escaped'.[65] He then moved his army on Haarlem, entrusting command to his illegitimate son Fadrique. Haarlem held out from 11 December 1572 to 12 July 1573 but it was bought at the cost of 10 000 of Alba's men and when the garrison of 2000 men surrendered on the guarantee of their safety they too were slaughtered. Haarlem was a massacre too many: far from encouraging other towns to surrender it hardened their determination not to do so, however straitened their circumstances became. The war now became now one of sieges, and Alba's brutality ensured that each was a fight to the death; surrender was no longer an option. When Alba besieged Leiden he came up against even more determined resistance.

Alba had failed, and at terrible cost. By the end of 1572 he had an army of nearly 70 000 men and yet the revolt, far from being crushed or even contained, seemed to be spreading. Moreover, Alba had failed to make the Low Countries pay for themselves and his great army was being supported almost exclusively by the Castilian taxpayer; of the 4 362 916 ducats that the government received in 1572–3 no less than 3 455 119 (79 per cent) came from Castile.[66] This level of expenditure simply could not be maintained. Rather than preparing the way for Philip's arrival as a beneficent and forgiving monarch, Alba had contrived to provoke a widespread revolt which cut right across the Low Countries and which involved all social classes. Rather than building support for the Crown, Alba had created revulsion towards Philip and to Spain, not just among the Protestants but among many Catholics and most moderates. His was a failure on an epic scale.

Philip was surprisingly prompt to recognise that Alba would have to be replaced, but having for once made a major decision with some alacrity he then grotesquely mishandled its implementation and in doing so inflicted further harm on his government in the Low Countries. He named as Alba's successor the duke of Medinaceli, who had been humiliated at Djerba in 1560. Medinaceli sailed for the Low Countries in December 1571 but a storm forced him to take refuge in Laredo, and not until April 1572 was he able to sail once again. He arrived in the Low Countries early in May but many of his larger ships found great difficulty in berthing in the Scheldt and eight were destroyed or captured by the Dutch. Medinaceli's fleet was the last one that succeeded in bringing soldiers from Spain to the Low Countries in Philip's reign, but probably fewer than 1000 survived the voyage to serve in the Army of Flanders. As if the sea voyage was not hazardous enough for the duke, Philip's instructions vested him with the unenviable brief of both investigating Alba's conduct and of replacing him. While, therefore, Alba was fighting the brutal campaign of 1572, he was having to defend himself against the accusations being raised by Medinaceli and fight off Medinaceli's attempt to take his place as Governor-General. It was entirely characteristic of Philip's government that at this moment of great crisis in the Low Countries, he should have not one but two captains-general *in situ*. Predictably, both Alba and Medinaceli failed, and Philip decided to replace Medinaceli before he had even entered into the exercise of his office. On 30 January 1573 he named Don Luis de Requesens as Governor and Captain-General in succession to Alba. Not until 17 November 1573 did Requesens arrive in Brussels, and even then Alba stayed a further month before deigning to leave.[67] This was misgovernment on an epic scale.

6

WAR IN THE LOW COUNTRIES

THE KING'S FRIEND

The appointment of Requesens to replace Alba, badly managed though it was, showed just how determined Philip was to resolve the situation in the Low Countries, for Don Luis was no ordinary adviser. Philip had known him for nearly forty years and trusted him deeply. Insistently, over the first two decades of his reign it had been to Requesens that Philip had turned when his own reputation had been at serious hazard: in 1563 he had sent him to Rome to find a settlement to the Carranza affair, and he had then trusted him to guide (and restrain) Don John in the campaigns in the Alpujarras and at Lepanto; in 1571 he had appointed him to the governorship of Milan so that he could both organise the despatch of troops and resources to Alba in the Low Countries and deal with the turbulence unleashed in the duchy by the enthusiasm with which Archbishop Carlo Borromeo had imposed the Tridentine reforms. Now, in 1573, Philip laid upon his friend the obligation of salvaging his own prestige in the Low Countries after the disasters of Alba's rule. He wrote to him: 'I entrust to you the greatest and the most important business that I have had or could have' and insisted that 'I will admit no excuses, nor must you for any reason give me [one] . . . I want you to serve me in this without making any reply'.[1] So that Requesens could serve him effectively Philip gave him much greater resources in terms of men and money than Alba had ever enjoyed.

For the campaign of 1574 in the Low Countries, prudence was not to be Philip's hallmark. Between December 1573 and March 1574 the Army of Flanders was increased in size by one-third, from 62 280 to

86235 men – not until 1640 would it surpass this level – and in 1574 it received twice as much money from Spain (3977151 ducats) as it had in 1573.[2] Such a commitment by Philip demanded absolute loyalty and competence from his commander; this was why Requesens was chosen. Don Luis would fight war on a new scale – but he would do so in order to make whatever peace he could, for Philip was determined that the climactic expenditure of 1574 would bring the war to an end. Unfortunately, Philip's despairing calculations took no account of the fact that Requesens was not the man he had been; although he was only forty-five years of age he was already in poor health, the result of a fragile constitution and various war wounds. Only with great reluctance did he accept the appointment and only very slowly did he make his way north.[3]

After some initial failures Requesens established his military credibility when in April 1574 his general Sancho Dávila crushed an invasion from France by Louis of Nassau at the battle of Mook. Louis (who in truth had led a charmed existence) paid with his life, as did another of Orange's brothers, Henry. It was Requesens's first victory but it was to be his only one, for on the very following day, 15 April, his triumphant army mutinied; despite the millions of ducats sent north by the Crown, the Spanish veterans who formed the core of the army had not been paid for three years and they threatened now to plunder Antwerp itself unless their pay was made good. That the great financial and commercial capital could be pillaged was unthinkable and so the campaign came to a halt for six weeks while Requesens found the money with which to placate his men. He never forgave the soldiers who had snatched his triumph away from him; bitterly, he insisted 'that it was not the prince of Orange who had lost the Low Countries, but the soldiers born in Valladolid and Toledo'.[4] When in June he offered a general pardon he did so from a position of weakness and few paid any heed to the offer, believing that it would be rescinded once he had regained control of his army. His period of success was over.

Requesens attempted to compensate for the mutiny by committing his army to capturing Leiden (where the siege had been temporarily lifted). But under the ferocious discipline of its Calvinist leaders the city held out, and Orange himself intervened decisively to insist that the dikes be breached to save the city. At the beginning of October a storm whipped the waters up and the Beggars were able to sail up to the walls of the city; the Spanish army broke ranks and fled, terrified as much of the waters as of the enemy. The siege of Leiden has been described as 'the costliest, hardest fought, and most decisive, as well as the most epic of the great sieges of the Revolt'. The relief of the town was a dramatic victory for the rebels. It was commemorated with poignant optimism by the foundation of the University of Leiden. The new university was specifically designed to compete with the Catholic universities of the Louvain and Douai; it was to train Protestant ministers and theologians and to educate its students in the need to defend their liberties. The State of Holland was in effect undertaking to train its own elite.[5] The demoralisation of the Spanish troops found reflection in yet another mutiny, which at the end of 1574 led to the abandonment of loyalist strongpoints in Holland. Philip made a further attempt to send reinforcements by sea, fitting out a fleet of 120 ships under the leadership of Pedro Menéndez de Avilés himself, but when Menéndez died in September the king decided to pay off the troops; Requesens would receive no help by sea.[6]

The 1574 campaign, therefore, far from being a resounding success, had been marked by two great mutinies, the failure before Leiden and the failure to send reinforcements by sea. The success at Mook was small compensation. The rebels were now doing rather more than merely surviving – and the Prince of Orange was beginning to build a reputation as an inspirational leader. The failure to send a fleet in 1574 was also a portent of a changing situation at sea; the growing threat from Protestant ships operating out of The Brill and Flushing, Le Havre and La Rochelle meant that Philip could only send reinforcements to the Low Countries when very large fleets could be assembled to transport them. Increasingly that was proving impossible for him to achieve, and he was having to accept that for the foreseeable future reinforcements for the Army of Flanders would have to go by the long, overland route that became known as 'The Spanish Road'. He was forced, too, to turn his mind to finding carrying agents who were able to bring goods from the Baltic and northern Europe to Spain; his attention began to settle on the members of the Hanseatic League.

Philip's gamble had failed; pouring men and money into the Low Countries had not turned his fortunes around. Rather, as Geoffrey Parker has brilliantly demonstrated, a cycle of self-inflicted and escalating damage had been created – the more soldiers Philip supported in the Low Countries, the more money he needed with which to pay them and as he was always unable to pay his army in full, so the more damage was done to his own cause by the inevitable mutinies of his own troops – more damage, sometimes, than was done to it by the enemy. In conclusion, the larger and more professional the army that Philip maintained in the Low Countries, the greater the damage done to his cause by its mutinies, which were themselves highly formalised and professional. Never had this been more fully demonstrated than in the 1574 campaign.[7] A further, complementary, defeat took place in September with the recapture of Tunis by the Turk. War on two fronts seemed to be leading simply to defeat on two fronts. Philip had no choice now but to seek to cut his losses; on 3 March 1575 negotiations with the States of Holland and Zeeland opened at Breda. The very fact of having to negotiate with his rebel subjects was profoundly humiliating to Philip. The discussions proved to be no less intractable than war, and after three months they broke down on the refusal of both sides to concede religious toleration within their territories. Time would show that the opportunity for a negotiated settlement that was lost in 1575 was the best that Philip would be presented with.[8] It would also show that the summer of 1575 was a decisive turning-point in the nature of the war, for in July the States of Holland considered formally for the first time the possibility of declaring independence from Philip of Spain, discussing a proposal 'that one ought soon to abandon the king as a tyrant who sought to oppress and destroy his subjects, and to seek another protector'.[9]

Castile sent nearly five million ducats to the Low Countries in 1575 and the effort broke her finances; on 1 September Philip declared a suspension of payments to his bankers. For Requesens, this was a catastrophe too far; he died on 5 March 1576. It was inevitably said that he died of a broken heart but in reality he had been unwell from the time of his appointment. He left a situation vastly worse than he had found it – an enormous army stranded in a land that would not pay for it at the behest of a government that could not pay for it, and in the absence of a governor who might control it. He left, too, the prospect of yet another hiatus of several months before a new governor could arrive in the Low Countries. It seemed that the situation could not get any worse.

THE 1570s: THE FUNDING OF WAR

The great war effort in the Low Countries in the years to 1575 was chiefly paid for by the Castilian taxpayer, and coming as it did on top of the expenses of the wars in the Alpujarras and the Mediterranean – the

Spanish contribution to the Holy League has been estimated at seven million ducats in the years 1571–3 alone – it had devastating consequences for the finances of Castile. By the mid-1570s the Crown was facing debts that totalled over eighty million ducats while it had a disposable income of a mere six million ducats a year.[10] But still Philip could not pull back; in the aftermath of the great bankruptcy of 1575 he determined to wring yet more resources from Castile with which to fight the war in the Low Countries.

Philip himself regularly despaired of his ability even to understand his financial situation let alone remedy it: 'You are aware of my ignorance as to financial affairs', he wrote on one occasion, going on to observe that 'I cannot tell a good memorial on the subject from a bad one. And I do not wish to break my brains trying to comprehend something which I do not understand now nor have ever understood in all my days.'[11] The king's modesty was misplaced, for deficient though his comprehension of finance undoubtedly was, it paled beside his inability at times of crisis and defeat to impose his undoubted political acumen upon his sense of dynastic and patrimonial responsibility. Consumed by the determination not to fail in his god-given responsibilities, Philip could never bring himself to accept defeat and when confronted by it he almost instinctively increased the stakes, gambling that with one more throw of the dice he could turn defeat into triumph. On 22 February 1575, therefore, he made an agreement with the procurators of the Cortes of Castile for an *encabezamiento general* which would bring in 3 091 362 ducats in 1575 and 3 716 362 in each of the subsequent nine years to 1584.[12]

It was one thing, however, to browbeat the thirty-six procurators in Madrid, quite another to ensure that their towns and cities actually produced the money. The cities with votes in the Cortes were so infuriated by the pusillanimity of their representatives that they refused to ratify the agreement. Accordingly, negotiations had to be re-opened and Philip decided to summon a new meeting of the Cortes so that he could make a fresh start. He issued the summons on 13 November 1575.

The cities of Castile were determined – possibly even as the result of some informal collusion – that they would not allow their procurators to commit them to taxes that they were not prepared to pay, and so the majority of them now issued their procurators with only limited powers and required oaths of obedience from them. Accordingly, the discussions in the Cortes were longer and more bitter than hitherto. It took a further two years to reach a settlement that the cities were prepared to sign up to; on 20 October 1577 Philip agreed to lower the *encabezamiento general* to 2 700 000 ducats a year. Reduced the amount may have been, but it was still over twice as much as had been paid in 1572 and governmental income from taxes in Castile in 1577 remained some 50 per cent higher than it had been a decade earlier.[13] However, with the new agreement the Crown was able to begin drawing a line under the financial crisis that had begun with the Suspension of Payments in 1575, and on 5 December 1577 it reached an agreement with its bankers (the *medio general*) whereby it revoked the decree of Suspension. Philip had access to credit once again.[14]

The long negotiations also redefined the relationship between the Crown and the Cortes of Castile.[15] Philip's insistent need for more money – and the municipalities' determination to have a say in what they contributed and how it was spent – meant that the towns and cities with votes in the Cortes would henceforth wield much greater political influence. The *encabezamiento general* lasted for four years (1578–81) and was then succeeded by a second that lasted for three years (1584–6), a third that lasted only for a year (1587) and a fourth for a further two years (1588–9).[16] In practice, therefore, after the bankruptcy of 1575 the Crown found itself locked into almost permanent negotiations with the cities and the procurators for the renewal of its grants. In these negotiations, a political development of potentially profound importance was taking place as the Cortes of Castile became almost a regular branch of government.

The growth in the importance of the Cortes contrasted signally with the position of the Council of Finance, for the crisis of the 1570s resulted in a diminution rather than an expansion of the Council's role. Even the dismissal of Espinosa (whose overarching power had inhibited the development of the Council) did not lead to a revival in its fortunes. Indeed, in 1573 Philip further undermined the Council by giving overall responsibility for financial affairs to the *Junta de Presidentes*, consisting of the presidents of Castile, Indies and Orders (Diego de Covarrubias, Juan de Ovando and Antonio de Padilla) and a number of senior councillors. Such a body could deal with major items of expenditure but by definition it could not oversee the daily management of the whole of the Crown's finances. Philip seems to have realised that he had made a mistake, for in 1574 he appointed Ovando as President of the Council of Finance. However, he could not bring himself to allow Ovando to leave the presidency of the Council of the Indies and so, as the Crown lurched towards the great bankruptcy of 1575, the presidency of the Council of

Finance was not even a full-time job. In the time that Ovando was able to devote to financial affairs he soon found out just how inadequate the Council of Finance was; indeed, he was not even able to discover what the responsibilities of the individual officers of the Council were. He therefore brought in some of his own men to help bolster his authority but in doing so he added greatly to the tensions within the Council and did nothing to resolve those between the Council and the *Junta de Presidentes.*[17] Financial management was impossible in these circumstances, and Ovando collapsed under the strain and died.

The flood of silver from the Indies came to the aid of the government (see Table 4.1). This treasure, in conjunction with the revenue raised by taxation in Castile, transformed Spain's political situation, allowing Philip to fund escalations of warfare in the 1580s which dwarfed even those that he had allowed in the 1570s. The windfall from the Indies, coming at. precisely the time when Spain had been unable to pay for the war in the Low Countries, had tragic consequences for Spain, though, for it enabled Philip to commit himself to more and more foreign adventures and to do so on a scale that would hitherto have been inconceivable. American treasure and Castilian tax-yields funded the gambles of the 1580s and 1590s that were the expression of Philip's desperate determination to reverse the defeats of the later 1570s.

Philip's resolve to tax Castile ever more heavily led him to look carefully at the informational bases upon which his government operated, and in the 1570s he instituted a series of major reforms designed to provide his government with proper statistical and juridical data. In the first instance, he set his ministers the task of establishing exactly how many people there were in Castile and where they lived. Questionnaires were sent out to each province in Castile in 1575 and again in 1578, asking how many inhabitants there were in each community, what their social composition was and what the secular and religious traditions of community were. The authorities in each city, town and village were required to fill in and return these questionnaires and they provided Philip with the most precise information about every community in the kingdom of Castile. Known as the *Relaciones Topográficas*, the replies amount to one of the great treasures of Spanish state records. They brought the Spanish government information that was much more detailed and complex than most contemporary rulers possessed.[18] With this information available, Philip set about the process of taxing his people of Castile ever more substantially.

Philip complemented this major enterprise by having the laws of Castile collated and published in 1567 in what became known as the *Nueva Recopilación*. This was followed by the beginning of the publication of the *Laws of the Indies* in 1571. The two projects meant that henceforth the laws under which Castile and the Indies were governed were readily accessible to the government; it could now exploit its rights more easily and more fully. Understanding that effective government required that the Crown should have full and immediate access to its own documentation Philip also set about reorganising the state archive. The state papers of the kingdom of Castile had been housed in the great castle of Simancas, twelve kilometres south of Valladolid, but they had not been properly maintained and Philip had been alerted to the inadequacies of the archive as early as 1556 when it had proved impossible to locate a document as important as the papal judgement given in favour of Katharine of Aragon some twenty years before; Philip was informed that 'no one knows who can have it'.[19] In 1561, Philip appointed Diego de Ayala as archivist in Simancas and observed in his title that the papers in Simancas had not been managed with 'the good order, distinction and clarity that is necessary' and were in a condition of 'confusion and disorder'.[20] Accordingly, Philip charged Ayala with organising and cataloguing the papers in the great archive. Neither king nor archivist appreciated the full enormity of the burden that was thereby placed on Ayala's shoulders. Certainly, the new archivist soon found out just how obstructive the king's administrators could be in refusing to co-operate by handing over their papers to him.[21] But at least the task had been begun. Philip's government would have a proper record of its actions. It was perhaps the most symbolic of Philip's acts in reforming and reorganising his governmental apparatus. It was certainly the most characteristic.

THE KING OF PAPER. PHILIP AND HIS SECRETARIES: ANTONIO PÉREZ AND MATEO VÁZQUEZ DE LECA

If the Crown's financial affairs were confused throughout the 1570s by a whole series of jurisdictional ambiguities and conflicts within government, the development of policy-making in foreign affairs and in many areas of domestic concern was stunted by Philip's determination to control everything himself. By the early 1570s he was living in the

Escorial for extended periods, and this made it easier for him to separate his own work from that of his administrators. He began to become more isolated from all but a select few of his advisers. It was in the 1570s that Philip truly became the king who ruled by paper, who resolved everything on paper. Unable to bring himself to delegate, he became now more and more concerned to be personally involved in every decision, to have the first and the last word on matters great and small. So that he could do so, he submitted himself to the most unsparing regime, working at his desk throughout the day and long into the night, allowing himself little recreation from the mountain of documents that arrived on his desk every day, often writing comments that were longer than the document that he was considering. But as he worked ever more intensively so Philip isolated himself from the main body of his advisers; working with paper enabled him to avoid meeting people who might try to argue with him over policy or bring unwelcome facts to his attention.

The extraordinary diligence with which Philip applied himself to his papers was the visible expression of his ideal of kingship – that he alone had the responsibility for making decisions. But it was also, perhaps less consciously, an expression of Philip's inability to take decisions quickly, for in endeavouring to read all important papers himself he actually put off the time when he would need to decide how to respond to the problems that they posed for him. In consequence, he often finished up by accomplishing very little.

To help him in his task, Philip turned chiefly to two secretaries, Antonio Pérez and Mateo Vázquez de Leca. Pérez, as secretary of the Council of State from 1568, was nominally only responsible for Italian affairs but in practice he dealt with the whole range of foreign policy and developed a special interest in the business of the Low Countries. Vázquez de Leca became Philip's private secretary in 1573 and concentrated on domestic affairs – most notably matters relating to patronage and appointments – and on the government of the Indies. Between them, therefore, the two men controlled the management of most of the important affairs of state in the 1570s other than financial affairs.

Both men were illegitimate by birth. Antonio Pérez was almost certainly the natural son of Gonzalo Pérez (although some thought that Ruy Gómez might have been his father) while Vázquez de Leca was a foundling who invented an ingeniously imaginative genealogy which traced his ancestry back to ancient Sardinian nobility.[22] The circumstances of their births made both men absolutely dependent upon the king himself. They were useful to Philip because they had the capacity for sustained work under high pressure; they could match the king in his long, grinding days and nights of administrative routine. Each normally saw him on a daily basis and travelled with him as he moved from residence to residence but despite their proximity to him the king insisted on writing to them on a daily basis. They in turn plied Philip with the smallest details of every problem and so he became at once more dependent upon them and less capable of distancing himself from the routine of his papers and of taking a broad, strategic view of the affairs of government. The king's dependence upon Pérez and Vázquez de Leca also made it easier for them to build up their own power bases and even to manipulate Philip in their own interests.

Antonio Pérez was never likely to be content to be a mere secretary. He had been educated at the universities of Alcalá, Louvain, Venice, Padua and Salamanca and was one of the most brilliant men of his time, a sophisticate who was effortlessly at ease in court and government. Extravagance marked everything about him – his abilities and his weaknesses, his friendships and his enmities. Above all, there was a carefree and arrogant ostentation about his lifestyle; his house in Madrid (which was known as 'La Casilla') became one of the social centres of the new capital, his hospitality the envy of political society. He owned one of the first great private collections of paintings in Spain. Pérez was proud of his knowledge of painting – indeed, he claimed to have sat at Titian's feet as a twelve-year-old while the great master expatiated upon the development of his own technique – and among the 127 paintings in La Casilla were an original *Adam and Eve* by Titian as well as works by Corregio and other Italian masters. Judiciously, Pérez collected portraits of Philip and his family; in all, he owned eight. It was widely known that Pérez accepted presents of pictures as well as of other valuables – tapestries, carpets, objets d'art and the like – and that people wishing to find favour with him could optimise their chances by presenting him with suitable gifts.[23] It was obvious to everyone at court – including to Philip himself – that Pérez was living substantially beyond his means, but until he fell from power in 1579 few dared criticise him, so powerful was he, so apparently secure in the king's favour. Pérez was, indeed, a man who lived on the edge and who was dangerous to everyone who dealt with him; brilliantly intuitive in his assessment of men's (and women's) weaknesses and ruthless in his exploitation of them, he bound people to him by the force of his personality and by fear of his purpose. Pérez was not an unprincipled politician – throughout his life he remained loyal to the principles that he had learned from Ruy Gómez – but he allowed nothing to stand in the way of his own advancement. It was characteristic of him that after his patron's death he should have formed an alliance – probably not a fully adulterous one – with Ruy Gómez's widow, Ana de Mendoza, Princess of Éboli. Antonio Pérez was a truly machiavellian politician.

This does not explain, of course, how he was able to beguile and manipulate Philip himself for a decade, much less how he contrived to involve him in a conspiracy to murder Juan de Escobedo, one of his own ministers, as he did in 1568. It may well be that Pérez was able in the first instance to gain ascendancy over Philip because he arrived in office at a time when the king was especially vulnerable after the personal losses of 1568. More enduringly, what was certainly true of Pérez was that he had the ability that Philip himself so lacked to cut through to the heart of problems, to perceive their essence and then to resolve them quickly and efficiently. It was this more than the extravagance of his personality that commended him to Philip: the count of Luna observed of Pérez that 'great men worshipped him; ministers admitted his superiority; the King loved him'.[24] Perhaps, too, Philip derived vicarious satisfaction from involving himself in the intrigues that were so much a part of Pérez's life. If so, it cost him dear: his reputation was never to recover from the devastation that Pérez wreaked upon it and he himself suffered agonies over two decades as a result of his intrigues with his brilliant but flawed secretary.

In Philip's defence, it must be said that others were as susceptible to Pérez's charms as he himself. Some of the leading figures in court and church bound themselves tightly to Pérez. Among his friends, for instance, were Cardinal Gaspar de Quiroga and Baltasar Álamos de Barrientos, two of the most honourable men of their age; both remained loyal to Pérez long after he fell from power. Others were as attached to him: among aristocrats, Don Pedro Fajardo, Marquis of Los Vélez, from Murcia; among churchmen, the Galician Antonio Mauriño de Pazos, president of the Council of Castile (1578–82) and Fray Francisco de Sosa, councillor of Inquisition and bishop of the Canaries (where he had been born). A pattern is clearly recognisable here, for while Pérez was only too pleased to receive support from any quarter it is undeniable that he had a talent for attracting the support of non-Castilians. He himself was from Aragon, and he certainly took special care to bind leading figures in the kingdom of Aragon to him – men such as

Don Martín de Gurrea y Aragón, duke of Villahermosa and Don Francisco de Aragón, count of Luna. Similarly, he had a coterie of Portuguese supporters, many of whom he had inherited from Ruy Gómez, and who were perhaps the more supportive of him when his opponents sneered at him as 'the Portuguese', in reference to the rumour that Ruy Gómez was his real father. The support that Pérez received from many members of the Society of Jesus may well have had its origins in the support given him by the Portuguese. Pérez had, too, a shadowy group of supporters in the Low Countries; it is all but certain that it was his intrigues with these men that finally persuaded Philip that he had to move against him.[25] It may well be, indeed, that Escobedo himself was about to reveal Pérez's intrigues with leading rebels in the Low Countries that persuaded the secretary that he had to have Escobedo murdered. But in dealing with Antonio Pérez we have always to remember that so much must always be speculative.

If many of Pérez's opponents came from the provinces, Castilians also figured prominently among his leading opponents, and chief among them were pillars of the establishment: aristocrats like the duke of Alba; Don Francisco Zapata de Cisneros, first count of Barajas and Diego de Cabrera y Bobadilla, third count of Chinchón; churchmen such as Fray Diego de Chaves, the king's Dominican confessor; lawyers such as Rodrigo Vázquez de Arce. These men were powerful individualists – it took strong, hard men to oppose Antonio Pérez – but they should not be thought of as forming a party or faction save in that they were united in their enmity to Pérez. More important than any of them was Mateo Vázquez de Leca; subtle, knowledgeable beyond compare of the personalities of court, Vázquez de Leca was the man who brought Pérez down. Others took their revenge after Pérez had fallen; Barajas (1582–91) and Vázquez de Arce (1592–9) presided over the Council of Castile while it investigated the fallen secretary, and indeed it was Vázquez de Arce who authorised the use of torture against him, and who sat in an adjoining room while Pérez was 'put to the question'. Pérez's power and his personality both helped, in short, to divide men and to create factions at court; rather as had been the case in the 1560s with Alba himself, men were either for Pérez or they were against him. There was no middle way.

One of Pérez's chief values to Philip was that he provided a barrier between the king and his Council of State. By the 1570s Philip was beginning to allow the council to sit fairly regularly and with a reasonably compact and stable membership, but he was nonetheless determined that it would have only an advisory purpose and that he would exclude the greatest of his nobles from it. Broadly, two groups of men attended the Council in the 1570s: aristocrats like the dukes of Alba, Sessa and Fernandina and the marquises of Los Vélez, Aguilar and Almazán; and senior churchmen and administrators who sat almost in an *ex-officio* capacity such as Quiroga, Inquisitor-General and archbishop of Toledo, and Diego de Covarrubias, president of the Council of Castile. Many other men held the title of 'councillor of State' but there had always been a distinction between those councillors who enjoyed the title in a merely honorary capacity and those who actually used it to sit at the council table and formally advise the king.

The most singular feature of the emerging Council of State in the 1570s was therefore that the greatest aristocrats – the men whose annual income exceeded 100000 ducats – did not attend it. In the later 1570s there were about 105 titled aristocrats in Castile (see Table 9.1). They varied enormously in wealth; five of them had incomes of over 100000 ducats a year while only forty-three had more than 20000 ducats a year and twenty had 10000 ducats or less. In all, they had a total rent roll of 2830000 ducats and an average income of 26952. The councillors of State came from the group below the leading five – chief among them, Alba, who with an income of 60000 ducats was the twelfth richest; Sessa, who with 34000 ducats a year was twenty-third on the list; and the marquis of Los Vélez (70000 ducats; tenth); the marquis of Aguilar had 24000 ducats a year and ranked only thirty-second among his peers.[26]

The nobles who sat on the Council of State in the 1570s, therefore, were mostly members of the service aristocracy, men who needed to win the king's favour by showing themselves to be diligent and attentive servants. Furthermore, because they were not the richest of the aristocracy these men had tended not to acquire significant foreign experience; only Alba and Sessa had served in major positions abroad. By definition, therefore, the active councillors of State were (with those two exceptions) not particularly well-qualified to advise the king on foreign policy. Indeed, their lack of experience greatly helped Philip and Pérez in their task of controlling the Council. Pérez convened the Council when the king ordered him to do so, read it the papers that formed the basis for discussion and then reported the views of the councillors back to the king. In doing so he was able to influence policy-making. When, for instance, in January 1574, three councillors met to discuss affairs in Germany,

Pérez duly informed the king that he himself would advise him the following day on what response should be made. When money had to be found for Flanders in 1577, Pérez convened a meeting of the two councillors who could be found and transmitted their views to the king.[27] To do this was to make policy – and it was also to discipline the councillors themselves. Perhaps this explains why Pérez was able to hold so many of them in thrall; as secretary of State, he was the master of the Council of State, and he was its voice.

Inevitably, the duke of Alba was the exception to the rule of quiet deference. That he had returned from the Low Countries in semi-disgrace did not inhibit Alba from arguing at the council table that Spain should wage stern, unremitting, war there.[28] Temperamental as always, Alba could also be relied upon to be obstructive and wilful; in 1575 he absented himself from a meeting and so the whole council had to reconvene the following day.[29] It fell to Antonio Pérez to discipline the duke, and he did so with subtle purpose; when in April 1576, Alba found himself unable to attend a meeting because of his ill-health, Pérez saw fit to inform the king that the duke's illness was not so severe as to force him to call off his plans to travel on the following day.[30]

Mateo Vázquez de Leca, in singular contrast to Antonio Pérez, was the soul of discretion, an almost invisible figure at the heart of power. He had learned his craft in the services of Juan de Ovando (1562–5) and of Cardinal Espinosa (1565–72) and was faithful to the principles he had learned from them. Indeed, Vázquez de Leca's whole career was built upon the advice that Ovando had given him – 'to remain in his place, to sew up his mouth, to continue serving as he had done in the past, and to show great humility and readiness to do whatever was asked'.[31] Vázquez de Leca transferred to Philip's service within a day of the Cardinal's death, taking with him Espinosa's invaluable book summarising the qualities and weaknesses of candidates for office.[32] Like Antonio Pérez, he had a keen appreciation of what he could offer the king; indeed, he wrote his own job description when he persuaded Philip that 'Your Majesty could summon me when he is alone during the day or the night to read the latest papers. Your Majesty could also order me to collect and keep the documents sent to me, and at the same time communicate whatever should prove necessary to the ministers of the Crown. My function would be to save Your Majesty inconvenience and worry . . .'[33] On 29 March 1573 Vázquez de Leca was appointed as Philip's private secretary, charged with organising the king's desk.[34] He remained at the king's side until his death in 1591.

Vázquez de Leca was fascinated by the minutiae of government but he was no mere clerk. Sitting at the king's right hand hour after hour gave him enormous influence and he used it, subtly but effectively. He held the administration together, working prodigiously long hours, dealing with the whole range of domestic business – political, administrative, ecclesiastical, American, papal, urban, fiscal. But more than anything else, he became the master of the Crown's patronage system, and he had a special interest in ecclesiastical affairs. By the 1580s few major positions were allocated without him having some input. This applied to courtly as much as to administrative offices; when, for instance, in 1579 a new *mayordomo mayor* had to be found for Queen Anna, it was Vázquez de Leca who summarised the characters and qualities of the candidates, and his comments were sufficient to rule men out of consideration – the marquis of Mondéjar, for instance, was 'acerbic'; Don Juan de Zúñiga was too shortsighted, while the duke of Béjar merited no comment at all. As a result of Vázquez de Leca's support, the count of Barajas won the position: how high the base-born secretary had risen![35]

Conciliar secretaries were not normally involved in the decision-making process but Vázquez de Leca created a role for himself by developing the use of inter-conciliar juntas as a fundamental instrument of government. Juntas were for the most part informal in their structure; they had no *ordenanzas* stipulating how often they should meet or who should sit on them and they had the advantage over the councils that they were more flexible. In particular they allowed Philip to bring in experts to discuss specific problems without allowing them to establish a prescriptive right to be consulted. Men could be used and if they did not measure up (or if they fell out with Vázquez de Leca himself) their services could be dispensed with. Knowledge could be compartmentalised, and only Vázquez de Leca held all the keys; he organised juntas on 'The Finances of Italy', on the Armada against England and on the government of the Indies but sometimes he did not even let the juntas know that other juntas existed. Like his king, he played men off against each other.[36]

As did Pérez, Vázquez de Leca raised supporters and like-minded men to high office, among them the duke of Medinaceli, the counts of Chinchón and Belchite and the financier Juan Fernández de Espinosa. He, too, therefore, became a great patron at court. His rivalry with Pérez was often hidden but it served to deepen and embitter those natural jealousies that were the daily stuff of life at court. Philip knew how intensely the two men were competing with each other and encouraged them; he mastered powerful and able servants by dividing them against each other. It was a basic fault-line in his kingship.

GASPAR DE QUIROGA, THE INQUISITION AND THE CHURCH IN THE 1570s

The Church had a much more tranquil time than did secular government in the 1570s. Philip had turned to Pedro Ponce de León, a career-bishop of no great distinction, to replace Espinosa as Inquisitor-General but he died within weeks and Philip then named Gaspar de Quiroga to take over. No more unlikely man ever filled the Inquisition's senior position. Quiroga was an intellectual of broad range, an accomplished politician and administrator, clear-sighted but subtle and patient. He had made his career by demonstrating his hostility to papal interference in church affairs in Spain and had been appointed to the presidency of the Council of Italy in 1567. In 1572 Philip raised him to the bishopric of Cuenca, and it seemed that at the age of sixty his career had reached its natural climax. However, in May 1573, Quiroga found himself (to his own great surprise) named as Inquisitor-General.[37]

Quiroga came into office at a time when the Inquisition of Valladolid had launched a series of attacks on distinguished intellectuals, perhaps with the intention of carrying on with the spirit of Valdés's work. In 1571, León de Castro, a professor at the University of Salamanca, laid charges against three of his colleagues of carelessness amounting to heresy in their theological writings – Luis de León, Gaspar de Grajal and Martín Martínez de Cantalapiedra. They were arrested and imprisoned in the spring of 1572 and were joined by Professor Alonso Gudiel of Osuna University, against whom León de Castro also laid charges. Quiroga dealt with the cases with sensitivity and courage. Alonso Gudiel died in prison in 1573, but Quiroga had him cleared posthumously of the charges against him. Fray Luis de León appealed to Quiroga, who referred his case back to the Inquisition of Valladolid with the suggestion that he be acquitted. This duly happened, and Fray Luis was presented with an official certificate of acquittal together with his arrears of pay from the University of Salamanca. When Fray Luis was arrested again in 1582 and charged over his involvement in a theological dispute, Quiroga personally interviewed him, accepted his promise of obedience and had him released. Although Martínez de Cantalapiedra remained in prison until 1577, in a succession of other cases, Quiroga moderated the zeal of his more backward inquisitors. He was deliberately bringing about a sea-change in the attitudes that governed the Inquisition.[38]

The protracted ordeal of Bartolomé de Carranza, archbishop of Toledo (see Chapter 2) finally came to its conclusion when on 14 April 1576 Pope Gregory XIII declared that no fewer than 1567 propositions in the archbishop's Catechism were of doubtful theological legitimacy. However, since Gregory only sentenced Carranza to abjure sixteen of them and suspended him for five years, the archbishop's supporters regarded the verdict as a vindication, particularly because the pope declared that Carranza had not been guilty of heresy and granted him money for his maintenance. To Carranza himself, vindication was satisfying but of little relevance, for he was at death's door and died on 2 May.[39]

Relieved at last of the case that had haunted him since 1559, Philip made no secret of the fact that he wanted to have his nephew, the archduke Albert of Austria, as archbishop of Toledo in succession to Carranza. Unfortunately, Albert was only eighteen years old and so Philip decided to appoint an elderly man who could serve for a few years while Albert acquired the necessary experience. Not unnaturally, he turned to Quiroga.[40] However, Philip's calculation went awry, for his temporary archbishop lived for another seventeen years and far from being compliant with royal wishes Quiroga seemed to take delight in opposing them. Quiroga realised full well that Philip was in a particularly delicate position; having lost one archbishop of Toledo the king could not risk losing another one. He therefore set the tone of his archbishopric by commissioning a sympathetic biography of Carranza and by having his portrait included among the holders of the primatial see. Moreover, Quiroga was self-confident enough to support the Society of Jesus despite Philip's suspicion of the Order; he founded two colleges for them in his archdiocese.

Vexed though he often was by Quiroga's independence, Philip had sufficient depth himself to recognise and value the qualities that Quiroga brought to the leadership of the Church. He went so far as to offer him the presidency of the Council of Castile, and had his status rounded out with a cardinal's red hat in 1578. Quiroga refused the presidency on the grounds that he had quite enough to do in pushing through the decisions of the Council of Trent in the great archbishopric. He held synods in 1580 and again in 1582 which tightened up on clerical discipline, insisting that benefice-holders should reside in their benefices. He took particular concern to enhance clerical standards – notably by imposing severe penalties upon confessors who made advances to female penitents – and to improve public decency and respect for the Church and its liturgy. In 1581 he issued his Manual of the Sacraments, which regulated the administration of the sacraments throughout Spain; Philip was so impressed by it that he paid it the tribute of having it printed at the Escorial. Quiroga issued an Index in two parts; in 1583, a Prohibitory Index and in 1584 one with the expurgations necessary to legitimise books. This innovation enabled him to allow many important works to be published with their excisions – again, an action that undermined the whole tenor of Valdés's long period of office. Quiroga could, however, be reactionary in policy; from the time that he became archbishop of Toledo he was gravely anxious about the number of *moriscos* living in his primatial city and he determinedly led opinion at court into a hostile attitude towards them.[41] He was so successful that by the time he died it was evident that the *moriscos'* days in Spain were numbered.

THE VICTOR OF LEPANTO

If the conjuncture of the suspension of payments in September 1575 and the death of Requesens in March 1576 brought the Spanish position in the Low Countries to the point of collapse, the events of the years 1576–8 reduced it almost to disintegration. Philip acknowledged the gravity of his predicament by appointing no less a figure than his own half-brother to succeed Requesens. At one level, this seemed to be no more than a reversion to the traditional practice of having a member of the royal family as Governor-General, but such was Don John's reputation that the appointment was generally understood to represent a determination on Philip's part to renew the war effort in the Low Countries with the fullest commitment. In fact, Philip's intention was the exact opposite; his instructions to Don John commanded him to find a way of ending the war, if need be by making substantial concessions. Unfortunately, the legend of the invincible and charismatic soldier obscured all this; Philip sent Don John to make peace, but all Europe assumed that he was sending him to make war.[42] In fact, Don John was not given the resources to fight a war, for in the wake of the suspension of payments of 1575 these were not available. Not for the last time, Philip was praying for a miracle – hoping that Don John's reputation alone would itself be sufficient to transform his affairs in the Low Countries. Reputation was no longer enough. Don John prepared slowly for his mission, and when he reached the borders of his new territories he found that only Luxembourg and Friesland were not in revolt and so he decided to make Luxembourg his base. He arrived there on 3 November. It had been seven months since his appointment.

Those months had led to a further fragmentation of the political situation as the parties in the Low Countries raced against time to secure their positions so that they could deal with Don John from a position of strength. The Army of Flanders took the lead; it conquered the town of Zierikzee on 2 July but then mutinied to secure its pay, replicating what it had done in 1574 after victory at Mook and after defeat at Leiden. It then demonstrated its terrible power by pillaging the loyalist town of Aalst (25 July), standing poised now to move against Brussels and Ghent. In turn, the Council of State of the Netherlands (which exercised royal authority while waiting for Don John to arrive) declared that the mutineers were outlaws who could be killed on sight (27 July). What remained of Philip's government had declared that his army was the enemy of all the people of the Low Countries, Catholic as much as Protestant.

In September the situation reached meltdown. With the connivance of much of the Catholic aristocracy of the south, the States of Brabant arrested the loyalist members of the Council of State and then invited the fourteen states other than Holland and Zeeland to send deputies to a meeting of the States-General in Brussels. Initially, representatives only turned up from the provinces of Flanders and Hainault. The three states together then invited Holland and Zeeland to meet with them in Ghent as the States-General of the seventeen provinces. It was the beginning of the process that would lead to revolution; although the States-General continued to profess their loyalty to the king himself they insisted that the Spanish troops had to be withdrawn and that Philip should re-establish the traditional privileges of the provinces.

The troops of the Army of Flanders had no thought of departure, appreciating only too well that if they did not now hold out for their back-pay they would never receive it. About 3500 of them moved on Antwerp, and this time they did not draw back. They arrived at the city on 2 November and on the following day, by agreement with the inhabitants, entered the city. They then embarked upon a systematic and organised sack of the great city. In eleven days of efficient butchery they killed thousands of people. Contemporary accounts put the dead as high as

17 000 but modern scholars consider that about 7500 died – 2500 in the fighting in the city itself and 5000 as they attempted to flee beyond it. It was said that the rich were killed because they had money and that the poor died because they had none. Even Catholic churches and religious houses had to yield up their coin – not even the Jesuits were spared! – and the town hall and other important civic buildings were destroyed. The dreadful details were quickly circulated throughout Europe, and they lost nothing in the telling – 'they neither spared age nor sex . . . person nor country: young nor old: rich nor poor . . . they slaughtered great numbers of young children'.[43] Coming as it did so soon after the Massacre of St Bartholomew's Day, the 'Spanish Fury' at Antwerp bolstered Protestant Europe in its conviction that Spanish power was rampant throughout the continent, that it would slaughter and despoil without mercy wherever and whenever it could. In reality of course neither massacre was attributable to the Spanish Crown, but that was of no consequence in the increasingly fevered atmosphere of the later 1570s.

The 'Spanish Fury' also destroyed the last vestige of legitimacy for the regime and united virtually all Netherlanders – royalist or opponent, Catholic or Calvinist, plebeian or aristocratic – against the rampaging monster in their midst. It raised an unbreakable resolve among Netherlanders that the Spanish troops had now at any cost to be removed as the very prerequisite of any settlement. On 8 November, the States-General of the loyalist provinces signed 'The Pacification of Ghent' with the rebel provinces of Holland and Zeeland, insisting that the Spanish troops be withdrawn and that all of the ancient privileges of the provinces should be guaranteed. The Spaniards and their supporters were declared to be 'a public plague' and the signatories pledged themselves to work for the restoration of 'the old privileges, customs and freedoms'. William of Orange was named as Stadholder of Holland and Zeeland for Philip, thus preserving the fiction that he was still loyal to the king, although a waspish reference to the restoration of the situation that had existed under Charles V stood as an explicit rebuke to Philip. The operation of the Placards was suspended and it was decided that there would be no alterations yet in the religious status quo; in effect this recognised the legitimacy of Calvinism as the dominant religion in Holland and Zeeland. Further condemnation of Philip's government came in the commitment to destroy the monuments erected by the duke of Alba, including (although it was not expressly mentioned) the infamous statue in Antwerp.[44]

It was to deal with this horrendous situation that Don John, with utterly hapless timing, arrived in Luxembourg. Unfortunately, Don John was not primarily concerned with resolving the situation in the Low Countries; his chief intention was rather to use the Low Countries as a base from which he could conquer England and win a crown for himself. He intended to overthrow Elizabeth and – most hazardous of manly ambitions! – to marry Mary Stuart. In doing so he would unite the kingdoms of England and Scotland and bring them both back to the Catholic faith. That was an ambition as worthy of his vaulting ambition as it was devoid of any grasp on reality, and since he did not disguise his intention he served only to antagonise Elizabeth of England, who began to move toward a more active involvement in the Low Countries. Philip himself was well aware of Don John's intentions, but in his Instructions only circumscribed his freedom of action by requiring that he had to reconquer the Low Countries before indulging in the overthrow of Elizabeth. As he had done with Alba earlier in the decade, Philip was hoping that his Governor-General of the Low Countries would take decisive action against Elizabeth on his own authority and that he himself would not have to make the dreadful decision to overthrow the queen.[45]

Don John's new subjects were not prepared even to recognise his authority until he had sent his Spanish troops away, and so for some months he had to remain in Luxembourg, virtually exiled from the lands over which he was nominally the ruler. He hit upon the ingenious solution of removing the troops by sea in the hope that they could surreptitiously land on English soil; in abandoning the Low Countries, they would gain the kingdom of England for him. However, the States-General, advised no doubt by Elizabeth, insisted that the troops leave by land and refused to allow them to embark by sea. In one swoop, therefore, Don John found all his ambitions frustrated and so on 12 February 1577 he issued 'The Perpetual Edict', agreeing that the Spanish troops would leave within a few weeks and accepting the terms laid down in the Pacification of Ghent. It took some time to organise the payment of the troops and their departure, but in April 1577 they marched south out of the Low Countries. Ashamed and embarrassed by their departure, Don John could not bring himself even to review them at their march past.[46] But at least he gained entry into his capital city; on 6 May he took the oath as Governor-General of the Low Countries in Brussels. It had been thirteen months since his appointment.

A Governor-General without his elite troops, Don John was a ruler without power and he sank into despairing inactivity. The legendary victor of Lepanto became increasingly spiteful and depressed. He had negotiations opened with Orange but won no concessions, and in the summer sent his secretary Juan de Escobedo back to Madrid to impress upon Philip just how serious the situation was. There can be little doubt that Escobedo's real mission was to urge Philip to send the Spanish troops back to the Low Countries and to justify to him the perilous course upon which Don John now embarked.

In the event, Don John did not even wait for Escobedo to reach court before indulging himself in the most irresponsible act of his career; on 24 July he seized the fortress of Namur. The element of surprise allowed him this success but his actions put his opponents on their guard; when a week later he tried to take Antwerp, his effort was contemptuously rebuffed. Don John's treachery at Namur also brought opprobium directly and unavoidably on to the Crown itself; since it was Philip's own brother who had behaved so treacherously it was no longer necessary for the king's opponents to upbraid his 'evil ministers' while maintaining loyalty to the king himself. Philip Marnix de Aldegonde, lord of St Aldegonde, published on behalf of the States-General a pamphlet in which he wrote, almost jubilantly, that 'it is common knowledge that Don John intends, as he has always done, to set the country ablaze with war'.[47] Moreover, war fought by impulsive and ineffectual gestures served only to unite the opposition; the cities of Antwerp and Brussels gave tumultuous welcomes to William of Orange (18 and 23 September) and the States-General, far from submitting to Don John, opened negotiations to bring in another member of the House of Habsburg as governor; in December 1577, the archduke Matthias accepted the sovereignty of the Low Countries. Matthias was only twenty years of age and was a willing tool of the States-General, who declared him to be 'lieutenant of the king and governor of these countries'.[48] The States-General were in all but name now acting as an independent body and they had a member of the royal family to validate their actions for them.

For Philip, Matthias's betrayal was a traumatic event. Until Matthias accepted the leadership offered by the States-General, Philip had been prepared to settle with his rebellious subjects: 'the King desires peace with Flanders at any price', it had been reported in October 1577.[49] But if anything in his life ever made Philip more angry than Matthias's disloyalty it is not recorded. When he first heard the news it was reported that he was 'in very dejected condition, and most averse to transacting business with any one' and that his wife and children shared his despair. When the report was corroborated Philip flew into 'a most violent passion'.[50] He promptly reversed policy and prepared for war; he decided to send the Spanish troops back to the Low Countries and entrusted their command to his nephew, Alexander Farnese. The appointment of a member of the royal family gave the lie to Matthias's presumption and emphasised Philip's absolute determination to re-establish his authority and reputation in the Low Countries.

For all that, the king had to justify his actions, if only to himself, and a revealing insight into his attitude to the Low Countries at this critical juncture is provided by the Instructions that he gave in January 1578 to his new ambassador in England, Don Bernardino de Mendoza. Philip stressed that he was a 'benign prince' who did not wish to go to war with his own subjects but who was driven to do so by their recognition of Matthias as their sovereign. He sent his Spanish troops back to the Low Countries, therefore, to maintain the two poles of 'the Roman Catholic religion and my authority'. Philip insisted that he had behaved very moderately in the Low Countries and that he had 'never desired to gain any advantage or fresh power there, other than what was enjoyed by my father the Emperor'. Far from seeking to circumscribe the privileges of his subjects he had wished to extend them and to increase their wealth and prosperity. He was genuinely puzzled by the hostility to him and ascribed it to the malevolence of a few accomplished rabble-rousers: 'it has been solely in consequence of the straying of evil-minded people in the States from the straight path, that the idea had been spread that my wish was to oppress them and treat them differently from the way in which they were treated by the Emperor, and that this has been a wicked invention spread by bad people, who try thereby to mislead others.'[51]

As Philip went back to war in the Low Countries he continued to try to avoid antagonising Elizabeth of England. In June 1577 he instructed Mendoza to 'continue to deal gently and amiably with the Queen and her ministers, this being the desirable course at present'.[52] But Philip's protestations were lost on Elizabeth; on 13 December Francis Drake led a small expedition of four ships and 164 men out of Plymouth. It was given out that Drake was headed for the Mediterranean but no one (least of all the Spanish ambassador) was deceived. Drake headed across the Atlantic, but not to raid the Caribbean; at the end of August he entered the Straits of Magellan. After a fortnight's passage he sailed into the Pacific Ocean. He was welcomed by a ferocious storm that tossed him around for a month and cost him the last of the three ships that had left Plymouth with him. Sailing now in the *Golden Hind* (as the

Pelican had been renamed) he then headed north for the coast of Peru.[53]
With only his flagship and less than half the men who had sailed out of
Plymouth with him, Drake would now shatter Spain's defences in the
Pacific.

As Drake sailed into the South Atlantic, Alexander Farnese led 3000
Spanish troops to the Low Countries. It is not clear whether Philip had
much confidence in Farnese; what was of paramount importance to him
was that the troops should be led by a member of his own family.
Farnese's troops were certainly well provided for; in December 1577 a
record shipment of silver arrived at Seville.[54] On 31 January, Farnese
routed the forces of the States at the battle of Gembloux, close to Namur.
Matthias and Orange fled from Brussels. But Don John did not have the
forces to follow up the success; his first victory in the Low Countries was
to be his last. Had he been more interested in the Low Countries, Don
John might have appreciated that there was more to be gained by dividing his opponents than by attempting to conquer them. When Calvinists
seized control of a number of southern cities, notably Brussels and
Ghent, Farnese noticed that their extremism was alienating many
Catholics and moderates, and that in the south as well as in the north
many were now fearing not only for the future of their religion but for
their lives and for their property.

Worse still for Don John was the situation in Madrid, where his position was undermined by the stridency with which Escobedo demanded
of Philip that he send Don John the troops and money that would enable
him to fight the Dutch properly – that, in effect, Philip reverse his policy
in the Low Countries to accommodate Don John's ambitions. Escobedo's
demands were hardly less offensive to Philip than the manner in which
he pressed them and, coming as they did at the moment that one royal
relative had publicly betrayed Philip, they doubtless allowed Pérez to
insinuate to the king that Don John was no better than Matthias and that
neither he nor Escobedo could be trusted.

In the wake of Matthias's treachery, it was but a small step for Pérez
then to convince Philip that both Don John and Escobedo were engaged
in treasonable discussions with the Dutch rebels. Pérez had a number of
reasons for turning Philip against Escobedo and at the heart of most of
them was his fear that Escobedo had found out too much about his own
activities, for in all probability it was Pérez himself who had been engaged
in secret (and treasonable) contacts with the rebels and Escobedo who
had discovered the truth. At all events, with that nerveless brilliance
that lay at the core of his personality, Pérez now persuaded Philip to

authorise Escobedo's assassination. The support of the marquis of Los Vélez in urging Philip to agree to the killing seems to have been crucial. Three attempts were made to poison Escobedo without success and so around midnight on 31 March 1578 he was stabbed to death in a Madrid street.[55] What seemed to be a murder by a gang of six desperadoes was in fact an execution authorised by the king himself.

As Philip's government collapsed into treachery and murder, the time came for him to move towards the greatest triumph of his career, the conquest of Portugal. Philip's nephew, Sebastián, had assumed control of government on reaching his fourteenth birthday in January 1568. He showed almost immediately how utterly unsuited he was for the task. Deeply religious, psychologically unstable, politically devoid of commonsense, Sebastián set himself to make good recent Portuguese losses in Africa and dedicated his reign as a crusade. He made little secret that it was the grand ambition of his life to reconquer the Holy Land for Christianity. As early as August 1574 he announced his intention of leading a campaign in Morocco. Nothing came of it but Sebastián was undeterred. Philip prudently kept his distance; he delicately side-stepped the proposal that Sebastián should marry Isabel Clara Eugenia and in December 1576 he met with Sebastián for ten days at Guadalope in an effort to dissuade him from his crusade in Africa. Once again, Philip avoided making commitments to his nephew and Sebastián returned to Lisbon disgusted with Philip's caution and determined to undertake his great enterprise. In June 1578 he embarked for Morocco with an army of 17000 men. He had no strategy other than to confront the Emperor of Morocco in battle and win military glory for himself, and he led his men to total defeat. On 3 August at Alcázarquivir, Sebastián was killed in combat and his army was destroyed; half of his men died in battle and virtually all the rest were taken into captivity, including most of Portugal's leading nobles. Only a hundred or so men escaped the rout and made it back to Portugal.

Sebastián's madcap adventure brought his country to its knees. The throne passed to his epileptic uncle, Cardinal Henry. The King-Cardinal declared his intention of seeking a papal absolution from his vow of chastity so that he could marry and secure the succession (31 January 1579) but he knew that he had no real prospect of success in Rome. Philip publicly supported him but had his ambassador to the Vatican work determinedly to ensure that the pope gave no such licence. Philip himself naturally had by far the strongest claim to succeed to the throne. His chief rivals for the succession were two members of the

Portuguese royal family – Catarina, duchess of Braganza and Antonio, prior of Crato. Both were of royal blood but were handicapped respectively by sex and illegitimacy. Other rivals – Alberto Ranucio di Parma, Emmanuel Philibert of Savoy and Catherine de' Medici of France – had no real possibility of gathering support. Philip himself had the advantage of proximity and of an iron resolve to gain the throne. He prepared the ground by sending as his envoys to Portugal two of his most trusted advisers – Pedro Téllez Girón, first duke of Osuna, and Christovão de Moura, a Portuguese courtier who had come to Spain with Juana in 1554 and who held the position of secretary of the Council of State.[56] Able men, Osuna and Moura set themselves to undermine Henry and to suborn what remained of the Portuguese ruling elite. In June 1579 they were joined by two Spanish lawyers sent to argue the legitimacy of Philip's claim.

As Philip reflected upon the momentous deaths of Escobedo and King Sebastián, opinion in the Council of State in Madrid was turning decisively against a continuation of the war in the Low Countries. In June and July 1578 the Council held a number of discussions to review the progress of the war and with the inevitable exception of Alba the councillors argued individually and jointly that a settlement had to be reached. Two men were especially persuasive: Quiroga confessed himself bemused by the complexity of the situation but, anxious about the burden on the Castilian taxpayer, he cited the Gospel to give Philip the example of the king who quite legitimately asked his enemy for peace because he recognised that he did not have the means with which to make war upon him. The duke of Sessa advised Philip that 'he holds the war to be very doubtful and full of difficulties, especially when considering how much has been spent there and will have to be spent in future'. The marquises of Los Vélez, Aguilar and Almazán also urged the king to seek a settlement. Of these councillors, Quiroga, Sessa and Los Vélez were close supporters of Antonio Pérez; the Ebolista policy of settling with the rebels was gathering strength. Alba stood alone in arguing that the war had to be pursued aggressively in order to be successful.[57] It may well have been the last straw for Philip; in January 1578 Alba was sent into internal exile in the fortress of Uceda, forty kilometres north of Madrid on the grounds that he had allowed his son Fadrique to marry Dona María de Toledo when he was already engaged to Doña Magdalena de Guzmán, a lady of the Queen's bedchamber.[58] With Alba removed from court, a settlement was clearly possible in the Low Countries: Antonio Pérez stood on the brink of triumph.

This was the more true because Don John himself contracted typhus and died on 1 October 1578, only thirty-three years of age. But for Philip, there was to be no escape from the murder of Escobedo: once he had digested the implications of Escobedo's death – and once he had studied Don John's papers after they were brought back from the Low Countries – he began to slowly absorb the awful knowledge that he had ordered the murder of an innocent man and – perhaps even worse – that his treacherous and brilliant secretary could prove that he had done so. Philip's reputation lay now in Pérez's safekeeping, and he knew how much reliance to place upon Pérez's integrity. After Escobedo's death, Pérez's own days in power were numbered. The question that tormented Philip was how to rid himself of Pérez while keeping him quiet and, much more importantly, how to get hold of the thirty cases of state papers that Pérez had in his possession, which told of secrets that Philip could not even contemplate having made into public knowledge. The papers held by Pérez were even more important than the Secretary himself, for what they told of terrified the king.

THE KING'S NEPHEW: ALEXANDER FARNESE AND THE BEGINNING OF RECOVERY IN THE LOW COUNTRIES

On his death-bed, Don John named Alexander Farnese as his successor, and so for the first time since 1559 there was no hiatus before the appointment of a new Governor-General in the Low Countries. Farnese's authority was only temporary while Philip decided who would succeed Don John but at least there was a Governor-General *in situ*. As time would soon tell there was a governor in office, for the first time in the reign, who was an accomplished soldier as well as an intuitive politician. Although he was only thirty-four years of age, Farnese had the gravity of manner to impress his new subjects and he had, too, the financial resources of an enormously rich man with which to impress his soldiers. Characteristically, Philip had no intention of keeping Farnese in his new position a moment longer than was necessary and so he persuaded Margaret of Parma, Farnese's mother, to return to the post that she had left with such relief in 1567. However, Alexander refused to serve under Margaret, and after she had laboriously crossed the Alps the old duchess had to turn home once again, her career finally at an end.[59] The young dandy had ruthless ambition in him.

He had, too, calculating judgement. An army serving the States under John Casimir was poised to confront Parma; the new governor disentangled himself from the need to fight it by the simple device of paying it off. Abortive peace negotiations were held at Cologne in May 1578 under imperial auspices, but Farnese's first campaign as governor made them irrelevant; on 29 June 1579 he captured Maastricht.

Politics went hand in glove with soldiering. Farnese appreciated that the enemies of Spain were held together in a fragile accord and he set himself to separate the Catholic south from the Calvinist north. On 6 January 1579 the states of Artois, Hainault and Douai formed the Union of Arras and undertook to negotiate a return to their loyalty to Philip. Farnese agreed that their provincial liberties would be guaranteed and that no Spanish troops would be billeted upon them. It was sufficient; on 17 May the southern provinces were restored to their loyalty to Spain. The north responded in kind; on 29 January 1579 the Union of Utrecht was signed between the states of Holland and Zeeland and Friesland, Utrecht, Gelderland and the Ommelanden of Groningen. The states pledged themselves to continue the fight, declaring that 'the Spaniards as well as Don John of Austria and more of their leaders and captains have sought and are still seeking by all means in their power to bring these provinces wholly or partly into subjection under their tyrannical government and into slavery'.[60] This was a Protestant, rebellious league and in the treaty the term 'The United Provinces' was used for the first time. The Netherlands had divided. On 15 June 1580 Philip put a price on William of Orange's head.[61]

Philip had taken his decision after consultation with Orange's old enemy, Cardinal Granvelle. The king had summoned Granvelle back in March 1579: 'I have absolute need of your person and your assistance: come to Spain as soon as possible.' Granvelle had waited twenty years for this moment and he arrived at the Escorial on 28 July; Philip greeted him with undisguised joy. He also took another action that he had long pondered; at midnight, Antonio Pérez and the Princess of Eboli were arrested.[62]

Granvelle was appointed president of the Council of Italy and given control of the major affairs of government.[63] He enthusiastically encouraged Philip in his determination to conquer Portugal and to pursue a forward policy in the Low Countries and he brought a driving commitment to his task, working with an energy and a determination that gratified the king. However, his term of real authority was counted in months rather than years, for when Philip left Madrid in March 1580 to claim the throne of Portugal, Granvelle stayed behind in Madrid and, denied proximity to the king, his influence rapidly waned. For all that, Granvelle left his mark on history, for while Philip was in Lisbon he persuaded him to accept the new calendar issued by the Pope Gregory XIII – the 'Gregorian Calendar' – which advanced time by ten days. Much of Protestant Europe refused to recognise the papal innovation and so from October 1582 the calendars of Catholic and Protestant Europe marched ten days adrift of each other as a poignant symbol of the religious division of the continent.[64]

While Granvelle's return to power was of relatively brief duration, in his shadow there began one of the great administrative careers of Habsburg Spain, for Granvelle brought with him from Italy Juan de Idiáquez, the son of an old colleague. Idiáquez was appointed Secretary of the Council of State in succession to Pérez. An unassuming but deeply diligent and quietly ambitious man, Idiáquez took some years to acquire the full confidence of the king, but when he did so he became one of the dominant figures in his administration during the last two decades of the reign. He then survived to serve Philip III until within a few months of his death in 1614.[65] Idiáquez's career was unique; no servant of the Habsburg state served the Crown for longer at as high a level as he.

In 1579, as the two alliances in the Low Countries began to reshape their war, the conflict between Spain and England reached around the globe as Francis Drake launched his first attack on Spain's Pacific possessions. On 5 December 1578 he began to pillage Valparaiso; in an act of provocative sacrilege he had the Church stripped of its silver. Returning to sea, he then seized a ship in Calloa (the port for Lima) and in March took the greatest prize of his career, a great galleon, the *Nuestra Señora de la Concepción*. It carried 263 272 ducats of gold and silver, of which 77 000 belonged to the Crown. Drake then sailed up to California and set out across the Pacific. He arrived in Plymouth on 26 September 1580, anxious only to verify that Elizabeth was still alive before unloading his precious cargo. His voyage had been a stunning financial success – its backers enjoyed a return on their investment of some 4700 per cent. Elizabeth had Drake knighted at Deptford in April 1581. The queen was committed now to an anti-Spanish policy and she no longer cared to pretend otherwise.[66] For his part, Philip as always learned from Francis Drake. In 1580 he established the *Armada del Mar del Sur* to patrol the Pacific coast of Peru to ensure that the treasure ships carrying the silver of Potosí from Callao to Panamá were properly protected; two large galleons and up to four smaller ships were used to patrol the coast. Drake's brilliant escapade was not to be repeated.[67]

By the time that Drake was knighted, another major change in Spain's international position had come about, for King-Cardinal Henry died on 31 January 1580. With him died the house of Avis and the independence of Portugal. Philip now moved to acquire Portugal for himself, and in doing so he transformed the politics of western Europe. The European world was turning to the Atlantic, the fount of Spain's new wealth and the battleground over which her new power would be fought. For Philip of Spain the Atlantic war would now take priority over the war in the Low Countries.

PART III
The Imprudent King

7

The Conquests of Portugal and the Azores and the Assault upon England

THE CONQUESTS OF PORTUGAL AND THE AZORES, 1580–3

By the autumn of 1579 Philip had spent twenty years in Spain as king – more than his father had done in the whole of his reign – and he had emphatically re-established the power of the monarchy. Certainly, the future of the dynasty seemed secure enough; Anna had presented Philip with three boys to add to his two daughters by Elizabeth and at thirty was still young enough to provide him with more children. Fernando, the eldest of Anna's boys, died on 8 October 1578; his death was a deep personal loss, for Philip probably loved him more than any of his sons. However, he still had two sons (Diego Felix and Felipe) and Anna gave birth to a daughter on 14 February 1580; she was christened María. With five children now alive, Philip could be confident that the succession was assured. He could be confident, too, that he had provided his monarchy with a functional capital city in Madrid, and since the construction of the Escorial was rapidly nearing completion he had the courtly complex that was so fundamental to his kingship. The dynasty had a stage that was worthy of it. Politically, Philip could be reasonably confident that neither France nor Turkey would drag him into major wars in the immediate future. He had resolved the threat to national security created by the *moriscos* of Granada. He had reasserted the authority of the Crown over the American colonies and was about to receive his reward; in the years 1581–90 nearly twice as much silver was registered at Seville than in the previous decade (see Table 4.1). This silver would, in conjunction with Castilian taxes, make it possible for Philip to expand his political ambitions almost beyond measure during the next two decades. He was about to reach the very pinnacle of his kingly stature and prestige by adding Portugal and its empire to his monarchy.

The acquisition of Portugal had profound political and indeed psychological importance for Philip and it led him to bring about a dramatic rescheduling of his priorities in foreign affairs. In the crucial years 1580–3 the conquests of Portugal and of its Atlantic islands of the Azores took precedence for Philip over affairs in northern Europe. It was perceptively remarked of him that he would 'rather surrender Flanders than this country [sc. Portugal]', and so it proved.[1] Philip was now the master of two global empires and there seemed to be no limits to his power. To both his friends and his enemies that power seemed to be unchallengeable. More importantly, it seemed to be so to Philip himself; from 1583 he undertook one gamble in foreign affairs after another, each greater and more risky than the last. The second half of his reign saw the once-prudent king gambling and failing – and doing both on the grandest of scales. But it also saw him becoming increasingly weakened physically, for in 1580, as he waited to enter his new kingdom, fever brought Philip perilously close to death and he never again enjoyed robust health. As he passed what proved to be the mid-point of his reign, Philip left behind him the last vestiges of his fabled prudence as well as his physical vigour; the gambles of the 1580s and 1590s were those of a man in physical decline, ever more conscious of his own mortality, increasingly aware of the need to resolve his problems before he died.

Philip prepared the ground methodically for the acquisition of Portugal.[2] He supplemented the work being done by Osuna and Moura in Portugal by writing to all secular and ecclesiastical authorities in the kingdom insisting on the legitimacy of his succession to the throne – that he had been called by God to be king of Portugal and that he accordingly now intended to take possession of his new realm peacefully and without loss of blood. He added the ominous rider that anyone who opposed him would be regarded as a rebel and subject to the appropriate penalties. King-Cardinal Henry, as one of his last acts, had five regents appointed to take charge of the realm after his death and Philip now subjected these men to intense pressure to declare for him.

Recognising that he would have to press his case by force of arms, Philip ordered all Spanish nobles who held land adjacent to Portugal to raise men and to seal off the frontier so that no one could enter or leave the country without permission: the counts of Lemos and Monterrey thus secured the frontier in Galicia; the duke of Alburquerque, the counts of Alva de Liste and Benavente, and the marquis of Villanueva del Rio did likewise in Extremadura and the dukes of Béjar and Medina Sidonia in Andalusia. Among other senior aristocrats who raised their own troops with the intention of leading them in person were the duke of Infantado and the marquises of Ayamonte and Mondéjar. In making use of the services and resources of his aristocracy on a grand scale Philip incurred obligations which he had to repay over succeeding years; with their involvement in the conquest of Portugal, Philip's aristocracy began to edge themselves back towards the heart of power. The great families of Spanish Italy also contributed; leading members of the Doria, Colonna and Medici family came to serve in person, anxious that they, too, would earn royal rewards by their loyalty. With the very greatest reluctance, Philip summoned Alba himself back from internal exile and gave him command of the army of invasion of some 23 000 men, aware that Alba's name alone would terrify many Portuguese into accepting Spanish rule. Philip placed the marquis of Santa Cruz in command of the naval arm. The fleet, which consisted of ninety-nine galleys, thirty royal ships and sixty supply and support ships and about 9000 men, has been described by Ricardo Cerezo as 'the last great galley fleet in the history of Spain'. It needed to be so large because it had to serve a number of functions: to combine with the army and disembark the infantry; to pre-empt a national rising in support of Dom Antonio; to prevent foreign help arriving by sea, and to protect the coast after the landings.[3] In all, there-fore, Philip prepared a force of about 32000 men for the conquest of Portugal. He himself left Madrid on 3 March 1580 for the Portuguese border. He made Badajoz his temporary capital so that he could super-vise the invasion; Badajoz was on the border, 130 kilometres from Lisbon. In May, Philip met two of the regents at Guadalope and gave them a month in which to declare for him, and on 6 June he wrote formally to all five regents insisting that they declare him to be the lawful monarch. To concentrate their minds he held a review of his army (13 June). No reply was forthcoming and four days later Philip sent a small force across the border. Elvas became the first town to fall, on 18 June. The conquest of Portugal had begun. By way of riposte, Portuguese loyalists crowned Dom Antonio as king at Santarém (19 June). Philip denounced Antonio as a traitor. On 30 June, Alba took the main body of his army across the frontier.

The Portuguese could offer little effective resistance; their military and aristocratic leaders had for the most part been slain or imprisoned after the disaster at Alcázarquivir and an untimely and severe outbreak of plague now afflicted the capital city, making it even more difficult for the populace to resist. As Alba reduced one fortress after another on the road to Lisbon, Santa Cruz sailed from Puerto de Santa María to join him at Setúbal. The two commanders then led an amphibious assault, landing at Cascais at the end of July and marching along the north bank of the Tagus to Lisbon.

Antonio led an army of 10000 men but it was no match for Alba when on 25 August the duke reached the outskirts of Lisbon. Battle was brief: 3000 of Antonio's men died in a couple of hours; it was said that 'the dead lay heap on heap like swine'. Determined not to sully the king's triumph by having Lisbon pillaged, Alba forbade his army to enter the capital but by way of compensation he allowed his men to plunder the suburbs, which they did with dreadful effect.[4] The battle for Lisbon, if it could be called that, was over. Dom Antonio fled to northern Portugal, where he spent seven months trying to rally support and evade capture. Few of his countrymen joined him, and in May 1581 he sailed for exile in France.

The conquest of Portugal was the high-point of Philip's reign and he exulted in it. With the conquest of Portugal (and of its empire, which tamely submitted in subsequent months) Philip acquired not just the prestige that went with adding a proud kingdom to his monarchy but also reinforced his own naval strength. Ten prime galleons belonging to the Crown of Portugal added substantially to Philip's navy while the acquisition of Lisbon provided him not only with a cosmopolitan and sophisticated city but with a large and impregnable harbour that was an ideal and historic watch-tower over the Atlantic coast.

It was fitting that as Philip acquired his new country the wealth cascading across the Atlantic should have begun to reach quite fabulous proportions; in September 1580, 14557125 ducats of silver were registered at Seville and a year later a further 9273208 were recorded.[5] But still it was not enough for Philip's needs; by April 1582 he had spent two and a half million ducats maintaining the army and navy that had conquered Portugal for him.[6] In Lisbon in 1582 Philip had to agree new *asientos* with his bankers to finance his ambitions.[7] It was a portent of what would happen with increasing frequency in the next two decades: a new scale of wealth, new opportunities, new commitments, a new scale of debts.

Philip and his court remained in Badajoz while Lisbon was secured, but the city did not have the facilities to house the court adequately and in the autumn of 1580 the royal households were infected by disease, which in all probability was typhus. Philip himself was struck down and for a fortnight was at the very point of death, his doctors despairing for his life. He survived but his wife did not; Anna died on 26 October.[8] For the fourth time, Philip was widowed; he was fifty-three years of age. He had now six children – three of each sex – and he evidently felt that the succession was secured for he never remarried. His tortured marital odyssey was at an end.

Philip led his court into Portugal early in December 1580. Even then he had to wait for the plague to die out in Lisbon and for the south of the country to be properly secured. He therefore moved no further than Elvas, where he was welcomed by senior Portuguese churchmen and dignitaries. Not until 16 March did he make his solemn entry into Tomar, eighty kilometres north-east of Lisbon, where the Cortes of Portugal were held. Over the next weeks he conferred titles and dignities upon the leading men of the kingdom to bind them to his service. Chief among those whom Philip honoured was the most powerful nobleman of the kingdom, Theodor, duke of Braganza; he appointed him constable of Portugal and invested him with the *toison* of the Order of the Golden Fleece in tacit recognition both of Braganza's decision not to press his own claim to the throne and of his own need for his support. Philip raised Don Francisco de Saá to the countship of Matusinos and Don Hernando de Noroña to that of Linares. He named Don Francisco Mascareñas as viceroy of India. He also granted a wide range of military habits, rents and offices to leading Portuguese.

Having displayed his regal generosity, on 16 April at Tomar, Philip received the fealty of the leading men of Church and State, led once again by Braganza. On the following day the dignitaries of the realm took the oath of loyalty to Diego Felix as heir. The Cortes formally recognised Philip as king of Portugal and he promised to maintain the privileges of the kingdom and not to hold cortes outside the kingdom. He guaranteed that Portugal would retain its own laws, government and coinage and issued a partial pardon for those who had rebelled against him, pointedly excluding Antonio himself and some fifty other named men. Philip recognised that he would not be able to live permanently in his new kingdom and went on to make a series of key promises – most notably that only native-born Portuguese would be appointed to the viceroyalty and to senior positions at home and in the colonies; and that Portugal's interests would be represented in Madrid by a Council of Portugal. Although Philip had conquered Portugal the settlement that he imposed was a moderate one, adhering to the principles adumbrated by the Eboli-Pérez grouping of ministers. Portugal was subsumed into

Philip's composite monarchy with guarantees for its continuing national integrity. However, Philip matched an *ebolista* gesture with one worthy of Alba himself when he placed a price of 80 000 ducats on the head of Dom Antonio.[9]

The Cortes concluded on 27 May, and two days later Philip made his formal entrance into Lisbon. It was in all probability the most joyous entry of his reign. He felt thoroughly at ease in his new capital – perhaps because it was the city in which his mother had been born? – and he explored the city, visiting its churches, religious houses, palaces and dockyards. His joy was deepened by an emotional reunion with his sister María, who had returned from Germany, a widow since the death of Maximilian in 1576. It had been twenty-four years since Philip and María had met. It is probable that Philip tried to persuade María to accept the viceroyalty of Portugal and that she refused to do so. María had in reality come to Lisbon to bid farewell to secular life, and she now returned to Madrid to see out her days living the life of a nun in the Descalzas Reales, dying there in 1603.[10] Philip found consolation in his correspondence with his daughters in Madrid, writing of how much he loved and missed them and of how he was pining to return home to them and to see once again his great monastery and its gardens, reporting to them on what he had seen in Portugal. His letters to Isabella and Catalina – which he signed as 'your good father' – are the most sensitive and human of all his correspondence.[11]

Philip never forgot that his hold on Portugal was precarious and that many of his new subjects deeply resented their subjugation to Castile. He was the more conscious of this because seven of the nine Portuguese islands of the Azores did not accept his claim to the throne. The islands occupied a strategic position in the Atlantic, astride the routes along which the Spanish fleets returned to Seville with their American silver and the Portuguese ships came to Lisbon with their precious goods from Asia and Africa. Although none of the islands were large, they extended some 640 kilometres in length and so covered a large area; they were therefore vulnerable to attack, not easily defended. Only the islands of São Miguel and Santa María immediately acknowledged Philip's sovereignty. The prospect of having the Azores fall into enemy hands and being used as a staging post from which his enemies could waylay the returning fleets was deeply worrying to Philip. Accordingly, in 1581 he despatched a fleet of six ships under Don Pedro de Valdés, General of the Squadron of Galicia, to prevent Antonio from landing a fleet in the Azores. Although Valdés only had 600 soldiers he decided to seek personal glory by conquering the islands himself. On 25 July he landed 350 men on Terceira. The defenders fled at the sight of Valdés's men, but then regrouped in the most extraordinary – and unmilitary – way; coming across a herd of bulls, they drove them at the Spaniards, whose lines broke. A massacre of Valdés's men then followed; only thirty or so escaped. On returning to Lisbon, Valdés was arrested on a charge of dereliction of duty.[12]

Valdés's failure left Philip exposed to ridicule and the Azores vulnerable to further assault. In February 1582 Philip heard that Filippo Strozzi, an Italian soldier of fortune who was related to Catherine de' Medici, was raising men in France to help Dom Antonio to secure the islands. He organised a major fleet to deal with the threat. Naturally, he gave the command to the marquis of Santa Cruz, and when the fleet joined up – half of it sailing out of Lisbon and half from Cadiz – it consisted of sixty-one ships and twenty-one galleys, totalling 24560 *toneladas*. Battle was joined off the island of São Miguel on 26 July but it was an uneven and brief affair; Santa Cruz destroyed the enemy fleet, capturing the *almiranta* and *capitana* and killing over 1200 of the enemy while himself losing only 224 men. Strozzi himself was among the dead in the *capitana*. Five hundred men were captured, among them about one hundred Frenchmen of rank. Santa Cruz exploited his victory ruthlessly. Claiming that the men who had fought against him were pirates or disturbers of the peace he executed seventy-seven gentlemen together with all ordinary soldiers and sailors who were over the age of seventeen. Philip approved (as he had the massacre at Matanzas) and went immediately to church to give thanks. He ordered that processions, fireworks and celebrations be held to mark the victory.[13]

Once again, triumph was followed by tragedy; on 21 November 1582, Diego Felix died in Madrid, a victim of smallpox at the age of seven. His death made it imperative that Philip return to Castile, and so on 30 January 1583 he had the Portuguese ruling elite take the oath to his last son and namesake, who was now nearly five years of age. Excusing himself for what he promised would be a short absence, Philip crossed the frontier into Spain on 11 February 1583. He left behind him as viceroy his nephew, Cardinal-Archduke Albert, with Don Carlos Galcerán de Borja, duke of Gandia, as Captain-General of a force that looked suspiciously like an army of occupation. As if to drive home the point that Portugal was subservient to Spain, Philip took the members of the new Council of Portugal with him to Madrid.[14] He never returned to Portugal.

Important though Santa Cruz's victory over Strozzi was, it still left the Azores in enemy hands, and so on 23 June 1583 the marquis sailed once again from Lisbon, this time to conquer the islands. He led a fleet of 98 ships totalling 22 749 *toneladas* and 15 372 soldiers, sailors and oarsmen. In a brilliant amphibious operation the galleys ferried the soldiers ashore and the French were routed. Once again, Santa Cruz executed his opponents; more than sixty Portuguese were hanged, and some of the bodies were then quartered. The Azores were secure – and the Spanish navy benefited from the accretion of some thirty-five ships. Philip regarded the conquest of the islands as a triumph fit to rival even those at Malta and Lepanto and so he proudly commemorated it on the walls of the Escorial. It was a particularly happy circumstance, therefore, that Santa Cruz's success was rounded out by the news that the Indies fleet would shortly bring eleven million ducats of Peruvian treasure and three million ducats' worth of other goods to Spain.[15]

Philip understood immediately that the defence of his new territories required the construction of a new type of navy. In 1580 he had used ninety-nine galleys in the conquest of Portugal, while in the Azores campaigns of 1582 and 1583 he had needed only twenty-one and fourteen respectively. The age of the galley was coming to a precipitate end. Philip needed galleons for the new warfare that would mark the 1580s. In 1576 he had established a fleet to protect the Indies run (the *Armada de la Guarda de la Carrera de las Indias*), and as soon as the conquest of Portugal was completed he convened a junta under the presidency of Santa Cruz to meet in Lisbon to assess how best to protect the Indies routes and the Azores themselves. The junta recommended that Philip should strengthen the *Armada de la Guarda* so that it could escort the silver fleets from the Azores to Cadiz. Philip agreed and authorised a new galleon-building programme. Nine new galleons were built in Santander in the years 1582–4 and the construction of some 15 000 tons of shipping was begun in Vizcaya. In 1584 the Indies galleons were completed.[16] With his new galleons added to his Portuguese ships and to those he had taken in the Azores, Philip now had the beginnings of an effective royal navy for the Atlantic and for the protection of the silver fleets on the final, precarious, leg of their journey home.

Philip's triumphs in Portugal and the Azores led him inexorably towards a more aggressive foreign policy. As he surveyed the Atlantic from his new kingdom Philip breathed in a dizzying air of self-confidence, believing that everything was possible, feeling that he could deal now with even the most intractable of his enemies. As early as March

1581 he had written ebulliently to his ambassador in England, setting a newly belligerent tone in his relations with Elizabeth. Mendoza was to

> represent to the Queen and her Ministers the dangers they incur by irritating me and causing me to look to my own affairs by troubling theirs; whereas if they do not provoke me further, they need have nothing to fear from my forces . . . You will intimate to them all I say here, so that fear of my forces may somewhat bridle them from further offending me; whilst at the same time they may not get desperate and lose hope of being forgiven for their past misdeeds, and thus be driven into new and pernicious leagues to the prejudice of Christianity and the public peace, and perhaps into plotting new evil in Flanders.[17]

Philip rewarded Santa Cruz for his successes in Portugal and the Azores by appointing him to two offices – as *capitán general del mar océano* and *capitán general de la gente de guerra de Portugal* – and by raising him to the grandeeship. When the marquis swore the oaths to his two offices he became formally responsible for the Atlantic fleet and for the defence of the Atlantic coast of Spain, Portugal and of the Azores. There was therefore very studied symbolism in Philip's decision to endow Santa Cruz with the *encomienda* that by tradition went to the king's most trusted adviser, that of Comendador Mayor de León in the Order of Santiago. The marquis stood pre-eminent now among all Philip's ministers.[18] When Santa Cruz sought to consolidate his new eminence by proposing in August 1583 that an armada be sent against Elizabeth of England Philip was especially receptive. However, he and Santa Cruz drew quite erroneous conclusions from the campaigns of 1580–3 and looked to attack England in an expanded version of the Azores campaign of 1583. Such an attack would involve the despatch of an enormous force from Iberian ports to make an amphibious landing in England. Philip ordered the duke of Parma to submit a plan for the invasion of England from the Low Countries.[19] Parma was much more sanguine than either Philip or Santa Cruz; it is likely that he never fully believed in the possibility of invading England from the Low Countries. No further detailed planning took place, but Philip began now to slowly mull over the possibility of committing himself to 'the Enterprise of England'.

The Prince of Orange understood only too well the implications of Philip's new power. After the débâcle of Matthias's 'governorship' of the United Provinces, in September 1580 Orange had the States-General offer the sovereignty to the duke of Anjou, Dauphin of France (and formerly duke of Alençon), on condition that Anjou obtained French support against Spain (Treaty of Plessis-lès-Tours). The Prince himself then proceeded to draw the logical conclusion from his act of rebellion; in December he published his *Apologia*, claiming that Philip was a tyrant. He justified his own conduct and protested at having had a price put on his head as if he were a common criminal. He denounced Philip as the murderer of his own son (Don Carlos), a vindictive and bigoted fanatic who was bereft of moral scruples. Most of Orange's charges were demonstrably false or exaggerated, but that mattered little in the European climate of the early 1580s. The Prince now accepted the title of count of Holland and Zeeland and on 26 July 1581 the representatives of the Union of Utrecht solemnly proclaimed the Edict of Abjuration, renouncing their loyalty to Philip.[20] There was no longer any pretence that the rebellion in the Low Countries was directed against the king's misguided ministers; it was now formally made clear that it was directed explicitly against Philip himself and against his claims of sovereignty over his former subjects. The breach had been made.

Relations with England deteriorated almost as rapidly. A rebellion against English rule had broken out in Ireland in 1579, and in 1580 Philip allowed some Spaniards to accompany the 800 papal troops transported to help the rebels, and he gave the command of the fleet that transported them to Ireland to one of his senior admirals, Juan Martínez de Recalde. It was an unambiguous act of war by the pope – and it was not too far short of it by Philip himself. The rebellion was soon overcome, but it confirmed Elizabeth in her appreciation that she would now be obliged to lead the opposition to the growth of Spanish power in order to protect herself. She determined to do so for as long as possible by proxy: 'We think it good for the King of Spain to be impeached both in Portugal and his Islands (sc. the Azores) and also in the Low Countries, whereto we shall be ready to give such indirect assistance as shall not at once be a cause of war.'[21] When Anjou returned to the Low Countries in February 1582 to swear the oath to the States-General he brought with him Elizabeth's secretary of State, Sir Francis Walsingham, and her personal favourite, Robert Dudley, earl of Leicester. Walsingham and Leicester were the leaders of the English war party. Elizabeth, in her inimitable way, was sending a message without making a commitment.

The duke of Parma responded to the likelihood of English involvement in the Low Countries by undertaking the capture of the ports on the coast of Flanders and by blocking the Scheldt below Antwerp.[22] He carefully avoided involving himself in a war with the heir to the French throne and it was probably because Parma did not actively oppose him that Anjou was able to capture Cambrai in the summer of 1581. In 1582 Parma began the systematic reconquest of Flanders and Brabant, and he began, too, to work at dividing his opponents, persuading the southern Estates to agree to the return of the Spanish *tercios*. With his elite troops once again at his command Parma would now show the full extent of his mastery of the arts of war.

HIATUS: THE RETURN TO MADRID AND THE JOURNEY TO ARAGON, 1583–6

Philip returned to Madrid at the end of March 1583. He was reunited with his last surviving son and together they made a splendid formal entry into the capital. Cardinal Granvelle led the welcoming party, but although Philip was especially gracious towards him he did not summon him to private audiences more than twice in the next four months.[23] Granvelle's time as a major figure in government was over. He had managed the affairs of the councils in Madrid during Philip's absence but had inevitably lost his pre-eminent position to the men who had travelled with Philip. Six men had played especially important roles as advisers to the king while he was in Portugal: the archduke Albert; Diego de Chaves, Philip's confessor; Mateo Vázquez de Leca, Christovão de Moura and Juan de Idiáquez – each of these three formerly a secretary but now in effect a minister; and Don Diego de Cabrera y Bobadilla, third count of Chinchón. Two other men had developed their power in Madrid itself, helping to undermine Granvelle; in October 1581 Francisco Zapata de Cisneros, first count of Barajas, was appointed to the presidency of the Council of Castile and at the end of 1582 Juan de Zúñiga y Requesens, brother of Luis de Requesens, returned to Madrid from Italy to serve as a general factotum for the king in the capital. Albert, of course, stayed behind in Portugal as viceroy and when Philip settled down once again in Madrid and the Escorial, Barajas and Zúñiga joined the other four at the heart of power. These men did not form a political party as such but they had several qualities in common (apart from their complete dependence upon the king) – by instinct they were centralisers in domestic policy and imperialists in foreign affairs; none of them were of the senior aristocracy and they all had good reason to hate Antonio Pérez. Their ascendancy both reflected and bolstered Philip's inclination towards a new stridency in foreign policy-making.

It was characteristic of Philip that even this intimate group should have had an inner core, consisting of Moura, Idiáquez, Vázquez de Leca and Chinchón. These were the men who had the fullest access to the king and who controlled the flow of paper to and from him. They now assumed responsibility for separate areas of policy. Moura naturally concentrated on Portuguese affairs but he also advised Philip across the whole range of domestic policy. With that easy affection that he gave to favoured Portuguese, Philip took Moura into his confidence. Before leaving Portugal he had placed Don Cristóbal (as Moura now became known by castili-anising his name) in charge of the Council of Portugal. As a special mark of his favour he allowed Moura to marry Doña Margarita de Corte Real, the daughter of a leading Portuguese nobleman; Philip himself attended the wedding and conferred a habit of the military order of Alcántara upon Moura.[24] Vázquez de Leca continued to specialise in ecclesiastical matters and his power-base was extended when on 13 March 1581 in Abrantes he was sworn in as secretary of the Council of Inquisition.[25] It may well be that Philip already had the intention of using the Inquisition to resolve the case of Antonio Pérez; at all events, Vázquez de Leca would keep the king informed of what was happening in *la Suprema* and he could most certainly be relied upon to keep the most vigilant of eyes on the development of Pérez's case. Juan de Idiáquez won no new advancement in Portugal but he consolidated his influence with the king and by 1583 was his chief adviser on foreign affairs. Chinchón was the only aristocrat among the inner group, but his was not a major title; it dated only to 1520 and was worth a mere 30 000 ducats of rent in 1595, placing him forty-third among the list of 116 nobles in that year. He succeeded his father as Treasurer-General of the Crown of Aragon and in that capacity sat on the councils of Aragon and Italy; he was the king's eyes and ears on those councils.[26] Moura, Vázquez de Leca, Idiáquez and Chinchón were practical men, concerned to make government function, and they stayed with Philip now, travelling with him to his country houses; most especially, they remained with him as he spent ever longer periods in the Escorial, which was completed exactly as he returned from Portugal. They pooled their common knowledge on juntas, particularly on what became known as the 'Junta of the Night' because it met in the late evening to review the government's work of the day. Individually and collectively, they developed their power and their control over the machinery of government; Vázquez de Leca lived only until 1591, but Moura, Idiáquez and Chinchón all survived until the end of the reign and exercised influence in a manner that became truly ministerial.[27]

Granvelle was bitterly angry at Philip's rejection and made no secret of his contempt for the men who had superseded him: 'God would want our sovereign to decide to work less and to choose better councillors; if he punished those who serve him badly and rewarded those who served well, it would not be long before affairs took a turn (for the better).'[28] It was not altogether surprising that Granvelle found himself in a minority of one; his arrogance was self-destructive.

It was therefore especially ironic that as Granvelle finally lost power and influence the policies that he was urging upon the king should have been carried through with conviction by the men whom he so despised. There was, too, a special irony in the fact that Alba himself died (12 December 1582) as a forward policy in the Low Countries was at last beginning to bear fruit. To the last Alba was unrepentant, telling his confessor that 'his conscience was not burdened with having in all his life shed a single drop of blood against it'.[29] The duke died as he had lived, convinced of his own rectitude, dismissive of doubt or of criticism.

During the summer of 1584 the political situation in the Low Countries was transformed by the deaths of Anjou and the Prince of Orange. Anjou had shown himself to be of marginal value as a military leader and had fallen into disgrace in January 1583 when his troops vainly attempted to storm Antwerp in order to overthrow the States-General and the Prince of Orange by force (the 'French Fury'). He left the Low Countries at the end of the year, already ill with the tuberculosis that ran so consistently in his family. He died on 10 June 1584. Inadequate though he was as a political leader and as a soldier, Anjou was a French prince of the blood and his death deprived the United Provinces of a leader who could claim some legitimacy. The Prince of Orange was assassinated on 10 July by Baltasar Gérard. It was said that his last words were 'My God, my God, have pity on me and on this poor people', and if he did utter them they truly reflected the dire situation of the United Provinces, for Orange had held the disparate states together and had brought in foreign help.[30] As Parma's army cut triumphantly and apparently irresistibly into rebel territory the loss of the Prince of Orange was a disaster for Parma's opponents. When it became known that Gérard had been a pupil of the Dominicans, his deed was laid at Philip's door – chilling proof, indeed, that no one was beyond his reach.

It was far from clear as yet that the death, in delivering Philip from one of his most able opponents in the Prince of Orange, had provided him with an even greater one by making the Prince of Navarre the heir-apparent to the French throne. Henry of Navarre seemed to have little chance of winning support in his quest for the French throne – he was widely distrusted by both Catholics and Huguenots for his multiple changes of faith – but he moved now with a sureness of touch that had been born of a lifetime of danger to establish his claim on the succession. He wrote lengthy tracts to the Parlement of Paris and to the Sorbonne, presenting himself as the rightful successor to Henry III and hinting that he might reconvert to Catholicism. He also presented himself as a genuinely independent Frenchman – a Protestant (for the while at least), but a patriot.

By contrast, French Catholics willingly looked abroad for support. The senior aristocracy of France traditionally claimed the right to revolt against a tyrant and, led by the House of Guise, the Catholics among them now availed themselves of this right in order to revive the Catholic League and to secure Spanish and papal assistance for it. After months of negotiation the Catholic League came once again into being at Joinville on the last day of 1584. The Guise brothers – Duke Henry, Cardinal Louis and Duke Charles of Mayenne – naturally took the lead and they were supported by their cousins, the dukes of Aumale and Elbouef. The League was in essence, therefore, Guisard and noble and it pledged itself to fight for the 'defence and preservation of the Catholic faith' and the extirpation of heresy. It united behind the candidature for the throne of the aged Cardinal of Bourbon. A number of provincial governors committed themselves and their provinces to support the League – those of Champagne, Burgundy, Brie, Picardy, Berry, Maine and Anjou notable among them. The Catholic League was therefore a formidable organisation, and it was rapidly becoming a nationwide one.

Other organisation took place less publicly. A few days after the League had come into being a secret society was formed for the protection of Catholicism in Paris. Consisting at first only of a few chosen men, it soon had disciplined cells established in each of the sixteen 'quarters' of the city. Accordingly it became known as 'The Sixteen'. Under the control of the Sixteen, Paris played a decisive role in the war that now broke out in France for the succession to the throne. Indeed, the city became during the course of the next decade the focal point of the struggle for control of France.[31]

Philip could not ignore the implications of Navarre's new eminence and so he acceded to the Treaty of Joinville and agreed to provide its partners with a generous monthly allowance to help raise and fund an army. In doing so, he effectively committed himself to intervening actively and decisively in the French civil wars. It was a momentous decision on Philip's part – perhaps the most profoundly important single decision that he took in his reign – and its implications transformed European politics over the course of the next fifteen years.

Philip's attitude to the politics of western Europe remained now, as it had always been, profoundly secular, but his growing belligerence in foreign policy coincided with the deepening of his conviction that Catholicism was losing ground in France, the Low Countries and in England. It also coincided, it should be added, with the fact that Philip now had only one son left to succeed him. As he aged, Philip became the more resolute in his determination to secure a settlement that would enable his son to succeed to a stable political situation in Europe.

By the early 1580s it seemed only a matter of time before Catholicism died out in England under the twin threats of persecution and indifference. In fact, renewal was already underway and it was led by priests who had been trained abroad and sent home to England as missionaries; the first English priests produced by the seminary of Douai in the Low Countries returned in 1574 and they were followed in 1580 by the first Jesuits (Edmund Campion and Robert Parsons). Survival in their homeland was not easy and many priests were quickly captured and executed. Philip was painfully conscious of the sufferings of the priests; in 1582, when he heard of the martyrdom of some English priests he wrote that 'I hope to God . . . that this and all the blood shed in England for the faith will cry aloud to Him for a remedy to be sent'.[32] But it was English activities in the Low Countries and in the Indies – and, increasingly, in Iberian waters – that most deeply affected Philip's policy.

The situation of Mary Queen of Scots continued to complicate Spain's relations with England, and in 1583 Ambassador Mendoza was implicated in a plot led by Nicholas Throckmorton to assassinate Elizabeth and replace her with Mary. Mendoza was expelled in January 1584, and Spain and England edged closer to the brink of war. In 1585 a man named William Parry was arrested and found to be carrying a letter from the pope's secretary approving his intention to assassinate Elizabeth.[33] The queen had no choice but to respond; the identification of Spain, the papacy, the Queen of Scots and her own Catholic subjects as enemies who were only waiting for the right moment to overthrow her forced her now to take positive action in her own defence. Elizabeth looked to find her salvation by opposing Philip in the Low Countries and in the Americas. She even sought an understanding with the Turk, appreciating that war with Spain was now all but inevitable.

Philip remained in Castile for less than three years after returning from Portugal. His health continued to deteriorate; attacks of gout (from which he had suffered since 1564) now began to force him to cut down his working hours. Death continued to strike at his family; he lost yet another child when María died at the age of three (4 August 1583) and was left now with only three children – Isabella, Catalina and Felipe. Increasingly frail, Philip found himself obliged to plan yet another major journey, to Aragon.

It had been twenty-one years since Philip had visited his eastern realms and now he had to address a range of political problems there, most of which had been exacerbated by his long absence. He needed, above all, to hold a meeting of the Cortes of the kingdom of Aragon. Respect for the Crown and the law was breaking down in Aragon as a result of festering conflicts between the Crown and local nobles over jurisdictional rights. In particular, the longstanding dispute between the Crown and the duke of Villahermosa over the county of Ribagorza had the most serious implications now that Philip was involving himself in a war with the heir to the French throne; the county of Ribagorza, which consisted of 200 or so small communities and some 400 people, abutted the frontier with France. The situation was further aggravated by spreading lawlessness as bands of robbers and *moriscos* ravaged the countryside. Philip had also to fulfil two major dynastic purposes in Aragon – to have his last son sworn in as heir to his eastern states and to bid farewell to Catalina Micaela, whom in 1583 he had affianced to Charles Emmanuel, prince of Savoy. Philip had his son take the oath as heir to Castile on 11 November 1584. He left Madrid on 19 January 1585; he was away until March 1586. These were momentous months during which the crises in northern and Atlantic Europe passed beyond Philip's control and during which his kingdom of Naples came perilously close to rebellion. The tide of good fortune, which had seemed to run so strongly for him in the years 1580–3 was now slowly but perceptibly turning against him.

Philip's departure cleared the way for the arrest of Antonio Pérez (31 January). Pérez had been charged in June 1584 with trading in state secrets and with having broken that oath of secrecy which defined his work as a royal secretary, but Philip had allowed him to remain at large in Madrid while he prepared his defence. Philip dared not, however, risk leaving Pérez at liberty while he himself was away from the capital in case he fled with the state papers that he had secreted away. Powerful friends rallied to Pérez; on the day after his arrest Cardinal Quiroga ostentatiously visited Pérez's wife Juana and her children in a gesture of solidarity that made it evident that the affair would not be quietly resolved. In January the verdict was published, and it was a very moderate one; Pérez was sentenced to two years' imprisonment and to banishment from court. He was to pay a fine of 32 749 ducats and to give up the valuables of the Princess of Éboli. The very leniency of the sentence made Pérez suspicious that he was to be done away with, probably by being poisoned. With the help of Álamos de Barrientos he therefore organised an escape attempt. It was unsuccessful and Pérez found himself confined in chains.[34]

Philip entered Zaragoza on 24 February 1585 and the wedding of Catalina Micaela and Charles Emmanuel was celebrated on 11 March, with Granvelle officiating. The marriage represented a radical departure in Crown policy, for Catalina was the only Spanish princess to marry outside the circle of the Holy Roman Empire, England, Portugal and France in the Habsburg period.[35] There were a number of reasons why Philip should have married his younger daughter to an Italian princeling and most of them reflected his anxieties at the emergence of Henry of Navarre as the heir to the French throne. Most obviously, the alliance with Savoy helped Philip to guarantee the security of the Milanese – always a priority of Spanish policy – while Philip hoped that Charles Emmanuel's new status as his son-in-law would encourage him to resist his natural inclination to play Spain and France off against each other. Moreover, the marriage helped push away the likelihood of a French succession to the duchy, since a French nobleman, the duke of Nevers, had a claim on the duchy of Savoy if Charles Emmanuel died without heirs. It also happened that Charles Emmanuel had a claim to the Portuguese throne; this was now discreetly dropped. There was, however, a serious risk in the Savoyard marriage, for if Philip's two other children failed to produce children, the sons of the duke of Savoy would have the next claim on the Spanish throne. As it happened, the marriage of Catalina Micaela was to be the most fertile of any member of the Spanish house of Habsburg; her first child, a boy who was named Victor Amadeo, was born in May 1586 and a further nine children followed in the years to 1597.

Early in April, Philip left Zaragoza for Barcelona. Weary, and anxious about the separation from his beloved daughter, he refused to let the city of Barcelona welcome him ceremonially, insisting that he was only visiting the city to conduct family business. On 13 June the newly-weds embarked at Barcelona, to the deep distress of Philip and both of his daughters; on the following day, Philip wrote to Catalina of his sadness at their parting and shortly afterwards he wrote to her of how he had scanned the horizon in the hope of seeing her fleet, but that it had already gone. From Barcelona, Philip and his household made their way up the mountains to Monzón, where on 28 June the General Cortes of the three eastern states were opened. They proved to be especially tiresome. The deputies made demand after demand before they would even begin to discuss the king's proposals. In the heat of late summer, feverish disease spread among the courtiers; soon no fewer than ninety had died. Philip himself collapsed with fever and for a fortnight (7–21 October) he was gravely ill. He made his confession and rewrote some details in his Testament. Again he survived, but his brush with death added urgency to the need to have his son sworn in as heir to the three eastern kingdoms; this was done between 6 and 14 November.[36] Philip's recovery was partial and incomplete. In 1585 he was, as it happened, exactly the age at which his father had died; doubtless he reflected upon the fact.

Philip made one important decision in Aragon, allowing the duke of Villahermosa to take possession of his title. In 1554, as Regent, Philip had decreed that the county of Ribagorza should be incorporated into the Crown's patrimony. Villahermosa appealed and won the case. Philip was not one to forget such a defeat but he now allowed the succession in order to placate the family at a time of acute political sensitivity. This was the more necessary because the tensions between the Crown and the Villahermosa family had deteriorated throughout recent years as the result of a vicious feud between the count of Chinchón and Villahermosa's son, the count of Ribagorza. In 1571 Ribagorza availed himself of an ancient prerogative to have his wife executed on charges of adultery. She was the niece of Don Pedro, second count of Chinchón, and at Chinchón's insistence Philip had Ribagorza himself publicly executed in 1573. When Don Pedro died in 1576 he was succeeded by his son Diego, and he developed the feud with unforgiving singlemindedness. It was almost certainly at the insistence of the new count of Chinchón that when Villahermosa died in 1581 Philip refused to admit his successor, Don Hernando de Gurrea y Aragón, to the exercise of the title. When Philip relented in 1585 it was then too late to diminish the resentment that the new duke felt towards both him and Chinchón. In two other cases the Crown was more successful; at the Cortes of Monzón the baronies of Ariza and Monclús were both taken into the royal patrimony. It was as part of the trade-off that the Crown allowed the lords of Aragon to exercise fuller control over rebellious vassals.[37]

The months that Philip spent in the hills of Aragon were a time of great stress for him. His physical isolation and his serious illness made it diffi-cult for him even to keep up with what was happening in the world at large let alone impose himself upon events. These were months during which the political situation in western Europe deteriorated dramatically. The most immediate danger arose in Philip's kingdom of Naples, which was torn by riots in the capital city which might have led to the develop-ment of full-scale revolt had they not been put down with spectacular brutality by the viceroy, the duke of Osuna. The city of Naples was the largest conurbation in Europe, with a population of over 200 000 – a pop-ulation which indeed made it almost as large as Madrid and Seville com-bined. Food shortages aggravated anti-Spanish feelings in the enormous city, and on 9 May 1585 a riot over bread prices resulted in the brutal and ritualised murder of Giovanni Vincenzo Starace, the representative of the people. The mob then paraded in front of the viceroy's palace pro-claiming 'Death to bad government and long live justice'. The city seemed to be on the point of rebellion. Other issues were involved in the disturbances, chief among them the resentment of the Neapolitans at the levies imposed upon them by the Crown; Naples's resources had been especially important in the naval campaigns in the Mediterranean in the 1570s and in the conquests of Portugal and the Azores in 1580–3. Indeed, those resources had also been cynically exploited in order to lessen the tax burden in Lombardy; in the years 1560–92 some 1 300 000 ducats were sent from Naples to Milan because Philip dared not risk the stability of the Milanese by demanding high taxes from its people. The immediate crisis was stabilised in Naples by the sale of grain from Sicily at artificially low prices, and when Don Pedro de Toledo arrived in July with forty galleys carrying soldiers the viceroy was able to re-establish control. Osuna terrorised the population of the capital, having thirty-one death sentences carried out and making use of torture that was even more brutal and ritualised than that which had been inflicted upon Starace. No fewer than 12 000 people fled the city, and in February 1586 Osuna razed the house of the chief ringleader, Giovanni Leonardo Pisano, and replaced it with a monument in which the hands and heads of the executed men and women were ceremonially displayed in individual niches.[38] The threat of rebellion was crushed.

The crisis in Naples may well have distracted Philip's attention from northern Europe and have thereby contributed to one of the major mis-calculations of his kingship. In May 1585 he ordered the seizure of all English ships in Iberian ports. It was probably Philip's intention to discourage Elizabeth from aiding the Dutch – this would explain why his decision was specifically announced as a temporary measure – but his action forced many English merchants to clamour for war against Spain so that their losses could be made good. Some of the ships had come to Iberia with grain to help relieve food shortages and had sailed under the Spanish government's promise of safe conduct. Philip's seizure of these ships therefore seemed to be simply treacherous. Merchants who had hitherto been insistent that Elizabeth should not break with Spain now urged her to do so. On 1 July, Francis Drake was commissioned to sail to Vigo and negotiate the return of English ships; in reality of course, Drake was once again charged to do such damage to Spain's defences and naval preparations as he could and, as always, he and his patrons hoped to intercept the Spanish treasure fleet. It was Drake's first major royal command; the pirate had become an admiral.[39]

The election of Felice Peretti as Pope Sixtus V in May 1585 further accelerated the drift to war. In 1584 Philip had made it a condition of taking action against England that the papacy should contribute substantially to the costs of the enterprise: 'if anything is to be effected (the pope) must contribute very largely'.[40] In Sixtus V, Philip found a pope who would support him in taking action against Elizabeth, for the new pope was determined to mark his pontificate with an enterprise that would redound to the credit of Christendom itself. Sixtus V had about him much of the simplicity – or clarity of purpose – of Pius V, and although he was deeply hostile to the advancement of Spanish power in Europe (and even professed admiration for Elizabeth of England) he set himself to bring about a Catholic crusade to remove Elizabeth from her throne. Accordingly, at the end of 1585 he renewed the *cruzada* for seven years to encourage Philip to fund an 'Enterprise of England'. The pope also joined Philip in urging Henry III to rescind all edicts granting any religious toleration to the Huguenots, and on 9 September 1585 he formally excommunicated Henry of Navarre and enjoined all French Catholics to turn on him. The pope's actions helped to precipitate yet another War of Religion in France – what was to be called 'The War of the Three Henries', fought between Henry III, Henry of Guise and Henry of Navarre. A Catholic crusade to prevent the accession of the Prince of Navarre was coming into being.

Philip was the more able to move against Elizabeth and involve himself in France because of the brilliant successes of Parma in the Low Countries. In 1583 Parma captured Dunkirk and Nieuport and in 1584–5 he triumphantly carried all before him as he took one great city after another: Brussels in March 1584; Bruges in April; Ghent (the leading Calvinist city in the south), September 1584; and – the greatest prize of all – Antwerp, which capitulated on 17 August 1585. Parma had made the siege of Antwerp a test, declaring that he would conquer the city or die in the attempt. He laid siege to it by building a fortified bridge across the Scheldt to cut Antwerp off from the sea and from allies. The construction of the bridge used up more than 10000 tree trunks and 1500 ships' masts were piled seventy feet down into the riverbed to support it. Thirty-two hulks were used to stabilise it. Construction took seven months, and when the bridge was completed in February 1585 it was one of the wonders of the age, an awesome masterpiece of military engineering. On 4 April the defenders of Antwerp mounted an attack by four fireships and thirteen support-ships – 'the hellships of Antwerp' – which terrified Parma's men and cut into the bridge. However, the breach was not exploited and the bridge survived, and with it the siege. Parma's slow, methodical strangulation of the great city seemed to many to be a metaphor for the fate that awaited the United Provinces themselves and when he made his triumphal entry into Antwerp on 27 August he seemed to be truly irresistible; in three years he had doubled the area of the Low Countries under Philip's control. Unfortunately, although Parma ensured that no reprisals were inflicted on the people of Antwerp, he could not make them accept conquest; in the four years after he marched in, some 38000 people, nearly half the population, left.[41] The golden age of Antwerp was at an end.

Philip was so gratified by the progress of the siege that he finally ceded Piacenza to Parma and his family, agreeing on 10 July to withdraw Spanish troops from the fort. The news that Parma had taken Antwerp came to Philip in the middle of the night and he rushed to Isabella's room and hammered on her door shouting 'Antwerp is ours!'[42] But in his excitement Philip misread the significance of events in northern Europe (as he had the capture of the Azores in 1583); the capture of Antwerp made it almost certain that England would be forced to intervene. So it proved; on 20 August, by the Treaty of Nonsuch, Elizabeth agreed to provide the United Provinces with an army of 6350 infantry and 1000 horse for the duration of the war, to be commanded by an Englishman of rank. In return, she would be allowed to place garrisons in the towns of The Brill and Flushing and the States would pay the costs of her army. Anxious about the legality of interfering in lands that belonged to a fellow monarch, on 1 October Elizabeth issued the 'Declaration of Richmond' in which she justified her actions to Europe by complaining that Philip had, in conjunction with the pope, sought to invade her territory in Ireland and that he had been involved in a series of conspiracies to assassinate her. The Earl of Leicester crossed the Channel on 19 December.[43]

By then Drake had sailed from Plymouth (14 September 1585), with a fleet of thirty-three ships and 1925 men. His orders enjoined him to do such damage as he could to the possessions of the king of Spain both in Europe and in the Caribbean. In all but name, Elizabeth was at war with Spain.[44] Philip himself seems to have crossed the line into war with England almost imperceptibly, perhaps even without realising fully the implications of what he was doing. Certainly, he had no clear idea as yet how exactly he would deal with England. He was, however, very clear in his purposes – to stop English help to the rebels in the Low Countries; to stop English attacks on the coasts and shipping of the Iberian countries; and to stop English incursions into the Caribbean. From the autumn of 1585 planning began in detail for what became 'the Enterprise of England'. The decision to send the fleet was taken at the turn of the year, and early in 1586 the marquis of Santa Cruz was informed that he was to be in charge of a new fleet that was to be stationed at Lisbon.[45]

Implicit in Philip's appointment of Santa Cruz to command the new fleet was clearly the decision that the marquis himself would lead the expedition against England. The choice was as well-judged as it was inevitable; Santa Cruz was unquestionably the most successful admiral in Europe, with a record of success in both Atlantic and Mediterranean going back to the early 1560s. Most notably, he had played the decisive role at the battle of Lepanto in 1571 and had already demonstrated a mastery of the complex techniques of amphibious warfare in the Azores in 1582 and 1583. But while Philip chose his admiral well, Elizabeth made a crass error of judgement in her choice of commander for her troops in the Low Countries. Robert Dudley, earl of Leicester, was a favourite of the Queen's and he proved almost at once to be an inept commander for his own soldiers and an abrasive ally for the Dutch. In January 1586, without consulting Elizabeth, he accepted the title of Governor-General of the Low Countries. He thereby committed Elizabeth to maintaining her support of the rebels as if she was herself monarch of them. Infuriated by Leicester's presumption, Elizabeth came close to recalling him but on reflection allowed him to remain in the Low Countries. He stayed until November 1586.[46]

The Cortes of the Crown of Aragon ended on 9 December 1585 and Philip paid a brief visit to Valencia before returning to Madrid in March

1586. His physical weakness continued to cause concern and was perhaps aggravated by his continuing anxieties over Antonio Pérez; he had Pérez brought back to Madrid while the investigation continued. As he began now to plan the armada against England, Philip could not escape from Pérez. In a sense, he was Pérez's prisoner.

The king was the prisoner, too, of another brilliant adventurer. Francis Drake spent a fortnight at the turn of September–October raiding in Galicia. Insulting though his action was to Philip, Drake contrived to miss two treasure fleets that he might have intercepted had he stationed himself off Cadiz. He destroyed a score or so of ships off the Portuguese coast before sailing on to the Canaries and across the Atlantic. He celebrated New Year's Day 1586 (in the English reckoning) by attacking Santo Domingo. He spent a month ashore but made little profit; Santo Domingo was poor and Drake had to settle for the paltry sum of 25000 ducats not to pillage it. He contented himself with desecrating churches and destroying some ships. He sailed on to Cartagena, where he stayed for a further six weeks. Here, he was more successful financially, wringing 110000 ducats from the populace for not destroying the town. Once again, however, he sacked churches as acts of calculated provocation. He sailed for home by way of Cuba and went north to Virginia, where he collected the settlers from the new colony of Roanoake, reaching England at the end of July 1586. Financially, the voyage was not an outstanding success; investors (including the Queen) received only 15 shillings in the pound. Moreover, the expedition cost the lives of 750 men, mostly through disease in the Caribbean.[47] But Drake had once again inflicted damage on Philip's defence system in the Caribbean that the king and his ministers simply could not tolerate.

Philip was in the depths of Aragon as he absorbed the news of Drake's onslaught, and it was there at the turn of 1585–6 that he committed himself to sending the Armada against England. In December he received a series of alarming despatches – on 5th, Parma's letter of 11 November explaining that English help to the rebels was growing progressively and that the Dutch were accordingly becoming ever more committed to continuing the war rather than with seeking peace (as had been the case after the capture of Antwerp in August); on 24th, Juan Bautista de Tassis's letter of 28 November from Namur in which he stressed that English help was bolstering the position of the Huguenots to the extent that Henry III might be forced to make peace. Philip's mind was made up; on 29 December he wrote to Parma from Tortosa that it was time to proceed to 'the principal business' ('el negocio principal'), and he instructed the duke to inform him of what resources he would need in order to carry it out. Philip insisted that a port would have to be conquered for the fleet to harbour in – 'without a port nothing can be done'. He followed this up by writing on 2 January 1586 to his ambassador in Rome, the count of Olivares, ordering him to negotiate a papal grant to support pay for the fleet – 'the justification and purpose of the Enterprise has to be to reduce that kingdom to the obedience of the Roman Church and to place the queen of Scotland in possession of [the Crown]'. While this was the ostensible justification for the Enterprise, Philip was insistent that Olivares should have the pope agree that the succession to Mary of Scotland could go to Philip's own daughter, Isabella. He further insisted that 'secrecy is everything'. The Armada would sail against England, and it was Philip's intention that it would do so during the course of 1586. On 13 January, the marquis of Santa Cruz himself wrote to Philip. Probably he had picked up the rumour that the king had decided to act against Elizabeth and was anxious not to be sidelined; at all events, Santa Cruz pointed out to Philip that the embargo was hurting Spanish merchants more than it was the English – that Philip's subjects had lost 'more than a million and a half ducats' by the embargo – and he suggested that the time was right to attack Spain's problems at their source, in England. The Turk was occupied elsewhere, France rendered incapable of action by internal divisions: it was, Santa Cruz insisted, time to act against England. Philip had Juan de Idiáquez reply favourably on his behalf – 'there are many things (in it) that are very well considered' – and Santa Cruz was ordered to establish 'a good armada' at Lisbon to police the Atlantic coast of Spain and Portugal and to protect the arrival of the Indies fleets. Unstated in the king's letter was the understanding, which Santa Cruz fully shared, that the fleet would be used against England. Philip ordered that the fleet was to be ready for action by the end of April, or at the very latest by the beginning of May.[48]

The Council of War in Madrid was outraged by Drake's actions and deeply angered by the 'little resistance' shown by the Spanish commanders in the Indies, who had failed to defend the king's territory from what was a comparatively small fleet. The Council spoke witheringly of the commanders' 'dishonour and shame' and demanded that they be brought to Spain in chains for trial. Even more serious than the damage done in the Caribbean was the self-confidence – the 'spirit and pride' – with which the English had returned home, confident that they could plan further attacks on Spain and her possessions whenever they wished.

Drake's success would have a cyclical effect as other seamen sought to emulate him.[49] The Council initiated a series of reforms to protect the silver fleet and the Indies themselves. In 1586 the fleet sailing to Panamá took with it a new governor for Cuba (Juan de Tejada) and an engineer, the Italian Juan Bautista Antoneli, who was charged with improving the fortifications of the cities and key strategic points of the Indies. After returning briefly to Spain for consultations, Antoneli stuck at his task in the Caribbean for twenty years.[50] Once again, Philip was quick to absorb the lessons that Francis Drake had taught him.

Among the side-effects of Drake's success was a further worsening of the situation in Portugal. In February 1586 Lisbon was reported to be 'in an uproar' on account of the damage that Drake had caused to Portuguese shipping and trade. Soon it was being noted that the Portuguese were reflecting that they had been safer under Sebastián than they were now under Philip.[51] Once again, there was confident talk at court in Madrid that Philip would travel to Portugal. As it happened, Santa Cruz's plans for the assault upon England reached Philip exactly as he returned to Madrid from Aragon in March 1586. The marquis's timing was exquisite: he insisted that he would be failing in his duty 'as a vassal of Your Majesty' if he did not give Philip a frank assessment of what ought to be done. Philip summoned Santa Cruz to the Escorial.[52] He also took a number of other actions to prepare for his great fleet. On 4 April, he ordered all Castilian bishops to have prayers offered in their dioceses for 'the affairs of Christendom and good success for public matters', and on 21st appointed Bernabé de Pedroso as Purveyor-General for the fleet that was to be assembled in Lisbon. On 1 May, Philip divided the secretaryship of the Council of War into two, one secretary specialising in affairs of Land and one in those of Sea, the better to prepare the expedition.[53] The planning for the 'Enterprise of England' had begun in earnest.

Santa Cruz's plan proposed a vastly expanded version of his campaign in the Azores in 1583, a sea-borne invasion that would comprise 510 ships with a total of 110750 *toneladas*, 86 galleys and galleasses and a force of 72812 men (16612 seamen, 55000 infantry and 1200 cavalry). The marquis estimated that the cost would be about 3500000 ducats.[54] He did not necessarily envisage a landing in England itself – Ireland or Wales might prove to be more appropriate – and with unwonted alacrity Philip gave permission in April for preparations to begin in Lisbon and in the dockyards of the Cantabrian and Andalusian coasts. The dockyards would never be able to build enough ships to satisfy Santa Cruz's plan but the task of preparing a fleet against England had begun – and once the ships began to roll off the production lines it became ever harder for Philip to back down.

Parma's plan arrived in June 1586. It proposed that 30 000 or so men cross from Flanders to England, probably at the end of the current campaigning season, and that they should then march on London. Action against England would have to be immediate; Parma noted that it was common talk in northern Europe that England was about to be invaded and insisted that the maintenance of secrecy was fundamental to the success of his plan. Philip seems never to have appreciated the need for maintaining secrecy and he certainly never attempted to iron out the fundamental differences between the plans of his two commanders.[55]

As Philip immersed himself in his planning, the central weakness of his government became ever clearer; obsessed by details, he failed to concern himself with strategy and, consulting with an ever-narrowing band of senior advisers, he did not open his plan up to impartial criticism and review such as might have improved it. He also came under great pressure, particularly from Santa Cruz and Granvelle, to move his capital to Lisbon so that he could organise the expedition against England and also counteract the growing unrest in the kingdom.[56] But Philip could not be persuaded; he had spent much of the previous six years away from Madrid, and in Badajoz in 1580 and in Monzón in 1585 he had been at death's door when forced to live in towns that did not have the facilities to house his court safely. It may well be, too, that the disturbances in Naples in 1585 reminded him of the need to keep the keenest eye on his Italian possessions; he was much better able to do this from Madrid than from Lisbon. He would travel no more, at least if he could avoid doing so. No doubt, too, Philip appreciated that he had to remain in Castile in order to satisfy the most generous of his realms; Castile would hardly be prepared to make the largest contribution to the costs of the expedition against England if Philip abandoned Madrid for Lisbon. And the Escorial was complete. The king would not change his capital city.

Granvelle died in September 1586 and his body was taken to Besançon for interment; he was a foreigner to the last. Juan de Zúñiga followed him to the grave in November and the men who had made their mark on the journeys to Portugal and Aragon consolidated their position at the heart of power. In particular, Moura and Idiáquez made further headway; Moura now slept in the king's ante-chamber (as only Ruy Gómez had done before him) and Idiáquez extended his influence on

foreign policy. With Philip beginning now to write less and less on documents, it was Idiáquez who wrote his comments for him on many important *consultas* and it was Idiáquez who conducted audiences in the king's
stead; the Venetian ambassador, having spoken with Idiáquez, observed
that the secretary's stature was such that his words 'were as though
spoken by the voice of the king'.[57] Both Moura and Idiáquez were raised
to councillorships of State so that they could represent the king's views
on the council – and keep vigilant eyes on their fellow councillors.

Early in 1586 Mary Stuart found a way of smuggling letters out of her
prison, unaware that it was Walsingham himself who had invented and
controlled her new conduit. As a result, in June 1586 a letter was found
inviting a Spanish or French invasion to free her and giving her approval
to a plot led by Anthony Babington to assassinate Elizabeth. It was Mary's
last intrigue; she was tried in October 1586 and found guilty of treason.
On 18 February 1587 she was beheaded. Mary's death removed the threat
of a Franco-Scottish succession to the English throne and made it easier
for Philip to push ahead with his plans for an armada against Elizabeth;
he did not have to worry that he might depose Elizabeth only to place a
pro-French Catholic queen on the throne. Sixtus V, perhaps relieved
by the death of the unstable and turbulent Catholic queen, in July
agreed to deposit a million ducats as a down-payment for the costs of the
Enterprise of England.[58]

Once again, Elizabeth set Drake loose. He sailed from Plymouth on 12
April 1587 with a commission to disrupt Philip's invasion plans by whatever means he could. He commanded a major fleet, of sixteen warships
and seven pinnaces, among which were four of the queen's galleons and
one that was owned by the Lord Admiral. There was no ambivalence
about Elizabeth's support for his expedition. Drake arrived off Cadiz on
29 April and found some sixty or so ships at anchor with many others
scattered around the harbour. In the most devastating of all his attacks
he destroyed twenty or so large ships (although characteristically he
claimed thirty-two victims). The duke of Medina Sidonia led the coun-
terattack the next day, sending fireships against the English fleet. Drake
was unflustered – he joked that the Spaniards were doing his work
for him by burning their own ships. However, it did not go unnoticed
by Philip that Medina Sidonia had shown energy and courage in confronting *el corsario*; few Spanish commanders had managed that. Drake
himself was impressed by the scale of Spanish preparations – 'the like
preparation was never heard of nor known', he observed. He went on to
capture the castle at Sagres and used the harbour as a base from which

he destroyed forty-seven small cargo vessels, most of which were designated to ferry men and provisions for the Armada. He abandoned his blockade of the coast when he heard that a great Portuguese ship, the *São Phelipe*, was headed with an enormous cargo of jewels and treasure for the Azores. Named as it was for the king himself, the *São Phelipe* was a symbol of Philip's rule over Portugal and its capture by Drake was especially wounding for him.[59] When Drake reached Plymouth this time (6 July 1587) he was weighed down by Philip's treasure and he had severely damaged the ships and supplies being prepared for the Armada. He had dislocated the Indies trade; in 1586 a record number of 148 ships had crossed from Cadiz to the Indies, but in 1587 only thirty-one did so. Drake had also, indirectly, caused significant damage to Philip's main fleet, for Santa Cruz had sailed from Lisbon on 16 July to protect the Azores and the *carrera de Indias* against Drake. The marquis spent three months at sea and when he returned to Lisbon on 29 September his fleet of 37 ships was badly in need of repairs and many of his men were weak or ill. The Armada would not sail in 1587.

There was, however, no longer any room for doubt that it *would* sail. Twice now, in 1586 and in 1587, the Enterprise of England had had to be postponed, and with each setback Philip (as was his custom) became the more determined to succeed. Parma's success in capturing the port of Sluys in August 1587 stimulated planning for the Enterprise. Sluys did not provide the deep-water port in which the Armada could shelter while it took troops on board but it could, in conjunction with the other coastal ports captured by Parma, notably Nieuport and Dunkirk, provide a point from which the Army of Flanders could embark on barges to be ferried out to the waiting fleet. When Santa Cruz limped back into Lisbon, therefore, it was to find that the king had issued his plans for the invasion of England. They bore the date of 14 September 1587.[60]

Philip had decided to reconcile the plans of his two commanders by merging them. It was probably on the advice of Juan de Zúñiga that he ordered that the Armada was to meet the Army of Flanders and transport its spearhead troops across to the 'Cape of Margate'. From there it would march on London.[61] In Philip's revised plan, therefore, the purpose of the Armada became to ferry Parma's troops across the Channel rather than to land soldiers itself, much less to engage the English fleet. It was a major structural change, foreseen by neither of his commanders, and it did not address the central logistical problem of how Parma's troops were to board Medina Sidonia's ships without a deepwater port in which the Armada could shelter and in the face of hostile English and Dutch fleets. Santa Cruz was so dismayed by the subordinate role now assigned him and his fleet that he seriously considered resigning. It was only with reluctance that he agreed to remain in office.[62]

The Council of War added its voice to the chorus demanding action against England. Its members, senior and highly professional men, were now convinced that military action was imperative.[63] But no one was more insistent than the king himself that the fleet should sail; Philip urged Santa Cruz to sail for England with such vehemence that the marquis felt obliged to defend himself against the implication of disloyalty. But even after the damage caused by Santa Cruz's foray to the Azores had been repaired, delay upon delay still occurred. On 16 November, thirty-nine ships were damaged, some seriously, by a storm; it was considered that it would take at least a fortnight to repair them.[64] Disease festered on the ships as they waited in harbour; at the end of November, Santa Cruz reported to Philip that 1400 men from the *tercio* of Naples had fallen ill in the six months that they had been embarked on ships in Lisbon. Insistently, he urged the king to let him disembark his men and have the ships cleaned. Ever more stridently, Philip refused to let him do so, stressing that if Santa Cruz did not get to sea all the men on board would fall ill, victuals be consumed and money devoured and all to no purpose.[65] On 2 December, Santa Cruz held a general muster. He found that 1180 (7 per cent) of the 16 260 sailors and soldiers in Lisbon were ill. Ten days later he informed the king that he thought that the fleet would be ready to sail after a further month. He hinted that he was himself becoming unequal to the task, noting that he would continue to work 'as long as life remains to me'.[66] On 18 January Philip ordered him to go to sea: 'I direct you and expressly order you that without losing an hour you should have the whole armada in the river'.[67] Philip despatched the redoubtable Pedro Enríquez, count of Fuentes, to Lisbon to see that Santa Cruz did so.[68]

King and admiral both crumbled under the strain. Philip collapsed at Christmas and was in bed for four weeks.[69] Endeavouring to sail in February 1588, Santa Cruz piled men, provisions and munitions on the fleet, ultimately without any order or priority other than to get them on board. The strain killed him: he contracted exanthematic fever when visiting sick seamen in hospital, collapsed and died on 9 February. Philip courteously promised the marquis's brother and son that he would remember his services but he allowed a more brutal reaction to become known at court, confessing himself relieved that Santa Cruz had died before the expedition set sail rather than after it had departed.[70]

The harshness of Philip's judgement reflected his obsessive concern; everything, but everything, depended on the Enterprise of England. In 1586–8 he had spent lavishly on the fleet and, exhausted though it was after its vain pursuit of Drake, it was still very substantial; by 1587 Philip was maintaining 117 ships in Lisbon, totalling 50846 *toneladas,* and he had about seventy galleys in the Mediterranean. He had a fleet that was large enough for the task that he was so insistently calling upon it to undertake. He himself, however, was exhausted; in February 1588 he was reported to be 'very languid and weak'.[71]

'OUR ARMADA'

On 14 February 1588 Philip informed his premier nobleman that he was to command the fleet against England. Alonso Pérez de Guzmán, seventh duke of Medina Sidonia, was the richest aristocrat in Spain, with an annual income of over 150000 ducats in rent, and he was an ideal choice as commander. Although he was only thirty-eight years old he was widely experienced in naval affairs and most especially in the provisioning of fleets. He knew the south-west coast of Spain in the greatest detail and had wide contacts in the kingdom of Portugal. His unique social standing ensured both that men would want to serve under him and that he would be able to impose discipline upon the fractious seamen who would command the ships of the Armada for him.[72]

The duke was horrified by his appointment and wrote to Juan de Idiáquez, begging him to have the king change his mind. He insisted that neither his health nor his financial resources were equal to the task, that he had knowledge neither of the sea nor of the state of preparation of the Armada. In fact, of course, Medina Sidonia had a very detailed knowledge of the fleet and was probably already convinced that it was heading for disaster. Philip dismissively insisted that the duke protested too much – 'I attribute this to your great modesty'.[73] On 18 February, Medina Sidonia wrote a second letter, which was so hostile to the Enterprise that Idiáquez and Moura professed that they dare not even pass it to the king. The two former secretaries did, however, remind Medina Sidonia that his reputation as a brave and honourable man 'would be at risk if what you write to us should become known'. The duke might not have been altogether reassured by the promise that Moura and Idiáquez gave him that they would 'look after his letter carefully'.[74] The two secretaries of State were virtually blackmailing Spain's premier nobleman into accepting the royal commission.

When Medina Sidonia arrived in Lisbon he found what Garrett Mattingly called 'a kind of frozen chaos'. The fleet consisted now of about 112 ships (48 490 *toneladas*) and 20 424 men – 5044 sailors and 15 380 soldiers.[75] The duke did the best he could, determined above all that men should not be allowed to disembark for fear that they would never be seen again. He added about 10 000 men and thirty ships to the fleet, but every extra man made the shortages of provisions the more acute and every extra ship added to the logistical difficulties confronting the duke.[76] For his part, Philip continued to work furiously at planning the expedition, but he cut himself off from contact with people who might have helped dissuade him from sending the fleet; he would not give audiences and relapsed into ever-increasing isolation from all but his closest advisers. By May he was not sleeping well, waking in the night to pray for the success of the Armada. As the summer of 1588 progressed he became increasingly withdrawn and irritable: 'every trifle annoys him', it was reported in July 1588.[77]

The rationale for sending the Armada was most authoritatively summed up by the Council of State in January 1588: 'the Enterprise should go ahead in the hope that God might favour such a just purpose as His Majesty has, taking it as His own, for this is the only way of assuring [the silver] that comes from the Indies and of freeing these coasts [of Iberia] from invasion and of giving security to Flanders, finishing by cutting out once and for good the root of the war there'. The Council recognised the importance of unanimity on this occasion and it recorded that 'although some councillors wanted to dissociate themselves from this everyone reached agreement'.[78] In the Council's view, Spain was fighting a defensive war to stop the English from helping the Dutch rebels and attacking the Iberian coasts and the Indies. The Dutch had resisted too long and it had cost Spain too much to fight them on land; if English aid was cut off the revolt in the Low Countries might be ended, or at the very least the rebels could be brought to the negotiating table. But there was no serious discussion of conquering or converting England: that was not a priority. Philip now had the support of his councils of State and War for the Enterprise of England. The fleet would sail against England for military and strategic and not for religious reasons and when it did sail it did so with the blessing of Spain's military and governmental elite.

Medina Sidonia's Instructions were despatched to him on 1 April. Like Philip's plans for the government of the Low Countries thirty years before, they were wide-ranging and detailed – and blithely optimistic. Philip ordered Medina Sidonia to:

> sail with the whole Armada, making for the English Channel, and pass through it until you reach Margate Cape, where you will join the Duke of Parma . . . You are to remove any obstacles and make secure his passage across the Channel, according to the plan arranged and according to my decision, with which you are both acquainted.

The duke was at all costs to avoid the risks of a naval battle, at least until he reached Margate. If battle was then forced on him, he could confidently anticipate being able to defeat the combined forces of 'the English Admiral and Drake' because the Spanish fleet 'will still be superior to both in quality, and also in the cause you are defending, which is God's . . .' Once Parma had landed, the Armada was to station itself at the mouth of the Thames and protect Parma's march towards London.[79] Secret instructions of the same day prepared Medina Sidonia for the unlikely eventuality of failure:

> If, however, through our sins it should fall out otherwise, and the Duke, my nephew, should not be able to cross to England, nor you for that reason meet him, then, after communicating with him, you will see whether you are able to capture the Isle of Wight, which is not so strongly defended as to appear able to resist you. Once captured, however, it can be defended, and you will have a secure port in which the Armada may take shelter and which, being a place of importance, would open the way for further action by you. It would therefore be well for you to fortify yourself strongly in it.[80]

Philip's plan predicated that the overwhelming strength of the Armada would enable it to dictate events, that English activity would be reactive. In fact, English strategy was based upon a keen understanding of the nature of the Spanish force and of its limitations. The subsidiary defects of the plan have been well-rehearsed by modern historians. Most obviously, there was no deepwater port in which the Armada could shelter while it took Parma's army – which may have numbered 26 000 men – on board. No specific provision was made to counter the possibility that the Dutch fleet could interfere with Parma's capacity to move his men along the Dutch coast in order to meet Medina Sidonia. The Spanish fleet was an Atlantic fleet and took with it only four large galleys; this was a serious deficiency, for galleys could have served a number of strategic functions, most notably in helping to protect Parma's army while it was ferried out to the great fleet. Santa Cruz had in 1583 wanted ten times as many galleys as actually sailed in 1588. Repeatedly, at key points in the campaign the shortage of galleys was to prove to be a fundamental weakness. These problems were compounded by the extraordinary difficulties of establishing and maintaining communication between the commanders. As to secrecy: the whole of Europe knew in detail what was being planned and betting books were opened on the likelihood of the success of the operation. Parma had urged Philip not to send the Armada if secrecy was broken but Philip became determined to send it precisely *because* secrecy was broken – his reputation demanded that because Europe was expecting him to send a great Armada against England he had to send one. Once again, the king demonstrated that when he had committed his prestige to a project he was incapable of pulling back from it.

It was Medina Sidonia's great achievement to get the fleet to sea. The duke was a punctilious book-keeper and in all the chaos of final preparations and departure we have a precise account of the strength of the great fleet as it prepared to leave Lisbon at the beginning of May; it consisted of 130 or so ships and 29453 men and carried 2431 pieces of artillery and 123790 cannon balls.[81] On 9 May, the fleet that had been so long in preparation finally edged out to sea. Unfortunately, it could not make progress beyond Belén in the face of strong winds and had to return to the safety of the harbour. It was a portent of something for which not even Philip could have planned: the summer of 1588 was to be especially foul.

If the weather was hostile to the Armada, events in France seemed all too likely to help it. By the end of 1587, the 'Sixteen' had organised their quarters of Paris and it was evident that Henry III was losing control of his capital. On 7 May he ordered house-to-house searches throughout Paris to discover evidence for use against the Sixteen. It was obvious that the king was preparing to move against his Catholic opponents and during the night of 11–12 May he had fifteen detachments of Swiss and French troops take up positions at strategic points throughout the city. Paris awoke on 12 May, therefore, to find itself a garrisoned city. The response of 'the Sixteen' showed that they had anticipated Henry's foolishness. With apparently miraculous co-ordination, they had barriers thrown up every thirty metres or so in each of their districts and the king and his garrisoning army found that it was they who were effectively imprisoned. Henry could do nothing and on the following day sneaked out of his capital, never to return. The Catholic League now controlled Paris. Henry would not be able to attack Parma's southern border or give any significant aid to Elizabeth.[82] The day passed into history as 'The Day of the Barricades'.

A final muster of the Armada was held on 28 May. It showed that the fleet had expanded in size even since the beginning of the month. It consisted now of 141 ships with a tonnage of 60151 *toneladas* and carried 7666 seamen and 19295 soldiers, a total of 26961 men. Even now, more men were piled on board; a Spanish naval historian, Hugo José O'Donnell, has demonstrated in a major reassessment that when the fleet sailed for England it carried as many as 33000–35000 men – equivalent to a medium-sized Spanish city. These men were truly cosmopolitan in their nationalities, reflecting the very nature of the monarchy of Philip II: the largest number (8000) were German mercenaries; there were 7000 Walloons and 6000 Spaniards; 3000 Italians and 1000 Irishmen and as many Burgundians. The spiritual needs of the men were served by about 150 friars and priests, their medical needs by seventy-four doctors and surgeons, and the notarial requirements of the fleet were supported by fifty scribes. The ships were divided into six fighting squadrons with a total of 63 fighting ships – the two royal squadrons of Castile and Portugal; a further two from Guipúzcoa and one each from Andalusia and the Levant. In addition, four large galleasses from Naples and four smaller galleys carried soldiers. Eleven small caravels carried soldiers but were intended as communication-ships, and twenty-three hulks were loaded with supplies.[83]

The commanders of the squadrons were massively experienced in different theatres of war: Don Alonso Martínez de Leiva, the second in command, had served as captain of infantry in the Low Countries, had commanded the galleys of Sicily in the Mediterranean and had fought on land against the *moriscos* of the Alpujarras; Don Pedro de Valdés had served as *maestre de campo* in the conquest of Florida under his kinsman Pedro Menéndez de Avilés and as admiral of the Armada defending the *carrera de las Indias* – he had ferried soldiers to Requesens in the Low Countries and commanded the galleons used in the conquest of Portugal in 1580; Don Juan Martínez de Recalde had also served in Flanders and had commanded under Santa Cruz in Portugal in 1580 and in the Azores in 1583; and Don Diego Flores de Valdés had served extensively in the Indies. These men (who were from northern Spain) had a wealth of military and naval experience. They did not, however, have high social rank, for it was a deficiency of the Spanish social and military systems that the navy (unlike the army) did not attract the scions of great noble families.[84]

The soldiers on board were commanded by Don Francisco Arias de Bobadilla, who had served three times as *maestre de campo general* in the Low Countries, and had fully earned a fearsome reputation (as befitted a descendant of Francisco Pizarro); discipline on the fleet was Bobadilla's responsibility. Distinguished soldiers commanded *tercios* under Bobadilla. For instance, Don Agustín Mexia led a *tercio* raised in Andalusia; Mexia had (like many soldiers on the Armada) served at Lepanto and had years of experience in the Army of Flanders. Similarly, Don Diego de Pimentel y Portugal, who commanded the *tercio* of Sicily, had served in the conquest of Portugal and had led cavalry in Italy. Both Mexia and Pimentel were younger sons of marquises (of la Guardia and Tavera respectively), and if their high social rank was a reminder of the priorities that governed appointments within the Spanish army, their professional excellence fully justified the positions they held. They both served on the Armada with distinction. So, too, did Don Baltasar de Zúñiga, brother of the count of Monterrey and noblemen such as Don Ramón Ladrón, son of the marquis of Terranova; Don Francisco Manrique, brother of the count of Paredes; Don Pedro Henrique, brother of the marquis of Villanueva del Rio; Don Bernardino de Velasco, brother of the Constable of Castile; Don Pedro de Zúñiga, son of the marquis of Aguilafuente, and so on. The social elite of Spain, and more particularly that of Castile, were strongly represented in every major ship of the fleet. So, too, were men of letters; Lope de Vega, who would become one of Spain's greatest dramatists, sailed on the Armada (as his great rival Miguel de Cervantes had served at Lepanto).[85]

The fleet sailed out of Lisbon once again over two days, on 28–30 May. Some of the food and drink was already going rotten, and within days rations had to be cut. The weather was so harsh that the great fleet took two weeks to sail the length of the Iberian coast, a distance of 160 sea miles. On 19 June, Medina Sidonia started to lead his fleet into the harbour of La Coruña to take on further provisions but only fifty ships had been securely berthed when at midnight a violent storm blew up and the ships outside the harbour were scattered, some of them being flung as far north as the Scilly Isles. It was an inauspicious beginning and Medina Sidonia did not lack the courage to protest to the king that many of the ships were quite inadequate. He wrote to Philip on 24 June that thirty-three ships were still unaccounted for and went so far as to suggest that the great storm was evidence of the Lord's lack of commitment to the Enterprise of England, a sort of divine hint that it should be abandoned. Certainly, disease was spreading on board; 500 men had to be taken off the ships in La Coruña and food and supplies for the fleet had to be brought from Lisbon. Medina Sidonia reiterated the technical shortcomings of the Armada and suggested that Philip would do better to seek a constructive peace with his enemies rather than to gamble everything on one throw of the dice. He concluded that 'it is essential that the enterprise we are engaged in should be given the closest scrutiny'. It was a courageous and honourable letter, from a man who was self-confident enough to risk his own standing with the most demanding of kings by pointing out to him the most obvious of his own shortcomings. Three days after writing to Philip, Medina Sidonia called a council of war to secure the support of his senior officers. The council agreed that the Armada was too weak to carry out its task.[86] Again, Philip paid no heed. His advisers at court supported him in insisting that his reputation demanded that the fleet proceed on its mission; an anonymous governmental note observed that 'if the Armada were now to remain in La Coruña, this would be construed as a proof of our weakness . . . (and) this would be the occasion for corsairs to fill the seas – to our shame; for the English, no longer fearing for their homes, to cross to the Indies'.[87] Philip accordingly dismissed Medina Sidonia's fears; on 1 July he wrote to him that 'the difficulties you raise as an argument for not continuing with the enterprise rest on no certain foundations' and insisted that 'I have dedicated this service to God, and have taken you as an instrument to assist me in it.' The duke was to sail for England.[88] Philip would not retreat on his commitment to despatch the Armada. Reluctantly, but having done his duty, Medina Sidonia prepared to obey. He was not able to take his fleet out again until 21–22 July. It had been nearly two months since he had first sailed from Lisbon, two months during which more than 30 000 men had been fed and supported without even coming close to engaging the enemy. He led 127 ships out of La Coruña – 20 galleons and four galleasses; 44 armed merchantmen; 38 auxiliaries and 21 supply ships. Even now, he lost some ships; when, nine days after leaving La Coruña, the fleet entered the Channel it consisted of 122 ships, five of which were used as despatch ships and took no part in the battles.[89] Medina Sidonia raised his banner as a declaration of intent to join battle.

It was probably Drake who insisted that the main English fleet should be based at Plymouth rather than at the Calais Roads. He had originally intended to attack the Armada off the coast of Portugal but delays caused by bad weather and the needs of national security obliged him to settle for fighting Philip's fleet in the Channel. Drake had had to settle, too, for serving under a leading nobleman, Charles, Lord Howard of Effingham. Like Medina Sidonia, Effingham was given command precisely because his social rank ensured that he could control the sea dogs who commanded Elizabeth's ships. Drake's behaviour in the Channel showed just how wise the queen's decision was. The English fleet gained the initiative by tacking out of Plymouth and winning the weather-gauge behind the Armada as it moved ponderously up the Channel. It was a brilliant operation and it gave the English the advantage of having the Spanish in view rather than having to wait for them (as Philip had always supposed they would) at the Straits of Dover. The English mobilised 226 ships (40 021 *toneladas*) against the 141 ships that Medina Sidonia had mobilised in Lisbon, and they were much smaller and more manoeuverable: only seventeen of their ships were more than 400 *toneladas* compared with sixty-five of the Spanish ships. They probably carried about 16 000 men.[90]

The Armada moved with consummate discipline in crescent formation but it moved at the pace of its slowest ships and the English shadowed it up the Channel, sailing close enough to keep in touch but far enough away to be out of serious danger. The Armada's first loss took place on 31 July when an explosion killed half of the 400 men on the *San Salvador* and horribly burned many others; Medina Sidonia saved the ship but then had to abandon her. On the following day he was unable – perhaps even unwilling – to rescue the *Rosario* under Pedro de Valdés when it failed to keep up with the fleet after a couple of collisions had damaged its bowsprit. Medina Sidonia ordered that the *Rosario* was abandoned and Drake himself – disobeying Effingham's orders – sneaked away from the English fleet in order to seize the prize for himself. Off Portland Bill, the fighting began in earnest as English ships used their superior sailing qualities and their rapid gunfire to assault the Spanish fleet, concentrating in particular on the flagship itself, the *San Martín*. But the English could not halt the Armada. They were, however, successful in preventing it from attempting to sail into the eastern Solent. Medina Sidonia was forced to decide that he would head for Flanders rather than for Margate, and he modified the formation of the Armada into a more compact crescent, ordering that any captain who deviated from his position should be hanged. He managed to save the *Gran Grifón* when it was damaged – by Drake? – but lost yet another galleon when the *Duquesa Santa Ana* was forced to take refuge in Le Havre (5 August).[91]

By now the problem of communicating with Parma was becoming acute. Parma would require several days to prepare his troops for the juncture with the Armada but apparently did not even know that the Armada was approaching, while Medina Sidonia thought that he would be waiting for him, prepared to embark his men. More serious still were the difficulties between the two commanders caused by the misunderstanding of each other's intentions and capacities. Medina Sidonia seems never to have realised that the flyboats of the Dutch would be able to prevent Parma from coming out of port to join him while Parma believed that it was Medina Sidonia's duty to secure his freedom to move out of port. The two commanders were operating on separate wavelengths – and with different purposes; one was committed to the Enterprise of England, and one was not.

Arriving off Calais on 6 August, Medina Sidonia found that all the worst possibilities materialised at once – there was no port for the Armada to sail into; Parma was prevented by a fleet of thirty or so Dutch cromsters from getting out to join him; the English had the command of the Channel and so there was no chance of retreat. As he waited, hoping against hope that Parma would come out to join him, the English massed their forces. On the night of 7–8 August, they began their main assault; eight fireships were towed towards the fleet. The Spanish themselves had used fireships against the English at San Juan de Ulúa in 1568 and at Cadiz in 1587 but it was from Antwerp in 1585 that so many of the soldiers on board remembered what these ships could do, and terror spread among the fleet as the hulks moved slowly towards them. In fact the fireships were not packed with explosives but the Spanish could not have known that and their fabled discipline broke. The ships of the Armada slipped their anchors and the following morning the English moved in, at last prepared to use their guns freely. After days of shadow-boxing up the Channel, battle was truly joined (Battle of Gravelines, 8 August) and it was quite unequal for the Spanish were in disarray and unable to cope with the greater manoeuvrability and more accurate firepower of the English, who now numbered perhaps 150 sail. Galleys would have been especially valuable in these critical days – in fending off the fireships and in helping the great Spanish galleons to manoeuvre away from the Dutch shoals. Medina Sidonia distinguished himself when he confronted virtually the whole English fleet with only five of his own ships for support. The Armada reformed but could not manoeuvre with the dexterity that distinguished the English fleet, and its ships were separated and attacked individually. Nor could they match English firepower; the Spanish ships had just under one-third of the number of long-range guns that the English had (172:497) and barely one-half of the number of heavy and medium guns (162:251). It has been estimated that the Spanish firepower was only about three-quarters of that of the English, and that indeed the Armada was carrying less than three times as much gunpowder as Santa Cruz had used in a single day's combat in the Azores in 1583. The Armada was outsailed at the Straits of Calais and it was outgunned. Professor Thompson has observed: 'what does seem certain is that the Spanish Armada was at such a decisive disadvantage in firepower, in both weight of shot and range, *that it was probably incapable of winning the sea battle on whatever terms it was fought.*' But the men of the Armada were not deficient in courage; they fought back and at the end of a dreadful day they had lost eight ships. It has been demonstrated by Capitán Gracia Rivas that on 8 August some 600 men died and a further 800 were wounded – nearly twice as many as had been killed or wounded in the days since battle had commenced on 31 July. In all, a total of 2636 men were lost in battle – 760 sailors and 1876 soldiers – just under 10 per cent of the force that had embarked in May. The ships had taken a terrible pounding, twenty times more fierce than the bombardment at Lepanto, according to some who were in a position to know. The *San Martín* absorbed 200 or more cannonballs.[92] It was no consolation that they had inflicted great damage on English ships; Drake's *Revenge* had been hit more than forty times. But had they known it, the men who survived the Battle of Gravelines still faced their most terrible and costly ordeal – the journey home.

On 9 August Medina Sidonia summoned his commanders for another council of war. It was decided to try once more to make the rendezvous with Parma. However, a strong wind then pushed the fleet out into the North Sea. At first Medina Sidonia welcomed this, for it blew him away from the shoals of the Dutch coast, but as the wind gathered force over three days it blew him deeper into one of the most inhospitable seas in the world. There was no possibility now of turning back to join with Parma. God's Protestant Wind had blown.

There was only one option, one route home. As the Armada edged tremulously north to begin rounding the British Isles, Medina Sidonia despatched Baltasar de Zúñiga to inform Philip of what had happened and to ask him to prepare help for such ships as managed to reach Spain. The fleet then set off on the journey around the north of the British Isles. As it did so, it left the enemy fleet behind, for the English commanders would not give further pursuit without sufficient provisions for their men. But for the Spanish there was no turning back; Medina Sidonia ordered his fleet (which consisted now of 110 ships) to give the rocky shores of Ireland as wide a berth as possible and the fleet headed north.

The weather deteriorated by the day and for the best part of a month the fleet was hammered by gales. It was now, rather than in the battles in the Channel itself, that the greatest losses took place; 6554 men were lost off Scotland and Ireland, many of them slaughtered after making it to land. Twenty-five ships were lost in these waters. By 3 September Medina Sidonia was delirious with fever. The mixture of relief and apprehension with which he sighted the Spanish coast can only be guessed at; on 21 September he led eight battered galleons into Santander. In the following weeks another forty-three ships made it to Santander, nine reached San Sebastian and six limped into La Coruña. Of the 127 ships that had left La Coruña in July, ninety-two returned home to Spain; three were lost in accidents and four in combat; twenty-eight were lost to the weather.[93]

Original reports arriving in Madrid cruelly suggested that the Armada had been victorious. On 18 August Philip himself wrote to Medina Sidonia congratulating him on his triumph over 'Drake's armada' and on the following day he informed Catalina Micaela that 'my armada had defeated that of England, or some of it'. Three days later, Mateo Vázquez noted that 'the most excellent news has come today from the Armada'. On 7 September the Council of War wrote cautiously to Philip that the Armada appeared to have succeeded but warned him that 'very great victories have (sometimes) been of more harm than profit' and advised him that the news might well prove to be bad. When twelve days later the Council heard that the Armada had sailed off into the North Sea it could scarcely credit the news. In an agony of uncertainty as to the fate of what it called 'our armada' it had to make plans for both offence and defence. Juan de Idiáquez wrote to Parma that Philip's agony was greater than could be imagined.[94]

Capitán Gracia Rivas has shown that 13 399 men returned to ports in Spain – 3834 sailors and 9565 soldiers. Poignantly, hundreds of men even died on their ships in port before they could be brought ashore, among them Miguel de Oquendo and Juan Martínez de Recalde.[95] Only about half of the ships that were saved proved to be of any use for further service. The Indies trade continued to be interrupted; for nearly three years (October 1586–March 1589) no convoy sailed for *Tierra Firme*.

Medina Sidonia left Santander on 5 October and arrived home at San Lúcar on 24th. Philip ordered Francisco de Bobadilla to write an assessment of the campaign and that sternest of soldiers freely recognised that Medina Sidonia had done as well as any commander could have done. But he went on to record that 'we found the enemy with a great advantage in ships, better than ours for battle, better designed, with better artillery, gunners, and sailors, and so rigged they could handle them and do with them what they wanted. The strength of our Armada was some twenty vessels, and they fought very well, better even than they needed, but the rest fled whenever they saw the enemy attack.'[96] To Medina Sidonia himself, Bobadilla's verdict can have been no consolation; his reputation had been ruined by a command which he had suspected to be doomed from the start and from which he had begged to be relieved. Philip was generous with his servant; he allowed no rebuke for Medina Sidonia to go unchecked and assured him of his continuing favour.[97]

The king's initial reaction was to vow that he would send another armada; he declared that he would 'imperill all his kingdoms in order to punish that wicked woman'. On hearing Zúñiga's report, he insisted (as was reported) 'that he is more than ever determined to follow out his enterprise with all the forces at his disposal', and to put out another fleet in March 1589. In October he vowed that he would if need be sell his own candlesticks to raise money so that he could do so. By the end of the month sufficient realism was breaking in for some advisers to accept that sending an armada in 1589 was not practical. Philip, however, insisted that he would overcome all difficulties. Some galleons arrived from Peru in October but brought only 1 500 000 ducats of silver for the Crown.[98] Philip turned yet again to the Cortes of Castile, asking the procurators to vote six million ducats over two years and to provide him with troops to resist any invasion of his territories by his enemies. Negotiations were long and hard for the procurators wanted to control the collection and disbursement of the money.[99]

The tumultuous year of 1588 ended with a significant defeat for the Army of Flanders when Parma failed, albeit narrowly, before Bergen-op-Zoom: it was his first major failure in the Low Countries. Almost unnoticed in the aftermath of the failure of the Armada, Charles-Emmanuel of Savoy took advantage of the weakness of the French Crown to invade and conquer the enclave of Saluzzo. More importantly, the year ended with Henry III making the most important of all his miscalculations. Drawing strength from the defeat of the Armada, Henry convened a meeting of the Estates-General at Blois. In December he summoned Henry of Guise for an audience; on entering the royal chambers, the duke was knifed to death (23 December). His brother the cardinal was arrested and was duly murdered on the following day. Henry III was, as it appeared, triumphant. He burnt the bodies of his two enemies so that no cult could develop to honour them.[100]

8

AFTER THE ARMADA: THE STRUGGLE FOR WESTERN EUROPE

NAVAL WAR WITH ENGLAND AND THE BURDEN ON CASTILE

In the later months of 1588, Philip slowly recovered his strength; by November he was once again working long hours at his papers and before the year was out he was conducting business with his ministers in person.[1] However, the last decade of his life was one of progressive physical decline and latterly of the unremitting agony of a long and lingering death. These years saw the king make a series of grievous errors of judgement – in his handling of the situation in Aragon; in his determination to risk so much on intervention in France and doing so at the expense of the war in the Low Countries; and in sending two more armadas against Elizabeth of England, both of which were ill-prepared and sailed unseasonably late in the year (1596 and 1597). The illnesses and the impairment of judgement were doubtless connected but what was most remarkable about Philip at the end of his life was the way in which he shed the indecisiveness that had characterised so much of his kingship. As he became more conscious of the approach of death, Philip became more determined to take any risk in order to bring his reign to a successful conclusion and to hand on a secure inheritance to his son.

Philip's senior ministers agreed with him that he was obliged to send another armada against Elizabeth to demonstrate that Spain's power remained unbroken. Indeed, in December 1588 the Council of War urged Philip to make offensive war precisely because defensive war would hearten his enemies and it insisted on the need to do something for reputation as much as for advantage. Accordingly, the Council of State

debated whether a new armada should best be directed to Ireland or
to Wales. Aware that resources were limited, the Council looked for
successes that could be gained cheaply; in July 1589 it even considered
despatching a galley fleet from Flanders to land in Hull in Yorkshire.[2]
The fertility – or desperation – of the Council's imagination did not
disguise the strategic imperative; defeat had made it inevitable that
Philip would send another armada.

Philip's first priority was of course to replace the ships that had been
lost in 1588, and in 1589–98 he had over sixty major ships built at the
Crown's cost. By the end of the reign he was once again maintaining a
fleet which had more than forty galleons at its core. Chief among the
new ships were the one thousand-ton galleons known as 'The Twelve
Apostles' – ships that were so-named because they were dedicated to
doing God's work – which were built in the Cantabrian dockyards in
1588–91. Despite his physical weakness, Philip was once again at his practical best here, and so the defeat of the Armada led to the creation of a
genuinely royal navy in the Atlantic – indeed, the adjective 'royal' was
added to the title of the Atlantic fleet in 1594 (*Real Armada del Mar
Océano*). The new fleet operated out of bases in Lisbon, Cadiz and La
Coruña to protect the whole of the Iberian Atlantic coast and the *carrera
de Indias* against the onslaught that inevitably followed the defeat of the
Armada.[3] The creation of the fleet was Philip's greatest success in his last
decade.

Philip began the process of persuading the Cortes of Castile to meet
the costs of these ships (and other defence expenditures) when in
September 1588 he summoned the procurators to the Escorial to agree
to a new grant. The negotiations were long and bitter and not until 4
April 1590 was agreement reached with the municipalities themselves on
the new tax; the Cortes undertook to provide the Crown with eight
million ducats over six years, at 1 333 333 ducats annually. Crown and
cities agreed that this was to be a temporary measure occasioned by the
national crisis and that it was not to be repeated.[4] When the details were
hammered out it was decided that the tax would be collected on the sale
of 'the four species' of wine, vinegar, oil and meat. The new levy was in
practice a tax upon the essentials of life; it not only increased the tax
burden on the poor but seemed to be targeted at them. Assessed in millions of *maravedís*, it became known as the *millones*.

Even this was not sufficient for Philip's needs and so in July 1589 he
once again summoned the procurators to the Escorial, urging them now

to increase the *encabezamiento general*. The procurators resisted, arguing that the damage done to Castile's prosperity and trade by the foreign wars had limited the kingdom's ability to pay yet more taxes. Philip would not give in and on 30 December the Cortes agreed to vote the *encabezamiento general*, at the rate of 2 755 555 ducats for six years.[5] The two taxes together, therefore, brought Philip some 4 088 888 ducats, an increase of about a third on the previous level. Further wealth flooded in from the Indies; in October 1589 the fleets of New Spain and Peru brought 19 721 811 ducats of silver.[6] Philip now had both the credit and the bullion with which to proceed on his grand projects. Even so, he looked anxiously to the future, concerned that the eight million ducats would not be sufficient for his needs; on 5 May 1592 a new session of the Cortes of Castile was opened so that the king could secure a renewal of the *millones* grant when it expired in 1596. Such was the bitterness of the debate about the king's request that the new Cortes outlasted Philip himself; not until the end of November 1598 was it brought to a close.[7]

Elizabeth of England was much more ready than many of her admirals and courtiers to admit how close Philip had come to success in 1588 and she remained fearful that he would put right his failure of that year. Both her fleet and her financial resources had suffered greatly in 1588 and Elizabeth therefore determined to inflict as much damage on Philip's surviving ships as she could so that they could not again sail against her. Elizabeth knew that over forty of these ships lay, damaged and largely unprotected, in the great harbour of Santander – a harbour so wide that it could not be readily defended by gun placements on the shore. She entrusted the task of destroying these ships to Francis Drake and Sir John Norris, a Flanders veteran. Her instructions to the commanders were unambiguous: 'Before you attempt any thinge either in Portugall or in the [Azores]; our express pleasure and comaundment is, that you first shall distress the shippes of warre in Guipuscoa, Biscay, and Galizia and in any other places that appertayne either to the kinge of Spayne or his subjects.'[8] Elizabeth's fleet was large enough to complete its primary mission; it consisted of more than 180 ships (including a score of Dutch ships that had conveniently become available) and 23 000 men, of whom no fewer than 19 000 were soldiers. The Armada veterans could be assaulted from the sea and, if necessary, finished off by an amphibious assault. The presence of such a large number of soldiers also told of Elizabeth's secondary strategy – that if she put a substantial army onto

Portuguese soil its presence alone might provoke a rising that would place Dom Antonio on the throne or at the very least force Philip to sue her for peace. Beyond this lay a third purpose to the great expedition – to waylay the treasure fleet at the Azores – and it was to this that the commanders were most deeply committed. If the expedition had too many purposes, soon it had too many commanders, for before they sailed Drake and Norris were joined by the earl of Essex, who fled from court to join the expedition in direct contravention of Elizabeth's command that he remain in London. They sailed from Plymouth on 8 May 1589.

The Spanish government had no doubt that Elizabeth's great fleet was directed against the ships in Santander and San Sebastian; indeed, as early as November 1588 the Council of War had advised Philip that 'reason dictates that what the enemy has chiefly to do is to burn the ships that have been collected from the Armada'. The Council sent north the few soldiers it could muster but it was deeply fearful of the outcome.[9]

Drake and Norris sailed straight to La Coruña, claiming that they had information that large numbers of Armada galleons were sheltering there; they arrived to discover that the port was virtually empty. They spent a fortnight ravaging the town and its countryside, wasting their own energies and supplies and enabling the defences of Lisbon to be reinforced before they arrived there. One Armada galleon (the *San Juan*) was destroyed, but by its own crew rather than by the English. It was a derisory success for such a large force.

The fleet then sailed for Portugal. Norris disembarked with his troops at Peniche, eighty kilometres north of Lisbon. He found the Portuguese were more intimidated by the presence of Spanish soldiers than they were animated by his own arrival; they stolidly refused to rise in support of Dom Antonio. In blistering heat, Norris marched on Lisbon but Cardinal-Viceroy Albert easily drove him off and by the time the English returned to their ships they had lost no fewer than 2000 soldiers to the heat and to enemy action.

Such cohesion as the expedition had now finally disintegrated. A storm hit the fleet off Portugal and with some difficulty the majority of the ships made their way to Vigo; Drake duly burnt much of the town before making a rather wan attempt to sail to the Azores and catch the treasure fleet. He could make little headway against strong winds, and with disease ravaging his overcrowded and ill-provisioned ships he reluctantly headed for home. He reached Plymouth at the end of June. More than

11 000 of the men who had sailed with him did not return – losses that compared with those suffered on the Armada – and these deaths were not compensated for by any strategic or financial gains, much less by any success in provoking a rebellion in Portugal. Drake had lost his touch; he could have crippled Spain's naval recovery, and he knew it. So, too, did Elizabeth; not until 1595 did she allow Drake to sail again on her service. Drake's failure allowed Philip to repair and re-rig his ships in the northern yards.[10] The losses of the Armada were rapidly being made good; the devastating blow that the English should have delivered after the victory of 1588 remained unstruck.

However, Spain was less able to win the daily war of attrition with the host of small expeditions that left England to attack her possessions in Europe and the Americas; in the years 1589–91 no fewer than 235 English ships attacked Spanish and Portuguese shipping wherever they could.[11] Spain was on the defensive across the Atlantic; in October 1589, for instance, it was reported that 'not a vessel has dared to put out from Mexico for fear of the English' while in November 'the sea round the Azores is swarming with pirates'.[12] The presence of large numbers of English ships did seriously dislocate the despatch of the fleets; in 1590 only twelve ships sailed for Spain from the Caribbean and in 1591 the departure of the treasure fleet for Spain was severely dislocated by the panic caused throughout the Caribbean by the fleet led by Hawkins and John Frobisher; seventy-seven ships were ready to leave Havana in July 1591 but not until the end of the year did they leave for Spain, arriving early in 1592. In 1592 itself, only nine ships sailed to Spain – the smallest homeward-bound royal fleet since Columbus's inaugural return voyage in 1493.[13] The *carrera de Indias* was buckling under the pressure of English attacks.

Some compensation came for Philip with the collapse of France into yet another civil war after the murder of the Guise brothers. The reaction to the murders was most immediate in Paris itself, where it was said that the arrival of the news 'made a 100000 Leaguers within an hour'. Within days the Sorbonne, the bastion of orthodox Catholicism, had condemned Henry III as a tyrant (7 January 1589), with the clear implication that he could legitimately be overthrown. Other towns and cities rushed to join the League – Rouen, Blois, Amiens, Reims, Dijon, Orléans, Toulouse and Marseilles. The pope, outraged by the murder of a prince of the church, summoned Henry III to Rome to account for his actions. The king ignored the pope and lost more credit in the eyes of his Catholic subjects. The murders also threw the League into more radical hands; the city of Paris, led by the Council of Sixteen (which was itself in close liaison with the Spanish embassy), was declared to be the new leader of the League. Charles, duke of Mayenne, the last surviving Guise brother, took the oath as commander of the League (13 March 1589). The murder of the Guise brothers had destroyed the reputation of Henry III and strengthened and radicalised the Catholic League.

Henry III had no choice but to ally himself with Henry of Navarre; at Plessis-lès-Tours on 30 April 1589 the two men agreed to join forces to fight the League. They made the capture of Paris their first priority, and it was when he was besieging the capital that on 1 August 1589 the king was assassinated by a Dominican, Jacques Clément. As he lay dying, Henry III recognised Henry of Navarre as his legitimate heir. France had a Protestant as her king.[14]

Philip decided with unwonted alacrity that he had to prevent Henry IV from establishing himself upon the throne and that he would if necessary downgrade the war in the Low Countries to do so. He also hoped to take advantage of the weakness of the French Crown to annex Provence and endow it upon the duke and duchess of Savoy. But just as Philip reordered the priorities of his foreign policy and moved towards open war with France for the first time since 1559 he found that his own frontier with France was vulnerable. The kingdom of Aragon was at the point of rebellion.

TUMULT IN ARAGON

When Philip decided to put Antonio Pérez on trial for murder he was naturally anxious that the case should be entrusted to a judge in whom he had complete confidence, and he turned to a fellow son of Valladolid, Rodrigo Vázquez de Arce. Don Rodrigo had made his name by his service to Don John in the Alpujarras and earned his elevation from the *oidoría* of the Chancellery of Granada to a councillorship of Castile.[15] He now faced up to Philip's complicity in the murder and forced the king to do likewise. He personally brought to Philip the paper that the king had written to Pérez, intimating that they had shared the secret of the murder. It may even have come as a relief to Philip to have to confront his own culpability after years of privately agonising about it. At all events, Philip wrote to Pérez (4 January 1590), ordering him to state the reasons that he had given him which had persuaded him to assent to Escobedo's death. Pérez naturally refused to incriminate himself and so Vázquez de Arce had him tortured (23 February 1590); unable to endure the eighth turn of the screw, Pérez confessed his guilt. On 1 July Vázquez de Arce condemned Pérez to be drawn through the streets and then be beheaded. He was also to lose all his property and possessions.[16]

The great intriguer now pulled off his masterstroke; on 19 April 1590 he escaped from prison and rode hard for Aragon.[17] Once he had crossed the border he threw himself upon the protection of the *fueros* of his native land, invoking the right of appeal which entitled him to be judged by the Justicia of Aragon without reference to royal (or Castilian) justice. Pérez could not have judged his moment better, for he arrived in Aragon exactly as the kingdom was being riven by acute tensions over a number of deeply sensitive (and divisive) constitutional, political and social issues. Chief among these was the question of whether Philip was legally justified in appointing a non-native viceroy; at the beginning of 1588 he had despatched Don Iñigo de Mendoza y de la Cerda, marquis of Almenara, to argue his case at the Justicia's court. Almenara was the cousin of Chinchón, and his appointment indicated that Philip intended now to follow the count's insistent advice that he should implement an aggressive policy of centralisation in Aragon. Almenara was greeted with intense hostility. When his house was set on fire by a mob he returned to Madrid to consult with Philip. The king sent him straight back, to serve as his special emissary and named the bishop of Teruel as viceroy. By a dreadful coincidence Almenara returned shortly before Antonio Pérez himself reached Calatayud.

Pérez was taken to Zaragoza in the coach of an official of the Justicia. He turned the journey into a triumphal procession, presenting himself at once as the champion of Aragon's liberties and as the victim of the king's vindictiveness. For thirteen months he remained in the Justicia's prison and he used the time to display the full range of his manipulative genius; he received the leading men of the kingdom of Aragon (and many of its scoundrels), showed off the scars from his torture and organised his defence. Not for nothing was the Justicia's prison known as 'the prison of liberty'; Pérez was the man to exploit the freedoms that it allowed its inmates.

Philip responded cautiously, anxious not to aggravate the situation at a time when it was becoming likely that he would be going to war with France. Philip was concerned, too, not to provoke a rebellion on Spanish soil that might be even more damaging to his authority than that in the Low Countries. Accordingly, he waited patiently for Aragonese justice to deal with Pérez. However, as he came to realise that his own case was going by default and that the Justicia was likely to set Pérez free, so Philip listened more readily to the voices of those advisers in Madrid who were urging severity upon him. Pérez's established enemies in the capital were now joined by the king's confessor, Fray Diego de Chaves, who urged Philip to use the Inquisition to resolve the case once and for all. The Inquisition was, Chaves argued, the only institution that could override the constitutional liberties of the Aragonese *fueros*.[18] The opponents of Pérez were joined, too, by Andrés de Prada, the respected secretary of the Council of War and formerly secretary to Don John himself. On 18 October 1590 Prada wrote to Philip, angrily rebutting Pérez's claim that Don John had been on the point of rebellion against Philip's authority when he died.[19] The king was driven to agree; in May 1591 he authorised the involvement of the Inquisition and withdrew from the process against Pérez. The secretary was now to be charged with heresy and sodomy – offences which carried the death penalty without involving king or ministers in giving evidence about the death of Escobedo. On 24 May Pérez was transferred to the Aljafería, the prison of the Inquisition.

The news provoked an explosion in Zaragoza. Stimulated by the partisans of Pérez, a mob once again besieged Almenara's house, and when the Justicia himself tried to lead Almenara to safety the marquis suffered a serious head wound. At the same time, another mob besieged the Aljafería. Panicking, the Inquisitors capitulated; Pérez was returned to his 'prison of liberty'. Almenara died from his injuries a fortnight later. When Philip was woken by Chinchón to be told the news he tugged insistently at his beard and made no comment other than 'they' had killed his viceroy.[20]

Reluctant as Philip was to send an army to fight against his own vassals, he now began to prepare an army to invade Aragon. He did so in the full knowledge that the very appearance of the army in Aragon might well unite all Aragonese against the Crown in defence of their privileges. He therefore determined – exactly as he had done in Portugal in 1580 – that his army would be of a size and of a quality as to brook no opposition. If he had to use force, Philip would use overwhelming force. He entrusted the command to Don Alonso de Vargas, a Flanders veteran of fierce reputation – he had led troops in 'the Spanish Fury' at Antwerp – and a councillor of war. Still, however, Philip was not prepared to give up all hope of a peaceful settlement, and so he sent the marquis of Lombay to Aragon in a last desperate attempt to calm the situation down; Lombay carried a letter for Miguel Martínez de Luna, count of Morata, an Aragonese nobleman, naming him as viceroy in succession to Almenara. Philip held on, too, to Vargas's commission: not until 14 August 1591 did he actually sign it.[21]

As Philip agonised over whether he should use force against his own vassals, Pérez insistently proclaimed from the Justicia's prison that his cause was that of Aragon and its liberties. The people of Aragon as a whole did not rally to the unlikely defender of their liberties but many lesser nobles did and the capital city itself was swayed to support Pérez.

The situation might have been contained even now had Aragon had the benefit of clear leadership. The two senior aristocrats of the kingdom, the duke of Villahermosa and the count of Aranda, were torn between their loyalty to their monarch and their commitment to their country and its *fueros*. Both were also, no doubt, mindful of the harsh treatment that they and their families had received from the king. Neither man had the clarity of purpose or political skill to resolve their dilemma. It was also to prove especially unfortunate that the Justicia, Juan de Lanuza, should have died at the very height of the crisis (22 September). He was succeeded by his son and namesake, Juan III. Twenty-eight years of age, the new Justicia had neither the political expertise nor the experience to impose himself upon the crisis.

On 24 September, the authorities tried once again to move Pérez to the Aljafería. A carefully orchestrated riot ensued and yet again Antonio Pérez escaped from custody. He headed for France, but then demonstrated his nervelessness by returning to Zaragoza, probably because he realised that he was safer in the capital than in the remote villages of the countryside. The Justicia and his family helped Pérez to hide in the city. The city of Zaragoza expelled all the king's supporters, and its magistrates distributed arms from the town hall. On 1 November 1591 the *Diputación* of the Kingdom declared war on Philip. Confronted by open and formalised rebellion, sanctioned by the leading judicial authorities and supported (if discreetly) by the country's leading noblemen, Philip could defer action no longer. On 6 and 7 November, Vargas led an army of 14800 men into Aragon – 11750 infantry, 1800 cavalry and 1300 artillery and support troops. These were prime troops – many of them were veterans of the Low Countries and Portugal – and among their leaders were some of the most senior and able of Philip's generals, notably Francisco de Bobadilla himself as *maestre de campo general* and Agustín Mexia. The army occupied the capital without resistance on 12

November. The Justicia raised a force of about 1500 men – it could not really be called an army – but it evaporated when called upon to confront Vargas and his hardened professionals. Vargas ensured that no incidents took place which might have provoked the local population into revolt. He also began to fortify northern frontier posts to prevent an invasion from France. Pérez fled and Villahermosa, Aranda, Juan de Luna and the Justicia took refuge in Épila, a walled town belonging to Aranda. They tried to reach an accommodation with Vargas while talking fearlessly of leading a rebellion in the mountains. But realising that they were defeated without having fought and fearing that they would be found guilty by association and by their absence, Villahermosa and Aranda returned to Zaragoza on 24 November. Lanuza joined them on 26th. Pérez crossed into France on 24 November, never to return to Spain.[22]

Philip had Villahermosa and Aranda arrested and taken to prison in Castile. The Justicia was arrested on 19 December as he went to hear Mass; Bobadilla curtly informed him that he had been sentenced to death. Lanuza rejected the charge of 'traitor', dejectedly responding only that he was 'not a traitor, but merely badly advised'. He was publicly beheaded on 21 December. His goods were confiscated and his home and castles were destroyed.[23] Villahermosa and Aranda both died in mysterious circumstances late in 1592 in their prisons in Castile. Garrisons were installed in all the principal towns of Aragon and the houses of the chief offenders were razed to the ground.

Philip issued a general pardon on 17 January 1592 but its exemptions led directly to the last act of the tragedy; Juan de Luna, Martin de Lanuza (brother of the dead Justicia) and Diego de Heredía – all of whom were excluded from the pardon – led an invasion from France of perhaps 600 men in February 1592. They received no significant support and Vargas dealt easily with them. Punishment was meted out on 19 October in Zaragoza, and in its savagery it reflected the niceties of social category: the noblemen, Luna and Heredía, were beheaded, Luna from the front and Heredía from the back; the gentlemen, Francisco de Ayerbe and Dionysius Pérez de San Juan, had their throats slit and were left to bleed to death while the commoner Pedro de Fuertes was garrotted and his body was then quartered. Brutality was added to the executions by the incompetence with which they were carried out – it took the headman twenty thrusts to remove Heredía's head from his body. The heads – or what remained of them in the case of Heredía's – were displayed on pikestaffs at key points in the city to remind the citizenry of the punishment waiting for rebels. On the following day, an *auto-de-fé* in Zaragoza condemned 500 people. Eight of them went to the stake and they were accompanied by an effigy of Antonio Pérez, burnt as a heretic and sodomite. A further score or so citizens of Zaragoza were flogged, expelled or sent to row in the galleys. In all – including Villahermosa and Aranda – forty-four people were executed as a direct result of the rising.[24]

The king now showed that he had learned one lesson from his mistakes in Flanders; ill and weak though he was, Philip travelled to Aragon to bring the revolt to a conclusion with a display of kingly forgiveness. He left Madrid on 12 May 1592, and he did so against the advice of his physician, Dr Vallés. To ensure that Castile remained firmly governed while he was away he appointed Rodrigo Vázquez de Arce as president of the Council of Castile (22 April).[25] However – as he had done in 1585 – Philip travelled circuitously and very slowly, spending several months in Old Castile before going to Pamplona so that his son could be sworn in as heir to the Kingdom of Navarre (22 November). Philip had the Cortes of the kingdom of Aragon opened in Tarazona on 15 June before he arrived, making it clear that he did not intend to sit through the discussions as he had had to do in 1585. The count of Chinchón himself arrived to expedite the conduct of business and the Cortes was brought to an end on 25 August. Two days later Francisco de Bobadilla was appointed to replace Vargas as commander of the army. Vargas had proved too pliant for the taste of the hardliners at court and Bobadilla had a reputation that ensured that he was obeyed without question. Bobadilla was a kinsman of Chinchón and his appointment rounded out the count's triumph; the kingdom of Aragon was now effectively governed for the king by members of Chinchón's own family and by his supporters.

Philip curtly used his new power to have the procedures of the Cortes of Aragon reformed so that a simple majority vote was sufficient in each of the four estates when new laws were being made. The king's right to appoint non-Aragonese viceroys and to remove an unsatisfactory Justicia were acknowledged. Fugitives were no longer to be allowed to appeal easily to the protection of the *fueros*. The construction of a royal fortress was begun within the Aljafería itself and the county of Ribagorza was absorbed into the royal domain as the culmination of thirty years of struggle on the part of the Crown. Philip conducted the chief business of his visit: on 2 December in the town hall of Tarazona Felipe was sworn in as heir to the kingdom of Aragon. Having achieved his purposes – and having ignored those of the people of Aragon – the king published a General Pardon on 4 December. He and his son left Tarazona on the following day; they reached Madrid on 30 December.

In military terms, the 'rebellion' of Aragon was much less serious than that of the Alpujarras had been in 1568–70 and certainly bore no comparison with the revolt in the Low Countries. It was much smaller and more localised, a disturbance or aristocratic tumult rather than a popular revolt, and it was dealt with comparatively easily once Philip had decided to act. The army was withdrawn in the spring of 1593 and the financial cost of the operation was 1 370 613 ducats.[26] But the rebellion in Aragon damaged everything that Philip held most dear in his reputation as a lawful monarch and it raised again, for all Europe to see, the spectre of the murder of Escobedo and the conduct of Philip himself in authorising it. Philip could not escape from his collusion with Antonio Pérez in the death of Escobedo and this had a draining effect on him. In a personal and perhaps even in a regnal sense, Philip's war with Antonio Pérez cost him more than his wars with foreign powers.

INTERVENTION IN FRANCE

The duke of Parma achieved little in 1589 before his campaign was brought to an end by yet another mutiny among his Spanish troops. It was perhaps because he had wasted a second successive year's campaigning that in October Parma urged Philip to seek a settlement with Holland and Zeeland. He advised the king to cede the right of private worship to the Calvinists of the north if they allowed the Catholics in their territories to practise their faith publicly. Philip initially rejected the suggestion, insisting that Holland and Zeeland would have to subject themselves to Rome and allow the free practice of Catholicism before he could consider making an agreement with them. On reflection, however, the king decided to allow Parma to make exploratory soundings. Unfortunately, by the time (in 1591) that he informed Parma that he would be prepared to concede toleration for a limited period in exchange for a return to allegiance by the rebels the moment had been lost. As always appeared to be the case when negotiating with his rebels, Philip contrived to win the worst of all worlds.[27] Moreover, as Philip concentrated his attention and resources on France, the great advances that Parma had made in the 1580s were lost by default. In truth they were almost abandoned. The Dutch army gathered strength; it stood at 20 000 men in 1588 and by 1595 had grown to 32 000. Moreover, in Maurice of Nassau, son of William of Orange, the Dutch army now had a general of real stature. In the 1590s Maurice captured forty-three towns and large swathes of five provinces: Gelderland, Overijssel, Drenthe, Groningen and north Brabant. His successes completed the transformation of the military situation; the Spanish never recovered the lands that Maurice took from them while they concentrated on France.[28]

Philip was not officially at war with France but from 1589 he was in all but name at war with a king of France. The contrast between the two monarchs could hardly have been greater. Philip was ill and immobile, while Henry was physically vigorous, ceaselessly on the move, leading his troops in person, rallying support, winning over opponents through personal contact. While Philip was increasingly rigid in his political objectives, Henry displayed a vigour and a subtlety that had been born of a lifetime of danger and of hardship. Both men now gambled desperately to win the throne of France.

Henry understood full well (although in fact he never claimed) that 'Paris was worth a mass' – that he could never sit firmly on the throne as The Most Christian King unless he was a Catholic. On 4 August 1589, therefore, he moved to win the support of his Catholic subjects, promising that he would 'maintain and conserve within the realm the Catholic, apostolic and Roman faith in its entirety, without altering anything'.[29] Philip's response was to the point; on 26 November 1589 he ordered Parma to lead his army into France.[30] Philip determined that his daughter Isabella should be his candidate for the succession to Henry III, if not as queen regnant then as queen-consort. In May 1590 he put forward Isabella's claim to the throne on the grounds that she was the granddaughter of Henry II. However, France's Salic Law expressly forbade a female succession and so Philip's action convinced many Frenchmen – among them, a growing number of Catholics – that they had to support Henry IV in order to preserve their national independence. Elizabeth of England had already been persuaded of the need to bolster Henry's position; in September 1589 she despatched 3600 men under Lord Willoughby to campaign with Henry in Normandy. The scene of conflict was shifting towards the northern coast of France.

On 14 March 1590 Henry won a great victory against the army of the League under Mayenne at Ivry and thereby opened up the road to Paris, some sixty kilometres away. Henry was in no hurry to besiege Paris, for hunger was doing his work for him, and not until 7 May did he open the siege. Even then, he allowed 3000 women and children to leave the city. In doing so he sent a powerful message to all Frenchmen about reconciliation and humanity. However, Henry then conducted the siege with brutal effectiveness; perhaps 30 000 of the population of 200 000 perished over the next months.[31] By the end of July it was clear that Paris could not hold out for more than a few weeks.

Philip decided that Paris was worth an army. He ordered Parma to lead the Army of Flanders into France. Parma protested strenuously that Philip was risking the loss of the Low Countries with little prospect of making substantive gains in France, but he had no choice than to obey. In mid-August he led an army of 14 000 infantry and 3000 cavalry into France. He joined Mayenne and the League forces at Meaux and duly saved Paris, entering in triumph on 19 September. He refused, however, to stay in France and in November returned to the Low Countries against Philip's express orders, leaving some 5000 men to help support the League.[32] In doing so, Parma gave his enemies at court the weapon with which to discredit him with the king; always bitterly resented by the aristocracy of the loyalist states and by the Spanish military elite in the Low Countries, he now found both groups working actively against him.

Philip's gamble in 1590 was not confined to north-eastern France. Brittany held out against Henry IV under the duke of Mercouer (who had a claim through his wife on the ancient Breton throne) and in October 1590 Philip sent 3000 Spanish troops under Don Juan de Aguila to support Mercouer. They landed at Blavet on the southern coast and began building a fortified base. Blavet would not accommodate Spain's largest galleons, but at least it provided a base near the Channel for her smaller galleons and for her galleys. Moreover, if Parma was able to effect a junction with forces operating out of Blavet, he would be able to bring the whole of northern France under Spanish control. A new armada against England would then have available to it not only Brest but the French Channel ports as well. For Elizabeth, this presented a more serious threat even than that of 1588 and she responded in May 1591 by sending Norris to Brittany with 3000 men and in August by despatching Essex to Normandy with another 4000 men. However, the forces raised with such cost proved to have little more than nominal value; Norris's men wasted away and three-quarters or so of them died, as much through hunger as in war.[33] The operations conducted from Blavet and from the Low Countries were not the sum of Philip's involvement in France, for in November Charles Emmanuel of Savoy led an army into Provence in the hope of extending his own lands by conquest, and he had some of Philip's soldiers in his army. In the autumn of 1591, therefore, Philip was supporting three separate armies in France. He was also maintaining his galley fleet at Blavet.

Far from redrawing the lines of conflict in Spain's favour, Philip's monumental effort proved to be quite as counterproductive as Parma had predicted. In 1591, Maurice of Nassau took Zutphen (20 May) and Deventer (20 June) before directly engaging Parma himself for the first time; Parma was besieging the fort of Knodsenburg when Maurice arrived and, in a deeply symbolic expression of the change in the balance of military power, Maurice forced Parma to abandon the siege. He went on to capture Hulst, a mere twenty or so kilometres away from Antwerp (24 September) and concluded a brilliant campaign by capturing Nijmegen (21 October). It was now evident not only that the Dutch had a general who could rival Parma but that the tide of the conflict in the Low Countries was turning against Spain, perhaps decisively; an Englishman wrote that 'for some years past the Spaniards carried all things before them and now they lose as fast'.[34] In the aftermath of the defeat of the Armada, Philip was struggling to maintain his position in the Low Countries.

He was also on the retreat in France, for Henry IV took Chartres (19 April) and Noyon (19 August) and in November besieged Rouen. If he succeeded in capturing the city Henry would control the whole of Normandy, be able to threaten the Low Countries from the south and to command the Seine as it coursed down towards Paris. His assault on Rouen therefore held the key to the control of north-eastern France and perhaps to the security of the loyalist lands in the Low Countries. Once again, Philip ordered Parma into France. King and Governor-General rehearsed their arguments of the previous year, and with the same results. At the turn of 1591–2 Parma entered France for a second time, commanding an army of 15 000 infantry and 3000 cavalry. On 20 April he duly lifted the siege of Rouen and then brilliantly escaped from Henry IV's pursuit and retreated towards the Netherlands. However, Parma was wounded at Caudebec (24 April) and lost a good deal of blood by refusing to have any medical attention before the engagement was concluded. Weakened, he fell into a fever. In danger of losing his arm if not his life, Parma made it back to the Low Countries. He wrote to Philip that he was 'more dead than alive' and went to Spa to recuperate; jaundice set in and Parma remained at Spa for five months.[35] He never recovered and did not know that Philip had decided to recall him. The count of Fuentes – another son of Valladolid – arrived in Brussels on 11 November to take over command of the army. Fuentes did not have time to deliver the documents informing Parma of his disgrace; on the night of 2–3 December the duke died at Arras.[36] He was forty-seven years of age. Parma was the greatest of Philip's servants but he had outlived his time; his successes ended when Philip repeatedly diverted the Army of Flanders away from its business in the Low Countries in the years 1588–92. Parma's gains were lost and were never recovered.

For Henry IV, characteristically, nothing succeeded like failure. The new king had to come to terms with defeat at Paris and Rouen and with the failure of the English to provide him with effective support; Essex's men, like Norris's, achieved nothing and the Earl himself returned home in January 1592. It was time for Henry to become a Roman Catholic. Circumstances helped him; two popes died in 1591 – Gregory XIV in October and Innocent IX in December – and Henry was able to take advantage of the weakness of the papacy to press for support at Rome. Philip made a determined effort to influence the conclave and the divisions within the College of Cardinals were so intense that for a time there was even talk of schism. On 20 January 1592 Ippolito Aldobrandini was elected pope. Only fifty-six years of age, he was likely to have a long pontificate. He took the name of Clement VIII and proclaimed his intentions by calling for prayers for France: Clement VIII understood full well the papacy's need to have France counterbalance Spain.[37]

In the loyalist Low Countries, control of affairs devolved upon the count of Fuentes after Parma's death.[38] He brusquely dismissed the claims of count Peter Ernest of Mansfelt to manage government and despatched Mansfelt's son, count Charles, to lead a third invasion of France. When the younger Mansfelt had a success in the capture of Noyon (1 April 1593) Fuentes claimed it as his own. Maurice of Nassau needed no encouragement to take advantage of the tensions at the heart of Spanish government in the Low Countries; on 25 June he captured Geertruidenburg, the only town held by the Spaniards in Holland.

On 25 July 1593 Henry attended Mass at Saint-Denis; dressed in white and carrying a candle, in front of the high altar he publicly abjured heresy and proclaimed that he would live and die in the Roman Catholic faith. He then went to confession and adopted the practice of attending Mass daily.[39] Henry's action outraged many of his Huguenot followers, who considered that he had sold his faith for a throne. However, the most grieved man of all at the conversion of 'the Béarnais' to Catholicism was the Catholic King, for at a stroke Henry did away with the justification for the existence of the Catholic League and for Philip's interference in France. Henry IV was crowned at Chartres on 27 February 1594. On 22 March he entered Paris at six in the morning; two hours later he heard Mass in Nôtre Dame. France had a Catholic king once again. Henry allowed the 3000 Spanish troops to march out of the city. The Sorbonne acknowledged the legitimacy of his title to the Crown, and the shops began to re-open for trade.[40]

Losing ground in both the Low Countries and in France, Philip reverted to the practice of having a member of his own family as Governor-General in the Low Countries. He chose the archduke Ernest, believing no doubt that since he had been educated for a decade in Spain he would be reliable. However, although Ernest was only forty-one years of age, he seemed already to be an old man, weakened by gout and lacking in vigour and determination. He showed no enthusiasm whatever for the task that Philip had imposed on him and only arrived in Brussels on 30 January 1594.[41] He recognised the weakness of his position by seeking a truce, but the States-General were unwilling to consider a cessation of hostilities; rather, they confirmed their power with the relatively easy conquest of Groningen, the last royalist stronghold in the north (22 July 1594).[42] Soon Ernest was letting it be known that he wanted to leave for Germany to press his candidature as king of the Romans. He had no appetite for defeat and humiliation in the Low Countries.[43]

By 1594 Philip himself was sufficiently weak to feel obliged to make his testament (7 March). The document bespoke at once Philip's deep religiosity and his love for his children and for his dynasty. He stipulated that 30000 masses were to be celebrated for the repose of his soul – the same number that his father had authorised in his own testament – and that masses were to be said in perpetuity on the anniversaries of his own birth and death. Further masses were to be said for the souls of his parents and his wives and children. The king left clothing for a hundred poor people and 10000 ducats for dowries for poor girls. He reserved 30000 ducats for the redemption of captives from the infidel. Philip prepared for death with the consolation that an important part of his life's work had come to fruition; on 30 August 1594 the basilica of the Escorial was consecrated.[44]

In December 1594 Henry survived an assassination attempt – one of three during that year alone – and on 17 January 1595 he formally declared war on Spain. He bitterly denounced Philip's interference in

France's internal affairs and prepared to lead his countrymen, Catholic and Protestant, in a national war against Spain.[45] Philip responded by insisting that he had intervened in France only to prevent the ruin of the Catholic religion and reiterated his support for the League.[46] Henry led, as always, by example; he hastened down to Burgundy to confront an army that the constable of Castile had led over the Alps, defeating it at the battle of Fontaine-Française in June 1595. He made a triumphant entry into Lyons early in September. Success brought more of his own countrymen flocking to his standard and it brought, too, the reward from the pope that Henry needed above all others; on 17 September 1595 the new Catholic was formally absolved from his sins and from his Huguenot past. Characteristically, Henry made it a condition of accepting absolution that he would not be required to abandon Elizabeth or any other of his allies. For his part, Clement VIII stipulated that Henry was to confess and communicate publicly at least four times per year and insisted that the decrees of the Council of Trent were implemented in France.[47]

The legitimation of Henry IV as The Most Christian King led to the final collapse of the Catholic League; on 20 September the duke of Mayenne, brother of the two murdered Guise brothers, concluded a three months' truce with the King. It was confirmed in January 1596 and during the summer of that year Mayenne's example was followed by the dukes of Joyeuse and Epernon. Only Mercoeur, isolated in remote Brittany, held out.[48] The Catholic League had fallen apart.

As Philip had for the first time in his reign to confront the full power of France in open war, the means for one last gamble became available to him. No treasure fleets had arrived in 1594 because of fear of English corsairs, and the treasure that they would have brought was scheduled to be transported in the fleet of 1595. That joint fleets would arrive made it easy for Philip to win credit and he committed himself to major *asientos* against the arrival of his enormous treasure. The fleets of New Spain and Peru reached Seville at the turn of April–May 1595, bringing some twenty-two million ducats, of which about one third were for the king. But the bounty disguised the debts into which Philip had fallen while he waited for his treasure, and it was calculated that if he paid these debts he would only have 1500000 ducats left.[49] In September a further eight million ducats' worth of silver arrived. In five months, therefore, well over thirty million ducats of bullion were unladen at Seville – an amount, it was noted, that 'surpasses any record in the memory of man'.[50] Philip had the resources, it seemed, for one last throw of the dice. And the Catholics of Ireland were begging him to help them. Philip had been defeated in battle by England, was in imminent danger of losing his war for the succession in France and was on retreat in the Low Countries. Might Ireland provide him with the means to bring Elizabeth to heel, and in doing so to reverse these losses? The reign was about to reach a thunderous crescendo.

9

CRESCENDO: FAILURE, SETTLEMENT AND DEATH

PRECONDITIONS OF DISASTER: HUNGER AND FAMINE

By the spring of 1595, Philip seemed to be surviving on willpower alone. His doctors marvelled at his courage and endurance; after he had weathered twenty-seven continuous days of fever in April–May 1595 they let it be known that 'his body is so withered and feeble that it is almost impossible that a human being in such a state should live for long'.[1] A year later, in April 1596, an attack of gout deprived him of the use of his right arm. He sank into deep depression; noting that an eclipse of the sun was due, he solemnly recalled that his father, his mother and other members of his family had died at such a time.[2] But battered though he was, Philip would not give up on his wars; he would make a settlement for his son, but he would do it on his own terms and even now, with his life ebbing away by the day, he would do it in his own time.

The country over which Philip ruled and from which he demanded ever-greater sacrifices mirrored his exhaustion. Hunger was widespread across the face of the Iberian peninsula (and indeed in Philip's possessions in the Mediterranean) during the last two decades of his reign. By the 1580s it was evident that the population was outstripping the capacity of the land to feed it.[3] It was against this background – and against his own determination to tax his vassals more fully through the *millones* – that Philip ordered that a census be taken to establish the exact population of Castile, and as importantly, its distribution. The census of 1591 (which became known as 'the census of the *millones*') showed that Castile's population had grown to 6 671 251 – an increase of 47 per cent since 1530. Using this information as a baseline, historical demographers have calculated that the total population of Spain in 1591 was 8 120 337, an increase of 42 per cent since 1530 (see Table 1). During Philip's own lifetime, therefore, the population of Spain had increased by nearly a half. There were most certainly now (in Braudel's phrase) 'too many people for comfort'.[4] At the end of a century in which Spain had become the first power of Europe, she could not feed her own people.

The hardships created by exceptional population growth were compounded by natural circumstances. It is now evident that the later years of the sixteenth century witnessed a significant climatic deterioration. This had especially severe consequences in Spain, where so much of the soil was of marginal use for agricultural production. The 1580s and 1590s were exceptionally harsh years in Spain; in 1590, for instance, Seville and its region were afflicted with 'many illnesses' caused by especially severe weather, while the historian of Granada referred to that year as seeing the beginning of 'a hunger caused by the great shortage of wheat from the last harvest'.[5] Widespread food shortages were the inevitable result; the city council of Cordoba, for example, was obliged as early as 1582–4 to purchase massive amounts of wheat so that its citizens could be fed.[6] The situation was worse in the central *meseta* of Castile; in Valladolid the price of wheat virtually trebled during the years 1587–94, reaching 682 *maravedís* per *fanega* – the highest level of the century – in 1594.[7] Population pressures were less extreme in the kingdom of Aragon but hunger was aggravated there by the growing problems of banditry on land and piracy on sea. Indeed, it was very much a sign of the times that some bandits became popular celebrities – in Aragon and Catalonia Lupercio Lattrass and Roca Guinarte basked in their fame, and in Naples the same was true of Marco Sciarra. In Portugal the situation was as bad if not worse. The natural poverty of the country had been compounded by the remorseless attacks of the English and the Dutch on Portugal's shipping and on its coast over the years since 1580; 'in Lisbon', it was recorded in April 1598, 'the cries of the people rise to heaven at the sight of their trade hampered and their city, so to speak, blockaded, and in straits for corn'.[8]

These pressures led inevitably to a flight from the countryside into towns and cities and this in turn placed an increased tax burden on the people who remained in the countryside. It also made it easier for urban authorities to tax the new arrivals. The sixteenth century had been a time of urban growth throughout Europe, and the most important towns and cities in Spain had grown substantially. In particular, the two great cities of Seville and Madrid – twin capitals, almost – acted as magnetic poles, drawing to themselves the resources of large swathes of the country. Seville probably had 125 000–130 000 people at the end of the century and was one of six largest cities in Europe, an extraordinary mixture of great wealth and extreme poverty. Madrid grew from about 67 800 people in 1590 to 83 000 at the turn of the century – respectively 424 per cent and 519 per cent on the Indicator of 1561 – and it did so despite losing 18–22 per cent of its population each year between 1595 and 1600 as over-population stretched its resources beyond breaking. It was sadly appropriate that in the last weeks of Philip II's life the people of Madrid were clamouring for food and that the bakers' shops were without bread.[9]

Across the face of the peninsula, therefore, the 1590s were a time of crisis, of deepening despair at the circumstances in which people were being forced to live. There were variants, certainly; coastal areas, particularly in the south, could be relieved by imports of grain more easily than, for example, places in the central *meseta*. But as Philip committed his people to ever-expanding wars in the 1590s it was undeniable that most of them were living in conditions of deepening hardship.

The great mobilisations of the 1580s and 1590s aggravated the pressure on food supplies. It has been estimated that the kingdom of Castile was supporting 20 000 men in its armed forces in 1580 but some 50 000 in 1598.[10] Towns and cities were therefore competing with royal purveyors for precious grain. The government was acutely aware of the problem and of the grave social tensions that its own demands were accentuating; on 1 August 1588 the Council of War wrote of 'the shortage of bread that there has been in Andalusia this year' and referred to the 'extreme need' of the region, of people dying of hunger, of deteriorating prospects of employment and of declining cultivation in the countryside. But the Council still insisted that the Enterprise of England had to be provisioned.[11] Military imperatives overrode the exigencies of civilian hunger.

Even more important than the levying and support of troops was the burden of direct taxation. The *millones* of 1590–6 brought the government's free revenue in Castile up to about twelve million ducats. However, by the 1590s Philip was spending ten million ducats annually on his military budgets alone, about twice as much as he had done twenty years before.[12] He made up the difference as best he could by mortgaging the Crown's remaining revenues for years ahead. The consequences at local level could be profoundly serious; in the province of Cordoba, for instance, the tax burden trebled from 4.5 million *maravedís* in 1557–61 to 13.6 million in 1590–5.[13]

During the 1590s there was an increasingly widespread perception that Spain was in crisis. The decade witnessed an upsurge in political debate and discussion – most of it, it is true, in coded form – about the nature and legitimacy of the demands made by the Crown on its subjects. The most natural focal point for these debates was the Cortes of Castile of 1592–8. The Cortes was in session for twice as long as any of its predecessors in testament to the gravity of the situation with which it was dealing and to the unyielding determination of the procurators and their cities not to be forced into making a further *millones* grant. The arguments about the concession and the collection of the *millones* were the more pointed because the Crown's policies were manifestly failing – the defeat of the Armada, the retreat in the Low Countries after 1590 and the interference in France inevitably raised fundamental questions about the purpose of Philip's foreign wars and why Castile should pay for them. The *millones* had, after all, been levied in the first instance to defend Castile against invasion by its foes; why they should be used – indeed, *whether* they could legitimately be used – to fight wars in Flanders or France was a question increasingly being asked, by procurators in the Cortes (of whom perhaps a third were openly hostile to Crown policies), by theologians and by political economists. Theologians also agonised over the legitimacy of the Crown's demands. The Jesuits Pedro de Ribadeneyra and Juan de Mariana led the way in criticising the demands that the government was making on its citizens, and they found support from political theorists at the universities.[14]

Discussion of grievance seemed about to give way to active sedition when on 21 October 1591 eight *pasquines* criticising the 'greed and tyranny' of the king were posted on prominent places in the city of Ávila. For king and ministers, the timing could not have been worse, for the *pasquines* appeared exactly as they were taking the decision to send Vargas and his army into Aragon (see chapter 8). The fear that Old Castile itself might follow Aragon into sedition, and perhaps even into rebellion, brought swift response. Philip despatched *alcalde* Pareja de Peralta to lead a commission to investigate the appearance of the broadsheets. Dr Pareja quickly rounded up seven ringleaders, among them two leading *caballeros* of the city – Don Enrique de Ávila and Don Diego de Bracamonte – and five representatives of the middle classes of the city: a priest, a doctor, a university graduate and a notary among them. The fear that one of the great cities of Old Castile was about to erupt into rebellion could not but remind Philip of the *Comuneros* revolt as well as of the situation in Aragon, and the punishment was swift and exemplary. On 14 February 1592, the two *caballeros* were sentenced to death and the priest (Marcos López) was sentenced to ten years in the galleys – which was in effect a death-sentence – to defrocking and to the payment of substantial fines. Two men received lesser sentences and two appear to have been found to have been innocent of the charges. The death sentence on Ávila was commuted but Bracamonte was decapitated on 17 February as a terrible example to the social elite of Old Castile.[15]

Not all debate was conducted within political or even indeed within educated circles. In May 1590 the Inquisition arrested Lucrecia de León, a twenty-one-year-old woman who was given to prophecy and who was personally known to many senior figures in government. When she was brought to trial she was investigated as a prophetess and some 400 of her dreams were analysed by the prosecutors. Some of her predictions had already been validated by events; seven months before the Armada sailed, Lucrecia had foretold that it would be defeated and be forced to sail off into northern waters. When, therefore, she castigated Philip as a tyrant who was 'responsible for the evil and ruin of Spain' and his senior ministers as men who were 'involved in dirty and abominable things' the government had good cause to be deeply anxious. Philip himself was benignly tolerant of Lucrecia, regarding her as a nuisance and nothing more, but the Inquisition was suspicious of her religious orthodoxy. Her ordeal lasted for five years before a moderate verdict was handed down.[16]

As Philip's physical condition declined, and as his political and military failures escalated, so men naturally looked to the heir for their futures. Political life, therefore, hung in a state of suspended animation. But as men waited for Philip to die, two developments were taking place that were to have profound importance in the years immediately after his death – in the welling political crisis, the apparatus of government was expanding and the aristocracy were settling themselves down in the capital city and preparing to take an increased role in courtly life and in government. Both developments were deeply unwelcome to the king himself, but while Philip hung grimly on to life and to power, men in governmental circles, and most especially the aristocracy, were preparing to move on.

THE EXPANSION OF GOVERNMENT

The pressures of population growth combined with the new levels of warfare and taxation to bring about substantial changes in the nature of government in Philip's last decade or so; the governmental councils became much more professionalised and well organised. Expression had been given to the developing importance of the councils by the creation of new bodies to deal with Portugal (1582) and Flanders (1588) but the most important (and enduring) changes took place among the established councils. Most notably was it true that the Council of State at last began to play a substantive role in policy-making. The preparation and despatch of the Armada stimulated the Council's importance while its defeat made Philip even more prepared to turn to the Council for support in crisis and in adversity; in August 1587 the Venetian ambassador noted that 'The Council of State sits three times a week, now, after never meeting for the last six years' and in January 1589 he noted that 'extraordinary meetings of the Council of State were held every night' in the house of Cristobal de Moura, secretary of the Council. By 1591 the Council was meeting regularly to deal with major affairs of state; its brief now extended to all matters of foreign policy and it also had lengthy discussions on important matters of domestic concern.[17] Philip still did not allow his senior aristocrats to attend the Council; the marquis of Almazán, Prior Don Fernando de Toledo, Cardinal Quiroga, the count of Barajas and of course Moura and Idiáquez sat in the 1590s, but the leading grandees such as the dukes of Medina Sidonia, Frias or Infantado did not. In 1593 Philip brought the archduke Albert back from Portugal so that he could support him at the centre of government and help in the education of his son. The Council of State still had some way to go before it was fully established as a regularly functioning component of government – in the event it remained for Philip III to allow that – but by the later 1590s it was certainly concerning itself with major affairs of foreign policy. Alongside it, the Council of War grew in importance, the volume and importance of its work increasing substantially with the demands of war. Six new councillors were appointed in 1586–7; they were soldiers of excellence who could give advice on the logistical conduct of wars and they sat on a council that was meeting much more regularly and with a more stable membership.[18]

The development of the Councils of State and War was matched by a growing specialisation among the Councils staffed by professional councillors. In the later 1580s Philip became increasingly conscious of the inadequacies of the Council of Castile and so in January 1588 he restructured it by establishing a Chamber (*Cámara*) on which the senior councillors sat with the President to control all major appointments in Church and State in Castile. Philip appointed the Count of Barajas as president of the Council and *Cámara* of Castile and charged him with implementing the changes. Barajas proved to have a heavy touch – suitable, perhaps, for dealing with Antonio Pérez but otherwise inappropriate for the holder of the senior judicial position in Castile – and he soon became widely unpopular. Protests against his conduct of his office gathered momentum and when on 19 March 1591 Fray Diego de Chaves wrote to Philip in his capacity as his confessor to insist that the king had to act against Barajas, the president's fate was sealed. Chaves insisted that Philip himself was approaching his own Day of Judgement and had to ensure that justice was properly administered in Castile. Alarmed by Chaves's warning, Philip ordered Barajas to ask him for permission to retire from court. In effect, the president had been dismissed.[19]

In 1593 it was the turn of the Council of Finance; in his *ordenanzas* reforming the Council Philip expressly recognised that the Council's jurisdictional rights and responsibilities had not been clearly delineated and established strict definitions of its areas of competence. He now carried through the sort of structural reforms that Juan de Ovando had urged on him twenty years before.[20]

Such reforms cost money. Philip's reign saw a three-fold growth in the cost of government and (as with military expenditure) the great leap forward came in the second half of the reign. In 1556 the payroll of the central councils had cost 8 011 582 *maravedís* (100 per cent) but by 1579 it had risen only to 10 120 740 (126 per cent); at the end of the 1570s, in other words, Spanish government was still recognisable as the apparatus of twenty years or so before. The great expansion then took place; by 1598 the cost had nearly trebled against the 1579 level, to 25 132 545 *maravedís* (314 per cent). Two-thirds of the rise in costs had taken place therefore in the second half of the reign.[21]

This rise came about in two ways – with a growth in the number of men serving the king and with increases in salary levels that allowed for inflation and for the extension of responsibilities. In 1556 the major central councils were supporting sixty-three full-time office-holders and in 1598 they had 126, twice as many. The greatest single area of growth was in the secretariat, reflecting the extent to which the volume of work being conducted by government had grown; in 1556 the central councils had needed only six secretaries and they had cost 760 000 *maravedís* (100 per cent) but in 1598 there were twenty-six and their salaries had risen to 2 073 217 *maravedís* (273 per cent). The secretaries were given officials to help cope with the volume of business. The case of the Council of War was typical; the division of the secretariat into two offices dealing with Land and with Sea in 1586 was followed in 1587 by the appointment of two officials for each secretary at the Crown's cost; in 1556 the secretariat had cost 100 000 *maravedís* while in 1598 it cost 700 000.[22] Other councils underwent expansion slightly later; for instance, on the death of Gabriel de Zayas in 1595, the secretariat of the Council of Italy was divided into three. The growth spread across the face of government and extended to the archive at Simancas; in June 1588 Philip appointed Antonio de Ayala, son of Diego, as official in the archive, noting that the great volume of papers that had been collected there meant that extra help was needed. To ensure stability in the management of the archive's papers, Philip gave Antonio the right to succeed his father when the time came.[23]

Philip did well by his administrators in increasing their salaries; in 1556, for example, the President of Castile earned 650 000 *maravedís* but by 1588 his salary had risen to 1 000 000 while the councillors of Castile saw their salaries increase from 100 000 *maravedís* in 1556 to 500 000 in 1588, with an extra 50 000 if they sat on the Cámara. The pattern was replicated on other councils. For instance, the Council of Inquisition had twenty people on its payroll in 1584 and their salaries came to 3 384 462 *maravedís*; by 1606 it had twenty-five but the cost of their salaries had doubled to 6 722 831 *maravedís*.[24]

As the problems of government became more complex and as the volume of business grew, so the most senior and trusted of Philip's advisers were given more extensive responsibilities. The Crown had always used juntas to deal with complex or urgent problems but from the 1580s more juntas were established on a permanent or semi-permanent basis – in military administration, the juntas of Galleys and of Fleets; in financial matters, those of Expedients (1586), of the Cortes (1588) and the *Junta Grande de Hacienda* (1591).[25] The juntas did not take the place of the councils but complemented the work they were doing, drawing them together, bridging gaps between them and performing specialist tasks. It was *because* the work of the councils was expanding that juntas were used to provide an overview of that whole range of areas where jurisdictions or responsibilities collided. The growing use of juntas also enabled the inner circle of Philip's advisers to spread themselves across the face of government and to report back to him on a more informed basis.

By the middle of the 1580s the members of the inner circle of senior advisers were meeting fairly formally at the end of the day to review business and to report to the king. The body on which they sat was not formally constituted but became known as the 'Junta of the Night' because of the hour at which it met (but also perhaps in resentful reflection of the secrecy with which it worked). But as that inner circle had expanded somewhat in the 1580s so it contracted in the 1590s. The death of Mateo Vázquez de Leca (5 May 1591) allowed for the further concentration of business in the hands of Moura and Idiáquez. Philip trusted and needed his two former secretaries the more as he became progressively more disabled and as the volume of business developed. He was indeed touchingly loyal to them; he attended the wedding of Moura's daughter and he ransomed Idiáquez's son when he was captured in the Low Countries.[26] The roles of Moura and Idiáquez helped to establish the principle that the king could use specialists in supra-conciliar, ministerial ways. Philip had always set himself against having his senior nobles as inner advisers but he ended his reign by allowing two comparatively low-born secretaries to exercise such a role. The grandees – and in particular, the marquis of Denia – took note.

THE KING AND HIS NOBLES

In his early years Philip had allowed favoured nobles to serve him in high administrative office; the marquis of Mondéjar, for instance, had been president of the councils of the Indies (1546–59) and of Castile (1559–64). But as Philip established his government in the 1560s he turned increasingly to lawyers – to men of whom Diego de Espinosa had been the supreme exemplar – and for the most part he confined his senior aristocracy to service abroad. Most especially, he allowed them to serve in the governorship-general of Milan, where it was imperative that the Crown was represented by a figure of unmistakable authority; only senior aristocrats had the social rank and the military expertise to serve this crucial position, and in Philip's reign it was held by, among others, the dukes of Sessa (1558–60), Alburquerque (1564–71) and Frias (1592–5). Philip was less keen on having senior nobles serve in the great Italian viceroyalties; the duke of Medinaceli (1557–64) was the only grandee to occupy the viceroyalty of Sicily in the first half of the reign and Alba's extraordinary tenure of office in Naples (1555) was the last by a senior aristocrat for nearly thirty years. Philip was prepared to use native-born Italians in major positions in the peninsular; for instance, the duke of Terranova (1566–7) and Marco Antonio Colonna (1577–84) served as viceroys of Sicily and of course the dukes of Savoy and Parma and Juan Andrea Doria were entrusted with leading military and naval commands. This did not amount to a policy of sharing responsibilities between the different nationalities of Philip's monarchy, but it went further towards doing so than has sometimes been recognised.

Philip was parsimonious in his creation of titles; he created less than fifty titles, and a third or so of those were honorary titles, given without an attachment of landed income.[27] Four of the new titles to which land was attached were dukedoms, the highest title of all, and all were endowed on men to whom Philip was particularly close in a personal sense: Alcalá de los Gazules in 1558 for Perafán de Ribera, marquis of Tavara; Osuna in 1562 for Pedro Téllez Girón, count of Urueña; Feria in 1567 for Gómez Suarez de Figueroa, count of Feria; and Pastrana in 1572 for Ruy Gómez de Silva (as he approached death). The Osuna dukedom might be taken as an illustration of how Philip was prepared to advance favoured aristocrats; it was certainly the most typical. Don Pedro Téllez Girón, fifth count of Urueña, had served Philip in England and the Low Countries, and was – a special commendation! – wounded at the battle of San Quentin. After recovering he was sent to Paris to conduct the marriage negotiations for the hand of Elizabeth of Valois. Grateful for his service, and indeed for his friendship, Philip created the dukedom of Osuna for him (5 February 1562) and in 1568 added further lustre to his family's greatness by establishing the marquisate of Peñafiel as an honorary title for his eldest son. Osuna fought in the War of Granada in 1568 and in 1570 he formally received Anna of Austria in the Low Countries and conducted her to Spain for her marriage to Philip. In 1579 Philip sent him on what he himself may well have regarded as the most important embassy of his reign, to Portugal as ambassador extraordinary to prepare (in company with Moura) the way for the conquest of that kingdom. As a reward for Osuna's brilliant success Philip then broke his own rule and appointed a duke to the viceroyalty of Naples. So lucrative was the viceroyalty of Naples that it was proverbially said that a man should not wish to be appointed to it because of the pain he would feel on leaving it. Philip allowed Osuna to serve two terms of office there (1582–6), and in doing so the duke made his fortune. On his return to Spain Osuna worked on the preparations for the Armada of 1588. When he died in 1590 he was only fifty-three years of age but he had spent his whole

238   The Imprudent King

life in the service of the Crown.[28] He had reaped prodigious rewards; at the time of his birth his family's rents were worth only 20000 ducats or so but shortly after his death they were worth 150000 ducats per annum, second only to those of Medina Sidonia (see Table 9.1). The king's grace was indeed lucrative.

Table 9.1   A Selection of Aristocratic Rent-Rolls (in ducats)

Title and rank	Date of foundation	1501	1539	1578	1595
No. of titles		54	73	105	116
Maximum income		50400	60000	150000	170000
Minimum income		2800	4000	4000	4000
Average income		10628	18769	26952	35750
Total rent-roll		573900	1464000	2830000	4147000
Medina Sidonia (d)	1445	39200[2]	55000[6]	150000[1]	170000[1]
Alba (d)	1465	33600[3]	50000[7]	60000[12]	120000[4]
Frias (d)	1492	50400[1]	60000[1]	42000[20]	65000[17]
Medinaceli (d)	1479	28000[5]	30000[1]	28000[28]	60000[18]
Infantado (d)	1475	28000[5]	50000[7]	100000[3]	120000[4]
Urueña (c)/Osuna (d)	1466/1562	16800[8]	20000[2]	112000[2]	150000[2]
Benavente (c)	1398	30800[4]	60000[1]	74000[9]	120000[4]
Denia (m)	1484	7000[30]	14000[3]	14000[6]	20000[58]
Mondéjar (m)	1512	–	15000[3]	50000[15]	40000[29]
(c) Count	(m) Marquis		(d) Duke		

Sources: The table is based upon an original by Helen Nader, 'Noble Income in Sixteenth Century Castile: The Case of the Marquises of Mondéjar, 1480–1580', Economic History Review, 2nd Series, 30 (1964) no. 4, pp. 411–28. Superscript numbers indicate ranking in order of wealth.

Dates of foundation
Juan Moreño de Guerra y Alonso, Guía de la Grandeza Historia Genealógica y Heraldica de todas las casas que gozan de esta dignidad Nobiliaria (Madrid: 1918 ?).
Josef Berní y Catalá, Creación, Antigüedad, y Privilegios de los Títulos de Castilla (Valencia: 1769).
Antonio Ramos, Aparato para la corrección y adición de la obra que publicó en 1769... J. Berní y Catalá... con el título: Creación, antigüedad, y prívilegios de los títulos de Castilla (Malagá: 1777).

Rental Incomes
1501   Anon., 'Relation du premier voyage de Philippe le Beau en Espagne, en 1501', Collection des voyages des souverains des Pays-Bas (Brussels: 1876), I, pp. 252–6.
1539   Lucas Marineo Sículo, De las cosas memorables de España (Alcalá de Henares: 1539)
1578   Anon., 'Grandes y Nobleza de España', British Library Harleian Manuscripts 5275, ff. 61–4.
1595   Pedro Núñez de Salcedo, 'Relación verdadera de todos los títulos que ai en España' (ed. Vicente Castañeda), Boletín de la Real Academía de Historia, LXXIII (1918), pp. 468–91.

Such an example led to emulation as much as to envy. Nobles could not maintain, much less expand, their territorial greatness and dignity without the king's favour, and to win this they needed to reside at court; in the later years of the reign they increasingly chose to do so. Although aristocratic incomes as a whole trebled during the course of the sixteenth century the fourfold rise in prices meant that the income of many aristocratic families fell behind the cost of living; these families were in effect living on diminished incomes. The king's favour could restore the fortunes of a family. There were indeed quite startling differences between the progress of aristocratic families during Philip's reign and two of the richest families might be taken as examples; the rental incomes of the dukes of Frias and Medina Sidonia were on a par at the time of Philip's accession but by 1598 a great disparity had opened up between them. The duke of Frias (who held the dignity of constable of Castile) was at the beginning of the sixteenth century the wealthiest nobleman in Spain, his family benefiting from the prosperity of Old Castile. During the first half of the century the family's rental income kept pace with inflation but when the wars which cut off the export trade with northern Europe afflicted the economy of Old Castile the fortunes of the family plummeted; in the half century to 1595 its income remained static. By contrast, in the south of Spain, the Medina Sidonia family benefited from the exploitation of the rich agricultural land of the Guadalquivir valley and from the booming trade with the American colonies; in the first half of the century its income rose only by some 2 per cent or so but during the years 1540–95 it then trebled. By the end of the century the family had rents that were nearly three times as valuable as those of the Frias family. The Medina Sidonia were now the richest family in Spain while the Frias had sunk to seventeenth on the list of rent-rolls (see Table 9.1).

Service followed from financial circumstances; the constable was prepared to serve as governor-general of Milan precisely because he needed to demonstrate his willingness to serve the Crown to win the rewards that only the king could give. Medina Sidonia, on the other hand, managed to fight off Philip's determined insistence that he serve in Milan in the early 1580s; he was quite prepared to do without the king's favour if it had to be earned by spending years in Italy which would involve great expenditure as well as the neglect of his own estates. However, his refusal to accept the governorship of Milan may well have made it impossible for him to withstand the order to command the Armada of 1588. That service in turn caused him to accumulate great debts; by the end of the reign he still owed the Crown over 100000 ducats.[29] The aristocrat's dilemma was precisely this: how to serve the Crown (and reap the rewards of loyal service) without bankrupting himself.

Philip could be generous; in 1595, for instance, he helped the Medinaceli family to restructure its debts by giving the Duke the right to impose 100000 ducats of mortgage (*censo*) on his estates.[30] Doubtless Philip chose to remember the services that the fourth duke of Medinaceli had rendered him (like the first duke of Osuna) in northern Europe in the 1550s and later in the Mediterranean. Philip had a long memory, and he remembered his friends. It is often said that the greater aristocracy did not do well under Philip; certainly it is true that it was only with the deepest reluctance that he allowed them to have access to powerful positions at court, but it is equally true that those aristocrats towards whom he was well disposed did very well during his reign – the careers of the fourth duke of Medinaceli and the first dukes of Osuna, Feria, Pastrana and Alcalá were testament enough to that.

Philip also remembered those whom he would not help. Francisco Gómez de Sandoval y Rojas, fifth marquis of Denia since 1574, was the son-in-law of the fourth duke of Medinaceli but he had rendered little service to the Crown and was living in humiliating poverty from the time that he inherited the title.[31] Philip refused to help him with office or with significant financial rewards but he did allow Denia to serve the heir to the throne as a gentleman of his chamber and was dismayed to find him insinuating himself into the favour of the impressionable young man. Philip therefore removed Denia from the Prince by appointing him as viceroy of Valencia in 1596. But it was too late; Denia had formed a relationship with the heir that survived his exile in Valencia and the king allowed him to return to court in November 1597, doubtless at the urging of his son. Denia now stood poised to benefit from his relationship with the new king when Philip died.

For all that Philip was so averse to expanding the size of his noble estate, he was in his later years less able to withstand the pressure for office exerted by the nobility and he became prepared to offer more governmental positions to chosen aristocrats. Francisco Zapata de Cisneros, first count of Barajas, served as president of the Council of Castile (1582–91) and Francisco de Rojas, third marquis of Poza, became president of the Council of Finance (1595–1602). So, too, in the Italian viceroyalties, Philip gave some ground; in Sicily, the counts of Alva de Liste (1585–91) and Olivares (1592–5) served as viceroys; in Naples, Osuna himself (1582–6) was followed by the counts of Miranda

(1586–95) and Olivares (1595–9). The way was being prepared, however tentatively, for the restoration of the aristocracy to a powerful role at the centre of court and government and it was being prepared, also, for the first of the great favourites of the seventeenth century.

THE CLIMAX OF THE WARS

As Philip edged towards the grave his wars with France, England and the United Provinces moved towards their climaxes. Some help came for Philip when a rebellion in Ireland under the leading noble, Hugh O'Neill, earl of Tyrone, forced Elizabeth to withdraw her forces from Brittany in February 1595. The Queen now had no soldiers serving at her expense on the mainland of Europe for the first time in nearly a decade.[32] Moreover, the build-up of Spain's Atlantic fleet made it possible for Philip to think once again of sending armadas into northern waters. Accordingly, he despatched Alonso de los Cobos to Ireland to make an exploratory assessment as to whether an armada might profitably be despatched to Ireland.

The death of the archduke Ernest also seemed to offer a way forward in the Low Countries; Philip replaced Ernest with his brother Albert. At thirty-seven, Albert was an experienced politician; he had a decade as viceroy of Portugal behind him and Philip held him in high regard and indeed in real personal affection. It is probable that Albert resisted the appointment to the Low Countries, for he was about to be consecrated as archbishop of Toledo when Philip named him to succeed Ernest. Albert seems to have had a genuine vocation for the ecclesiastical life and it was only with real reluctance that he divested himself of his ecclesiastical garb. Philip secured a papal brief postponing Albert's ordination as a priest and named García de Loaysa to serve as Albert's deputy in the great archbishopric.[33]

Philip revived the war effort in the Low Countries by ordering Fuentes to campaign in Picardy while he awaited Albert's arrival. The count obeyed to spectacular purpose; he took Doullens on 24 July (and slaughtered the garrison) and then moved swiftly to capture Cambrai (9 October) before Henry IV was able to move to its defence. Fuentes made his way back to Brussels in triumph.[34] Albert joined him there on 11 February 1596. However, Fuentes effectively refused to serve under Albert, resentful (like most of the Castilian military elite) of the leadership of a foreigner in the Low Countries.[35] He returned to Spain.

Albert may not have enjoyed Fuentes's confidence but he was certainly the first Governor-General of the Low Countries whom Philip fully trusted from the time of his appointment. He soon demonstrated that he was a man of independence by recognising the need to make a settlement. He set about securing a position of strength from which he could do so. He besieged Calais with 21 000 men; within eighteen days he had taken the town (17 April) and after a further ten days later the citadel capitulated. Albert had the men of the garrison put to the sword and gave the town itself over to a sack which was conducted with real enthusiasm.[36] The new Governor-General had announced himself. Albert's success compensated for prestige lost elsewhere and although the capture of Calais did not facilitate an invasion of England – for it did not provide a deep water port – it nevertheless meant that Spanish forces stood at either end of the Channel. It also gave notice that Spain once again had a general of stature in the Low Countries.

At court in London, Elizabeth was able to hear Albert's guns assaulting Calais and the fall of the town almost certainly confirmed to her the need to re-engage with Spain on the mainland as well as maintaining the war at sea.[37] Certainly, Elizabeth had been moving back to a more belligerent pursuit of the war in recent months, stimulated by her fear of Spain's naval revival and, more especially, by the realisation that Philip's new galleons might be used to ferry men to Ireland. During the course of 1595 she therefore decided to unchain Drake once again (for the first time since 1589) and to send a major expedition to damage Philip's renewed fleet in Spain. Drake sailed in September 1595 and a great fleet under Lord Howard of Effingham and the earl of Essex moved on Cadiz in June 1596.

The Queen's new belligerence was formalised by the Treaty of Greenwich (24 May 1596) in which she and Henry IV committed themselves to a defensive and offensive alliance and agreed not to make peace separately with Spain. Elizabeth undertook to provide 4000 English soldiers for six months in northern France and Henry agreed to pay for them. In October, the United Provinces joined the alliance. As Philip's life drained away, his three northern enemies were uniting formally against him.

Drake sailed on 17 September 1595 with six of the queen's galleons (or one-fifth of the royal navy) and with orders to be back in England by the early summer of 1596 to help national defence against another armada. He took John Hawkins with him. The two men proved no more able to work together than they had been in 1568 and they found that the Spanish commanders were much more capable and determined than those of 1585–6 had been. Hawkins died off Puerto Rico on 12 November and Drake captured Nombre de Dios in a poignant reminder of his golden days before succumbing to disease and dying on 28 January 1595 off Puerto Bello. The news of Drake's death buoyed Philip up and it was observed that he 'shows the keenest delight and declares that this good news will help him to get well rapidly'.[38] In times past Drake had demoralised the king; now his death helped to restore Philip's spirits.

Effingham arrived off Cadiz on 30 June with 120 sail to find that the great harbour contained no fewer than sixty ships, half of them galleons that were fully laden in preparation for their journey to the New World. There were also six royal galleons to escort them and fifteen galleys for the defence of the port itself. After some hesitation, Effingham ordered an assault on the galleons. Four of them were 'Apostles', and two (the *San Felipe* and the *Santo Tomás*) were burned, while the other two (the *San Mateo* and the *San Andrés*) were captured, to be added to Elizabeth's navy. This success was not matched against the merchantmen; Effingham allowed the Spanish to negotiate with him over these ships, which lay huddled against the shore and laden down with perhaps twelve million ducats' worth of merchandise for the Indies. As discussions dragged on, the Spanish burned over thirty of the ships rather than yield their cargoes to the English.

Essex himself then led the assault on the town of Cadiz, systematically gutting the town for nearly two weeks. So thrilled was Essex with his triumph that he urged Effingham to allow him to remain in Cadiz with a garrison that would both defy attack from the land and prevent the Spanish from using the harbour. Effingham, however, insisted on departing and on 14 July, after setting much of the town alight, the expedition sailed away. It moved along the coast for a week but achieved nothing of note. Effingham considered heading for the Azores to waylay the treasure fleet but foul weather made up his mind for him, and he sailed for home, arriving in Plymouth on 18 August. Elizabeth was at first delighted – 'let the army know I care not so much for being Queen as that I am sovereign of such subjects' – but when she realised how much plunder had been appropriated by her soldiers and sailors rather than by her commissaries and when she understood what she had lost when the merchantmen went up in smoke she was furious with her commanders.[39] The English expedition of 1596, like that of 1589, had failed in its primary purpose.

For its part, the Spanish government was simply dumbfounded by the attack on Cadiz. As recently as 4 July, the Council of State had assured Philip that it was extremely unlikely that the English would mount an attack on the coastal towns and that if they did so, 'nowhere could they inflict less damage than in Cadiz and the other ports of Andalusia' because of the promptness with which forces could be moved to defend those places. Philip was in Toledo when the news came of the attack; Moura did not dare to wake him and waited three hours until the king had awoken and dressed before he told him the news. So shaken was the Council of State that not until 9 July did it even rouse itself to make detailed responses to the attack.[40]

The assault on Cadiz was the greatest humiliation of Philip's reign, the most deeply wounding assault on his kingly reputation. For a fortnight, an enemy (and heretical) force had camped on his own soil and sacked his most important seaport without any significant response having been made. The only consolation that could be grasped was that the English had missed the treasure fleet that arrived at San Lúcar on 27 September after a particularly fast crossing from Havana. The fleet brought twelve million ducats' worth of silver, eight for private individuals and four for the Crown.[41] However, the attack on Cadiz brought the Indies trade to a halt; not until February 1598 did the next fleet from the Indies return to Seville.[42]

Prince Felipe had been outraged by the attack and gallantly offered to lead troops to free Cadiz. The king refused, but perhaps encouraged by his son's enthusiasm, allowed Felipe to sit as president of the Council of State from 9 July.[43] In the autumn, Philip commissioned a report on Felipe's progress. It was sent to him on 20 October by García de Loaysa. Young Felipe was described as a deeply religious and obedient young man, and García de Loaysa glossed over the tutors' doubts about his intellectual capacity, merely observing that the Prince had not yet acquired the gravity that went with kingship, although he knew how to disguise his own feelings. Nor did the tutors make any mention of their concern about the influence that the marquis of Denia clearly held over the heir.[44]

Philip decided that his revenge for the attack on Cadiz would take the form of an armada sent to Ireland to help the rebels against Elizabeth. Learning from one of his mistakes in 1588, the king tried to keep the destination of the fleet a secret. Once again he chose a nobleman of rank as his commander. Don Martín de Padilla y Manrique, hereditary Adelantado Mayor of Castile, had the social status for the task, for his countship of Buendía compared in seniority with Medina Sidonia's dukedom, dating from 1475. His wealth, however, was vastly inferior to his predecessor's; his rents were worth only about 30000 ducats in 1596. The Adelantado had served with distinction in many theatres of war. He had begun his career at the battle of St Quentin and gone on to serve in the Alpujarras and at Lepanto. In 1585 he had been created Captain-General of the Galleys of Spain and in 1587 was given the county of Santa Gadea in reward for his services. He had fought against the English at Lisbon in 1589, and in 1596 was appointed Captain-General of the Atlantic Fleet.[45] He had therefore a detailed and broad knowledge of war on land and on sea. He was, however, an abrasive man, known for the shortness of his temper; humility was alien to him.

The Adelantado's appointment to command the second Armada had an element of the accidental about it, for he was officially sent to Lisbon in July 1596 to reassure the citizenry that the city would be defended in the aftermath of the English attack on Cadiz. In reality, his mission was to ensure that no rising took place in support of Dom Antonio. He took prompt action, commandeering some Dutch boats and preparing them to serve in his fleet. Philip ordered ships from the northern coast and from Andalucia to join the Adelantado. Soon he had sixty ships at his command – which were to form the core of the Armada of 1596.

The fleet that arrived at Cadiz at the beginning of October brought 12000000 ducats, and it may have been the happy coincidence of having a fleet available and the money to fund it that led Philip to decide that he could at last send the second Armada upon which he had so long determined. By early October he had decided to go ahead. He ordered that prayers were to be said throughout Spain for his purposes and that the fleet be made ready to sail. Perhaps even now Philip was not clear about the purposes of the fleet, although when an Irish bishop boarded it speculation inevitably grew that it was headed for Ireland.

Many of the events of 1588 now replayed themselves. Philip insisted that the fleet should sail even though it was not properly supplied or provisioned. The Adelantado summoned his captains and asked them on oath whether they thought the fleet was ready to leave. They insisted that it was not, and the Adelantado then drew up a memorial which they all signed and sent to Philip, urging him to hold back until the fleet was properly prepared. As in 1588, Philip rejected the advice of his commander.

The Adelantado brought his fleet from Lisbon to Ferrol to shorten the journey – one of the lessons of 1588 was certainly learned – and at Ferrol he counted ninety-eight ships, twenty-seven of them royal galleons, with about 15 000 men on board. Philip's insistence that the fleet sail at once for Ireland seemed sadly unrealistic; it was as much as the Adelantado could do to leave port, for so foul was the weather that he only made it out of Ferrol at the fourth attempt (16 October). Predictably, the fleet sailed into a violent storm: off Cape Finisterre on 20 October, seven galleons, twenty-five larger merchantmen and many smaller craft and 2000 men were lost. The Adelantado returned to Ferrol for shelter. Even now, Philip insisted that he sail on, at the very least so that the fleet could reach Brittany (despite the fact that the harbour at Blavet was not large enough to hold the fleet). The English did not know what had happened and made expensive preparations to receive the Armada; not until the end of the year would they be certain that the Adelantado would not appear in the Channel.[46]

Once again the failure of an armada was followed by plans to send a replacement in the following year, and once again Philip found himself in agony, now with bowel trouble, and suffering from disturbed sleep.[47] His advisers began to push for a settlement of the wars. In November 1596 the Council of State urged him to reduce his commitments; suggesting that 'peace is the purpose of wars', the Council advised the king to pursue a suspension of arms with Henry IV because this would at least enable him to retain the places he had taken in France while the making of peace would involving returning them.[48]

Once again, however, silver flooded in from the Indies to enable Philip to increase the stakes for which he was fighting so desperately; in 1596 two fleets arrived, carrying perhaps fifteen million ducats of silver. But as always, great wealth had to be measured against great debts; Philip owed Genoese bankers ten million ducats on short-term contracts, and the Council of Finance calculated that the shortfall in its revenues for 1597 would amount to seven million ducats and that it was some twenty-five million ducats adrift of its needs for the years 1596–9. The king was now without any income from the *millones*; the grant made in 1589 had expired in 1596 and although Philip secured an agreement with the procurators of the Cortes for a new grant he had yet to secure permission from a majority of the eighteen towns and cities to raise the money. In practice, the new grant was waiting on Philip's death; the procurators and their municipal masters appreciated that there was little point in making a grant to a king who would not live long enough to reward them with his favour. In November 1596 Philip declared a suspension of payments to his bankers and forbade the export of specie.[49]

The financial crisis deprived Albert of the means to mount a serious campaign, and in 1597 he achieved little of any real significance. The Army of Flanders captured Amiens in March but lost it again in September. Philip recognised with surprising rapidity that the war against Henry IV was lost, and that 'the Prince of Béarn' was now secure on his throne. This made it easier for him to concentrate on revenging himself on Elizabeth of England. He determined that the Adelantado would sail once again with an armada in 1597. Urgency was added to Philip's insistence that the Adelantado sail by the news that Elizabeth was preparing a large fleet under the earl of Essex to attack Spain and the Azores. The Adelantado was ordered to seize Falmouth and to intercept Essex's fleet on the way home; it would be the Spanish who, in a fine turn of destiny, would be waiting in the Channel for the English. Philip had at least learned that it was easier to defend the Channel than to attack in it. He and Elizabeth both prepared great fleets.

The Adelantado's fleet was larger than those of 1588 or 1596 but carried fewer men: it comprised 136 ships, of which 44 were royal galleons and carried 12 634 men. For the third time, Philip harried his commander to sail before he was ready; the fleet was despatched with a shortage of sailors and provisions. Once again the Adelantado sailed unseasonably late in the year (18 October), knowing that he had little prospect of success. Notwithstanding this, he made good time; by 12 October the fleet was approaching the Lizard, but as the Adelantado called a council of war to prepare his assault a wind arose which scattered the fleet. When the Adelantado found that he had only three galleons accompanying him he ordered the return to Spain, and he arrived in Ferrol on 20 October. Over the next two weeks 108 ships returned to La Coruña and Ferrol. Although the number of ships lost was comparatively small, two of the 'Apostles' went down – the *San Bartolomé* and the *San Lucás* – and so in 1596–7 Philip was deprived of six of the Twelve Apostles that had been the pride of his revived naval forces. For all that, the Adelantado had come close to success. He had arrived off the English coast to find that fourteen of England's twenty-six major fighting ships were away, apparently off the Azores. The English admiral Monson observed that Spain had 'never had so dangerous an enterprise on us'.[50] But there was no escaping the central logic of a third failure of a massive assault upon England by Philip; God's winds *were* Protestant.

Essex's voyage was as unsuccessful as the Adelantado's. Elizabeth must have known that her impetuous favourite would go his own way, and Essex duly set himself to achieve a whole variety of objectives in order to make his position at court impregnable: to destroy Spanish naval power; to capture the treasure fleet; and then to turn to an attack on the West Indies themselves. After a false start, when a storm blew him back into Plymouth, Essex sailed on 27 August. He ran into a storm in the Bay of Biscay and abandoned his attempt on Ferrol in favour of intercepting the treasure fleet at the Azores. Probably this had been his intention all along. He missed the fleet (which sailed, unseen, between two English squadrons) and headed for home. He ran into the same storm that devastated the Adelantado's fleet. By 31 October he had dismissed his men. The Indies fleet arrived in Seville on 21 February carrying seven million ducats' worth of silver, of which 2 500 000 belonged to the Crown.[51] But it was not enough for more wars; Philip had to look now to making a final settlement of Spain's affairs, and to preparing for his own death. In a dreadful prelude to his own demise, in December he heard of the death of his beloved Catalina Micaela after her tenth pregnancy in eleven years. There was little left for him to live for now except to make his final provisions.[52]

THE SETTLEMENTS OF 1598 AND THE DEATH OF PHILIP

At the end of February 1598 Henry IV set out for Brittany with a formidable army; sensibly, Mercoeur came quickly to terms. Henry then proceeded to sign a composite edict in Nantes on 13 April which granted limited freedom of conscience and full equality before the law to Huguenots and allowed them to hold their services in many towns and chateaux. The Edict of Nantes (as it became known) aroused much opposition and it was to be several years before Henry had it ratified by the *parlements*, but it had signalled his intention to allow the Huguenots to live in tolerable freedom under his rule.[53]

The settlement with Mercoeur and the Edict of Nantes completed Henry's triumph; he was now truly and fully king of France. He was also in a position from which he could make peace with Spain, and he did so through negotiations with Albert's emissaries at the small town of Vervins in Picardy. The Peace of Vervins (2 May 1598) effectively restated the conditions and terms of the Peace of Câteau-Cambrésis in 1559. Unstated was Philip's acceptance that Henry IV was the legitimate king of France and that France was once again the equal of Spain in European affairs; as an expression of this Spain gave up all the towns that she still held in France, including Blavet and Calais. Only the marquisate of Saluzzo, conquered by Savoy in 1588, remained alienated from the French royal domain. The Dutch and the English did everything they could to prevent Henry from making peace with Spain, but on 21 June, in a magnificent ceremony in Nôtre-Dame, the king solemnly swore to observe the peace. Albert followed suit on 12 July.[54] The United Provinces and England would have to fight on without France.

Philip could not bring himself to publish the treaty. Recognising that many in Spain felt that too many concessions had been made he took refuge in the pretence that he did not need to make peace because he had never declared war on France. Few were fooled. Vervins was a dramatic defeat and the count of Fuentes spoke for many when he exclaimed that 'we are ashamed of it; and it was concluded by those who don't understand the use of arms'. Not until 9 September, four days before Philip himself died, did the government publish the terms of the peace and it deliberately employed minimal ceremony in doing so.[55]

In the spring of 1598 Philip's doctors weakened him still further by bleeding him yet again. Only now did he turn to the settlement of his affairs. Philip had decided to marry both Felipe and Isabella to Austrian relatives. Arrangements had been made for young Felipe to marry one of the daughters of the archduke Charles of Styria, but the eldest two girls died precipitately and so Philip now confirmed his son's engagement to the third daughter, Margaret, who was thirteen years old. Isabella was to marry Albert himself, who was of course Charles's brother.

On 6 May, Philip renounced the Low Countries and the County of Burgundy in favour of his daughter as her dowry. He restated the conditions that his father had imposed when he abdicated responsibility for the Low Countries in 1555. He kept for himself (and his heirs) the Grand Mastership of the Order of the Golden Fleece and retained control for his army over five major fortresses in the Low Countries, notably those of Antwerp, Ghent and Cambrai. Isabella was thirty-two years old and if she died without heirs Albert was to remain governor, holding the position for his lifetime. If, on the other hand, Albert predeceased Isabella, the infanta was not to marry again without consent of her brother. The formal devolution of authority would, Philip hoped, lead to a more efficient conduct of the war and to some remission of the demands made by it upon Spain. But to men like Fuentes, handing over even restricted authority to Albert was itself something of an abdication. Accordingly, they regarded it as a point of honour to undermine Albert from the beginning of his rule in the Low Countries.[56]

Philip's two settlements of May 1598 acknowledged the failure of the aggressive foreign policy that he had pursued during the last fifteen years or so. However, he committed himself to the settlements less from a conviction that the policies themselves had been ill-considered than from a desire to lighten the burden on his son. While he still hoped for a negotiated settlement in the Low Countries, he fully intended that the war was to continue, not least because the Dutch were attacking his overseas possessions; with fine timing, it was in 1598 that the Dutch appeared for the first time in the Pacific. The war with Philip's Dutch rebels, far from being wound down, was about to escalate across the face of the globe, and in doing so to threaten the greatest achievement of his reign, the unification of Spain and Portugal and of their empires. As ominously, it was spreading too into the Mediterranean, where the Dutch and the English appeared with increasing frequency during the last years of his reign. In 1598 the English appeared off Ibiza and it was noted that 'they have begun to make themselves felt' in the Mediterranean.[57]

Philip could not bring himself to make peace with England. Like Elizabeth he was being forced to appreciate the expensive futility of the war but neither monarch was yet ready for peace; both of them would have to depart the stage before that was possible. Elizabeth had little choice but to continue to support the United Provinces in their struggle and on 6 August 1598 her government signed a mutual defence agreement with the Dutch. Philip responded by continuing to give such aid as he could to Elizabeth's rebels in Ireland.

On 1 July, Philip left Madrid to go to the Escorial for the last time. He travelled against his doctors' advice, determined that he would die in his beloved monastery. Such was his agony that it took him six days to travel the forty kilometres. He still had some limited mobility by the time that he arrived in the Escorial but it ebbed away from him, and on 22 July he was carried to his bed for the last time; he remained there for fifty-three dreadful days and nights, unable to move and in searing and fulminating agony. His body began to suppurate in open wounds and his flesh to tear off with the bed sores. He lost control of his bowels and so intense was his agony that his doctors were unable to move him to clean him properly. His servants had to cut a hole in his mattress so that his bodily waste could flow away and the stench was so bad that one of his doctors became ill. But not a word of complaint came from Philip.[58]

On 5 August, Philip urged his son to continue to use the junta of ministers that he was bequeathing to him and particularly commended the new archbishop of Toledo to Felipe, noting that 'I have placed him in this dignity so that he can serve my son'. On 15 August he accepted the inevitable and appointed the marquis of Denia as *sumiller de corps* and *caballerizo mayor* to the heir; in the first capacity Denia had access to the prince whenever he was in the palace, while in the second he had the right to accompany Felipe wherever he went on horseback. He was thereby entitled to be close to the prince at any time, inside or outside the palace. On 16 August Philip watched the consecration of the new archbishop of Toledo and in a document that was signed with a movingly feeble monogram he once again commended García de Loaysa to his son, noting that the archbishop had been sworn in as a councillor of State. He further charged his son to retain his councillors of State 'all the time that they live and have health and strength to continue'. He appointed Moura as *camarero mayor* of the prince and named Idiáquez as Margaret's *caballerizo mayor*. Philip intended to govern Spain from the grave. It was of course a forlorn hope; the king could hardly have done more to ensure that his men did not survive under his son.[59]

By the end of August it was evident that Philip's death was imminent. Still the king dragged out his life, displaying 'incredible patience in his acute sufferings'. He planned his funeral, ordering black drape for the Escorial and having his lead shirt and coffin brought in for him to inspect. He summoned his children and exhorted them to govern their states well and gave the prince two sealed envelopes to be opened after his death. He tried to settle outstanding matters, notably by restoring the estates of the duke of Villahermosa to his heir. But – mindful perhaps of his father's regret at abdicating? – even now he could not bring himself to shed his authority. So weak was he that on 3 September those around his bedside thought that he had died and he was given extreme unction. He awoke and requested that he be given his father's crucifix. Moura asked him whether it was time for the prince to take responsibility for government. Philip refused.[60] On 11 September Philip issued the last order of his reign, writing to Albert to inform him that he accepted the papal offer to conduct the two marriages.[61]

Philip's instructions for his son ordered him to be present at his deathbed so that he could see how kingship ended. He commanded Felipe always to defend the Catholic faith and to dispense justice impartially. Pointedly, he defined a good minister as one who sought to bolster the king's authority rather than his own and – clearly with the marquis of Denia in mind – he strongly urged his son not to abandon the responsibilities of government to anyone. Philip and Isabella were brought to him, and he gave them his blessing and dismissed them; they kissed his hands and bade him farewell, tears filling their eyes. García de Loaysa read the Passion of St John and the Prior of the Escorial read the Commendation of the Soul to God. Philip's last words, uttered in breathless agony, affirmed that he died as a Catholic in obedience to the Roman Church. He died at about 5 a.m. on Sunday, 13 September 1598. He was holding his father's crucifix and candle, one in each hand. In accordance with his instructions, his body was washed and dressed by Moura and Fernando de Toledo. With deep symbolism, however, it was the marquis of Denia himself who formally handed the coffin over to the new king. Philip III made his first confession as king and then retired with Denia to an antechamber. He returned to announce that the marquis had been appointed to the Council of State. Philip II had been correct: favouritism and the Council of State would go hand-in-hand. On the following day, and without having been embalmed, Philip was interred in the Escorial. No music was played for him, no pomp was displayed.[62]

EPILOGUE

Long anticipated though it had been, Philip II's death was a momentous event in European history. Contemporaries certainly believed that a great figure had passed on and that the political landscape had shifted substantially with his death. That historians have failed to find agreement on the verdict to be passed on him is hardly surprising, for Philip's reign lay at the heart of so many of the issues of political and national development, of religious and cultural identity that have helped to define Europe. Debate has been further complicated by Philip's extraordinary personality, which has lent itself so readily to extreme interpretations. It is perhaps useful to remember how much the ambitions of Philip's last decade have served to accentuate the division of opinion about him. If Philip had died at Badajoz in 1580 or at Monzón in 1585 his reputation would surely now outshine that of all his contemporaries; he would be seen as the creator of Spain, the victor over Suleiman the Magnificent at Malta, the comptroller of an Atlantic economic and political system and of a pan-Pacific trading system. As it is, Philip is most often remembered for the unbridled intensity with which he pursued the war in the Low Countries, launched his armadas against England and intervened in the civil wars in France in the 1590s.

In truth, Philip's successes and his failures both had something of the epic about them. His greatest achievement was to recreate Spain after the decades of neglect that had characterised his father's rule and to defend her strategic interests in both the Mediterranean and the Atlantic. But so many of the characteristic features of his kingship derived from (or were the expression of) the comparatively narrow base of Philip's concern with the principles and polity of Castile: his residence in Castile

253

and his neglect of his eastern kingdoms; the creation of Madrid as the capital of the monarchy (and of the Escorial as its cathedral); the determination to hold on to the Low Countries at almost any cost to Castile; the resolve to exclude interlopers from Castile's territories in the New World. But the over-taxation that Philip imposed on Castile had, like the colossal failures of the last decade, the most serious consequences for Spain well into the seventeenth century.

Both successes and failures had their roots in Philip's impossibly high concept of his kingly greatness and the congenital indecisiveness that made it seem at times impossible for him to make a decision until he was forced to do so by events – or indeed, was left behind by them. With his unyielding view of kingship went his efforts to create a personality that was devoid of emotion. But while his gravitas impressed (or intimidated) so many people it also made it possible for his enemies to smear him as the great intriguer, the king who was behind so many foul events in Europe. And in truth, Philip was behind enough foul events for the charges to seem to have truth in them. While he was (at a stretch) entitled to place bounties on the heads of William of Orange and Prior Antonio of Crato because they were rebellious subjects, there was no justification for his involvement in repeated attempts to assassinate Elizabeth of England. Nor could there be even the pretence of legitimacy in his complicity in the death of Juan de Escobedo. There was, too, serious political miscalculation here. In the Low Countries, Egmont and Hornes in 1568 and the Prince of Orange in 1584 paid with their lives for Philip's failure to comprehend how essentially moderate their political demands had been. So, too, in ghastly secrecy in Simancas in 1570, did Egmont's brother, Montigny, garrotted in a dreadful charade of justice. It is all but certain that the count of Aranda and the duke of Villahermosa suffered similar fates in Castilian prisons in 1592.

Philip was especially unfortunate in the quality of his opponents; Elizabeth I, William of Orange and Henry IV were all great national heroes and figureheads, the personification of the glory of their nations, and in his conflicts with them Philip seemed incapable of seizing the high ground. Perhaps this was partly because he thought that they were lesser figures than he was – the first a woman, the second a rebel and the third a Protestant – but it was certainly because he could not have anything but contempt for people who could trim or even change their political or religious allegiances to suit the needs of the moment. Philip believed himself to be guided immutably and immovably by principle and conviction. In practice he was every bit as erastian and as malleable as his three great opponents; he would have found decision-making much easier if he had recognised the fact. But he did not measure himself against his contemporaries; to the end of his life he was locked into a competition with his father. Only days from death, after forty-two years as king of Spain, Philip felt the need to be certain that it was proper for him to be buried in Franciscan garb and so he had two unfortunate friars from the Escorial open up his father's coffin to verify that Charles V had indeed gone to meet his maker dressed as a member of the Order of St Francis. They confirmed that the emperor had done so, and Philip was satisfied that he too should make his last journey robed as a Franciscan.[1] But for all his inhibitions when confronted by the greatness of his father, Philip II was a greater king than Charles V; he wrestled with a world that had become much more complex, embittered at once by the deepening of religious conflicts and by their extension over the Atlantic and even into the Pacific. Unlike his father, too, Philip confronted his own despair and uncertainties by redoubling his commitment to his kingship rather than by abdicating from it. Was it the example of Charles V that brought about in Philip his determination never to yield – be it to enemies or to debility and even to old age?

With all his faults and failures, Philip remains the most powerful and perhaps even the most interesting figure of his time, an intriguing mixture of certainty and of doubt, of high purpose and of low methods, of unyielding determination and of limitless procrastination. The age that he so dominated is properly named after him, not so much as a result of his personal qualities as because he ruled at a time when his country became the first modern superpower both within Europe and beyond. When he died men were beginning to question whether Spain's very power was not in danger of declining precisely because he had over-extended it. The overwhelming power of Philip II's Spain had been restrained in the 1580s and 1590s only by the alliance of much of western Europe against it but in substantial part that power was itself the result of the accident of French weakness. If France had been able to exercise her natural power in the 'Age of Philip II', Spain's own historical development might have been much more healthily balanced. So, too, might have been the view that history has held of Philip himself.

Glossary

adelantado holder of a position conferred by the king, normally the governorship (or captaincy-general) of a frontier province

alcabala sales tax of 10 per cent on value of goods sold in Castile

almiranta ship on which the admiral of a fleet sailed (but did not necessarily command)

armada fleet or navy

Armada de Barlovento fleet defending the Caribbean, operating out of Cartagena and the Greater Antilles

Armada del Mar del Sur fleet protecting Peruvian silver shipments to Panama

Armada para la Guarda de la Carrera de las Indias fleet guarding the approach to Spain of the fleet from the Indies

auto-de-fé Act of Faith conducted by the Inquistion; the formal publication of sentences in cases of alleged heresy

campo grande large open public space used for communal events

capitán general Captain-General commanding soldiers and/or a kingdom or province

capitana flagship of a fleet or squadron

Casa de la Contratación House of Trade in Seville regulating the Indies trade

Comendador Mayor holder of the senior *encomienda* in the Military Order of Santiago

comuneros soldier in the popular army rebelling in 1520

conquistador conqueror of a province or kingdom, usually in the Indies

Consulado monopolistic corporation of merchants of Seville

corsario privateer

Cortes parliament (Castile and Aragon)

Corts parliament (Catalan)

cruzada tax authorised by papacy, originally to fight the war of Granada but subsequently to maintain galleys for crusade against the infidel

ebolista adherent to views of Ruy Gómez de Silva, prince of Éboli

encabezamiento general register of householders for fiscal purposes

encomienda endowment of a rent in a Military Order

entrada military expedition of conquest, usually in the Indies

etiqueta definition of ceremonial used at a royal court

excusado tax levied on parish tithes in Castile, authorised by papacy, originally to fund the war in the Low Countries, subsequently for Mediterranean galleys fighting against the infidel

flota fleet; in Indies trade, the fleet sailing from Spain to New Spain

fuero constitutional privilege of town, region or kingdom in Crown of Aragon

galeón galleon, large sailing ship

galeones in Indies trade, fleet sailing from Spain to collect the Peruvian silver at Cartagena

galeota small galley, with 16–20 banks of oarsmen

galeote galley slave

galera real royal galley

gobernador governor

Gran Soccorso large expedition relieving Malta in 1565

infante prince

infanta princess

junta committee, usually governmental

juro government bond

La Casilla the Little House (ironic)

La Suprema the Council of Inquisition

libras unit of currency in Crown of Aragon, worth slightly less than one Castilian ducat

limpieza de sangre purity of blood, free of Jewish blood

maestre de campo colonel

mar océano the Atlantic

mayordomo chief officer of a household

medio general settlement between Crown and its creditors after a suspension of payments by Crown

morisco (a) a Christian of Moorish extraction

Nueva Recopilación revised version of laws of Castile

oidor judge or councillor

ordenanza   Crown regulation or decree
patronato   patronage
plaza de armas   parade ground
plaza mayor   main square
quintal   a hundredweight
reconquista   reconquest of Spain from the Moors
Relaciones Topográficas   topographical descriptions
repartimiento   division for purposes of tax assessment
servicio   tax paid to Crown
subsidio   tax on clergy, authorised by papacy, for galleys to be used
  against the infidel
sumiller de corps   court officer in charge of supervising the dressing and
  undressing of a king and everything to do with the royal bedchamber
supremo   a court of appeal; a governmental council from whose judgement there was no right of appeal (except to the king)
tercio   infantry regiment
título   titled nobleman
tonel   the tonnage of a ship (some 10 per cent variation between
  Cantabrian and Andalusian shipbuilders)
tonelada   originally an accounting unit, by the time of the Armada it normally referred to the dimensions of a ship in *toneles machos*

NOTES

INTRODUCTORY NOTE

The study of Philip II and his reign has been transformed in recent years. Attention is drawn in the footnotes to many of the more important new works, but students wishing to develop their understanding of recent advances might look profitably at the following, many of which have detailed bibliographies:

Casey, J., *Early Modern Spain. A Social History* (London: 1999)
Checa, F., *Felipe II [Mecenas de las artes]* (Madrid: 1997)
Fernández Álvarez, M., *Felipe II y su tiempo* (Madrid: 1998)
Glete, Jan, *Warfare at Sea, 1500–1650. [Maritime Conflicts and the Transformation of Europe]* (London: 2000)
Kamen, H., *Philip of Spain* (New Haven: 1997)
Martin, C. and Parker, G., *The Spanish Armada* (Manchester: 1999)
Martínez Millán, J. (ed.), *La Corte de Felipe II* (Madrid: 1994)
Martínez Millán, J. (dir.), *Felipe II (1527–1598). Europa y la Monarquía Católica* (5 vols, Madrid: 1999)
Parker, G., *The Grand Strategy of Philip II* (New Haven: 1998)

The catalogues of three major exhibitions in the series entitled *Felipe II. Un monarca y su época* contain a wealth of information and analysis: *La monarquía hispánica* (Madrid: 1998); *Las tierras y los hombres del Rey* (Madrid: 1998) and *Un príncipe del Renacimiento* (Madrid: 1998–9). The papers delivered at the major conference held in Madrid in 1998 have been published by J. Martínez Millán (ed.), as *Felipe II (1527–1598). Europa y la Monarquía Católica* (5 vols, Madrid: 1999)

Probably the greatest single advance of recent years has been made in studies of the Armada of 1588 (see chapter 7, n. 54). Attention is drawn here to the extraordinary project of publishing all the Spanish papers relating to the Armada, *La Batalla del Mar Océano* (*BMO*), (eds, J. Calvar Gross, J. I. González-Aller Hierro,

M. de Dueñas Fontán and M. del C. Mérida Valverde, (3 vols, Madrid: 1988–93). Thus far the collection has covered the years from 1568 to the beginning of 1588; it incorporates many major series of published documents, and I have indicated in the footnotes where documents published in England have been included in it. Chief among collections in English on the reign are the *Calendar of State Papers*; I have used three series: the Spanish [*CSPS*] *I–IV Elizabeth* (London: 1892–9); the Foreign [*CSPF*], most usefully 1564–5, 1566–8 and 1579–80, (London: 1870–1904]; and the Venetian [*CSPV*] (vols V–IX), (London: 1873–97).

1   PREPARATION FOR POWER

1. P. de Sandoval, [*Historia de la vida y hechos del Emperador] Carlos V* (ed. C. Seco Serrano, Madrid: *Biblioteca de Autores Españoles* [*BAE*] 80–82: 1955–6), at II, p. 247.
2. F. A. Yates, *Astraea. The Imperial Theme in the Sixteenth Century* (Harmondsworth: 1977), pp. 1–28.
3. V. Cadenas y Vicent (ed.), *Diario del Emperador Carlos V (Itinerarios, permanencias, despacho, sucesos y efemeridades relevante de su vida)* (Madrid: *Hidalguía*, 1992) and J. de Vandenesse, 'Diario de los Viajes de Carlos V', in J. García Mercadal (ed.) *Viajes de Extranjeros [por España y Portugal]*, (3 vols, Madrid: 1952–9), I, pp. 911–44. R. Tyller, *The Emperor Charles V*, (London: 1956), pp. 321–50.
4. M. J. Rodríguez-Salgado, *The Changing Face of Empire: Charles V, Philip II and Habsburg Authority, 1551–1559* (Cambridge: 1988), pp. 34–5.
5. M. Fernández Alvarez, *Charles V. Elected emperor and hereditary ruler* (London: 1975), pp. 114–16.
6. A fine biography, J. M. Boyden, *The Courtier and the King. Ruy Gómez de Silva, Philip II, and the Court of Spain* (Berkeley: 1995); on the Portuguese connection, J. Martínez Millán, 'Familia Real y Grupos Políticos: La Princesa Doña Juana de Austria', in the important collection of essays edited by J. Martínez Millán, *La Corte de Felipe II* (Madrid: 1994), pp. 73–105.
7. L. Cabrera de Córdoba, *Felipe Segundo, Rey de España*, [*Felipe II*] (4 vols, Madrid: 1876–77), I, pp. 3–6; J. M. March, *Niñez y Juventud de Felipe II*, (Madrid: 1942), *passim*; A. Losada, *Juan Ginés de Sepúlveda a traves de su "Epistolario" y nuevos documentos* (Madrid: *Consejo Superior de Investigaciones Científicas [CSIC]*, 1973), pp. 93–5; M. Lafuente, *Historia General de España* (30 vols, Madrid: 1850–67); XII, chapter XXXI, 'El Príncipe Don Felipe', pp. 372–408; on music, H. Anglès, 'Latin Church Music on the Continent – 3 Spain and Portugal', *The New Oxford History of Music*, vol. IV, *The Age of Humanism, 1540–1630* (ed. G. Abraham), (Oxford: 1968), pp. 372–418.
8. J. M. March, *El Comendador Mayor de Castilla Don Luis de Requeséns en el Gobierno de Milan 1571–1573* (Madrid: 1943), pp. 9–21; I. Clopas Batlle, *Luis de Requesens. [El Gran Olvidado de Lepanto]* (Martorell: 1971), pp. 38–9.
9. M. Fernández Alvarez, *Corpus Documental de Carlos V* [*CDC*] (4 vols, Salamanca: 1973–9), II, pp. 135–40 and 165–6.
10. Ibid., II, pp. 90–118.

11. Ibid., pp. 187–8.
12. P. Gachard, *Don Carlos y Felipe II* (Madrid: 1984), pp. 37–8.
13. See, for instance, *CDC*, II, pp. 187–204. On Charles V and Philip, Rodríguez-Salgado, *Changing Face of Empire*, pp. 75–7 and 105–10.
14. J. L. G. Novalín, *El Inquisidor General Fernando de Valdés (1483–1568). Su vida y su obra* (Oviedo: 1968), pp. 163–6.
15. H. Kamen, *The Spanish Inquisition. An Historical Revision* (London: 1997), pp. 236–54.
16. Sandoval, *Carlos V*, III, pp. 281–97.
17. H. Trevor-Roper, *Princes and Artists. Patronage and Ideology at four Habsburg Courts 1517–1633* (London: 1976), pp. 47–83.
18. L. van der Essen, *Alexandre Farnése, Prince de Parme, Gouveurneur Général del Pays-Bas (1545–1592)* (5 vols, Brussels, 1933–7), I, chapters I–III, pp. 10–56; L. de Salazar y Castro, *Glorias de la Casa Farnese, ó resumen de las heroycas acciones de sus Principes* (Madrid: 1716), pp. 91–136.
19. R. G. Trewinnard, 'The Household of the Spanish Monarch: Structure, Cost and Personnel 1606–65', unpublished Ph.D. thesis, (University of Wales, Cardiff, 1991).
20. *CDC*, III, pp. 31–6; see also R. Rodríguez Raso, *Maximiliano de Austria, Gobernador de Carlos V en España. Cartas al Emperador* (Madrid: CSIC, 1963). On Philip's journey, C. Calvete de Estrella, *El felicissímo viaie [d'el muy alto y muy poderoso príncipe don Phelippe . . .]* (Antwerp: 1552) and A. de Santa Cruz, *[Crónica del emperador] Carlos V* (5 vols, Madrid, 1920–5), V, chapters XXV–XXVII and XXXI–XXXII.
21. On the reception in Augsburg, *CDC*, III, pp. 100–1.
22. For a map of Philip's tour of the Low Countries, Geoffrey Parker, *The Dutch Revolt* (Harmondsworth: 1979), p. 24.
23. Calvete de Estrella, *El felicissímo viaie*, p. 220.
24. R. Strong, *Art and Power. Renaissance Festivals, 1450–1650* (Woodbridge: Boydell, 1984), pp. 7–8, 47–8, 66–7, 76–7, 87–9, 91–3 and J. de Iongh, *Mary of Hungary Second Regent of the Netherlands* (London: 1959), pp. 232–4. On Philip and the arts (and much else besides), Checa, *Felipe II*, especially, pp. 76–85.
25. Rodríguez-Salgado, *Changing Face of Empire*, pp. 38–40.
26. Trevor-Roper, *Princes and Patronage*, pp. 37–9.
27. Rodríguez-Salgado, *Changing Face of Empire*, pp. 60–72.
28. Lafuente, *Historia de España*, XII, pp. 410–11.
29. David Loades, *Mary Tudor: A Life* (Oxford: 1989), pp. 201–10.
30. Egmont to Philip, London, 21 Jan. 1554, Archivo General de Simancas [AGS] E[stado] 808, f. 2.
31. This Álvaro de Bazán was the father of the celebrated Marquis of Santa Cruz of the same name; *CDC*, IV, pp. 105–17; Loades, *Mary Tudor*, pp. 220–2, and Rodríguez-Salgado, *Changing Face of Empire*, pp. 79–92; R. B. Wernham, *Before the Armada. The Growth of English Foreign Policy 1485–1588* (London: 1966), pp. 208–20.
32. 'A letter relating Philip's voyage to England and marriage', Jul. 1554, *CSPS*, XIII, 11; J. de Vandenesse, 'Diario de los viajes de Felipe II' in García Mercadal (ed.) *Viajes de Extranjeros*, II, pp. 1064–9.

33. *CSPV*, V, 922 and 923; on Milan, Philip to Charles V, Richmond, 16 and 17 Aug. 1554, AGS E. 808, ff. 31 and 32, and Boyden, *Courtier and the Prince*, pp. 174–5, n. 10.
34. *CSPS*, XIII, 7.
35. Ibid., 30.
36. From Antoncurch, 2 Sept. 1554, AGS E. 808, f. 38.
37. Wallace MacCaffrey, *Elizabeth I* (London, New York: 1993), p. 23; on Elizabeth's acknowledgement that they had met, see main text, pp. 124–5.
38. Loades, *Mary Tudor*, pp. 234–8.
39. Copy of letter to Gómez Suarez de Figueroa, London, 12 March 1555, AGS. E. 809, f. 14.
40. Ibid.
41. John Guy, *Tudor England* (Oxford: 1998), pp. 237–9.
42. Loades, *Mary Tudor*, pp. 234, 248; *CSPV*, VI/I, 138, 209; Vandenesse, 'Viajes de Felipe II', in García Mercadal (ed.) *Viajes de Extranjeros*, II, p. 1068.

2 KING OF SPAIN

1. *CSPV*, VI/I 214, 253, 254; Sandoval, *Carlos V*, III, pp. 473–85. For modern assessments, M. Van Durme, *El Cardenal Granvela [(1517–1586).* *Imperio y Revolución bajo Carlos V y Felipe II]* (Barcelona: 1957), pp. 190–3 and Rodríguez-Salgado, *Changing Face of Empire*, pp. 101–35.
2. *CSPV*, VI/I, 301, 496, 513.
3. 'He then continued that he was naturally so desirous of being freed from having the care of vassals, that if the first-born of the King of the Romans, after his remaining six years childless, had not been a female, he would never have married, and would have left him successor to all his States', ibid., 353; Sandoval, *Carlos V*, III, 486–9 prints documentation; on departure, *CSPV*, VI/I, 573, 590, 602, 610, 617.
4. Ibid., 449, and VI/II, 760, 884, 1064, 1071, with the description of Philip at pp. 1060–66.
5. Ibid., I, 453, and *CSPS*, XIII, 183, 196, 197.
6. *CSPS*, XIII, 296.
7. *CSPV*, VI/II, 884, p. 1063.
8. Rodríguez-Salgado, *Changing Face of Empire*, pp. 101–18; *CSPV*, VI/I, 24,
9. Vandenesse, 'Viajes de Felipe II', in García Mercadal (ed.), *Viajes de Extranjeros*, II, p. 1070.
10. Ibid., and Wernham, *Before the Armada*, p. 231.
11. *CSPV*, VII/I, 635 and II, 1039; W. Maltby, *Alba: A Biography of Fernando Álvarez de Toledo, Third Duke of Alba, 1507–1582* (Berkeley: 1983), pp. 86–109.
12. An account of the battle, *CSPS*, XIII, 336.
13. Ibid., 367 and 380.
14. Sandoval, *Carlos V*, II, 509–16, Vandenesse, 'Viajes de Felipe II', in García Mercadal (ed.), *Viajes de Extranjeros*, pp. 1075–91 and Strong, *Art and Power*, pp. 95–6.; on death of Mary, *CSPS*, XIII, 502.

15. Feria to Philip, London, 14 and 29 Dec. 1558, copies, AGS. E. 811, ff. 99 and 105; Rodríguez-Salgado, *Changing Face of Empire*, pp. 315–28; MacCaffrey, *Elizabeth I*, p. 71.
16. *CSPV*, VII, 47, 54–8; Rodríguez-Salgado, *Changing Face of Empire*, pp. 305–37.
17. J. Garrisson, *A History of Sixteenth-Century France, 1483–1598* (Basingstoke: Macmillan, 1995); on faction, pp. 256–78.
18. Parker, *Dutch Revolt*, pp. 48–52.
19. C. J. de Carlos Morales, 'El Poder de los Secretarios Reales: Francisco de Eraso', in Martínez Millán (ed.) *La Corte de Felipe II*, pp. 107–48.
20. Boyden, *The Courtier and the King*, p. 63
21. M. Cavalli, 'Relación' of 1551, in García Mercadal (ed.), *Viajes de Extranjeros*, at I, 1057.
22. Boyden, *The Courtier and the King*, p. 55.
23. H. Pizarro Llorente, 'El Control de la Conciencia Regia. El confesor real Fray Bernardo de Fresneda', in Martínez Millán (ed.) *La Corte de Felipe II*, pp. 149–88, at pp. 153–64.
24. Novalín, *El Inquisidor General Fernando de Valdés . . . Su Vida y Obra*, pp. 287–347, and *idem*, 'Fernando de Valdés', in Q. Aldea and others, *Diccionario de Historia Eclesiástica de España [DHEE]* (5 vols, Madrid: 1972–5 and 1987), IV, pp. 2684–5; Rodríguez-Salgado, *Changing Face of Empire*, pp. 215–18, 226–7; minute re. Valdés, London 10 June 1557, AGS E. 810, f. 43.
25. J. Martínez Millán, 'Familia Real y grupos políticos', in Martínez Millán (ed.), *La Corte de Felipe II*, pp. 91–2.
26. R. G. Villoslada, 'JESUITAS (Compañia de Jesús, SI)', *DHEE*, II, pp. 1231–7.
27. Novalín, *El Inquisidor General Fernando de Valdés . . . Su Vida y Obra*, pp. 277–80.
28. *Cédulas* of 22 Aug. 1559, AGS. E. 550, no folio; on the stadholderships, J. Israel, *The Dutch Republic. Its Rise, Greatness, and Fall 1477–1806* (Oxford: 1995), pp. 138–41.
29. G. Redworth, '"Matters Impertinent to Women": Male and Female Monarchy under Philip and Mary', *English Historical Review [EHR]*, 1997, XCII, June 1998, pp. 597–613.
30. M. Sangrador Vitores, *Historia de la Muy Noble y Leal Ciudad de Valladolid*, 2 vols, Valladolid 1851–4, I, pp. 386–94, with a list of the victims at the *autos-de-fé* of 21 May and 8 Oct. 1559; Gachard, *Don Carlos y Felipe II*, p. 64.
31. Printed by Sandoval, *Carlos V*, III, pp. 552–61.

3 THE RE-ORDERING OF SPAIN

1. Gachard, *Don Carlos y Felipe II*, p. 66.
2. F. Braudel, *The Mediterranean and the Mediterranean World in the Age of Philip II* (2 vols, London: 1972), II, p. 964.
3. *CSPV*, VII, 150.
4. G. de San Agustín, *Conquistas de las Islas Filipinas – 1565–1615* (ed. Pedro G. Galende, Manila: 1998), pp. 210–13.
5. R. L. Kagan (ed.), *Ciudades del Siglo de Oro. Las Vistas Españolas de Anton Van den Wyngaerde* (Berkeley: 1986); this beautifully produced volume

includes an appreciation by E. Haverkamp-Begemann, 'Las Vistas de España de Anton Van den Wyngaerde', pp. 54–67; a map of Wyngaerde's journeys, p. 11. See also M. J. Rodríguez-Salgado, 'Christians, Civilised and Spanish: Multiple Identities in Sixteenth-Century Spain', *Transactions of the Royal Historical Society*, Sixth Series, VIII, (1998), pp. 233–51.

6. I. A. A. Thompson, *War and Government in Habsburg Spain, 1560–1620* (London: 1976), 'Table A. The Finances of Castile', p. 288.

7. Ibid., pp. 67–8. In recent years a powerful revisionist approach has transformed our understanding of the importance of the Cortes of Castile; see, in particular, Thompson's 'Crown and Cortes in Castile, 1590–1665', *Parliament, Estates and Representation* [*PER*], II (1982), pp. 29–45; C. Jago, 'Habsburg Absolutism and the Cortes of Castile', *American Historical Review* [*AHR*], LXXXVI (1981), pp. 307–26 and 'Philip II and the Cortes of Castile: The case of the Cortes of 1576', *Past and Present* [*PP*] 109 (Nov. 1985), pp. 24–43; J. I. Fortea Pérez, 'The Cortes of Castile and Philip II's fiscal policy', *PER* (1991), II (2), pp. 117–38; and L. González Antón, *Las Cortes en la España del Antiguo Régimen* (Madrid: 1989). On the financial history of the reign, M. Ulloa, *La Hacienda Real de Castilla en el Reinado de Felipe II* (Madrid: 1977).

8. Braudel, *The Mediterranean*, I, p. 533.

9. Ulloa, *La Hacienda Real de Castilla*, pp. 759–65.

10. Cabrera de Córdoba, *Felipe II*, I, pp. 396–9; Gachard, *Don Carlos y Felipe II*, pp. 93–104; J. Reglà Campistol, *Felip II i Catalunya* (Barcelona: 1956), pp. 19–20.

11. A. Martínez Llamas, *Isabel [Elizabeth] de Valois, reina de España. Una historia de amor y enfermedad* (Madrid: 1996); *CSPV*, VII, 133, 245, 268.

12. *CSPS, 1 Eliz.*, 285.

13. Martínez Llamas, *Isabel de Valois*, pp. 230–47; Cabrera de Córdoba, *Felipe II*, I, pp. 597–600.

14. *CSPV*, VII, 104.

15. *CSPS I Eliz.*, 163.

16. Gachard, *Don Carlos y Felipe II*, pp. 75–91.

17. Ibid., pp. 123–4.

18. Ibid., p. 127.

19. Cabrera de Córdoba, *Felipe II*, I, pp. 557–66, 588–91; *CSPF*, 1566–68, 1969, 2475; D. de Colmenares, *Historia de la Insigne Ciudad de Segovia y Compendio de las Historias de Castilla* (2 vols, Segovia: 1970), II, pp. 285–6; Boyden, *The Courtier and the King*, pp. 132–3.

20. See, for example, *CSPV*, VII, 155.

21. 'Correspondencia de Felipe II y de otros personajes con Don Juan de Austria desde 1568 hasta 1570 . . .', *Colección de Documentos Inéditos para la Historia de España* [*CODOIN*], XXVIII (Madrid, 1856).

22. On the wedding, Colmenares, *Historia de Segovia*, II, pp. 293–317; on the children, G. González de Avila, *Teatro de las Grandezas de Madrid, Corte de los Reyes Católicos de España* (Madrid: 1623, reprint, Madrid: 1986), pp. 145–6; A. de León Pinelo, *Anales de Madrid (desde el año 447 al de 1658)* (Madrid: 1971), pp. 111–29, and L. Cortes Echanové, *Nacimiento y crianza de personas reales en la corte de España, 1566–1886* (Madrid: CSIC, 1958), pp. 12–30.

23. A. Alvar Ezquerra, *El Nacimiento de una Capital Europea. Madrid entre 1561 y 1606* (Madrid: 1989); I have used the population figures from this important study, pp. 15–104. See also, M. F. Carbajo Isla, *La Población de la Villa de Madrid: desde finales del siglo XVI hasta mediados del siglo XIX* (Madrid: 1987), V. Pinto Crespo and S. Madrazo Madrazo (eds), *Madrid. Atlas Histórico de la Ciudad, Siglos IX–XIX* (Madrid: 1995), S. Juliá, D. Ringrose and C. Segura (eds), *Madrid: historia de una capital* (Madrid: 1995) and J. Camacho Cabello, *La población de Castilla–La Mancha (siglos XVI, XVII, XVIII): crisis y renovación* (Toledo: 1997). On the inadequacy of Toledo, *CSPV*, VII, 144, 148.

24. Checa, *Felipe II*, pp. 36–69 and 111–34.

25. Manuel Fernández Alvarez, 'El Establecimiento de la Capitalidad de Espana en Madrid', in *Madrid en el Siglo XVI* (Madrid: *CSIC*, 1962), p. 12.

26. Even historians of Madrid in the seventeenth century were not sure exactly when the city had become the capital; León Pinelo noted that 'it is only known that on 22 February (1561) the Council was in Toledo and that on 19 July it was despatching business in Madrid . . .', *Anales de Madrid*, p. 85; Jerónimo de Quintana thought that the court had moved there in 1563, *A la Mvy Antigva, noble y coronada villa de Madrid: historia de su antiguedad nobleza y grandeza* (Madrid: 1629), f. 331b.

27. *CSPV*, VII, 263.

28. Calculation based on the list in González Davila, *Teatro de . . . la Villa de Madrid*, pp. 234–99 and on Pedro Texeira's map of Madrid in 1656. I am obliged to Helen Rawlings for guidance on these foundations.

29. Alvar Ezquerra, *Madrid entre 1561 y 1606*, pp. 15–105 and Carbajo Isla, *La Población de la Villa de Madrid*, p. 200.

30. J. de Sigüenza, *Fundación del Monasterio de el Escorial por Felipe II* (Madrid: 1927), pp. 559–61; Sigüenza based his calculation on the royal *cédulas* and receipts from the *pagadores*, and estimated that the costs of decoration brought the total up to 6 200 000 ducats. An architectural study, A. Bustamante García, *La octava maravilla del mundo. (Estudio histórico sobre El Escorial de Felipe II)* (Madrid: 1994).

31. AGS Casa y Sitios Reales [CySR], 259, ff. 59, 368; on woods for the monastery, AGS GA 140, f. 53.

32. Sigüenza, *Fundación*, pp. 15 and 19.

33. L. Wyts, 'Viaje por España', in García Mercadal (ed.), *Viajes de Extranjeros*, at I, p. 1175.

34. 'Relacion de las rreliquias que su Md del rey nro señor ha traydo a este su M[onasteri]o De Sanct lorenco el rreal . . . , XII de Julio 1570', AGS CySR 259, f. 635; on Guzmán de Silva, Sigüenza, *Fundación*, pp. 74–5.

35. The following paragraphs draw on Sigüenza, *Fundación*, 'Discurso XVII, pp. 506–27; Checa, *Felipe II*; Jonathan Brown, *Painting in Spain 1500–1700* (New Haven, London: 1998); George Kubler, *Building the Escorial* (Princeton, 1982); Trevor-Roper, *Princes and Artists*; and Mary Hollingsworth, *Patronage in Sixteenth-Century Italy* (London: 1996). I am obliged to David Davies for his generous guidance on the significance of Coxcie and Bosch.

36. Sigüenza, *Fundación*, p. 520.

37. Ibid., p. 517.

38. Anglès, 'Latin Church Music', and R. Stevenson, 'Madrid', in *The New Grove Dictionary of Music and Musicians* (ed. S. Sadie) (London: 1980), 11, pp. 457–8.

39. M. J. Rodríguez-Salgado, 'The Court of Philip II', in R. G. Asch and A. M. Birke (eds) *Princes, Patronage, and the Nobility: The Court at the Beginning of the Modern Age, c. 1450–1650* (Oxford: 1991), pp. 205–44, especially pp. 216–18.

40. Boyden, *The Courtier and the King*, pp. 60–1.

41. Madrid, 25 June 1565, printed by A. González Palencia, *Gonzalo Pérez, Secretario de Felipe Segundo* (2 vols, Madrid, 1946), II, p. 510.

42. Boyden, *The Courtier and the King*, pp. 105–111; *CSPV*, VII, 198, 121, 129, 148, 176. On the divisions on the Council of State, P. D. Lagomarsino, 'Court Factions and the Formulation of Spanish Policy towards the Netherlands (1559–67)', unpublished Ph.D. thesis (Univ. of Cambridge: 1973).

43. *CSPV*, VII, 198.

44. Ibid., 201.

45. Boyden, *The Courtier and the King*, p. 17.

46. Maltby, *Alba*, pp. 121–4.

47. J. Arrieta Alberdi, *El Consejo Supremo de la Corona de Aragón (1494–1707)* (Zaragoza: 1994); J. J. Salcedo Izu, *El Consejo Real de Navarra en el Siglo XVI* (Pamplona: 1964); E. Schäfer, *El Consejo de las Indias*, 2 vols (Seville: 1935–43).

48. Title to office, Brussels, 30 Jan. 1557, AGS Quitaciones de Corte [QC] 39. On the Council of Finance, C. J. de Carlos Morales, *El Consejo de Hacienda de Castilla, 1523–1602. Patronazgo y clientelismo en el gobierno de las finanzas reales durante el siglo XVI* (Junta de Castilla y Leon: 1996).

49. On court politics and the career of Espinosa, J. Martínez Millán, 'Grupos de poder en la corte durante el reinado de Felipe II: la facción ebolista, 1554–1573' in Martínez Millán (ed.), *Instituciones y élites de poder en la monarquía hispana durante el siglo XVI* (Madrid 1992), pp. 137–97 and 'En busca de la ortodoxía: El Inquisidor General Diego de Espinosa', in Martínez Millán (ed.) *La Corte de Felipe II*, pp. 189–228. The first of these articles is one of the seminal modern pieces on Spanish government.

50. Boyden, *The Courtier and the King*, pp. 116–50.

51. Alba to Espinosa, Segovia, 10 Aug. 1565, British Library [BL] Additional Manuscripts [Add] 28344, f. 18 and Ruy Gómez to the same, Estremera, 11 April 1566, ibid., f. 192.

52. Boyden, *The Courtier and the King*, pp. 130 and 136.

53. On Ovando see main text, p. 183–7 and Vázquez de Leca, pp. 281–96; on Espinosa's decline, Martínez Millán, 'Grupos de poder en la corte durante el reinado de Felipe II' in Martínez Millán (ed.), *La Corte de Felipe II*, pp. 189–228.

54. Requesens to Margaret of Parma, (Rome ?), 17 Nov. 1563, and same to Philip II, 6 April 1564, *Pio IV y Felipe Segundo. Primeros Diez Meses de la Embajada de Don Luis de Requesens en Roma 1563–64* (Madrid: *Colección de Libros Españoles Raros ó Curiosos*, 1891), XX, pp. 94–5 and 278.

55. To Don Juan de Zúñiga, (Rome ?) 18 Aug. 1564, ibid., p. 424.

56. I am obliged to Helen Rawlings for this information.

57. F. Ruiz Martín, 'Demografía eclesiastica de España hasta el siglo XIX', *DHEE*, II, pp. 682–733.

58. C. Gutiérrez, 'Concilio de Trento 1545–1563', ibid., I, pp. 483–96.

59. P. Janelle, *The Catholic Reformation* (London: 1975), pp. 89–90.

60. J. Tejada y Ramiro, *Coleccion de Cánones de todos los concilios de la Iglesia de España*, V, (Madrid: 1855), *Concilio Provincial de Toledo 1565–66)*, pp. 220–1.

61. Cabrera de Córdoba, *Felipe II*, II, p. 354.

62. H. E. Rawlings, 'The Secularisation of Castilian Episcopal Office under the Habsburgs, c. 1516–1700', *The Journal of Ecclesiastical History*, 38, 1, (1987), pp. 53–79, at p. 68.

63. Tejada y Ramiro, *Colección de Cánones*, 'Sesion II. De Reforma', pp. 228–60.

64. Gutiérrez, 'Concilio de Trento 1545–1563', *DHEE*, II, p. 491.

65. *Tres Indices Expurgatorios de la Inquisición Española en el Siglo XVI* (Madrid: Real Academía de Historia, 1952).

66. Novalín, *Fernando de Valdés . . . Su Vida y Obra*, pp. 269–86; on the Carranza case and Valdés's fall, ibid., pp. 349–79. Valdés died on 9 December 1568.

67. J. Contreras and G. Henningsen, 'Forty-four thousand cases of the Spanish Inquisition (1540–1700): Analysis of a Historical Data Bank', in Henningsen and J. Tedeschi (eds), *The Inquisition in Early Modern Europe. Studies on Sources and Methods* (Northern Illinois Univ. Press: 1986), pp. 100–29. On the Inquisition, Kamen, *Spanish Inquisition*, and S. Haliczer (ed.), *Inquisition and Society in Early Modern Europe* (London: 1987).

68. S. T. Nalle, *God in La Mancha: Religious Reform and the People of Cuenca 1500–1650* (Baltimore, London: 1992), p. 34.

69. Novalín, *Fernando de Valdés . . . Su Vida y Obra*, pp. 369–79.

70. R. G. Villoslada, 'Jesuitas', *DHEE*, II, 1232–4.

71. E. Allison Peers, *Mother of Carmel. A Portrait of St. Teresa of Jesus* (London: 1945) p. 146.

4   THE WEALTH OF THE INDIES

1. R. Cerezo Martínez, *Las Armadas de Felipe II* (Madrid: 1988), pp. 78–81; P. Bakewell, *A History of Latin America* (Oxford: 1997), p. 201.

2. *Recopilación de leyes de los Reynos de las Indias*, (4 vols, reprint of edition of 1681, Madrid: 1973), III, fol. 1.

3. See 'Instrucción a Martín Enriquez', Aranjuez, 7 Jun. 1568, *Los Virreyes Españoles en America durante el Gobierno de la Corona de Austria*, BAE, 273 (ed. L. Hanke, Madrid: 1976), pp. 189–202.

4. P. Gerhard, *A Guide to the Historical Geography of New Spain* (Cambridge: 1972), pp. 22–8.

5. Ibid., 'Table D. *Epidemics in Nueva España*', p. 23.

6. N. Wachtel, *The Vision of the Vanquished. The Spanish Conquest of Peru Through Indian Eyes 1530–1570* (Trowbridge: 1977), especially pp. 85–140.

7. *Recopilación de leyes de . . . las Indias*, III, ff. 55b–62b.

8. P. J. Bakewell, *Silver Mining and Society in Colonial Mexico. Zacatecas, 1546–1700* (Cambridge: 1971), 'Table 10b. Five-yearly totals of mercury produced at Almadén and Huancavelica. . . . 1571 to 1700', p. 256.

9. M. Grice-Hutchinson, *Early Economic Thought in Spain 1177–1740* (London: 1978), p. 104; quoted by J. H. Elliott, *Imperial Spain 1469–1716* (Harmondsworth: 1963), p. 191.

10. *Recopilación de leyes de . . . las Indias*, III, ff. 130b–158b.

11. J. L. Casado Soto, *Los Barcos Españoles del Siglo XVI [y La Gran Armada de 1588]* (Madrid: 1988), p. 11; for a summary in English of Casado's important work, see his 'Atlantic Shipping in Sixteenth-Century Spain and the 1588 Armada', in M. J. Rodríguez-Salgado and S. Adams (eds), *England, Spain and the Gran Armada. Essays from the Anglo-Spanish Conferences London and Madrid 1988* (Edinburgh: 1991), pp. 95–133.

12. A. Domínguez Ortíz, 'La Baja Andalucía' in *idem* (ed.) *Historia de Andalucía*, IV, *La Andalucia del Renacimiento* (Madrid, Barcelona: *c.* 1980), at p. 238.

13. P. E. Hoffman, *The Spanish Crown and the Defense of the Caribbean, 1535–1585. Precedent, Patrimonialism, and Royal Parsimony* (Baton Rouge and London: 1980), pp. 64–70, at p. 68.

14. K. R. Andrews, *The Spanish Caribbean. Trade and Plunder 1530–1630* (New Haven and London: 1978), pp. 83–4.

15. *CDC*, IV, pp. 429–35 and 441–2.

16. C. M. Vigil, *Noticias biográfico-genealógicas de Pedro Menéndez de Avilés Primer Adelantado y Conquistador de la Florida* (Avilés: 1982), and E. Lyon (ed.), *Pedro Menéndez de Avilés*, vol. 24, *Spanish Borderlands Sourcebooks* (New York and London: 1995); see in particular, Lyon's 'The Enterprise of Florida', pp. 61–72 and 'Pedro Menéndez de Avilés', pp. 3–29. I have drawn from these important essays in the following paragraphs.

17. Philip II to Menéndez de Avilés, Madrid, 12 May 1566, printed by E. Ruidiaz y Caravia, *La Florida. Su Conquista y Colonización por Pedro Menéndez de Avilés* (2 vols, Madrid: 1893), II, p. 363.

18. *CSPS I Elizabeth*, 340.

19. See, for instance, Guzmán de Silva to Philip II, 'Relacion de los Nauios que dizen q[ue] van a las Indias', n. d., AGS. E. 816, f. 48 and same to same, London, 11 July 1567, ibid., f. 106.

20. J. Cummins, *Francis Drake* (London: 1995), p. 28; see also 'The third troublesome voyage made by the *Jesus of Lubeck*, the *Minion*, and four other ships, to the parts of Guinea and the West Indies, in the years 1567 and 1568, by Master John Hawkins', R. David (ed.), *Hakluyt's Voyages* (London: 1988), pp. 397–405.

21. On the convoy system, Hoffman, *The Spanish Crown and the Defense of the Caribbean*, pp. 109–212; J. H. Parry, *The Spanish Seaborne Empire* (London: 1996), pp. 254–5; D. Goodman, *Spanish Naval Power, 1589–1665. Reconstruction and Defeat* (Cambridge: 1997), p. 3.

22. Cummins, *Drake*, pp. 33–64.

23. After the death of Luis de Velasco a group of about 120 colonists were involved in a conspiracy to overthrow the viceregal government and replace it with a monarchy led by Martín Cortes, son of the conqueror. Cortes may not have even known what was happening and nothing much came of

it; see M. C. Meyer and W. L. Sherman, *The Course of Mexican History* (5th edn., Oxford: 1995), pp. 158–60 and B. García Martínez, *El Marquesado del Valle. Tres siglos de régimen señorial en Nueva España* (Mexico City: 1969), pp. 74–5.

24. Martínez Millán, 'En busca de la ortodoxía: el Inquisidor General Diego de Espinosa', in Martínez Millán (ed.), *La Corte de Felipe II*, pp. 222–3.
25. Bakewell, *Silver Mining and Society*, p. 171.
26. 'Memorial que Don Francisco de Toledo dió al Rey Nuestro Señor . . .', L. Hanke (ed.), *Los Virreyes Españoles en America durante el Gobierno de la Casa de Austria, Perú I* (Madrid, 1978), BAE, vol. 280, pp. 128–49. Another version, AGS Guerra Antigua [GA] 140, f. 77.
27. R. Ricard, *The Spiritual Conquest of Mexico. An Essay on the Apostolate and the Evangelizing Methods of the Mendicant Orders in New Spain, 1523–1572* (Berkeley: 1966), pp. 61–82.
28. R. Recolons, 'Mejico', *DHEE*, II, pp. 1456–65 and 'Peru', ibid., III, pp. 1974–9; see also V. Rodríguez Valencia, 'Mogrovejo, Toribio de', ibid., p. 1499.
29. A. W. Lovett, 'Juan de Ovando and the Council of Finance' (1573–1575), *The Historical Journal*, [*HJ*], XV, 1 (1972), pp. 1–21; H. F. Cline, 'The "Relaciones Geográficas" of the Spanish Indies, 1577–85', *Hispanic American Historical Review* [*HAHR*], 44, 1964, pp. 341–74; L. Suárez Fernández, *El Consejo de Indias en el siglo XVI* (Valladolid: 1970); and E. Martiré, 'La política de Juan de Ovando y su actividad recopiladora', *Historia General de España y America* (Madrid: Ediciones Rialp, 1982), VII, pp. 455–63.
30. Title to office, Madrid, 28 Aug. 1571, AGS. QC. 28.
31. Lovett, *Philip II and Mateo Vázquez de Leca*, pp. 63–4; on the presidency of Finance, p. 63, n. 16.

5 CRUSADE, CRISIS AND REVOLT IN THE LOW COUNTRIES

1. Braudel, *The Mediterranean*, II, p. 970. Braudel's is the indispensable study on the Mediterranean in this period. On galley warfare, J. F. Guilmartin Jr, *Gunpower and Galleys. Changing Technology and Mediterranean Warfare at Sea in the Sixteenth Century* (Cambridge: 1974), and on warfare in general, Glete, *Warfare at Sea, 1500–1650*.
2. Braudel, *The Mediterranean*, II, p. 882.
3. C. Fernández Duro, 'El Desastre de los Gelves (1560–1561)', in his *Estudios Históricos del Reinado de Felipe II* (Madrid: 1890); CSPF, III, 128, 187, 494; A. Clot, *Suleiman the Magnificent. The man, his life, his epoch* (London: 1992); and Guilmartin, *Gunpowder and Galleys*, quotation at p. 130.
4. On La Herradura, Cabrera de Córdoba, *Felipe II*, I, p. 357 and CSPF, XVII, 407; P. Castillo Manrubía, 'Naufragio de la Armada Española en La Herradura (Granada): 19 de Octubre de 1562', *Revista General de Marina*, 199, (1980), pp. 57–69; Thompson, *War and Government*, pp. 165–71. Guilmartin, *Gunpowder and Galleys*, p. 133.

5. Thompson, *War and Government*, p. 16.
6. Goodman, *Spanish Naval Power*, p. 13.
7. *CSPF Elizabeth 1564–5*, 637.
8. Toledo to Duke of Alburquerque, Canal de Malta, 7 Sept. 1565, printed by E. García Hernán, *La Armada Española en la Monarquía de Felipe II [y la Defensa del Méditerraneo]* (Madrid?: 1995), pp. 150–1. T. Pickles, *Malta 1565. Last Battle of the Crusades* (Oxford: 1998); National Maritime Museum, *The Maritime Siege of Malta 1565*, (1965); I. C. Lochhead and T. F. R. Barling, *The Siege of Malta 1565* (London: 1970).
9. Guilmartin, *Gunpowder and Galleys*, pp. 192–3.
10. Braudel, *The Mediterranean*, II, p. 1020; *CSPS* 1 Eliz., 327.
11. The following account is based upon D. Hurtado de Mendoza, *Guerra de Granada* (Madrid: *Clásicos Castalia*, 1970); L. del Marmol Carvajal, *Historia de la Rebelión y Castigo de los Moriscos [del Reyno de Granada]* (2 vols, Madrid: 1797); F. Bermúdez de Pedraza, *Historia eclesiástica de Granada* (facsimile of 1639 edition, Granada: 1989); A. Marin Ocete, *El Arzobispo Don Pedro Guerrero y la Política Conciliar Española en el Siglo XVI* (2 vols, Zaragoza: 1970), and Braudel, *The Mediterranean*, II, pp. 1055–82.
12. Bermudez de Pedraza, *Historia eclesiástica*, pp. 229–241b and Marmol Carvajal, *Historia de la Rebelión y Castigo de los Moriscos*, I, *libros* 2 and 3.
13. D. Ortiz de Zúñiga, *Anales Eclesiásticos y Seculares de la Muy Noble y Muy Leal Ciudad de Sevilla* (5 vols, Madrid: 1796), IV, pp. 48–9; Thompson, *War and Government*, pp. 148–9, 237.
14. Hurtado de Mendoza, *Guerra de Granada*, pp. 198–217; Marmol Carvajal, *Historia de la Rebelión y Castigo de los Moriscos*, I, pp. 511–13; Cabrera de Córdoba, *Felipe II*, II, pp. 5–86.
15. Marmol Carvajal, *Historia de la Rebelión y Castigo de los Moriscos*, I, pp. 514–18.
16. Hurtado de Mendoza, *Guerra de Granada*, p. 307, n. 417.
17. *CODOIN*, XXVIII, pp. 54–6; Braudel, *The Mediterranean*, II, p. 1096.
18. The history of the Spanish *moriscos* is best approached through A. Dominguez Ortíz and B. Vincent, *Historia de los moriscos: vida y tragedia de una minoría* (Madrid: 1978).
19. On the Holy League and the Lepanto campaign, Braudel, *The Mediterranean*, II, pp. 1088–1142; Requesens' appointment, Antoni Borrás I Feliu, *Luis de Requesens, Cataluña y Lepanto* (Barcelona: 1971), Title to office, pp. 9–10 and 13–14. The account of Lepanto is based upon the anonymous *La Batalla Naval del Señor Don Juan de Austria Segun un Manuscrito Anónimo Contemporaneo* (Madrid: 1971); the figures for men and fleet (with the exception of the number of Turkish galleys which I have increased from his 208). See also J. M. Martínez-Hidalgo y Terán, *Lepanto. La Batalla. La Galera 'Real'* (Barcelona: 1971), pp. 15, 23, 35. See also Cerezo Martínez, *Las Armadas de Felipe II*, pp. 213–31, where an important account of the battle has even larger forces involved on both sides. See also R. Vargas-Hidalgo, *La Batalla de Lepanto según cartas inéditas de Felipe II, Don Juan de Austria y Juan Andre Doria e informes de embajadores y espías* (Santiago, Chile: 1988), p. 270.
20. Don John of Austria to Philip II, Las Islas Escocelaras, 9 Oct. 1571, printed by Vargas-Hidalgo, *La Batalla de Lepanto*, pp. 273–4; M. de Cervantes, *Don*

Quixote, trans. J. M. Cohen, (Harmondsworth: Penguin Classics, 1950), p. 348.

21. García Hernán, *La Armada Española en la Monarquía de Felipe II*, p. 81.

22. 'cada dia se va soltando mas contra la religion', Duke of Feria to Philip II, London, 14 Dec. 1558, AGS E 811, f. 99, a copy; see also same to same 29 Dec., ibid., f. 105.

23. Wernham, *Before the Armada*, pp. 259–77.

24. *CSPS*, I Eliz., 300.

25. Parker, *Dutch Revolt*, p. 46 and Israel, *The Dutch Republic*, p. 136; my account of the Dutch Revolt relies consistently on these two standard works and on E. H. Kossman and A. F. Mellink (eds), *Texts [concerning the Revolt of the Netherlands]* (Cambridge: 1974). See also Parker's *The Army of Flanders [and the Spanish Road 1567–1659]* (Cambridge: 1972), and J. Giménez Martín, *Tercios de Flandes* (Madrid: 1999). On the background to the revolt, J. D. Tracy, *Holland under Habsburg Rule 1506–1566. The Formation of a Body Politic* (Berkeley, Los Angeles, Oxford: 1990).

26. Parker, *Dutch Revolt*, p. 46.

27. Ibid., pp. 47–8 and Israel, *Dutch Republic*, pp. 141–3.

28. Van Durme, *El Cardenal Granvelle*, pp. 256–61.

29. Parker, *Dutch Revolt*, p. 68.

30. *CSPS I Eliz.*, 322, 327.

31. Quotations from the letter of 17 October, printed by Kossman and Mellink, *Texts*, 1, pp. 53–6.

32. Parker, *Dutch Revolt*, p. 68.

33. *CSPS, I Eliz.*, 334.

34. The 'Compromise' and the 'Request', printed by Kossman and Mellink, *Texts*, 3 and 4, pp. 59–64; quotations at pp. 60 and 63.

35. Parker, *Dutch Revolt*, pp. 72–82, map at p. 77; Israel, *Dutch Republic*, pp. 146–54.

36. Kossman and Mellink, *Texts*, 6, pp. 69–75, quotation at p. 74.

37. Cabrera de Córdoba, *Felipe II*, I, pp. 490–7; Boyden, *The Courtier and the King*, pp. 130–1.

38. Parker, *Dutch Revolt*, pp. 90–101.

39. Wernham, *Before the Armada*, p. 290.

40. Braudel, *The Mediterranean*, II, pp. 1040.

41. Salazar y Castro, *Indice de las Glorias de la Casa Farnese*, pp. 641–2.

42. Granvelle's verdict, Giménez Martín, *Tercios de Flandes*, p. 64; Israel, *Dutch Republic*, pp. 155–68.

43. 'Execution of Count Egmont and Count Horn in Brussels', V. von Klarwill (ed.), *The Fugger News-Letters [FNL]*, (2 vols, London: 1924–6), II, no. 1.

44. Parker, *Dutch Revolt*, p. 111; and B. Rekkers, *Benito Arias Montano (1527–1598)* (London: 1972), pp. 13–28.

45. Printed by Kossman and Mellink, *Texts*, 11, pp. 84–6, at p. 86.

46. Parker, *Army of Flanders*, Fig. 21, p. 232.

47. Guzmán de Silva wrote to Philip that Elizabeth had observed 'que no la conocera V(uestra) M(agesta)d por esta mudada y flaca . . .', London, 3 Feb. 1567, AGS. E. 816, f. 19; see also same to same, 15 July and 4 Nov. 1566, 3

Feb. 1567, 21 Feb. 1568, ibid., ff. 6, 10, 19b, 36–7; *CSPS* II Eliz., 7; see Maltby, *Alba*, pp. 182–204.

48. *CSPS II Eliz.*, 14, 45b.
49. Ibid., 49.
50. Ibid., 80, 87.
51. Ibid., 165 [*BMO* 25].
52. Ibid., 184.
53. Ibid., 193, and Wernham, *Before the Armada*, pp. 305–6.
54. *CSPS II Eliz.*, 193.
55. Ibid., 567.
56. Ibid., 259.
57. N. Williams, *Thomas Howard, Fourth Duke of Norfolk* (London: 1964), pp. 168–248.
58. Wernham, *Before the Armada*, pp. 312–14.
59. *CSPS I Eliz.*, 314; MacCaffrey, *Elizabeth I*, p. 177.
60. Printed by Kossman and Mellink, *Texts*, 14, pp. 93–7, quotation at pp. 95–6.
61. 'Instruction and advice for . . . Philip Marnix . . .', ibid., 15, pp. 98–101.
62. A. Soman (ed.), *The Massacre of St. Bartholomew. Reappraisals and Documents* (The Hague: 1974); N. M. Sutherland, *The Massacre of St Bartholomew and the European Conflict, 1559–1572* (London: 1973); P. Benedict, 'The Saint Bartholomew's massacres in the provinces', *HJ*, 21, 1 (1978), pp. 205–25; Garrisson, *Sixteenth-Century France*, pp. 352–63 and M. Greengrass, *France in the Age of Henri IV. [The Struggle for Stability]* (London and New York: 1984), pp. 4–6.
63. Cabrera de Córdoba, *Felipe II*, II, p. 165.
64. Greengrass, *France in the Age of Henri IV*, pp. 22–3.
65. Parker, *Dutch Revolt*, p. 142.
66. *Idem*, Appendix G, 'The Financing of Spanish Imperialism in the Netherlands, 1566–76', *Army of Flanders*, p. 287, and pp. 139–42.
67. A. W. Lovett, 'A new governor for the Netherlands: the appointment of Don Luis de Requesens, Comendador Mayor de Castilla', *European Studies Review*, 1971, 1, no. 2, pp. 89–103; M. Pi Corrales, *España y las potencias nórdicas. ['La otra invencible' 1574]* (Madrid: 1983), p. 81; Casado Soto, *Los Barcos Españoles del Siglo XVI*, p. 40.

6   WAR IN THE LOW COUNTRIES

1. A. Annoni, *S. Carlo el il suo tempo* (Rome: 1986); see also Clopas Batlle, *Luis de Requesens* and March, *El Comendador Mayor de Castilla Don Luis de Requesens*.
2. Parker, *Army of Flanders*, Appendix A, 'The Size and Composition of the Army of Flanders, 1567–1661', pp. 271–2; see also pp. 233–4 and fig. 21 'The receipts of the *pagaduría*, 1: 1567–76', p. 232.
3. Philip II to Requesens, 30 Jan. 1573, printed by Clopas Batlle, *Luis de Requesens*, p. 162.
4. Parker, *Army of Flanders*, p. 185.

5. Israel, *Dutch Republic*, p. 181; Kossman and Mellink, *Texts*, 'Introduction', p. 21.
6. Pi Corrales, *España y las potencias nórdicas*, pp. 153–69.
7. This is the theme of Parker's *Army of Flanders*.
8. 'Brief and true account of what happened at the peace negotiation of Breda, 20 March 1575', printed by Kossman and Mellink, *Texts*, 22, pp. 124–6; Parker, *Dutch Revolt*, pp. 166–7.
9. Kossman and Mellink, *Texts*, 'Introduction', p. 21.
10. A. W. Lovett, 'The Castilian Bankruptcy of 1575', *HJ*, 23, 4 (1980), pp. 899–911; C. Jago, 'Habsburg Absolutism and the Cortes of Castile', *American Historical Review*, 86, 1981, pp. 307–26; Carlos Morales, *El Consejo de Hacienda*, pp. 122–7.
11. Lovett, 'Ovando and the Council of Finance', p. 7.
12. J. I. Fortea Pérez, *Monarquía y Cortes en la Corona de Castilla: las ciudades ante la política fiscal de Felipe II* (Valladolid: 1990), pp. 88–9.
13. Thompson, *War and Government*, Table A, 'The Finances of Castile', p. 288.
14. A. W. Lovett, 'The General Settlement of 1577. An Aspect of Spanish Finance in the Early Modern Period', *HJ*, 25, 1 (1982), pp. 1–22.
15. Jago, 'Philip II and the Cortes of Castile', p. 38.
16. Fortea Pérez, *Monarquía y Cortes*, p. 109.
17. Carlos Morales, *El Consejo de Hacienda*, pp. 120–31; Lovett, 'Ovando and the Council of Finance', pp. 1–21 and 'Castilian Bankruptcy', pp. 907–11.
18. On the *Relaciones Topográficas*, N. Salomon, *La Vida Rural Castellana en Tiempos de Felipe II* (Barcelona: 1982). On the peasantry, F. Brumont, *Campo y campesinos de Castilla la Vieja en tiempos de Felipe II* (Madrid: 1984).
19. *CSPS I Eliz.*, 424, 426, 428, 431.
20. Ayala's title, Toledo, 19 May 1561, AGS QC 11; and Cabrera de Córdoba, *Felipe II*, I, pp. 504–5.
21. A. W. Lovett, *Philip II and Mateo Vázquez de Leca: the Government of Spain (1572–1592)* (Geneva: 1977), p. 31.
22. Lovett, *Philip II and Mateo Vázquez de Leca* and G. Marañon, *Antonio Pérez 'Spanish Traitor'* (London: 1954).
23. A. Delaforce, 'The Collection of Antonio Pérez, Secretary of State to Philip II', *Burlington Magazine*, CXXIV, 957, 1982, pp. 742–52.
24. Marañon, *Antonio Pérez*, p. 13.
25. Ibid., pp. 124–37.
26. Almázan does not appear on the list of aristocratic titles for 1578 (Table 4) although he certainly sat on the Council at this time.
27. Pérez to Philip II, no place, 17 Jan. 1574 and 13 Feb. 1577, BL Add. 28 262, ff. 70 and 239.
28. *Consulta* [*cnta.*] 7 Sept. 1577, AGS E 2843, f. 8.
29. Pérez to Philip II, no place, 28 Nov. 1575, BL Add. 28262, f. 90.
30. Same to same, no place, 11 April 1576, ibid., f. 139.
31. Lovett, *Philip II and Mateo Vázquez*, p. 15.
32. *Idem*, 'A Cardinal's Papers: the rise of Mateo Vázquez de Leca', *EHR*, CCCXLVII, 1973, pp. 241–61.
33. *Idem, Philip II and Mateo Vázquez*, pp. 37–8.

34. Title to office, San Lorenzo, 29 March 1573, AGS QC 34.
35. Vázquez de Leca to Philip II, El Pardo, 20 Feb. 1579, BL Add. 28263, f. 212.
36. Lovett, *Philip II and Mateo Vázquez*, pp. 144–5; Carlos Morales, *El Consejo de Hacienda*, pp. 113–27; Thompson, *War and Government*, pp. 40–1.
37. M. Boyd, *Cardinal Quiroga, Inquisitor-General of Spain* (Dubuque, Iowa: 1954), pp. 45–6.
38. Boyd, *Quiroga*, pp. 65–75; Kamen, *Spanish Inquisition*, pp. 123–5; A. Grive, 'Quiroga y Vela, Gaspar de', *DHEE*, III, pp. 2041–2.
39. Novalín, *El Inquisidor General Fernando de Valdés . . . Su Vida y Obra*, pp. 369–72.
40. Cabrera de Córdoba, *Felipe II*, II, pp. 353–4; J. Roco de Campofrio, *España en Flandes. Trece Años de Gobierno del Archiduque Alberto (1595–1608)* (Madrid: 1973), p. 3, and Boyd, *Quiroga*, pp. 24–7.
41. See, for example, *cntas*. St. 14 Nov. 1589, 3 May and 11 Aug. 1590, AGS E 165, ff. 349, 351 and 350.
42. Parker, *Dutch Revolt*, pp. 176–7.
43. George Gascoigne, 'The Spoyle of Antwerpe', (London?: 1576); Parker, *Dutch Revolt*, p. 178; Giménez Martín, *Tercios de Flandes*, pp. 116–20.
44. 'The Pacification of Ghent, *8 November 1576*', Kossman and Mellink, *Texts*, 23, pp. 126–32, at p. 127.
45. Marañon, *Antonio Pérez*, pp. 106–7.
46. A. Carnero, *Historia de las Guerras Civiles, que ha avido en los Estados de Flandes . . .*, (Brussels: 1625), pp. 108–9; A. Marichalar, *Julián Romero* (Madrid: 1952), pp. 428–33.
47. 'A short account of the true causes and reasons which have forced the States General of the Netherlands to take measures for their protection against Don John of Austria, 1577', Kossman and Mellink, *Texts*, 27, pp. 139–40.
48. 'Articles by which Archduke Matthias was accepted as governor and captain-general of the provinces of the Netherlands, 1577', ibid., 28, pp. 141–4.
49. *CSPV*, VIII, 688.
50. Ibid., 691, 692.
51. *CSPS II Eliz.*, 475 [*BMO* 89].
52. Ibid., 511 [*BMO* 511].
53. J. Cooke and W. Legg (?), 'The famous voyage of Sir Francis Drake into the South Sea . . .', printed in David (ed.), *Hakluyt's Voyages*, pp. 514–36 and Kelsey, *Sir Francis Drake*, pp. 75–89.
54. H. and P. Chaunu, *Séville y l'Atlantique, 1504–1650* (8 vols, Paris: 1955–60), VI/I, pp. 120–36.
55. Marañon, *Antonio Pérez*, pp. 165–84.
56. A. Danvila, *Felipe II y el Rey Don Sebastián de Portugal*, (Madrid: 1954), *passim*; on the conquest of Portugal, *idem, Felipe II y la Sucesión de Portugal* (Madrid: 1956).
57. Gabriel de Zayas to Philip II, 14 and 23 June 1578, AGS E 578, ff. 119 and 118, quotations from f. 119; *pareceres* of Quiroga, Aguilar and Almazan, 23 June 1578, ibid., f. 120; of Sessa, f. 121 and another by Aguilar, f. 125. See also, report on meeting of 12 July 1578, AGS E 2844, f. 14.
58. Maltby, *Alba*, pp. 274–9.
59. Philip II to Margaret of Parma, Madrid, 26 Oct. 1578, in L. P. Gachard, *Correspondance [de Philippe II sur les affaires des Pays-Bas]* (5 vols, Brussels,

1848–79), I, 682; Salazar y Castro, *Glorias de la Casa Farnese*, pp. 97–8; G.
Parente et al., *Los Sucesos de Flandes de 1588 en relacion con la Empresa de Inglaterra* (Madrid: 1990), pp. 71–7.

60. 'Treaty of the Union, eternal alliance and confederation made in the town of Utrecht by the countries and their towns and members, 29 January 1579', Kossman and Mellink, *Texts*, 37, pp. 165–73, at p. 165.

61. Parker, *Dutch Revolt*, p. 196; and Israel, *Dutch Republic*, pp. 196–205.

62. Van Durme, *El Cardenal Granvelle*, pp. 343–9.

63. Copy of title as President, San Lorenzo, 1 Sept. 1579, AGS. *Secretarias Provinciales [SP]*, lib. 634, f. 1; the *ordenanza* for the Council, El Pardo, 20 Oct. 1579, ibid., ff. 8–14. On the Council of Italy, M. Rivero, *Felipe II y el Gobierno de Italia* (Madrid: 1998).

64. Granvelle to Juan de Idiáquez, Madrid, 11 Dec. 1582, and copies of *cédulas*, 17 and 28 Sept. 1582, ordering that ten days be added to the calendar from 15 October, AGS GA 139, ff. 65, 72, 73.

65. Title as secretary, San Lorenzo, 8 Sept. 1579, AGS QC 27; on his career, see F. Pérez Minguez, *D. Juan de Idiáquez, embajador y consejero de Felipe II* (San Sebastián: 1934).

66. Cummins, *Francis Drake*, pp. 87–129 and Kelsey, *Sir Francis Drake*, pp. 214–19.

67. Goodman, *Spanish Naval Power*, p. 4.

7 THE CONQUESTS OF PORTUGAL AND THE AZORES AND THE ASSAULT UPON ENGLAND

1. Lisbon, 26 Feb. 1580, *The Fugger News-Letters*, [*FNL*] II, 69.

2. On the conquest of Portugal, Cabrera de Córdoba, *Felipe II*, II, pp. 512–693 and III, pp. 5–9 and Salazar de Mendoza, *Monarquía de España*, *libro* V; Danvila, *Felipe II y el Rey Don Sebastián de Portugal* and *Felipe II y la sucesión de Portugal*; F. Caeiro, *O Arquiduque Alberto de Áustria* (Lisbon: 1961). Several illuminating essays are included in F. Bouza, *Imagen y propaganda. Capítulos de Historia Cultural del Reinado de Felipe II* (Madrid: 1998); on the preparation for the invasion, IV, 'De archivos y antiguas escrituras en la pretensión al trono portugués de Felipe II', pp. 121–33. I am obliged to Dr Lorraine White for her guidance on the conquest of Portugal.

3. On the size of the force, Maltby, *Alba*, pp. 283–305; Casado Soto, *Los Barcos Españoles del Siglo XVI*, pp. 45–6 and Cerezo Martínez, *Las Armadas de Felipe II*, pp. 288–9 (quotation).

4. Lisbon, 1 Sept. 1580, *FNL*, II, 33.

5. Morineau, 'Tableau 6, Arrivage des métaux précieuse de 1580 á 1620', p. 72; my conversion at 1.375 pesos per ducat.

6. 'Resolucion del tanteo . . . del dinero . . . para los gastos desta Jornada de portugal', Lisbon, 22 April 1582, AGS GA 140, f. 69.

7. Asientos with Fuggers, ibid., ff. 1–22.

8. *CSPF 1579–80*, 463, 503.

9. Danvila, *Felipe II y la Sucesión de Portugal*, caps. XXI–XXIII; Salazar de Mendoza, *Monarquía de España*, *Libro* V, pp. 216–21.

10. On Maria's later years, M. S. Sánchez, *The Empress, The Queen, and the Nun. Women and Power at the Court of Philip III of Spain* (Baltimore: 1998).

11. F. Bouza has edited the letters from Portugal, and their continuation after 1585, to Catalina, now Duchess of Savoy, *Cartas de Felipe II a sus hijas* (Madrid: 1988).

12. C. Fernández Duro, *La Conquista de las Azores en 1583* (Madrid: 1866), pp. 11–17; *CSPV*, VIII, 49; Cerezo Martínez, *Las Armadas de Felipe II*, pp. 291–2 and Casado Soto, *Los Barcos Españoles del Siglo XVI*, p. 46.

13. *BMO*, 332, 340; AGS GA 139, ff. 200, 210, 230; *CSPV*, VIII, 95, 103, 104; Casado Soto, *Los Barcos Españoles del Siglo XVI*, p. 47.

14. Danvila, *Felipe II y la Sucesión de Portugal*, p. 336; Caeiro, *O Arquiduque Alberto*, pp. 81–2.

15. Anon., *Svcceso de la iornada expvgnación y conquista de la ysla de la Tercera* (Lisbon?: 1583); *CSPV*, VIII, 145, 148, 151, 158, 161; Cerezo Martínez, *Las Armadas de Felipe II*, pp. 298–304 and Casado Soto, *Los Barcos Españoles del Siglo XVI*, pp. 49–50.

16. Casado Soto, *Los Barcos Españoles del Siglo XVI*, pp. 45–51; Thompson, *War and Government*, pp. 32–3, and Goodman, *Spanish Naval Power*, p. 3.

17. *CSPS III Eliz.*, 71.

18. Luis de Salazar y Castro, *Los Comendadores de la Orden de Santiago* (Madrid: 1949); Diego de la Mota, *Libro del principío de la orden de la Cavalleria de S. Tiago del Espada* (Valencia: 1599), pp. 277–8; *BMO*, 379, 380.

19. Santa Cruz to Philip II, La Terceira, 9 Aug. 1583, printed by C. Fernández Duro, *La Armada Invencible* (2 vols, Madrid: 1884–5), I, pp. 241–3; Martin and Parker, *Spanish Armada*, pp. 88–9.

20. 'Apology or Defence of His Serene Highness William . . . prince of Orange', Kossman and Mellink, *Texts*, 48, pp. 211–16 and 'Edict of the States General of the United Netherlands . . . , 26 July 1581', ibid., 49, pp. 216–28.

21. Wernham, *Before the Armada*, p. 360.

22. Parker, *Dutch Revolt*, pp. 208–16.

23. Van Durme, *El Cardenal Granvelle*, p. 363.

24. Danvila, *Felipe II y la Sucesión de Portugal*, pp. 331–2.

25. Title to office, AGS GA 139, f. 82.

26. S. Fernández Conti, 'La Nobleza Cortesana; Don Diego de Cabrera y Bobadilla, Tercer Conde de Chinchón', in Martínez Millán (ed.), *La Corte de Felipe II*, pp. 229–70.

27. An observation first made to the author by Geoffrey Parker.

28. Van Durme, *El Cardenal Granvelle*, pp. 357–66.

29. Maltby, *Alba*, p. 305.

30. Israel, *Dutch Republic*, p. 216.

31. Garrisson, *Sixteenth-Century France*, pp. 307–16 and Greengrass, *France in the Age of Henri IV*, pp. 26–9 and 39–40.

32. *CSPS 3 Eliz.*, 192 [*BMO* 258].

33. Wernham, *Before the Armada*, pp. 340, 381.

34. Philip's journey to Aragon, E. Cock, 'Anales del Año Ochenta y Cinco', in García Mercadal (ed.), *Viajes de Extranjeros*, II, pp. 1293–1412 and Marañon, *Antonio Pérez*, pp. 220–8.

35. I am obliged to Dr Robert Oresko for his advice on the Savoyard marriage.
36. Philip II to Catalina Micaela, Barcelona, 14 June and Martorell, 18 June, printed by Bouza, *Cartas de Felipe II a sus hijas*, pp. 115–18; Cock, 'Anales del Año Ochenta y Cinco', in Garcia Mercadal (ed.), *Viajes de Extranjeros*, I, pp. 1293–1447.
37. V. Vázquez de Prada, 'Conflictos socio-políticos en la Corona de Aragón en el reinado de Felipe II', *Revueltas y Alzamientos en la España de Felipe 11* (Valladolid: 1992), pp. 41–64.
38. R. Villari, *The Revolt of Naples* (Cambridge: 1993), pp. 19–55; A. Calabria, *The Cost of Empire: the Finances of the Kingdom of Naples in the time of Spanish Rule* (Cambridge: 1991), p. 89; G. Galasso, *En la periferia del imperio. La monarquía hispánica y el Reino de Nápoles* (Barcelona: 2000), pp. 117–43; L. de Rosa, 'Motines y rebeliones en el Reino de Nápoles en el S. XVI', in *Revueltas y Alzamientos en la España de Felipe II*, pp. 97–116.
39. A list of ships embargoed in Cadiz and Sanlúcar between 8–16 June, *BMO*, 411. S. Adams, 'The Outbreak of the Elizabethan Naval War against the Spanish Empire: The Embargo of May 1585 and Sir Francis Drake's West Indies Voyage', in Rodríguez-Salgado and Adams, *England, Spain and the Gran Armada*, pp. 45–69; Cummins, *Francis Drake*, pp. 132–4 and Kelsey, *Sir Francis Drake*, p. 241.
40. *CSPS* 3 Eliz., 382.
41. On the siege, Carnero, *Historia de las Guerras Civiles*, pp. 184–201, van der Essen, *Farnese*, IV, *Le Siège d'Anvers (1584–1585)*, (Brussels: 1935), A. W. Lovett, *Early Habsburg Spain 1517–1598* (Oxford: 1986), pp. 180–1; Parker, *Dutch Revolt*, pp. 214–15; Giménez Martín, *Tercios de Flandes*, pp. 173–87.
42. *CSPV*, VIII, 284; Van der Essen, *Farnese*, pp. 136–7.
43. *BMO*, 435, 454; Wernham, *Before the Armada*, pp. 371–2.
44. 'The discourse and description of the voyage of Sir Francis Drake and Mr. Captain Frobisher', printed by J. S. Corbett (ed.), *Papers Relating to the Navy during the Spanish War 1585–1587* (Aldershot: 1987 reprint), pp. 1–27; Cummins, *Francis Drake*, pp. 135–7 and Kelsey, *Sir Francis Drake*, pp. 242–3.
45. See main text, See pp. 189–90.
46. Wernham, *Before the Armada*, pp. 376–9.
47. *CSPV*, VIII, 290, 300, 304, 333, 354; Cummins, *Francis Drake*, pp. 135–60; K. R. Andrews, *The Spanish Caribbean. Trade and Plunder 1530–1630* (New Haven: 1978), pp. 146–53. For reports reaching Madrid of Drake's activities, *BMO*, 474, 480.
48. Parma to Philip II, Antwerp, 11 Nov. 1585; Bautista de Tassis to same, Namur, 28 Nov. 1585; Philip II to Parma, Tortosa, 29 Dec. 1585; to Olivares, Tortosa, 2 Jan. 1586; Santa Cruz to Philip II, 13 Jan. 1586 and Juan de Idiáquez to Santa Cruz, San Lorenzo, 26 Jan. 1586, *BMO*, 485, 491, 498, 503 and 518.
49. *Cnta.* War, 11 Sept. 1586, AGS GA 190, f. 504.
50. Andrews, *The Spanish Caribbean*, pp. 153–5.
51. *CSPV*, VIII, 320, 327.
52. Santa Cruz to Philip II, Lisbon, 13 Jan. 1586, *BMO*, 518.
53. I. A. A. Thompson, 'The Invincible Armada', in *War and Society in Habsburg Spain. Selected Essays*, 'Part II: The Spanish Armada' (Aldershot, 1992).

54. Casado Soto, *Los Barcos Españoles del Siglo XVI*, pp. 158–61. On the *BMO*, above, 'Introductory note' to the footnotes. The most accessible Spanish documentation not yet incorporated into the *BMO* is printed by E. Herrera Oria, *La Armada Invencible. Documentos precedentes del Archivo General de Simancas* (Valladolid: 1929, Archivo Histórico Español, II). English translations of several important documents are published by G. P. B. Naish as 'Documents Illustrating the History of the Spanish Armada' in D. W. Waters, *The Elizabethan Navy and the Armada of Spain* (National Maritime Museum Monographs, XVII: Greenwich, 1975). English documentation is published in two reprints by The Navy Records Society (Aldershot, 1987): J. S. Corbett (ed.), *Papers Relating to the Navy during the Spanish War 1585–1587* and John Knox Laughton (ed.), *State Papers relating to the defeat of the Spanish Armada, Anno 1588*. An important series of monographs were published in Spain for the 400th anniversary of the Armada as the *Colección Gran Armada*: J. L. Casado Soto, *Los Barcos Españoles del Siglo XVI*; C. Gómez-Centurión Jiménez, *Felipe II, la Empresa de Inglaterra y el Comercio Septentrional (1566–1609)* (Madrid: 1998) and *La Invencible y la Empresa de Inglaterra* (Madrid: 1998); M. Gracia Rivas, *Los Tercios de la Gran Armada* (Madrid: 1989) and La *Sanidad en la Jornada de Inglaterra (1587–1588)* (Madrid: 1990); H. J. O'Donnell, *La Fuerza del Desembarco de la Gran Armada contra Inglaterra (1588): Su origén, organización y vicisitudes* (Madrid: 1989); G. Parente et al., *Los Sucesos de Flandes de 1588 en Relación con la Empresa de Inglaterra* (Madrid: 1990). English historians also published major works, notably Colin Martin and Geoffrey Parker, *The Spanish Armada* (London: 1988), M. J. Rodríguez-Salgado (ed.), *Armada 1588–1988* (London: 1988); F. Fernández-Armesto, *The Spanish Armada: The Experience of War in 1588* (Oxford: 1988); N. A. Rodger, *The Armada in the Public Records* (London: 1988). Two important collections of essays were also produced for the anniversary: Rodríguez-Salgado and Adams (eds), *England, Spain and the Gran Armada* and those produced by the National Maritime Museum, Greenwich, *Royal Armada* (apparently without an editor). Some important advances are made in I. A. A. Thompson's *Selected Essays* (above, n. 51). Three fine biographies provide a wealth of information: P. Pierson, *Commander of the Armada: The Seventh Duke of Medina Sidonia* (New Haven: 1989), H. Kelsey, *Sir Francis Drake* and J. Cummins, *Francis Drake*. Among older books, G. Mattingly, *The Defeat of the Spanish Armada* (London: 1959) is a classic. R. B. Wernham's trilogy on the Armadas (*Before the Armada*; *After the Armada*; *Return of the Armadas*) is indispensable.

55. Martin and Parker, *Spanish Armada*, pp. 93–4.

56. *CSPV*, VIII, 327, 328; F. Bouza, '*Sola* Lisboa *Casi* Viuda. La ciudad y la mudanza de la corte en el Portugal de los Felipes', *Imagen y propaganda*, pp. 95–120.

57. Ibid., 453.

58. Martin and Parker, *Spanish Armada*, pp. 105–6.

59. On the Cadiz raid, Corbett (ed.), *The Spanish War 1585–1587*, pp. 97–206; Drake's claim, p. 32; Kelsey, *Sir Francis Drake*, pp. 280–304, and Cummins, *Francis Drake*, pp. 161–78; and Casado Soto, *Los Barcos Españoles del Siglo XVI*, p. 163.

60. Philip II to Cardinal Archduke Albert, n. p., 14 Sept. 1587, printed by Herrera Oria, *La Armada Invencible*, pp. 33–7; on the ships going to the Indies, Chaunu, *Séville y l'Atlantique, 1504–1650*, VI/I, pp. 127–32.
61. Martin and Parker, *Spanish Armada*, pp. 96–7.
62. Thompson, 'The Invincible Armada', pp. 5–6.
63. *Cnta.* War, 4 May 1587, AGS GA 208, f. 272.
64. Anon., 'Daños que sufrió la armada durante el temporal del día 16 de noviembre', *La Batalla del Mar Océano (BMO)* 3348.; Casado Soto, *Los Barcos Españoles del Siglo XVI*, pp. 169–71.
65. Philip II to Santa Cruz, El Pardo, 30 Nov. 1587, *BMO*, 3412; M. Gracia Rivas, *La Sanidad en la Jornada de Inglaterra (1587–1588)* (Madrid: 1988), pp. 96–8.
66. Santa Cruz to Philip II, Lisbon 16 January 1588, *BMO*, 3752; on illnesses, Gracia Rivas, *La Sanidad en la Jornada de Inglaterra*, pp. 102–4.
67. Philip II to Santa Cruz, Madrid, 18 January 1588, *BMO*, 3773.
68. Same to same, (Bosque de Segovia), 21 Oct. 1587, *BMO*, 3142; on Fuentes, Philip II to Santa Cruz, 23 Jan. 1588 in Herrera Oria, *La Armada Invencible*, pp. 53–4, 117, 123.
69. Martin and Parker, *The Spanish Armada*, p. 121.
70. Philip II to Don Alvaro and Don Alonso de Bazán, Madrid, 15 Feb. 1588, *BMO*, 4143 and 4144; *CSPV* VIII, 628. On Santa Cruz's fever, Gracia Rivas, *La Sanidad en la Jornada de Inglaterra*, pp. 98–101.
71. Casado Soto, *Los Barcos Españoles del Siglo XVI*, p. 167; *CSPV*, VIII, 627 (quotation); Rodríguez-Salgado (ed.), *Armada*, p. 29; Thompson, *War and Government*, pp. 191–2.
72. Philip II to Medina Sidonia, Madrid, 14 Feb. 1588, *BMO* 4141, Naish, 'Documents', pp. 57–8; I. A. A. Thompson, 'The Appointment of the Duke of Medina Sidonia to the Command of the Spanish Armada', reprinted in *War and Society in Habsburg Spain*.
73. Philip II to Medina Sidonia, Madrid, 20 Feb. 1588, Herrera Oria, *La Armada Invencible*, pp. 150–1.
74. Moura and Idiáquez to Medina Sidonia, Madrid, 22 Feb. 1588, ibid., p. 152.
75. Mattingly, *The Defeat of the Spanish Armada*, p. 184; Casado Soto, *Los Barcos Españoles del Siglo XVI*, pp. 172, 180.
76. Ibid., and Thompson, 'The Invincible Armada', pp. 3–4, 10–11.
77. *CSPV*, VIII, 656, 684 (quotation).
78. Minute of meeting of 20 Jan. 1588, AGS E 2855, no folio.
79. Philip II to Medina Sidonia, Madrid, 1 April 1588, in Naish (ed.), 'Documents', p. 59.
80. Same to same, same date, ibid., p. 62.
81. Anon., 'Relacion de los Galeones, Navios Pataches y Zabras . . .', Lisbon, 9 May 1588, printed by Herrera Oria, *La Armada Invencible*, pp. 384–435; Martin and Parker, *Spanish Armada*, pp. 26–7 and 261–8.
82. Garrisson, *Sixteenth-Century France*, pp. 378–9 and Greengrass, *France in the Age of Henry IV*, pp. 40–7.
83. O'Donnell, *La Fuerza del desembarco de la Gran Armada*, p. 402; on priests, doctors and scribes, Gracia Rivas, *La Sanidad en la Jornada de Inglaterra*, pp. 211–38; on the ships, Casado Soto, *Los Barcos Españoles del Siglo XVI*, p. 180 and Thompson, 'The Invincible Armada', p. 4. Ten of the 141 ships were

humble carrying vessels and are often excluded from estimates of the fighting fleet itself. Note, however, that an even higher figure (of 151 ships) is given by M. Barkham, 'Rival Fleets', in Rodríguez-Salgado (ed.), *Armada*, pp. 151–63.

84. On the commanders, Salazar y Castro, *Comendadores de....* *Santiago*, pp. 260–1; de la Mota, *Libro del principio de la orden de la Cavalleria de S. Tiago del Espada*, pp. 276, 295, 305, 310.

85. On Mexia and Pimentel, A. López de Haro, *Nobiliario Genealogico de los Reyes y Títulos de España* (2 vols, Madrid: 1622), II, pp. 191 and 481–2; Salazar y Castro, *Comendadores de... Santiago*, p. 223; de la Mota, *Caballeros de Santiago*, pp. 302–3 and González Davila, *Teatro de las Grandezas de Madrid*, pp. 92–6; 'Relacion de las Galeones . . .', printed by Herrera Oria, *La Armada Invencible*, pp. 406–11; O'Donnell, *La fuerza de desembarco de la Gran Armada*, pp. 400–2. On the size of the fleet, Casado Soto, *Los Barcos Españoles del Siglo XVI*, p. 180.

86. Casado Soto, *Los Barcos Españoles del Siglo XVI*, pp. 176–7; Martin and Parker, *The Spanish Armada*, p. 142.

87. Anon., 'The reasons why the difficulties raised concerning the prosecution of the task begun are without foundation', n. d., printed by Naish, 'Documents', pp. 63–4.

88. Two letters of Philip II to Medina Sidonia of 1 July 1588, printed by Herrera Oria, *La Armada Invencible*, pp. 208–9 and 213–14; English versions printed by Naish, 'Documents', p. 64.

89. Casado Soto, *Los Barcos Españoles del Siglo XVI*, pp. 177–9.

90. Ibid., p. 229; Martin and Parker, *The Spanish Armada*, pp. 64–5; Rodríguez-Salgado, *Armada*, pp. 154–8. On the intention to attack the Armada off the Portuguese coast, Drake to the Privy Council, Plymouth, 30 March 1588 (OS), printed by Rodger, *The Armada in the Public Records*, pp. 42–3. See also Kelsey, *Sir Francis Drake*, pp. 310–21.

91. Martin and Parker, *Spanish Armada*, pp. 167–78.

92. The study of Armada gunnery has been revolutionised by I. A. A. Thompson, 'Spanish Armada Guns', reprinted in *War and Society in Habsburg Spain* (quotation, at p. 370), and by the superb chapter in Martin and Parker, *Spanish Armada*, chap. 11, 'Anatomy of failure', pp. 195–225. Gracia Rivas, *La Sanidad en la Jornada de Inglaterra*, p. 290.

93. P. Coco Calderón to Philip II, Santander, 27 Sept. 1588, in Herrera Oria, *La Armada Invencible*, pp. 294–6; on the losses, Casado Soto, *Los Barcos Españoles del Siglo XVI*, p. 245, Gracia Rivas, *La Sanidad en la Jornada de Inglaterra*, pp. 300–1, and Martin and Parker, *Spanish Armada*, pp. 227–50.

94. Philip II to Medina Sidonia, 18 Aug. 1588, printed by Herrera Oria, *La Armada Invencible*, p. 272; same to Catalina Micaela, Escorial, 19 August, printed by Bouza, *Cartas de Felipe II a sus hijas*, p. 158; Vázquez de Leca to Philip, San Lorenzo, 21 Aug. (1588), BL Add. 28 263, f. 481; *CSPV*, VIII, 715, 718; *cnta.* War 7 Sept. 1588, AGS GA 235, f. 71; *cnta.* War 19 Sept. 1588, ibid., f. 89 (quotation); Idiáquez to Parma, San Lorenzo, 31 Aug. 1588, *Correspondance*, II, 841. On Philip's reaction, M. J. Rodríguez-Salgado, 'Philip II and the Post-Armada crisis: foreign policy and rebellion, 1588–1594', in Instituto de Historia y Cultural Naval, *IX Jornadas de Historia Marítima, Después de la Gran Armada* (Madrid: 1993), pp. 51–89, at 52–7.

95. Gracia Rivas, *La Sanidad en la Jornada de Inglaterra*, pp. 319–20, 327–33; 339; Martin and Parker, *Spanish Armada*, pp. 257–9.
96. Ibid., pp. 265 and 267–8, and Thompson, 'The Invincible Armada', p. 17 (quotation).
97. *CSPV*, VIII, 750, 754, 780.
98. Ibid., 735 (quotation), 745, 770.
99. A. W. Lovett, 'The vote of the *Millones* (1590)', *HJ*, XXX (1987), pp. 1–20.
100. Garrisson, *Sixteenth-Century France*, pp. 380–2, and Rodríguez-Salgado, 'Philip II and the Post-Armada crisis', pp. 65–9.

8 AFTER THE ARMADA: THE STRUGGLE FOR WESTERN EUROPE

1. *CSPV*, VIII, 780; see Philip's responses to *cntas*. War, AGS GA 235.
2. *Cnta*. War 17 Dec. 1588, AGS GA 235, f. 213 and 'Puntos de los q[ue] Su M[agesta]d mandó q se platicasse Visp[er]a de Santiago 1589', AGS E 2855, no folio number.
3. Thompson, *War and Government*, pp. 192–3; Cerezo Martínez, *Las Armadas de Felipe II*, pp. 111–12; Casado Soto, 'Atlantic shipping', in Rodríguez-Salgado and Adams, *England, Spain and the Gran Armada*, p. 113; M. Vaquerizo Gil, 'Presencia de Santander en la Política del Reino', in J. L. Casado Soto *et al.* (eds), *Cantabria a través de su historia. La crisis del Siglo XVI* (Santander: 1979), pp. 178–9; Goodman, *Spanish naval power*, p. 8.
4. A. W. Lovett, 'The vote of the *millones* (1590)', *HJ*, 30, 1 (1987), pp. 1–20; Fortea Pérez, *Monarquía y Cortes*, pp. 132–4.
5. Fortea Pérez, *Monarquía y Cortes*, pp. 132–78, 461–505.
6. Morineau, *Incroyables Gazettes*, 'Tableau 6', p. 73.
7. I. A. A. Thompson, 'Oposición Política y Juicio del Gobierno en las Cortes de 1592–98', *Studia Histórica. Historia Moderna*, 17, (1997), pp. 37–62.
8. Cummins, *Francis Drake*, pp. 194–223, Kelsey, *Sir Francis Drake*, pp. 341–64 (quotation, pp. 347–8), and Wernham, *After the Armada*, pp. 92–130. An important essay by Simon Adams, 'English Naval Strategy in the 1590s', in Instituto de Historia y Cultura Naval, *Después de la Gran Armada*, pp. 57–72.
9. *Cnta*. War, 22 Nov. 1588, AGS GA 235, f. 154.
10. Cummins, *Francis Drake*, pp. 206–23.
11. K. R. Andrews, *Elizabethan Privateering: English Privateering during the Spanish War, 1585–1603* (Cambridge: 1964) and *idem*, *The Spanish Caribbean: Trade and Plunder 1530–1630* (New Haven and London: 1978).
12. *CSPV*, VIII, 883, 893 (quotation).
13. 'Abstract of divers Spanish letters', 4, 4 and 6 March 1595, Public Records Office [PRO], State Papers [SP] 94/IV, ff. 96–9, and J. Wroth to Burghley, Venice, 25 Feb. 1595, ibid., SP 99/I, f. 172; Morineau, *Incroyables gazettes*, p. 73; Chaunu, *Séville et l'Atlantique*, VI/I, pp. 132–5.
14. Garrisson, *Sixteenth-Century France*, pp. 382–3 and Greengrass, *France in the Age of Henry IV*, pp. 47–52.

15. Don John of Austria's praise of Vázquez de Arce, to Philip II, Granada, 19 Nov. 1570, BL Add. 28, 264, f. 140; title as councillor of Castile, Madrid, 26 Nov. 1570, AGS QC 39.

16. Marañon, *Antonio Pérez*, pp. 238–40, 258–9.

17. On the revolt of Aragon, Cabrera de Córdoba, *Felipe II*, III, *Libro* V, 'Capitulo Adicional', pp. 520–612; Salazar de Mendoza, *Monarquía*, II, pp. 146–222; Marañon, *Antonio Pérez*, *passim*. M. Gracia Rivas has written an important account of the military operation, *La 'Invasion' de Aragón en 1591. Una Solución Militar a las Alteraciones del Reino* (Zaragoza: 1992); S. Fernández Conti, 'La Profesionalización del Gobierno de la Guerra: Don Alonso de Vargas', in Martínez Millán (ed.) *La Corte de Felipe II*, pp. 417–50; A. W. Lovett, 'Philip II, Antonio Pérez and the Kingdom of Aragon', *European History Quarterly*, 18 (1988), pp. 131–53. J. Gascon Pérez has compiled a valuable bibliography, *Bibliografía crítica para el estudio de la Rebelión Aragonesa de 1591* (Zaragoza: 1995).

18. Fernández Conti, 'La Nobleza Cortesana', in Martínez Millán (ed.), *La Corte de Felipe II*, pp. 255–64.

19. Cabrera de Córdoba, *Felipe II*, III, pp. 536–7.

20. Ibid., p. 554.

21. Ibid., p. 582; title printed by Gracia Rivas, *La 'Invasion' de Aragón*, pp. 291–2.

22. Gracia Rivas, *La 'Invasion' de Aragón*, p. 102; Marañon, *Antonio Pérez*, p. 294.

23. Cabrera de Córdoba, *Felipe II*, III, p. 591.

24. Saragossa, 11 Nov. 1592, *FNL*, II, 146; on Heredía's agony, Gracia Rivas, *La 'Invasion' de Aragón*, p. 168, and on the number of executions, p. 175.

25. Cabrera de Córdoba, *Felipe II*, III, p. 596; on Vázquez de Arce's appointment, AGS QC 39; on the journey, Cock, 'Anales del Año Ochenta y Cinco', in García Mercadal (ed.), *Viajes de Extranjeros*, I, pp. 1293–1412.

26. Gracia Rivas, *La 'Invasion' de Aragón*, pp. 277–8.

27. Parker, *Dutch Revolt*, pp. 222–4.

28. Israel, *The Dutch Republic*, pp. 241–54.

29. M. Wolfe, *The Conversion of Henry IV. Politics, Power, and Religious Belief in Early Modern France* (Cambridge Mass.: 1993); on the famous aphorism, p. 1.

30. Van der Essen, *Farnese*, V, pp. 279–80.

31. Garrisson, *Sixteenth-Century France*, p. 388.

32. Van der Essen, *Farnese*, V, pp. 272–310; Giménez Martín, *Tercios de Flandes*, pp. 204–7.

33. M. Gracia Rivas, 'La Campaña de Bretaña (1590–98). Una Amenaza para Inglaterra', Instituto de Historia y Cultural Naval, *Después de la Gran Armada: La Historia Desconocida* (Madrid: 1993), pp. 41–56; Wernham, *After the Armada*, pp. 400–20.

34. Sir R. Sidney to Burghley, Flushing, 13 Oct. 1591, PRO SP 84/XLIII, f. 100; Carnero, *Historia de las Guerras Civiles*, pp. 259–61.

35. Van der Essen, *Farnese*, V, pp. 323–55 and Giménez Martín, *Tercios de Flandes*, pp. 208–12.

36. Ibid., p. 356; Van der Essen, *Farnese*, V, pp. 356–84; on Fuentes, J. Fuentes, *El Conde de Fventes y su tiempo. Estudios de Historia Militar Siglos XVI á XVII* (Madrid: 1908), 2 parts, I, p. 64.

37. 'News from Rome', 18 Jan. 1592, PRO SP 101/LXII, f. 61 and J. Wroth to Burghley, Venice, 21 and 29 Jan. 1592, ibid., 99/I, ff. 162, 164; A. Borromeo, 'España y el problema de la elección papal de 1592', *Cuadernos de investigación histórica*, II (1978), pp. 175–200.
38. Parker, *Dutch Revolt*, p. 230.
39. 'Instructions for Sir T. Wilkes', *c.* 17 Sept. 1593, PRO SP 77/V, f. 132 and A. de Mouy to Burghley, London, 30 Jul. and 9 Aug. 1593, ibid., 101/XXVII, f. 99.
40. Sir R. Sidney to Lord Burghley, Paris, 12 March 1594, PRO SP 78/XXXIII, f. 136; Garrisson, *Sixteenth-Century France*, p. 391.
41. Fernández Duro, *Fuentes y su Tiempo*, p. 473, n. 1.
42. Carnero, *Historia de las Guerras Civiles*, p. 310.
43. 'Provisions for Ostend', Nov. (?) 1594, PRO SP 84/XLVII, f. 203.
44. M. Fernández Alvárez (ed.), *Felipe II. Testamento* (Madrid: 1982); Carlos M. N. Eire, *From Madrid to Purgatory. The Art and Craft of Dying in Sixteenth-Century Spain* (Cambridge: 1995), pp. 283–5.
45. Buisseret, *Henry IV*, p. 56.
46. 'The King of Spain's declaration in answer to the Prince of Béarn', Brussels, 12 March 1595, PRO SP 94/V, f. 11.
47. R. Mousnier, *The Assassination of Henry IV. The Tyrannicide Problem and the Consolidation of the French Absolute Monarchy in the Early 17th Century*, (London: 1973), pp. 106–16.
48. Garrisson, *Sixteenth-Century France*, pp. 391–4.
49. *CSPV*, IX, 348; Morineau, *Incroyables gazettes*, 'Tableau 6', p. 73. Morineau's figures for silver imports in the 1590s are significantly higher than Hamilton's; see Note to Table 4.1.
50. *CSPV*, IX, 349.

9 CRESCENDO: FAILURE, SETTLEMENT AND DEATH

1. *CSPV*, IX, 348.
2. Ibid., 416, 418, 422.
3. A. García Sanz, 'Castile 1580–1620: economic crisis and the policy of reform', in I. A. A. Thompson and B. Yun Casalilla (eds), *The Castilian Crisis of the Seventeenth Century. New Perspectives on the Economic and Social History of Seventeenth-Century Spain* (Cambridge: 1994), p. 22.
4. E. Garcia España and A. Molinié-Bertrand, *Estudio Analítico* (Madrid: 1986); Braudel, *The Mediterranean*, I, p. 403.
5. Ortiz de Zúñiga, *Anales Eclesiásticos y Seculares*, vol. IV, pp. 150, 156; F. Henríquez de Jorquera, *Anales de Granada. Descripción del Reino y Ciudad de Granada. Crónica de la Reconquista (1482–1492). Sucesos de los años 1588 a 1646*, (ed. A. Marín Ocete, 2 vols, Granada: 1987), II, p. 529.
6. J. I. Fortea Pérez, *Córdoba en el Siglo XVI: Las bases demográficas de una expansión urbana* (Cordoba: 1981), p. 207.
7. Bennassar, *Valladolid*, p. 262; see also *idem*, 'Valladolid en el Reinado de Felipe II', in L. A. Ribot García et al. (eds), *Valladolid. Corazon del Mundo Hispánico. – Siglo XVI* (Valladolid: Historia de Valladolid, III, 1981), pp. 71–133.

8. *CSPV*, IX, 682.
9. Domínguez Ortíz, 'La Baja Andalucía', p. 238, and Alvar Ezquerra, (who estimates Madrid's population at 83 000–90 000), *Madrid entre 1601 y 1606*, pp. 19–21; on Madrid, September 1598, *CSPV*, IX, 728. On the 1590s, J. Casey, 'Spain: A Failed Transition', in P. Clark (ed.) *The European Crisis of the 1590s. Essays in Comparative History* (London: 1985), pp. 209–28.
10. Thompson, *War and Government*, p. 36.
11. *Cnta* War, 1 Aug. 1588, AGS GA 235, f. 3.
12. Thompson, 'Table A. The Finances of Castile', *War and Government*, p. 288.
13. Fortea Pérez, *Cordoba*, p. 139.
14. Thompson, 'Oposición Política', pp. 41–6; C. Gómez-Centurión Jiménez, 'The New Crusade: Ideology and Religion in the Anglo-Spanish Conflict', in Rodríguez-Salgado and Adams (eds), *England, Spain and the Gran Armada*, pp. 264–59.
15. Cabrera de Córdoba, *Felipe II*, II, p. 504; J. M. Carramolino, *Historia de Ávila, su provincia y obispado*, (3 vols, Madrid: 1872), III, pp. 253–60.
16. Richard L. Kagan, *Lucrecia's Dreams. Politics and Prophecy in Sixteenth-Century Spain* (Los Angeles and Oxford: 1990).
17. *CSPV*, VIII, 567, 805; see, for example, the *consultas* and minutes in AGS E 2855, and S. Fernández Conti, *Los Consejos de Estado y Guerra de la Monarquía hispana en tiempos de Felipe II (1548–1598)* (Valladolid: 1998), pp. 208–69.
18. *CSPV*, VIII, 439, 497, 780, 788.
19. *Novísima Recopilación*, III, pp. 152–6; J. Martínez Millán, 'Las luchas por la administración de la gracia en el reinado de Felipe II. La reforma de la Cámara de Castilla, 1580–1593', *Annali di Storia moderna e contemporanea*, 4, (1998), pp. 31–72; on Barajas, Cabrera de Córdoba, *Felipe II*, III, pp. 471–4.
20. Carlos Morales, *Consejo de Hacienda*, pp. 162–7, and *Novisima Recopilación*, III, pp. 152–5.
21. P. Williams, 'El Auge Desaforado de los Consejos', in J. Martínez Millán (ed.) *Felipe II (1527–1598) Europa y la Monarquía Católica*, I, *El Gobierno de la Monarquía (Corte y Reinos)* (Madrid: 1998), pp. 975–84.
22. 'Nomina de los Consejos', 1556–98, AGS Contadurías Generales [CG], 886, ff. 27–63 and 887, ff. 1–11; Thompson, *War and Government*, pp. 38–41 175–7.
23. On Italy, *cédula*, Madrid, 28 June 1595, AGS SP., libro 634, f. 118; Ayala's title, San Lorenzo, 3 June 1588, AGS QC 7.
24. Philip II to Juan de Carriaco, May/Jun. 1584, Archivo Histórico Nacional [AHN], Inquisición, libro [lib.]361, ff. 270v–271v, and Juan Bautista de Acevedo to Francisco Buelta, Valladolid, 5 February 1606, ibid., lib. 367, ff. 146v–148v.
25. Thompson, *War and Government*, pp. 40–1, 175–7; and Carlos Morales, *El Consejo de Hacienda*, pp. 113–17.
26. Quintana *Madrid*, f. 363; *CSPV*, IX, 362.
27. I. Atienza Hernández, *Aristocracia, poder y riqueza en la España moderna. La Casa de Osuna siglos XV–XIX* (Madrid: 1987). A tentative list (comprised essentially from the sources attached to Table 4.1) has forty-six new titles, of which the underlined names seem to have no landed income – dukes: Alcalá, Osuna, Fería, Pastrana, <u>Baena</u>, <u>Huescar</u>; marquises: Mirabel, la Mota, Adrada, El Algava, Santa Cruz, Estepa, Fromesta, Almazán, Villanueva del

Rio, Villamanrique, Velada, Auñon, Aguilafuente, el Carpio, la Guardia, Ardales, Alcalá; *Algecila, Peñafiel, la Flechilla, la Bañeza, Almenara, Huélamo, Cuellar, Lanzarote, Navarra*; counts: Santa Gadea, Barajas, Fuentes, Montalbán, Luna, la Puebla de Montalbán; *Galve, Villardonpardo, Villanueva de Cañedo, Mayalde, Fuensaldaña, Plasencia, Uceda*. I am obliged to Professor I. A. A. Thompson for his help in compiling this list.

28. F. Fernández Bethencourt, *Historia Genealógica y Heráldica de la Monarquía Española* (10 vols, Madrid: 1897–1920), V, pp. 263–5; V. M. Marquéz de la Plata and L. V. de Bernabé, *El Libro de Oro de los Duques* (Madrid: 1994), pp. 26–7, 134–5, 266–8 and 276.

29. Pierson, *Medinasidonia*, pp. 1–18. There is no study of the Constable of Castile's family.

30. Fernández Bethencourt, *Historia Genealógica*, V, p. 264.

31. P. Williams, 'Philip III and the restoration of Spanish government, 1598–1603', *EHR*, LXXXVIII, 349, (1973), pp. 751–69.

32. Wernham, *Return of the Armadas*, p. 22.

33. Roco de Campofrio, *España en Flandes*, pp. 5–6.

34. Carnero, *Historia de las Guerras Civiles*, pp. 363–74, and Fernández Duro, *Conde de Fuentes*, pp. 534–5.

35. Fernández Duro, *Conde de Fuentes*, p. 481.

36. Roco de Campofrio, *España en Flandes*, pp. 38–107; *CSPV*, IX, 440.

37. Wernham, *Return of the Armadas*, p. 66.

38. *CSPV*, IX, 437; K. R. Andrews (ed.), *The last voyage of Drake and Hawkins* (Cambridge: 1972).

39. Wernham, *Return of the Armadas*, pp. 82–129, quotation at p. 115; S. and E. Usherwood, *The Counter-Armada 1596. The Journall of the Mary Rose* (London: 1983).

40. *Cntas*, State 4 and 9 July 1596, AGS E 2855, ff. 23, 25; *CSPV*, IX, 469.

41. *CSPV*, IX, 493; Morineau, *Incroyables gazettes*, 'Tableau 6', p. 74.

42. Ibid.

43. León Pinelo, *Anales de Madrid*, p. 34.

44. G. González Davila, *Historia de la Vida y Hechos del Inclito Monarca, Amado y Santo D. Felipe Tercero* in Salazar de Mendoza, *Monarquía de España*, III (Madrid: 1771), at pp. 20–2.

45. López de Haro, *Nobiliarío Genealogico*, I, p. 308.

46. On the armada of 1596, Fernández Duro, *Armada Espanola*, III, pp. 129–31; *CSPV*, IX, 497, 506–8, 511, 519; Wernham, *Return of the Armadas*, pp. 114–40 and 144.

47. *CSPV*, IX, 528.

48. Minute of Council of State, 13 Nov. 1596, AGS E 2855, no folio.

49. Thompson, *War and Government*, p. 72; Morineau, *Incroyables gazettes*, 'Tableau 6', p. 74.

50. *CSPV*, IX, 626, 629, 634; Fernández Duro, *Armada Española*, III, p. 166 and Wernham, *Return of the Armadas*, pp. 171–90, quotation at p. 190.

51. Essex's voyage, Wernham, *Return of the Armadas*, pp. 171–83; *CSPV*, IX, 666.

52. 'Parecer de los 3 de Xbre 1597 en el Pardo sobre dos materias graues', AGS E 2855, no folio.

53. Buisseret, *Henry IV*, pp. 70–4.

54. Ibid.

55. *CSPV*, IX, 697, 708, 711 (quotation), 734.

56. 'Condiciones le la renunciación que hizo el rey don Felipe Segundo, de los Estados de Flandes en la infanta doña Isabel su hija', Madrid, 6 May 1598, *CODOIN*, XLII, pp. 218–25.

57. *CSPV*, IX, 682; J. Israel, *The Dutch Republic and the Hispanic World 1606–1661* (Oxford: 1982), pp. 1–28.

58. On Philip's death, Antonio Cervera de la Torre, 'Testimonio Auténtico y Verdadero de las Cosas Notables que Pasaron en la Dichosa Muerte del Rey N. S. Don Felipe II . . . ,' (Valencia, 1599); *CSPV*, IX, 727, 728, 731, 732, 734, 737; Eire, *From Madrid to Purgatory*, pp. 255–368; R. Vargas Hidalgo, 'Documentos inéditos sobre la muerte de Felipe II y la literatura funebre de los siglos XVI y XVII', *BRAH*, CXCII (1995), pp. 377–453.

59. Philip II to Prince Philip, San Lorenzo, 5 Aug. 1598, AGS Patronato Real [PR] 29, f. 37, and Codicil to Testament, San Lorenzo, 16 Aug. 1598, ibid., f. 38.

60. *CSPV*, IX, 727, 732.

61. Philip II to Albert, San Lorenzo, 11 Sept. 1598, *Correspondance*, IV, 1461.

62. Denia to Juan de Borja (?), San Lorenzo, 13 Sept. 1598, BL Add. 28422, f. 4; González Davila, *Felipe III*, pp. 29–32 and idem, *Teatro de las Grandezas de Madrid*, pp. 46–8.

EPILOGUE

1. Eire, *From Madrid to Purgatory*, pp. 323–4.

INDEX

287